ISSUES PAST and PRESENT

An American History Sourcebook

VOLUME II

ISSUES PAST and PRESENT

An American History Sourcebook

VOLUME II

EDITED BY

Phillip S. Paludan
University of Kansas

Robert M. Calhoon
*University of North Carolina
at Greensboro*

Michael A. Moore
Bowling Green State University

Jonathan G. Utley
University of Tennessee, Knoxville

BIOGRAPHIES BY

Donald C. Lord
Unity College

D. C. HEATH AND COMPANY
Lexington, Massachusetts   Toronto

Acknowledgment is made to the following sources for permission to repro-
duce pictures from their collections:

Cover: The Bettmann Archive, Inc.
          Ellis Herwig/Stock, Boston, Inc.

p. 11:   Courtesy Illinois State Historical Library.
p. 67:   Courtesy University of Illinois Library at Chicago Circle Campus,
          Jane Addams Memorial Collection.
p. 141:   Courtesy Department of Archives and Manuscripts, Louisiana State
          University, Baton Rouge.
p. 217:   Courtesy U.S. Office of War Information, the National Archives.

Published simultaneously in Canada.

Printed in the United States of America.

International Standard Book Number: 0-669-00954-7

Library of Congress Catalog Card Number: 77-78614

Preface

Our concerns in presenting this book are contemporary—we believe that modern problems can be clarified by studying the past. Our major assumption is that at certain periods in American history, men and women faced problems that still exist today and that their efforts must be considered if *our* confrontation is to be understood. We gather around us, then, people like Jonathan Edwards, Benjamin Franklin, Sam Adams, Daniel Webster, Henry David Thoreau, Abraham Lincoln, Andrew Carnegie, Woodrow Wilson, Jane Addams, Oliver Wendell Holmes, Jr., Franklin Roosevelt, and ask their advice. We also call to us people less well known to history—a former slave, an early immigrant, an assembly of unknown women organizing to fight slavery, a black historian, a labor organizer, a veteran trying to survive the Depression, a couple of Peace Corps workers — and ask their counsel. Finally, we bring men and women who have confronted these problems in our own times, and we solicit their understandings and proposals. We ask of the historical figures, "When you faced issues like those confronting us, how did *you* try to resolve them?" We require a dialogue about the enduring issues in American life with both our contemporaries and our ancestors.

There are limitations in the answers provided by the past. Earlier Americans confronted the issues at times when the structure of society, beliefs about man's place in the universe, and other fundamental concepts and experiences were quite different from today. We must perceive therefore how these differences may limit potential answers to today's problems.

But the fact of limitations does not invalidate the method. The best demonstration of its validity is provided by reading the documents themselves. When the Puritans dealt with the question of creating a sense of community, they were as aware as we are of the vital role played in the process by the family, the individual's moral sense, the school, and the state. When the people of the Civil War era agonized over whether or not war could be justified, they posed a question yet to be answered: Will the result of victory be worth the numbers of the dead? When Americans at the turn of the century calculated the cost of achievement, they wrestled as we do with the question "What will getting ahead cost my family, my society, my own humanity?" When we discover that our parents' generation also wondered how their government could be responsive to the needs of "little people," the "generation gap" narrows a bit.

Finding answers in the past will not uncover a blueprint for today — will not ensure resolution of modern dilemmas. In order to deal with today's problems, we need to understand clearly today's world. Knowledge of the past, however, will make us recognize the dimensions of the issues which have troubled men and women for centuries. We shall become aware of alternative responses extending beyond our time. Studying the past frees us from the present, providing us greater opportunity to shape our future, because we are able to expand our options and increase our choices. As T. S. Eliot put it, "This is the use of memory, for liberation — not less of love, but expanding of love beyond desire, and so liberation from the future as well as the past." Here, then, is the ideological foundation for this text.

There is a pedagogical foundation also. We believe that, for students, "doing history" is as important as reading it and that reading the sources and coming to conclusions based on them is an imperative preliminary step to evaluating what historians or anyone else — past and present — write and say.

Our format for "doing history" pivots on the issues, juxtaposing the past and the present in several ways: first, by an introductory essay which provides the background needed to understand a topic in its time as well as its meaning for us today; second, by a biography of a prominent person whose efforts in dealing with an issue altered existing beliefs; third, by introductory comments preceding the documents which suggest questions thoughtful persons might ask themselves were they living at the time; and finally, by a modern essay which illustrates today's discussion of an issue.

The *introductory essays* to each section of the book are designed to show how these issues remain vital and suggest the range of argument that they have provoked. Though the Puritans are gone, the central problems of their life continue to demand answers of us. Though John Brown's body "lies a molderin' in the grave," the issues tormenting his soul go marching on. Though Jane Addams is dead, the conflicts which threaded through her life exist today also. Though Franklin Roosevelt is no more, many of the problems he wrestled with remain.

The *biographies* following the introductory essays help make the issues more vivid by relating them to the lives of thoughtful, interesting men and women. They offer readers a chance to examine why people like William Byrd, Thomas Hart Benton, William Jennings Bryan, Paul Robeson responded as they did to these persistent problems. We hope that the biographies will also provoke you to question how your life relates to the issues today: What is *my* community based on? Can it, should it, endure? What would *I* fight, kill, or die for? What price am I willing to pay for success? How much of my comfort would I give up so that others might live?

The *documents* bring to life the conflicts of the past. They recreate the sense of being alive in another age, of listening, as it were, to an ancient radio and hearing history being made in the accents and dialects of the time. By reflecting a wide range of opinions on issues, they suggest the past be viewed not in black and white but rather in infinitely subtle shades of gray. The editors' comments and questions which precede each document are designed to stimulate thought, discussions, and argument. They encourage the reader to ponder the complex evolution and subsequent mutations of the issues through time. Indeed, encountering the issues again in the *modern essays,* the reader realizes how bound we are to today's imperatives and how important it is to call forth yesterday's forgotten insights, in order to understand the dimensions of problems which have persisted throughout the American experience.

We believe that *Issues Past and Present* will stimulate an encounter with and respect for this nation's roots by showing that the tree which has emerged from these roots flourishes in our own time. Students in introductory American history courses will benefit from confronting a past shown to be relevant to modern dilemmas. But this book is not just a text for students in school. It is offered for all people who are concerned about the world they live in and who recognize that the issues our ancestors wrestled with in the past continue to shape the present. We cannot afford to ignore their experiences as we try to shape our future.

P. S. P.
R. M. C.
M. A. M.
J. G. U.
D. C. L.

Acknowledgments

Although this work is the product of much mutual discussion and criticism, each of the authors has made specific contributions. Robert Calhoon prepared "Colonial and Revolutionary America" and "The Young Republic." Phillip Paludan is responsible for "Manifest Destiny and Reform" and "Civil War and Reconstruction." He collaborated with Calhoon on the section on colonial community. Michael Moore wrote and edited "The Gilded Age" and "The Progressive Era." Jonathan Utley wrote and edited "Prosperity and Depression" and "An Insecure World." Donald Lord prepared the biographies. Paludan coordinated the efforts and acted as general editor.

We have accumulated debts to others who have contributed to this effort, and they must be recognized. We would like to thank Clifford Griffin, Donald McCoy, Mark Rose, and John Lomax of the University of Kansas; William Bruce Wheeler, Charles W. Johnson, Stephen V. Ash, James A. Burran, Nancy-Ann E. Min, Bonnie B. Gilley of the University of Tennessee, Knoxville; and Kathleen Swiger and David C. Roller.

Our families sustained the effort with their love, their diversions, and their encouragement, and to them we also owe our thanks.

Contents

PART II

The Progressive Era

PART III

Prosperity and Depression

PART IV

An Insecure World

PART I

The Gilded Age

1

Introduction

Success and Survival:
Coping with the American Dream

National birthdays have been times of celebration and reflection. In both the centennial celebration in 1876 and the bicentennial anniversary in 1976, the American people congratulated themselves on having survived as long as they had, and for the progress they had made since the nation's founding. They took pride in their economic wealth, their great cities, their dazzling array of inventions, their political system, and, perhaps most of all, their belief that America had remained a "land of opportunity," offering to all the chance to improve their material and spiritual well-being. In both 1876 and 1976, equal opportunity, individual self-improvement, and economic prosperity for all were thought to be essential ingredients of the "American Dream," a dream that had come true for many.

Certainly the Philadelphia Exposition of 1876, created in honor of the nation's centennial, celebrated the success of that Dream. There was the Corliss steam engine, a mammoth machine capable of generating thousands of horsepower of energy, and exhibitions of the tremendous advances that energetic Americans had made in industry, commerce, and construction. Orators sang America's praises, looking back with pride at the accomplishments the nation had made in a mere one hundred years, and looking forward to an even brighter destiny. That was the "American way," using history as a confirmation that we were on the right track toward a future that would offer even more fulfillment than had the past. There was no limit to what we could do or become.

Other voices at Philadelphia were less optimistic, however. As they reflected on America's past and future, they found much about which to be concerned. To them, America was still a great social "experiment" whose results could lead either to chaos or continuity. One such observer was an Englishman, Thomas H. Huxley, who pinpointed the potential problems of America with chilling accuracy:[1]

> ... To an Englishman landing upon your shores for the first time, travelling hundreds of miles through strings of great and well-ordered cities, seeing your enormous actual, and almost infinite potential, wealth in all commodities, and in the energy and ability which turn wealth to account, there is something sublime in the vista of the future. Do not suppose that I am pandering to what is commonly understood by national pride. I cannot say that I am in the slightest degree impressed by your bigness, or your material resources, as such. Size is not grandeur, and territory does not make a nation. The great issue, about which hangs a true sublimity, and the terror of overhanging fate, is what are you going to do with all these things? What is to be the end to which these are to be the means? You are making a novel experiment in politics on the greatest scale which the world has yet seen. Forty millions at your first centenary, it is reasonably to be expected that, at the second, these states will be occupied by two hundred millions of English-speaking people, spread over an area as large as that of Europe and with climates and interests as diverse as those of Spain and Scandinavia, England and Russia. You and your descendants will have to ascertain whether this great mass will hold together under the forms of a republic, and the despotic reality of universal suffrage; whether state rights will hold against centralisation, without separation; whether centralisation will get the better, without actual or disguised monarchy; whether shifting corruption is better than a permanent bureaucracy; and as population thickens in your great cities, and the pressure of want is felt, the gaunt spectre of pauperism will stalk among you, and communism and socialism will claim to be heard. Truly America has a great future before her; great in toil, in care, and in responsibility; great in true glory if she be guided in wisdom and righteousness; great in shame if she fail.

It is important to understand Huxley's comments because they form the framework for this chapter. He pointed to a number of paradoxes that could unravel the fabric of American life at that time: the clash of interest groups versus the myth of a "classless society," the growing nationalization of life and activity versus the tradition of small towns and decentralized government, the increasing gap between the very rich and the masses of poor people, the tradition of an open government versus the tendency to centralize the presidency into a monarchy, and the razor's edge between corruption and a permanent

---

[1] Thomas H. Huxley, *American Addresses* (New York: D. Appleton & Co., 1877), pp. 125 ff.

class of government bureaucrats. Even though Huxley was speaking in 1876, could not his observations have been equally relevant in 1976?

Huxley was pointing at something about which many Americans were beginning to worry: the society that had given rise to the American dream was fading, being replaced by a social, economic, and political set of realities that threatened the tradition of self-help, rugged individualism, the family, and personal responsibility that had formed the core of most Americans' beliefs since the beginning of the Republic. Huxley was calling attention to the formation of an urban proletariat, a phenomenon with which Thomas Jefferson was unfamiliar, but about which Karl Marx had written very perceptively. Huxley talked about the rise of the federal government in the wake of the Civil War and the emergence of political machines that paralleled the growth of the cities, something of which the writers of the Constitution were unaware, but which had become a way of political life to the swarms of "bosses" who pulled strings in nearly every major city in the country.

In short, Huxley was painting a picture that stood in stark contrast to the prevailing belief systems of the time. The gap between rhetoric of individualism and the reality of industrialism was constantly growing wider, making people wonder just what was necessary in order to survive or to succeed. Beliefs die hard, particularly the belief in America as a land of equal opportunity. To be sure, most immigrants found life in this country more bearable than from where they had emigrated. Even as hard as factory labor was in this country, it was still "a damn sight better than . . . to slave for fourteen hours a day with manure all over your boots," as one historian noted.[2] Yet, while an immigrant from Europe or a migrant from the farm to the city might be able to chart progress from the standpoint of where he or she had been, what were the prospects for continued survival or success? Greater opportunity was not the same as equal opportunity, yet the failure to distinguish between the two created a host of problems.

The "old beliefs," or, the American Dream, as many preferred to say, were based upon the expectation that individuals would be able to achieve as much upward social and economic mobility for themselves or their children as their desires and abilities could attain. At a time when the acquisition and exploitation of land represented individual success and social standing, this had been a reasonably attainable ideal (for whites). Unlike Europe, which was beginning to experience a population squeeze, America could boast a frontier line (less than two people per square mile) until 1890, which, when coupled with the vast mineral deposits and rich agriculture, led the Scottish historian Thomas Carlyle to admonish an American correspondent: "Ye may boast o' dimocracy, or any ither cracy, or any kind o' poleetical roobish; but the rea-

---

[2] Stephan Thernstrom, "Urbanization, Migration, and Social Mobility in Late Nineteenth Century America," in Barton J. Bernstein, ed., *Towards a New Past: Dissenting Essays in American History* (New York: Vintage, 1969), pp. 161–162, 163. Copyright © 1967, 1968, by Random House, Inc.

son why yer laboring folk are so happy is thoth ye have a vost deal o' land for a verra few people." [3] Carlyle's observation was confirmed in this country: "I wasn't worth a cint and bejabbers to-day I'm worth me thousands upon thousands," [4] said one Irish immigrant. Or as a farmer testified: "You can see it in people's faces, you can feel it in the aire. Everybody and everythings' goin' places." [5]

The basis for the American definition of success was *material*. The qualitative worth of individuals was measured in quantitative terms. If you were a worthwhile human being it was assumed that you worked hard, and conversely, if you worked hard, you would have something to show for it. Although there were other measures of human value and dignity, they did not have the force of the materialistic yardstick: the acreage under cultivation, the increase in the gross national product, the miles of railroad track laid, the amount of land wrested from the environment and the Indians, and after 1890, the number of islands added to the American Empire. Such "progress" was seen as the result of hard work by individuals and therefore evidence of strong moral character; failure by definition was seen as an admission of personal weakness or laziness. Our material success was a sign of God's favor. Thus, the Episcopal bishop of Massachusetts, the Reverend Thomas Lawrence, could write in all sincerity in 1890 that "Godliness is in league with riches," raising the intriguing possibility that one's standing with the Almighty was directly proportional to the size of one's bank account. Americans, conditioned to believing that material success and moral character were but two sides of the same coin — whose motto, after all, was "In God We Trust" — could accept at face value the statement that "God gave me my money," even though it was John D. Rockefeller who said it.

This materialism that underlay American concepts of success and moral character was so pervasive that it blended together many ideological threads. The prevailing economic philosophy was based upon Adam Smith, whose concepts of laissez faire, the laws of the market place, and the "invisible hand" assumed that free, selfish individuals in their collective struggle for wealth all would work together for the welfare of the entire community. Much of the religious thought was based upon what historians have called the "Protestant ethic," a system of belief that stressed hard work, sobriety, thrift, investment of profits, respect for property, and obedience to authority as the way to achieve salvation in the afterlife. Indeed, the traits that identified the religious person were precisely those of Adam Smith's ideal "economic" person, and they motivated William Jennings Bryan no less than Andrew Carnegie.

Not only were hard work, material growth, and thrift economically and morally correct; such traits were also patriotic. As a young country America

---

[3] David Potter, *People of Plenty* (Chicago: University of Chicago Press, 1954), p. 126, n.
[4] Eric Goldman, *Rendezvous with Destiny* (New York: Vintage Books, 1952), p. 7.
[5] Ibid., p. 1.

needed hard workers to accomplish its national goals: taming the environment, opening up the West, developing foreign trade, laying railroad track, growing food, and working in the mills. All of these activities, and more, contributed to America's manifest destiny, a mystical, optimistic faith that it was America's fate to grow and to dominate the North American continent.

Therefore, the American Dream, resting as it did on the triple foundation of profits, piety, and patriotism, was deeply imbedded in most Americans' way of identifying themselves and each other. It was a dream that taught both a sense of individual vindication — and guilt. It was also a dream that was taught to the young at an early age, as *McGuffey's Eclectic Readers* illustrate. The *Readers,* first published in the 1830s, were the basic reading text for generations of American school children; some 22,000,000 copies were sold. Although they contained literary selections superior to the content of later readers (such as the *Fun with Dick and Jane* series), they were also intensely and narrowly moralistic, reflecting a small-town, agrarian, and culturally homogeneous society of self-reliant individuals. McGuffey did not include stories of labor unions, immigrants, the hardships of living in the city; there were no references to the problems of large government, monopolies, or of population density. Such phenomena simply did not exist in McGuffey's view of the world. To him, individuals were primarily responsible for their own futures, and if they made a mess of it, they were at fault.

Horatio Alger, a popular writer of boys' books in the late nineteenth century, made the same point. Ragged Dick, one of his heroes, was the archetypical individual who overcame adversity and poverty, took care of his sick mother, behaved like a "good boy," and climbed the ladder of (material) success to achieve his reward. Alger wrote over ninety books, all of them based upon the same formula, and all preaching the gospel of success.

It is the purpose of this chapter to examine two of the problems raised by Huxley: (1) What were the requirements for impoverished but ambitious people to "get ahead," to achieve upward mobility; and (2) what was the cost that industrialism exacted from people who simply tried to survive? To be sure, these two questions are interrelated; the line between success and survival is sometimes indistinct. Yet there are some essential differences that make these problems worth examining separately.

First, people seeking simply to survive were not necessarily threats to the existing social order. The lonely farmer "busting sod" on the prairie, the anxious immigrant seeking work, the industrial worker fighting disease and despair, or the young people growing up in Meadville, Pennsylvania, were not so concerned at the time about changing the social order as they were in trying to find meaning for their individual lives. Thus, their world was often their immediate neighborhood. Many of the less fortunate had come from circumstances much harsher than what they were presently enduring, and this may explain why they were willing to put up with so much deprivation. Others still hoped that in this land of opportunity, things would improve if only they could hold out just a little longer. After all, had not Andrew Carnegie started at the bottom?

Yet there were others — themselves often poor — who wanted more out of life than simple survival: they wanted to succeed and make the American Dream a reality for their own lives. These people, however, faced another problem. If they were factory workers like Samuel Gompers, or if they were black like Booker T. Washington, they had additional obstacles to overcome in order to succeed. Anti-unionism and racism were quite prevalent during the Gilded Age because unions and blacks were seen as threats to the social order, and were therefore "un-American." Thus Gompers and Washington had to ask themselves: "How do I and my followers get something out of the system without appearing to threaten it, or appearing to sell out to the other side?" Although Richard Nixon is neither a black nor a union member, he faced the dilemma of the price an impoverished person had to pay in order to succeed. In linking Washington, Gompers, and Nixon to the rhetoric of success we come face to face with a fundamental struggle in American life: Does the kind of "success" described by Carnegie, McGuffey, Twain, Altgeld, and Garry Wills force us to be something other than what we would like to be?

Second, the problem of survival was a *social* problem, whereas the problem of success was, to an extent, an *individual* one. Even though McGuffey and others implied that it was your own fault if you were poor, the realities of industrialization began to force many to ask whether poverty indeed was caused by "the system." If so, was there a need for some kind of social control to prevent exploitation so that every individual had a chance to prove his or her worth? This was the question that the Populists tried to answer in 1892 and which led to the prominence of William Jennings Bryan in 1896. Bryan's Cross of Gold speech (page 48) was significant because it attacked the old myth that people's failure was their own fault. In taking dead aim at the industrial system as a cause of failure, he opened a debate that continues to the present day.

The struggle for success is somewhat more optional than the struggle for survival. Samuel Gompers did not have to run for president of the American Federation of Labor; Booker T. Washington did not have to establish a black college at Tuskegee, Alabama; Richard Nixon did not have to go into politics. It is possible to argue that these men could have found more modest goals for themselves and would have avoided the problems they were to confront. But they did not; they chose to "play the game."

The problem that confronts us today is whether to play the game: to decide what we want for our lives, and risk the consequences of failure or psychological stress. To be sure, we may not be able to alter the game's rules; yet are we to be enslaved by them?

William Jennings Bryan's career exemplifies the dilemma of success and survival. Raised in small-town America, he devoutly believed in personal success and responsibility. Yet the realities of industrialism forced him to realize that these personal characteristics were no longer enough. If the old virtues were still to produce success, there needed to be some changes in the system. But what kind of changes? Bryan, like so many of the people in the following documents, could only fight with the weapons that he knew; like so many others he could make out the nature of the "enemy," but not totally identify and conquer it. That was the dilemma of many in the Gilded Age.

Personalizing the Issues

William Jennings Bryan: The Great Commoner

It was a rare moment in history. The scene was a political convention, but this time the delegates were not sitting in quiet boredom, or making dutiful responses to the usual political harangue; the delegates to the 1896 Democratic convention were enraptured. The speaker, a young politician–editor from Nebraska, spoke as if the world were on fire and only his words could quench the flames. In turn he appealed to the delegates' humanity, their anger, and their Christianity as he dramatized the plight of the western farmer caught in the frightening vice of falling farm prices and rising costs. He had

come, he said, to speak to them "in defense of a cause as holy as the cause of liberty — the cause of humanity." Then, as the delegates sat basking in their humanity, he appealed to their militancy. "We have," he continued, "petitioned and our petitions have been scorned; we have entreated and our entreaties have been disregarded; we have begged and they mocked when our calamity came." Then as they acknowledged their agreement by jumping and shouting, he exclaimed, "We beg no longer; we entreat no more; we petition no more. We defy them!" When the deafening roar which greeted that defiant statement diminished, the speaker went on slowly, surely, building his argument, using and responding to his listeners' rapture. The climax came as the young man served notice on the enemies of humanity that they would "not press down upon the brow of labor this crown of thorns"; [they would] "not crucify mankind upon a cross of gold."

Before the thirty-six-year-old William Jennings Bryan rose to address the convention, the leaders of the Democratic party had been more responsive to their eastern rather than their western constituency, as they had since the end of the Civil War; when he sat down, they could no longer ignore the mood of the party's discontented rural element. In the previous three elections Grover Cleveland of New York had been the party's nominee. It made no difference to many of the delegates that he had been twice victorious, or that at the moment he sat in the White House. What mattered to them was that no one seemed to understand or care about their plight.

The rebellious delegates were eager for change. They felt themselves helpless victims of a system which gripped them like an octopus, and no single part of that system strangled them more than railroads. The iron tentacles of the nation's railway network seemed to choke western agrarians in many ways. Railroads were usually given grants of public lands and supported by public taxation. Then they ungraciously bled the public. Although many of the farmers' charges were exaggerated, it should be noted that it was cheaper to ship a load of grain from Chicago to Liverpool by boat than it was to send the same load from the Dakotas to Minneapolis by train. This phenomenon is one reason why 11,000 families lost their farms to foreclosure in Kansas between 1889 and 1893.

While the railroad represented the first "soulless corporation" to the struggling agrarians, the scarcity of money was considered by many to be the basic cause of the farmer's plight. Money was indeed scarce. Frightened by the inflation caused by the issue of greenbacks during the Civil War, fiscal conservatives and moderates were able to persuade the Congress to return to the gold standard and retire the greenbacks then in circulation. This caused monetary deflation just as farm prices tumbled. At the close of the war, wheat had sold for $2.50 a bushel; by the 1890s it had dropped to 50¢ a bushel. The seriousness of the situation can be easily illustrated. Most farmers were debtors. If they had borrowed $1000 when wheat was selling at $1.00 a bushel and had to repay the loan when wheat was 75 cents a bushel, they needed 333 more bushels of wheat to end their indebtedness than they had needed when they contracted their loan. Thus when Bryan spread his arms like the crucified Christ and stated that the people would not be crucified upon a cross fashioned from the gold standard, he vividly demonstrated for the delegates their own frustrations.

Economists have since pointed out that Bryan's remedy for the plight of the farmers, the free coinage of silver at the ratio of sixteen silver dollars to one gold dollar, would not have corrected the deflationary situation, but neither he nor his flock understood that concept. In the 1890s, the grasp of economics at all levels of society was limited, and few national leaders advocated government action of any kind no matter how serious the situation became. This was not because they were callous to human suffering, but because they believed that hidden forces beyond human control regulated economic matters. During the Depression of 1893, for example, Cleveland waited for the economy to straighten itself out. Thus when the charismatic Bryan spoke at the Democratic convention three years later, he found a willing audience.

Even though the country was in the biggest uproar since the election of 1876, it is still surprising that this man who had served two terms in Congress and who recently had been defeated for a seat in the United States Senate could acquire the nomination of his party, particularly since he had little understanding of many of the major changes brought about by urbanism, industrialism, immigration, and the growing nationalization of American politics. He was always a provincial; he was a spokesman for a rural America which assumed that success in America during the Gilded Age was achieved just as it would have been in early America. He believed that industry and Christian morality, coupled with a government crackdown on "corporate evil," would conquer all obstacles. He never deviated from his beliefs that cities were equated with vice, that the Democratic party was on the side of the angels, and that reason, tempered with love, could conquer force.

Such simplicity of belief deserves an explanation. Born in Salem, Illinois, in 1860, Bryan grew up as what Hamlin Garland called a "Son of the Middle Border." While other midwesterners like Sherwood Anderson and Edgar Lee Masters became famous for exposing the provincialism of middle America (that is, the Middle Border), Bryan became famous for espousing its virtues. Basically he was a product of two inseparable forces: agrarian Protestant Christianity and the *McGuffey Readers.*

As noted earlier, the *McGuffey Readers* stressed that the agrarian way of life was the purest form of living. Indeed, morality permeated every page. The main point of each lesson was moral: "waste not, want not"; "try, try again"; "virtue is always rewarded"; and so on. Despite a widespread belief that America was a land built on the separation of church and state, God was omnipresent in the *McGuffey Readers,* but the readers also had their worldly side. Since virtue was always rewarded, kind, honest, thrifty people were successful, and disobedient, greedy, and rude ones were punished. Additional subjects included patriotism and philosophy. Many orations were printed, particularly those that called for a "girding of the loins" to achieve great things in the face of adversity.

The impact of the *McGuffey Readers* on both Bryan and his constituents was pervasive. Whatever their faults, the *Readers* created several generations of statesmen who shared common ties and a common body of illusion. The agrarian myth they perpetuated, and the simple concept of a not-so-simple-world, motivated both the Populists and the Bryan Democrats.

The Christian fundamentalism expressed in the *Readers* was also evident in Bryan's religious education. His belief in the infallibility of the Bible and the necessity of living the Golden Rule was also shared by his constituents. Not until the Scopes Monkey Trial of 1925, when Clarence Darrow exposed some of the weaker points of Bryan's theology, was his religious dedication a liability. His testimony disappointed fundamentalists and angered the liberals, causing H. L. Mencken to conclude that "The President of the United States [Coolidge] may be an ass, but at least he doesn't believe that the earth is square, and that witches should be put to death, and that Jonah swallowed the whale." Yet according to Bryan's beliefs, his reasoning was not illogical. He believed that there was no civilization without morality, morality came from religion, religion rested on a belief in God, a belief in God rested on a belief in the Bible, and Darwinism undermined the Bible. For these reasons, he appeared as the champion of reaction in the Scopes trial.

Usually, Bryan's intuition was much more rational, due partly to the strong influence of the democratic ideals of Thomas Jefferson, and the belief of the Russian novelist Tolstoy that love was more powerful than the sword. Even his detractors — and they were numerous — admitted that his sympathy for the underprivileged was genuine, and that he was no demagogue. He believed what he said and for most of his life he was an amazingly consistent politician.

Bryan's honesty, decency, and compassion were rewarded in 1890 and 1892 when he was elected congressman from Nebraska. In 1894, when state legislatures still elected senators, he failed in his effort to join "the world's most exclusive club." For the next two years he edited the Omaha *World-Herald* and traveled the Chautauqua circuit, developing the oratorical excellence that earned him the title of "the Golden-Voiced Orator of the Platte." It mattered little to his constituents and devoted followers that his detractors said he was much like the River Platte, very shallow and a "mile wide at the mouth"; his constituency saw him as the delivering angel who combined common sense and showmanship.

After his defeat in 1894, the Nebraskan concentrated his efforts on working for the Democratic presidential nomination. This seemed presumptuous to Democratic politicians, who refused to take his candidacy seriously. They failed to understand that as he traveled across the nation, perfecting his style and developing his arguments, he was participating in a political revolution. In 1896, when he threw his hands above his head and slowly pulled them toward his temples as he announced that no one would "press down upon the brow of labor this crown of thorns," symbolically he pulled down a political way of life that had been changing for over a decade.

Prior to Bryan's nomination, the American government had dealt unsuccessfully with the problems created by the nationalization of American life, mainly because few politicians came to grips with the need for effective government. In the years 1896–1915, in which he was a viable force in the Democratic Party, the structure of politics did not change as both parties became the parties of reform, but the nature of politics changed drastically. After 1896, presidential candidates discussed issues that had long been ignored. Later, in 1906, when Theodore Roosevelt was president, his annual State of the Union message was referred to by the New York *World* as the Bryan-Roosevelt merger. According to the editor, Roosevelt, a man who had considered Bryan a dangerous radical in the 1890s, adopted all of the Democrat's "radical" ideas except those on the regulation of the railroads and the reduction of the tariff. The editor could have gone further: as the Progressive Republican William Allen White said, the "Republicans caught the Populists [and thus Bryan] in swimming and stole their clothes except for their tarnished underwear of silver."

The so-called Bryan-Roosevelt merger was an important step forward effective government in America, as Taft and Roosevelt channelled the rural and urban impulses for reform into a meaningful program. It emphasized Bryan's role as one of the most successful failures in America and reiterated his belief that the American government functioned best when there were two parties: the radical and the conservative. The radical party would force the conservative party to move, and the conservative one would make sure the radicals would not move too fast or too far.

Bryan's oversimplified analysis was unacceptable to many voters in 1896, but it is interesting to note that the Democrats called for trust-busting, an end to both high tariffs and labor injunctions, and a graduated income tax, all considered radical innovations at the time. Bryan's demand for increasing the supply of money by coining silver was considered his most radical demand. Such was the fear generated by the western spokesman that eastern workers were told that his election would mean a 50-cent dollar and no work. After his defeat, rational journals like *Harper's Weekly* and *The Nation* claimed that America "escaped Socialism" and that "civilization" had defeated "barbarism." To this McKinley's national and intelligent campaign manager, Mark Hanna, added: "God's in his heaven, all's right with the world!"

In many ways the campaign of 1896 was one of America's most significant political elections. Although it can be said that it really symbolized adjustments already in motion before 1896, it was through this campaign that the issues of the 1890s were brought into clearer focus and the quest for adjustment to the modern world begun. This was due in great part to Bryan's tireless labors. He traveled over 1,800 miles and gave 600 speeches. Neither his voice nor his energy wavered despite the handicaps under which he labored. Money was a constant problem. Standard Oil and J. P. Morgan gave a combined total of $500,000 to the Republican campaign. This was more than the entire fund raised by the Democrats. Near the close of the campaign when Mark Hanna was returning unneeded and unsolicited funds, Bryan kept his "Barefoot Campaign" going on a day-to-day basis, never missing an opportunity to speak to his devoted followers. Once when he was interrupted while shaving, he stuck his lathered face through an open window and gave an impromptu address. Whenever halls were filled, he went outside and spoke briefly to his overflow audiences and continued his spellbinding effect upon rural América. As he said, when he finished his sentences there was a roar of approval; when he started the next one, "the room was still as a church."

Bryan's approach worked, but only in the depressed areas of the South and the West that had once been Populist strongholds. He lost the election by 600,000 votes, but since McKinley carried the most populous sections, Bryan lost even more decidedly in the electoral college (271–176). As Hanna said, the Great Commoner "talked silver too much," thus the cities went overwhelmingly Republican. Only twelve of the eighty-two cities over 45,000 in population went for Bryan, and seven of those were in the Democratic South. Bryan failed to carry a single county in New England, and only one in New York. Even New York City went Republican. Prosperous farm states like Iowa, Wisconsin, and Minnesota also went to McKinley. Yet Bryan received more popular votes than any previous candidate in history. He aroused the electorate as few others had, but like all dynamic people, he aroused both support and opposition.

Bryan never again came as close to the presidency as he had in 1896. Twice more — in 1900 and 1908 — he tried for the White House and failed, but he remained an important force within the party. In 1904, even though he was rejected in favor of an eastern candidate, he campaigned for him as the lesser of two evils against William Howard Taft. In 1912, he helped initiate the swing toward Woodrow Wilson in the Democratic convention when it appeared that New York was trying to get the nomination for Champ Clark. Later, as Wilson's Secretary of State, he used his influence with considerable effect to push Wilson's New Freedom legislation through Congress. Only when he resigned from Wilson's cabinet because the president seemed inconsistent in his foreign policy — professing neutrality during Europe's war, but actually following policies that Bryan thought were not — did the "Great Commoner's" influence within the party ebb. For the next ten years he did little to add to his stature and much to detract from it, and when he died quietly in his sleep in 1925, five days after the close of the Monkey Trial, he was no longer the giant of a man who left his impact upon his country.

But these actions were anticlimactic. Bryan's greatest contributions had been made during the Gilded Age as he led the farmers' crusade for social justice. Most of the so-called radical causes which he and the Populists championed became realities, either through the efforts of the Progressives or the New Dealers. Progressive historian Paolo E. Coletta has argued that Bryan was as successful in defeat as other politicians have been in success. Most of his cherished goals, including income and inheritance taxes, tariff reform, abolition of crushing labor injunctions, banking and currency reform, the direct election of senators, and direct primaries, were achieved by later politicians. Coletta concluded that "all that was reasonable in Bryanism . . . was eventually" achieved.

Not all historians accept Coletta's evaluation of the "Great Commoner." To them Bryan was a provincial who drew attention to national problems, but offered only provincial and decentralized solutions which pitted section against section. Bryan may have changed the nature of politics, they argue, but it was Roosevelt and Taft who provided the necessary structure — a national party — to bring about necessary political reforms. Furthermore, it is possible that the "Golden-Voiced Orator" was the Gilded Age's Don Quixote, jousting at windmills with outdated weapons, with all of the nobleness and futility that that effort implies. But if this is true, like Don Quixote, he left the world a better place in which to live, because he was willing to confront the issues of his age even if he did not understand all their subtlety. The important and dramatic changes in America that took place between 1896 and 1914 were in part due to his constant efforts. He had the courage, if not the wisdom, to move the nation through these years.

Issue

The Price of Achievement

The striver can never stop striving. It is because Nixon is so totally this sweaty moral self-doubting self-made bustling brooding type, that he represents the integral liberalism that once animated America and now tries to reassert itself.

Garry Wills, 1970

There is no excellence without great labor. It is the fiat of fate, from which no power of genius can absolve you.

McGuffey's Reader, 1879

A freshman once described his parents as "workaholics" — people so driven by ambition and the lure of success that they thought of nothing other than getting ahead on the job. We all know of workaholics — the "go-getters," those who are "going places," someone whose first coronary (before the age of 40) symbolizes a purple heart won on the battlefields of business.

"Competitive stimuli are active from the cradle to the grave," a noted scholar once said, in describing the kind of social environment in which we grow up.[1]

We may solemnly swear that we will never allow ourselves to be caught in the "rat race," but it is a promise that becomes increasingly difficult to keep in a culture that seems so dedicated to success, competition, ambition, and achievement.

How are we to measure "achievement" — the way in which it can spur people on to do more than they thought they could do, as well as the cost it often exacts from people? The purpose of this section is to provide a perspective on these questions by examining some evidence from an earlier era (the Gilded Age) that stretches from the end of the Civil War to the end of the nineteenth century. When it comes to the drive for success, the "rags-to-riches" myth, and stories of poor folks who made good, the Gilded Age has few equals. The period also provides us with a chance to look at ourselves, because the Gilded Age was the beginning of modern America.

As you read the following documents, you might start out by asking: "What are the possible consequences — beneficial as well as detrimental — of having a belief system that is based upon materialistic values?"

◆ DOCUMENTS ◆

Laying Down the Ground Rules for Achievement

MCGUFFEY'S READER

McGuffey's Readers *helped shape the values of countless Americans. What values does this selection advance? Why should these values be respected? What would be wrong in just plain loafing? Of what aspects of life would full devotion to these ideals deprive us?*

---

[1] Karen Horney, quoted in David Potter, *People of Plenty,* p. 55.

Source: From William Holmes McGuffey, *McGuffey's Fifth Eclectic Reader, 1879 Edition* (reprint by New American Library, 1962), pp. 71, 242–244.

Work

1. Work, work, my boy, be not afraid;
     Look labor boldly in the face;
   Take up the hammer or the spade,
     And blush not for your humble place.

2. There's glory in the shuttle's song;
     There's triumph in the anvil's stroke;
   There's merit in the brave and strong
     Who dig the mine or fell the oak.

3. The wind disturbs the sleeping lake,
     And bids it ripple pure and fresh;
   It moves the green boughs till they make
     Grand music in their leafy mesh.

4. And so the active breath of life
     Should stir our dull and sluggard wills;
   For are we not created rife
     With health, that stagnant torpor kills?

5. I doubt if he who lolls his head
     Where idleness and plenty meet,
   Enjoys his pillow or his bread
     As those who earn the meals they eat.

6. And man is never half so blest
     As when the busy day is spent
   So as to make his evening rest
     A holiday of glad content.

No Excellence without Labor

1. The education, moral and intellectual, of every individual, must be chiefly his own work. Rely upon it that the ancients were right; both in morals and intellect we give the final shape to our characters, and thus become, emphatically, the architects of our own fortune. How else could it happen that young men, who have had precisely the same opportunities, should be continually presenting us with such different results, and rushing to such opposite destinies?

2. Difference of talent will not solve it, because that difference is very often in favor of the disappointed candidate. You will see issuing from the walls of the same college, may, sometimes from the bosom of the same family, two young men, of whom one will be admitted to be a genius of high order, the other scarcely above the point of mediocrity; yet you will see the genius

sinking and perishing in poverty, obscurity, and wretchedness; while, on the other hand, you will observe the mediocre plodding his slow but sure way up the hill of life, gaining steadfast footing at every step, and mounting, at length, to eminence and distinction, an ornament to his family, a blessing to his country.

3. Now, whose work is this? Manifestly their own. They are the architects of their respective fortunes. The best seminary of learning that can open its portals to you can do no more than to afford you the opportunity of instruction; but it must depend, at last, on yourselves, whether you will be instructed or not, or to what point you will push your instruction.

4. And of this be assured, I speak from observation a certain truth: THERE IS NO EXCELLENCE WITHOUT GREAT LABOR. It is the fiat of fate, from which no power of genius can absolve you.

5. Genius, unexerted, is like the poor moth that flutters around a candle till it scorches itself to death. If genius be desirable at all, it is only of that great and magnanimous kind, which, like the condor of South America, pitches from the summit of Chimborazo, above the clouds, and sustains itself at pleasure in that empyreal region with an energy rather invigorated than weakened by the effort.

6. It is this capacity for high and long-continued exertion, this vigorous power of profound and searching investigation, this careering and wide-spreading comprehension of mind, and these long reaches of thought, that

> Pluck bright honor from the pale-faced moon,
> Or dive into the bottom of the deep,
> And pluck up drowned honor by the locks;

this is the prowess, and these the hardy achievements, which are to enroll your names among the great men of the earth.

A Million Bucks' Worth of Achievement?

JOHN PETER ALTGELD

Altgeld was a penniless German immigrant who became wealthy and later was elected governor of Illinois. He sacrificed his political career by courageously pardoning some of the men convicted of murder in the Haymarket

From John Peter Altgeld, *Live Questions* (Chicago: George P. Bowen, 1889), p. 476.

Square rioting. In this selection, is Altgeld issuing a warning veiled in sarcasm? Would McGuffey have thought that Altgeld was needling him?

How to Make a Million

Springfield, March 17, 1895.

C. R. Macloon, The Tribune, Chicago:

Dear Sir: — You ask what would be my advice to the young man of to-day who is ambitious to become a millionaire.

While I am not the right man to answer your question, I should say to the young man, "Go it alone and hustle." That is, rely on yourself — keep your word — keep your manhood — keep your own counsel — do your own errands and look ahead. No matter how often you fail, keep on. But if you wish to get very rich quickly, then bleed the public and talk patriotism. This may involve bribing public officials and dodging public burdens, the losing of your manhood and the soiling of your fingers, but that is the way most of the great fortunes are made in this country now.

Respectfully,

JOHN P. ALTGELD

Poking Fun at the Success Ethic

MARK TWAIN

The following story would never have appeared in any editions of McGuffey's Readers. *And while Andrew Carnegie might have laughed at Twain's tale, it is doubtful that he would have cared for some of the implications of what Twain was saying. Was Twain trying to be more than humorous? Was he, in effect, needling McGuffey and Carnegie? Were his observations about success more or less accurate than McGuffey's?*

The man lived in Philadelphia who, when young and poor, entered a bank, and says he: "Please, sir, don't you want a boy?" And the stately personage said: "No, little boy, I don't want a little boy." The little boy, whose heart was too full for utterance, chewing a piece of licorice stick he had bought with a cent stolen from his good and pious aunt, with sobs plainly audible, and with great globules of water rolling down his cheeks, glided silently down the marble steps of the bank. Bending his noble form, the bank man dodged behind a door, for he thought the little boy was going to shy a stone at him. But

---

From Mark Twain, "Poor Little Stephen Girard," in Anna Randall-Diehl, ed., *Carleton's Popular Readings* (New York, 1879), pp. 183–184.

the little boy picked up something, and stuck it in his poor but ragged jacket. "Come here, little boy," and the little boy did come here; and the bank man said: "Lo, what pickest thou up?" And he answered and replied: "A pin." And the bank man said: "Little boy, are you good?" and he said he was. And the bank man said: "How do you vote? — excuse me, do you go to Sunday school?" and he said he did. Then the bank man took down a pen made of pure gold, and flowing with pure ink, and he wrote on a piece of paper, "St. Peter;" and he asked the little boy what it stood for, and he said "Salt Peter." Then the bank man said it meant "Saint Peter." The little boy said: "Oh!"

Then the bank man took the little boy to his bosom, and the little boy said, "Oh!" again, for he squeezed him. Then the bank man took the little boy into partnership, and gave him half the profits and all the capital, and he married the bank man's daughter, and now all he has is all his, and all his own too.

My uncle told me this story, and I spent six weeks in picking up pins in front of a bank. I expected the bank man would call me in and say: "Little boy, are you good?" and I was going to say "Yes"; and when he asked me what "St. John" stood for, I was going to say "Salt John." But the bank man wasn't anxious to have a partner, and I guess the daughter was a son, for one day says he to me: "Little boy, what's that you're picking up? Says I, awful meekly, "Pins." Says he: "Let's see 'em." And he took 'em, and I took off my cap, all ready to go in the bank, and become a partner, and marry his daughter. But I didn't get an invitation. He said: "Those pins belong to the bank, and if I catch you hanging around here any more I'll set the dog on you!" Then I left, and the mean old fellow kept the pins. Such is life as I find it.

Justifying One Standard of Achievement
ANDREW CARNEGIE

How many opportunities for success would poor but industrious people have under the kind of system that Carnegie describes? Should we accept Carnegie's assumption that there are going to be losers as well as winners? What would Carnegie define as success? Does he understand the price of it? Is he right about the "laws" of society and nature?

From Andrew Carnegie, "Wealth," *North American Review* (June 1889), CXLVIII, 653–656, 661–663.

The problem of our age is the proper administration of wealth, so that the ties of brotherhood may still bind together the rich and poor in harmonious relationship. The conditions of human life have not only been changed, but revolutionized, within the past few hundred years. . . .

It is easy to see how the change has come. One illustration will serve for almost every phase of the cause. In the manufacture of products we have the whole story. It applies to all combinations of human industry, as stimulated and enlarged by the inventions of this scientific age. Formerly articles were manufactured at the domestic hearth or in small shops which formed part of the household. The master and his apprentices worked side by side, the latter living with the master, and therefore subject to the same conditions. When these apprentices rose to be masters, there was little or no change in their mode of life, and they, in turn, educated in the same routine succeeding apprentices. There was, substantially, social equality, and even political equality, for those engaged in industrial pursuits had then little or no political voice in the State.

But the inevitable result of such a mode of manufacture was crude articles at high prices. To-day the world obtains commodities of excellent quality at prices which even the generation preceding this would have deemed incredible. In the commercial world similar causes have produced similar results, and the race is benefited thereby. The poor enjoy what the rich could not before afford. What were the luxuries have become the necessaries of life. The laborer has now more comforts than the farmer had a few generations ago. The farmer has more luxuries than the landlord had, and is more richly clad and better housed. The landlord has books and pictures rarer, and appointments more artistic, than the King could then obtain.

The price we pay for this salutary change is, no doubt, great. We assemble thousands of operatives in the factory, in the mine, and in the counting-house, of whom the employer can know little or nothing, and to whom the employer is little better than a myth. All intercourse between them is at an end. Rigid Castes are formed, and, as usual, mutual ignorance breeds mutual distrust. Each Caste is without sympathy for the other, and ready to credit anything disparaging in regard to it. Under the law of competition, the employer of thousands is forced into the strictest economies, among which the rates paid to labor figure prominently, and often there is friction between the employer and the employed, between capital and labor, between rich and poor. Human society loses homogeneity.

The price which society pays for the law of competition, like the price it pays for cheap comforts and luxuries, is also great; but the advantages of this law are also greater still, for it is to this law that we owe our wonderful material development, which brings improved conditions in its train. But, whether the law be benign or not, we must say of it, as we say of the change in the conditions of men to which we have referred: It is here; we cannot evade it; no substitutes for it have been found; and while the law may be sometimes hard for the individual, it is best for the race, because it insures the survival of the fittest in every department. We accept and welcome, therefore, as conditions to which we must accommodate ourselves, great inequality of environment, the concentration of business, industrial and commercial, in the hands of a few, and the law of competition between these, as being not only beneficial, but essential for the future progress of the race. Having accepted these, it follows that there must be great scope for the exercise of special ability in the merchant and in the manufacturer who has to conduct affairs upon a great scale. That this talent for organization and management is rare among men is proved by the fact that it invariably secures for its possessor enormous rewards, no matter where or under what laws or conditions. The experienced in affairs always rate the MAN whose services can be obtained as a partner as not only the first consideration, but such as to render the question of his capital scarcely worth considering, for such men soon create capital; while, without the special talent required, capital soon takes wings. Such men become interested in firms or corporations using millions; and estimating only simple interest to be made upon the capital invested, it is inevitable that their income must exceed their expenditures, and that they must accumulate wealth. Nor is there any middle ground which such men can occupy, because the great manufacturing or commercial concern which does not earn at least interest upon its capital soon becomes bankrupt. It must either go forward or fall behind: to stand still is impossible. It is a condition essential for its successful operation that it should be thus far profitable, and even that, in addition to interest on capital, it should make profit. It is a law, as certain as any of the others named, that men possessed of this peculiar talent for affairs, under the free play of economic forces, must, of necessity, soon be in receipt of more revenue than can be judiciously expended upon themselves; and this law is as beneficial for the race as the others. . . .

This, then, is held to be the duty of the man of Wealth: First, to set an example of modest, unostentatious living, shunning display or extravagance; to provide moderately for the legitimate wants of those dependent upon him; and after doing so to consider all surplus revenues which come to him simply as trust funds, which he is called upon to administer, and strictly bound, as a matter of duty to administer in the manner which, in his judgment, is best calculated to produce the most beneficial results for the community — the man of wealth thus becoming the mere agent and trustee for his poorer brethren, bringing to their service his superior wisdom, experience, and ability to administer, doing for them better than they would or could do for themselves. In bestowing charity, the main consideration should be to help those who will help themselves; to provide part of the means by which those who desire to improve may do so; to give those who desire to rise the aids by which they may rise; to assist, but rarely or never to do all. Neither the individual nor the race is improved by alms-giving. Those worthy of assistance, except in rare cases, seldom require assistance. The really valuable men of the race never do, except in cases of accident or sudden change. Every one has, of course, cases of individuals brought to his own knowledge where temporary assistance can do genuine good, and these he will not overlook. But the amount which can be wisely given by the individual for individuals is necessarily limited by his lack of knowledge of the circumstances connected with each. He is the only true reformer who is as careful and as anxious not to aid the unworthy as he is to aid the worthy, and, perhaps, even more so, for in alms-giving more injury is probably done by rewarding vice than by relieving virtue.

Black Rules for White Man's Achievement

BOOKER T. WASHINGTON

Booker T. Washington explains the requirements for black achievement at the Atlanta Exposition in 1895. What is the key to success for the blacks? Should political rights be dependent on economic achievement? Is it necessary for the disadvantaged and the minorities to play according to establishment rules? If not, by what rules should they play?

One-third of the population of the South is of the Negro race. No enterprise seeking the material, civil, or moral welfare of this section can disregard this element of our population and reach the highest success. I but convey to you, Mr. President and Directors, the sentiment of the masses of my race when I say that in no way have the value and manhood of the American Negro been more fittingly and generously recognized than by the managers of this magnificent Exposition at every stage of its progress. It is a recognition that will do more to cement the friendship of the two races than any occurrence since the dawn of our freedom.

Not only this, but the opportunity here afforded will awaken among us a new era of industrial progress. Ignorant and inexperienced, it is not strange that in the first years of our new life we began at the top instead of at the bottom; that a seat in Congress or the state legislature was more sought than real estate or industrial skill; that the political convention of stump speaking had more attractions than starting a dairy farm or truck garden.

A ship lost at sea for many days suddenly sighted a friendly vessel. From the mast of the unfortunate vessel was seen a signal, "Water, water; we die of thirst!" The answer from the friendly vessel at once came back, "Cast down

From Booker T. Washington, *Up From Slavery* (Cambridge: Houghton Mifflin, 1928), pp. 218–225. Originally published in 1901.

your bucket where you are." A second time the signal, "Water, water; send us water!" ran up from the distressed vessel, and was answered, "Cast down your bucket where you are." And a third and fourth signal for water was answered, "Cast down your bucket where you are." The captain of the distressed vessel, at last heeding the injunction, cast down his bucket, and it came up full of fresh, sparkling water from the mouth of the Amazon River. To those of my race who depend on bettering their condition in a foreign land or who underestimate the importance of cultivating friendly relations with the Southern white man, who is their next-door neighbour, I would say: "Cast down your bucket where you are" — cast it down in making friends in every manly way of the people of all races by whom we are surrounded.

Cast it down in agriculture, mechanics, in commerce, in domestic service, and in the professions. And in this connection it is well to bear in mind that whatever other sins the South may be called to bear, when it comes to business, pure and simple, it is in the South that the Negro is given a man's chance in the commercial world, and in nothing is this Exposition more eloquent than in emphasizing this chance. Our greatest danger is that in the great leap from slavery to freedom we may overlook the fact that the masses of us are to live by the productions of our hands, and fail to keep in mind that we shall prosper in proportion as we learn to dignify and glorify common labour and put brains and skill into the common occupations of life; shall prosper in proportion as we learn to draw the line between the superficial and the substantial, the ornamental gewgaws of life and the useful. No race can prosper till it learns that there is as much dignity in tilling a field as in writing a poem. It is at the bottom of life we must begin, and not at the top. Nor should we permit our grievances to overshadow our opportunities.

To those of the white race who look to the incoming of those of foreign birth and strange tongue and habits for the prosperity of the South, were I permitted I would repeat what I say to my own race, "Cast down your bucket where you are." Cast it down among the eight millions of Negroes whose habits you know, whose fidelity and love you have tested in days when to have proved treacherous meant the ruin of your firesides. Cast down your bucket among these people who have, without strikes and labour wars, tilled your fields, cleared your forests, builded your railroads and cities, and brought forth treasures from the bowels of the earth, and helped make possible this magnificent representation of the progress of the South. Casting down your bucket among my people, helping and encouraging them as you are doing on these grounds, and to education of head, hand, and heart, you will find that they will buy your surplus land, make blossom the waste places in your fields, and run your factories. While doing this, you can be sure in the future, as in the past, that you and your families will be surrounded by the most patient, faithful, law-abiding, and unresentful people that the world has seen. As we have proved our loyalty to you in the past, in nursing your children, watching by the sick-bed of your mothers and fathers, and often following them with tear-dimmed eyes to their graves, so in the future, in our humble way, we shall stand by you with a devotion that no foreigner can approach, ready to lay down our lives, if need be, in defence of yours, interlacing our industrial, commercial, civil, and religious life with yours in a way that shall make the interests of both races one. In all things that are purely social we can be as separate as the fingers, yet one as the hand in all things essential to mutual progress.

There is no defence or security for any of us except in the highest intelligence and development of all. If anywhere there are efforts tending to curtail the fullest growth of the Negro, let these efforts be turned into stimulating, encouraging, and making him the most useful and intelligent citizen. Effort or means so invested will pay a thousand per cent interest. These efforts will be twice blessed — "blessing him that gives and him that takes."

There is no escape through law of man or God from the inevitable: —

> The laws of changeless justice bind
> Oppressor with oppressed;
> And close as sin and suffering joined
> We march to fate abreast.

Nearly sixteen millions of hands will aid you in pulling the load upward, or they will pull against you the load downward. We shall constitute one-third and more of the ignorance and crime of the South, or one-third its intelligence and progress; we shall contribute one-third to the business and industrial prosperity of the South, or we shall prove a veritable body of death, stagnating, depressing, retarding every effort to advance the body politic.

Gentlemen of the Exposition, as we present to you our humble effort at an exhibition of our progress, you must not expect overmuch. Starting thirty years ago with ownership here and there in a few quilts and pumpkins and chickens (gathered from miscellaneous sources), remember the path that has led from these to the inventions and production of agricultural implements, buggies, steam-engines, newspapers, books, statuary, carving, paintings, the management of drug-stores and banks, has not been trodden without contact with thorns and thistles. While we take pride in what we exhibit as a result of our independent efforts, we do not for a moment forget that our part in this exhibition would fall far short of your expectations but for the constant help that has come to our educational life, not only from the Southern states, but especially from Northern philanthropists, who have made their gifts a constant stream of blessing and encouragement.

The wisest among my race understand that the agitation of questions of social equality is the extremest folly, and that progress in the enjoyment of all the privileges that will come to us must be the result of severe and constant struggle rather than of artificial forcing. No race that has anything to contribute to the markets of the world is long in any degree ostracized. It is important and right that all privileges of the law be ours, but it is vastly more important that we be prepared for the exercises of these privileges. The opportunity to earn a dollar in a factory just now is worth infinitely more than the opportunity to spend a dollar in an opera-house.

In conclusion, may I repeat that nothing in thirty years has given us more hope and encouragement, and drawn us so near to you of the white race, as this opportunity offered by the Exposition; and here bending, as it were, over the altar that represents the results of the struggles of your race and mine, both starting practically empty-handed three decades ago, I pledge that in your effort to work out the great and intricate problem which God has laid at the doors of the South, you shall have at all times the patient, sympathetic help of my race; only let this be constantly in mind, that, while from representations in these buildings of the product of field, of forest, of mine, of factory, letters, and art, much good will come, yet far above and beyond material benefits will be that higher good, that, let us pray God, will come, in a blotting out of sectional differences and racial animosities and suspicions, in a determination to administer absolute justice, in a willing obedience among all classes to the mandates of law. This, this, coupled with our material prosperity, will bring into our beloved South a new heaven and a new earth.

Senate Hearings on Labor Rules for Capitalist Achievement

MORRIS HILLQUIT and SAMUEL GOMPERS

Socialist Morris Hillquit and antisocialist labor leader Samuel Gompers debate strategies for labor to achieve its ends in a capitalist system. What is Hillquit's goal? What is Gompers'? Which strategy is most consistent with the existing system? Which is more likely to bring achievement to the workers? Is Gompers urging the same philosophy as Washington?

Mr. Hillquit: Now, Mr. Gompers, . . . is it your conception, Mr. Gompers, or that of the Federation, that workers in the United States to-day receive the full product of their labor?

Mr. Gompers: I think, but I am not quite so sure, that I know what you have in mind.

Mr. Hillquit: Do you understand my question?

Mr. Gompers: I think I do, but in the generally accepted sense of that term, no.

Mr. Hillquit: In any particular sense, yes?

From U.S., Congress, Senate, *Final Report and Testimony to the Commission on Industrial Relations,* 64th Cong., 1st sess., 1916, pp. 1526–1529, 1541.

Mr. Gompers: No. . . .

Mr. Hillquit: Then one of the functions of organized labor is to increase the share of the workers in the product of their labor, is that correct?

Mr. Gompers: Yes, sir; organized labor makes constantly increasing demands upon society for reward for the services which the workers give to society, and without which the civilized life would be impossible.

Mr. Hillquit: And these demands for an increasing share of the reward of the product of labor continue by a gradual process all the time?

Mr. Gompers: I am not so sure as to gradual process. Sometimes it is not a gradual process, but it is all the time.

Mr. Hillquit: All the time?

Mr. Gompers: Yes, sir.

Mr. Hillquit: Then, Mr. Gompers, you assume that the organized-labor movement has generally succeeded in forcing a certain increase of that portion of the workers in the share of the general product, do you?

Mr. Gompers: Yes, sir.

Mr. Hillquit: And it demands more now?

Mr. Gompers: Yes, sir.

Mr. Hillquit: And if it should get, say, 5 per cent more within the next year, will the organized-labor movement rest contented with that and stop?

Mr. Gompers: Not if I know anything about human nature.

Mr. Hillquit: Will the organized labor movement, or the labor movement of the country generally, stop in its demands for an ever greater share in the product at any time before it has received or does receive the full product, and before in its eyes complete social justice shall have been done?

Mr. Gompers: That question again that you have bobbed up with quite serenely in regard to the share of the product of labor, say that the working people — and I prefer to say working people and speak of them as real human beings — the working people, as all other people, they are prompted by the same desires and hopes of a better life, and they are not willing to wait until after they have shuffled off this mortal coil for the better life, they want it here and now, and they want to make conditions better for their children so that they may meet the other, the newer problems in their time. The working people are pressing forward, pressing forward, making their claims and presenting those claims with whatever power they have, to exercise it in a normal, rational manner, to secure a larger, and constantly larger share of the products. They are working to the highest and best ideals of social justice.

Mr. Hillquit: Now, the highest and best ideals of social justice, as applied to the distribution of wealth, wouldn't that be a system under which the workers, manual, mental, directive, executive and all other lines together get the sum total of all the products we supply them?

Mr. Gompers: Really, a fish is caught by the tempting bait; a mouse or a rat is caught in a trap by the tempting bait; the intelligent, comprehensive, common-sense workmen prefer to deal with the problems of to-day, the problem which confronts them to-day, with which they are bound to contend if they want to advance, rather than to deal with a picture and a dream which has never had, and I am sure never will have, any reality in the affairs of humanity, and which threaten, if it could be introduced, the worst system of circumscriptional effort and activity that has ever been invented by the ken of the human kind.

Mr. Hillquit: That is what I want to get from you, Mr. Gompers, but I would like to get an answer. In your experience with the labor movement and in its ever forward march toward greater and greater improvement, and a greater and greater share of social justice, can you point out any line where the labor movement will stop and rest contented so long as it may receive short of the full product of its work?

Mr. Gompers: I say that the workers, as human beings, will never stop in any effort, nor stop at any point in the effort to secure greater improvements in their condition, a better life in all its phases. And wherever that may lead, whatever that may be, so far in my time and my age I decline to permit my mind or my activities to be labeled by any particular ism.

Mr. Hillquit: Do not try to attach any ism to me, please; but the question I ask is whether you maintain — whether the American Federation of Labor, and its authorized spokesmen have a general social philosophy, or work blindly from day to day?

Mr. Gompers: I think your question ――

Mr. Hillquit (interrupting): Inconvenient.

Mr. Gompers: No. I will tell you what it is, it is a question prompted to you, and is an insult.

Mr. Hillquit: It is not a question prompted to me.

Mr. Gompers: It is an insult.

Mr. Hillquit: Why? Why, Mr. Gompers?

Mr. Gompers: To insinuate that the men and women in the American Federation of Labor movement are acting blindly from day to day.

Mr. Hillquit: I have not insinuated ――

Mr. Gompers (interrupting): Your question implies it.

Mr. Hillquit: I am giving you an opportunity to deny.

Mr. Gompers: If a man should ask me whether I still beat my wife, any answer I could make would incriminate me if I answered yes or no. If I answered that I did not, the intimation would be that I had stopped. If I answered that I did, that I was continuing to beat her.

Mr. Hillquit: But Mr. Gompers, this question bears no analogy to that story ――

Mr. Gompers (interrupting): Your question is an insult and a studied one.

Mr. Hillquit: Now, will you state whether you will or whether you will not answer my question?

Mr. Gompers: Will you repeat the question?

Mr. Hillquit: My question was whether the American Federation of Labor as represented by its spokesmen has a general social philosophy, or whether the organization is working blindly from day to day? Now, that is a plain question.

Mr. Gompers: Yes; it is a plain question; it is a plain insult.

Chairman Walsh: Do you refuse to answer it on the ground that it is insulting?

Mr. Gompers: Yes, sir.

Chairman Walsh: That is all, then.

Mr. Hillquit: Then, inform me upon this matter: In your political work of the labor movement is the American Federation of Labor guided by a general social philosophy, or is it not?

Mr. Gompers: It is guided by the history of the past, drawing its lessons from history, to know of the conditions by which the working people are surrounded and confronted; to work along the lines of least resistance; to accomplish the best results in improving the condition of the working people, men and women and children, to-day and to-morrow and to-morrow — and to-morrow's to-morrow; and each day making it a better day than the one that had gone before. That is the guiding principle and philosophy and aim of the labor movement — in order to secure a better life for all.

Mr. Hillquit: But in these efforts to improve conditions from day to day you must have an underlying standard of what is better, don't you?

Mr. Gompers: No. You start out with a given program, and everything must conform to it; and if the facts do not conform to your theories, why, your declarations, or, rather, your actions, betray the state of mind "so much the worse for the facts."

Mr. Hillquit: Mr. Gompers, what I ask you is this: You say you try to make the conditions of the workers better every day. In order to determine whether the conditions are better or worse you must have some standards by which you distinguish the bad from the good in the labor movement, do you not?

Mr. Gompers: Certainly. Well, is that ——

Mr. Hillquit (interrupting): Now, just ——

Mr. Gompers (interrupting): Well, one moment. Does it require much discernment to know that a wage of $3 a day and a workday of 8 hours a day in sanitary workshops are all better than $2.50 a day and 12 hours a day and under perilous conditions of labor? It does not require much conception of a social philosophy to understand that.

Mr. Hillquit: Then, Mr. Gompers, by the same parity of reasoning, $4 a day and seven hours a day of work and very attractive working conditions are still better?

Mr. Gompers: Unquestionably.

Mr. Hillquit: Therefore ——

Mr. Gompers (interrupting): Just a moment. I have not stipulated $4 a day or $8 a day or any number of dollars a day or eight hours a day or seven hours a day or any number of hours a day, but the best possible conditions obtainable for the workers is the aim.

Mr. Hillquit: Yes; and when these conditions are obtained ——

Mr. Gompers (interrupting): Why, then, we want better.

Mr. Hillquit (continuing): You will still strive for better?

Mr. Gompers: Yes.

Mr. Hillquit: Now, my question is, Will this effort on the part of organized labor ever stop until it has the full reward for its labor?

Mr. Gompers: It won't stop at all.

Mr. Hillquit: That is a question ——

Mr. Gompers (interrupting): Not when any particular point is reached, whether it be that toward which you have just declared or anything else. The working people will never stop ——

Mr. Hillquit: Exactly.

Mr. Gompers (continuing): In their effort to obtain a better life for themselves and for their wives and for their children and for humanity.

Mr. Hillquit: Then, the object of the labor union is to obtain complete social justice for themselves and for their wives and for their children?

Mr. Gompers: It is the effort to obtain a better life every day.

Mr. Hillquit: Every day and always ——

Mr. Gompers: Every day. That does not limit it.

Mr. Hillquit: Until such time ——

Mr. Gompers: Not until any time.

Mr. Hillquit: In other words ——

Mr. Gompers (interrupting): In other words, we go further than you. [Laughter and applause in the audience.] You have an end; we have not. . . .

Mr. Hillquit: Then, you would not think it is perfectly proper for an official representative of the American Federation of Labor to cooperate with well-known capitalist employers for common ends? . . .

Mr. Gompers: That is not the question. I will appeal to the devil and his mother-in-law to help labor if labor can be aided in that way.

Conscience vs. Achievement

WILLIAM DEAN HOWELLS

Novelist William Dean Howells describes a crisis in the life of a fictional businessman, Silas Lapham. What would be Carnegie's attitude toward Lapham? What values are in conflict in this selection? What are Howells's opinions on the price of achievement in the Gilded Age?

From William Dean Howells, *The Rise of Silas Lapham* (Boston: Houghton Mifflin, 1884), pp. 60–65.

Lapham drove there with his wife after he had set Bartley Hubbard down at the *Events* office, but on this day something happened that interfered with the solid pleasure they usually took in going over the house. As the Colonel turned from casting anchor at the mare's head with the hitching-weight, after helping his wife to alight, he encountered a man to whom he could not help speaking, though the man seemed to share his hesitation if not his reluctance at the necessity. He was a tallish, thin man, with a dust-coloured face, and a dead, clerical air, which somehow suggested at once feebleness and tenacity.

Mrs. Lapham held out her hand to him.

"Why, Mr. Rogers!" she exclaimed; and then, turning toward her husband, seemed to refer the two men to each other. They shook hands, but Lapham did not speak. "I didn't know you were in Boston," pursued Mrs. Lapham. "Is Mrs. Rogers with you?"

"No," said Mr. Rogers, with a voice which had the flat, succinct sound of two pieces of wood clapped together. "Mrs. Rogers is still in Chicago."

A little silence followed, and then Mrs. Lapham said —

"I presume you are quite settled out there."

"No; we have left Chicago. Mrs. Rogers has merely remained to finish up a little packing."

"Oh, indeed! Are you coming back to Boston?"

"I cannot say as yet. We some think of so doing."

Lapham turned away and looked up at the building. His wife pulled a little at her glove, as if embarrassed, or even pained. She tried to make a diversion.

"We are building a house," she said, with a meaningless laugh.

"Oh, indeed," said Mr. Rogers, looking up at it.

Then no one spoke again, and she said helplessly —

"If you come to Boston, I hope I shall see Mrs. Rogers."

"She will be happy to have you call," said Mr. Rogers.

He touched his hat-brim, and made a bow forward rather than in Mrs. Lapham's direction.

She mounted the planking that led into the shelter of the bare brick walls, and her husband slowly followed. When she turned her face toward him her cheeks were burning, and tears that looked hot stood in her eyes.

"You left it all to me!" she cried. "Why couldn't you speak a word?"

"I hadn't anything to say to him," replied Lapham sullenly.

They stood a while, without looking at the work which they had come to enjoy, and without speaking to each other.

"I suppose we might as well go on," said Mrs. Lapham at last, as they returned to the buggy. The Colonel drove recklessly toward the Milldam. His wife kept her veil down and her face turned from him. After a time she put her handkerchief up under her veil and wiped her eyes, and he set his teeth and squared his jaw.

"I don't see how he always manages to appear just at the moment when he seems to have gone fairly out of our lives, and blight everything," she whimpered.

"I supposed he was dead," said Lapham.

"Oh, don't *say* such a thing! It sounds as if you wished it."

"Why do you mind it? What do you let him blight everything for?"

"I can't help it, and I don't believe I ever shall. I don't know as his being dead would help it any. I can't ever see him without feeling just as I did at first."

"I tell you," said Lapham, "it was a perfectly square thing. And I wish, once for all, you would quit bothering about it. My conscience is easy as far as he's concerned, and it always was."

"And I can't look at him without feeling as if you'd ruined him, Silas."

"Don't look at him, then," said her husband, with a scowl. "I want you should recollect in the first place, Persis, that I never wanted a partner."

"If he hadn't put his money in when he did, you'd 'a' broken down."

"Well, he got his money out again, and more, too," said the Colonel, with a sulky weariness.

"He didn't want to take it out."

"I gave him his choice: buy out or go out."

"You know he couldn't buy out then. It was no choice at all."

"It was a business chance."

"No; you had better face the truth, Silas. It was no chance at all. You crowded him out. A man that had saved you! No, you had got greedy, Silas. You had made your paint your god, and you couldn't bear to let anybody else share in its blessings."

"I tell you he was a drag and a brake on me from the word go. You say he saved me. Well, if I hadn't got him out he'd 'a' ruined me sooner or later. So it's an even thing, as far forth as that goes."

"No, it ain't an even thing, and you know it, Silas. Oh, if I could only get you once to acknowledge that you did wrong about it, then I should have some hope. I don't say you meant wrong exactly, but you took an advantage. Yes, you took an advantage! You had him where he couldn't help himself, and then you wouldn't show him any mercy."

"I'm sick of this," said Lapham. "If you'll 'tend to the house, I'll manage my business without your help."

"You were very glad of my help once."

"Well, I'm tired of it now. Don't meddle."

"I *will* meddle. When I see you hardening yourself in a wrong thing, it's time for me to meddle, as you call it, and I will. I can't ever get you to own up the least bit about Rogers, and I feel as if it was hurting you all the while."

"What do you want I should own up about a thing for when I don't feel wrong? I tell you Rogers hain't got anything to complain of, and that's what I told you from the start. It's a thing that's done every day. I was loaded up with a partner that didn't know anything, and couldn't do anything, and I unloaded; that's all."

"You unloaded just at the time when you knew that your paint was going to be worth about twice what it ever had been; and you wanted all the advantage for yourself."

"I had a right to it. I made the success."

"Yes, you made it with Rogers's money; and when you'd made it you took his share of it. I guess you thought of that when you saw him, and that's why you couldn't look him in the face."

At these words Lapham lost his temper.

"I guess you don't want to ride with me any more to-day," he said, turning the mare abruptly round.

"I'm as ready to go back as what you are," replied his wife. "And don't you ask me to go to that house with you any more. You can sell it, for all me. I sha'n't live in it. There's blood on it."

• MODERN ESSAY •

Achievement for What?

GARRY WILLS

What is it about our economic and social system that often makes "getting ahead" such an intense personal struggle, full of inner conflicts? Is it because American values have become so materialistic? Is there something in our culture that forces ambitious people to be something that they really aren't — a trait often ascribed to Richard Nixon? Is it because we have defined words such as "success," "ambition," and "achievement" in such a way that there have to be winners and losers? Is the kind of problem that was eating away at Silas Lapham also consuming Richard Nixon? On the other hand, are there admirable things about these values? Is the price of achievement a price we must pay to achieve all we have?

And finally, what of our own desires for success and our own ambitions? In reading about Carnegie, Washington, Howells, or Nixon, can we recognize similar traits in each of us?

Nixon was the most distasteful part of the Eisenhower regime, because he epitomized all those traits liberals wanted to ignore when they celebrated the American "mainstream." He was more self-made than Eisenhower. He was

From Garry Wills, *Nixon Agonistes: The Crisis of the Self-Made Man,* pp. 581–583, 165–166, 585–586, 587. Copyright © 1969, 1970 by Garry Wills. Reprinted by permission of Houghton Mifflin Company.

more religious — Ike started going to church when he sought office; Nixon "brought the church home with him" when he entered the White House. He was more competitive, *much* closer to the common man, and full of that resentment our emulative ethic breeds. And — here was the true scandal, the stumbling block even brightest analysts could not get over — Nixon logically completed the picture by being more deeply and consistently liberal than Eisenhower. Phrases like "equal opportunity" and "self-determination" mean something to Nixon. To Eisenhower, they were just phrases; he had not been educated enough to believe in the learned myths. Nixon is a politician, and — like all politicians — he must use every margin left him for maneuver. But his basic beliefs are in that very system toward which the fifties thinkers groped their way. Nixon is at one with Woodrow Wilson and Herbert Hoover in all things that united those earlier Presidents. He believes in, he summarizes, he is the apt spokesman for (and the final product of) classical liberalism. Eisenhower was a cover, like so much else in the fifties — he disguised the basic shift taking place, a shift back toward the man Eisenhower thought so little of, toward his own Vice-President.

Even now commentators do not see that Nixon is the authentic voice of the surviving American liberalism. They speak of his policy as a matter of zigs and zags, a welter of compromises, a muddling through the moment under prods of hope or fear. "Conservatives" (i.e., Thurmond and Mitchell) are played off against "liberals" (i.e., Finch and Moynihan), North is pitted against South. Nixon is guided, we are told, not by principle but by an inbuilt instinct for omnidirectional placation ("Give him a choice from one to ten and he will always choose five"). Yet there has been a connectedness in the programs Nixon personally espoused. "Black capitalism," for instance, is not a mere sop to the Negro community (ineffectual sop) — Nixon believes in civil rights, only he believes man's first right is the right to earn. His diversion of civil rights energy into the North, though it may soothe Senator Thurmond, is based on the liberal principle of Interchangeability, a principle Nixon, no less than its major spokesman (Moynihan), accepts. A tough line toward student protesters and marchers is part of John Mitchell's strategy for winning Wallace types to Nixon, but it is in perfect accord with Nixon's own compulsive sense of tidiness and order. The President's devotion to "self-determination for the Vietnamese" is not a mere cover for our actions in Vietnam; it is a Wilsonian ideal very dear to Nixon. The voluntarization of the draft is meant to buy off student opposition to the war — but it is also in line with Nixon's general hope (officially handed over to George Romney and Mrs. Nixon) that private action can make governmental compulsion unnecessary in many spheres of life.

The coherence of Nixon's own views has not generally been recognized, and for an important reason: this would involve the admission that American liberalism and the emulative ethic cohere — inhere, rather, in each other. All our liberal values track back to a mystique of the earner. . . . [T]he self-made man has to concentrate on the thing he is making, on his product and end and whole excuse — on himself. When Nixon writes that "adversity breaks the weak but makes the strong," he is not simply repeating a platitude. Making the self strong is the task proposed to man by the Whittier of his youth, by the moral old America of Emerson.

The true significance of nineteenth-century liberalism was not so much that products are tested on the open market of free enterprise, or that truth will triumph in the free market of the academy, as that man himself must be spiritually *priced,* must establish his value ("amount to something"), in each day's trading. To experience one's worth in the real testing place, in the active trading of today's market, is the sole aim of America's moral monsters. That is why Emerson trumpets the need to "bring the past for judgment into the thousand-eyed present and live ever in a new day . . . a true man belongs to no other time or place, but is the center of things." That is the spirit of Nixon's cult of crisis — his eagerness, always, to be "in the arena," his praise of others for being cool under pressure, for being "tested in the fires."

But what if, having entered the market, one's stock falls? Who or what is there to lend support in that case? The merit, for an Emerson, is all his own if he stands independent, freed of help from the centuries. And if the merit is each man's without debt, then the failure must be one's own as well. Nixon puts it this way: "Chief Newman, my football coach in college and a man who was a fine coach but an even more talented molder of character [that's the real game, all right, mold the self, make a new little free-standing Emerson], used to say: 'You must never be satisfied with losing. You must get angry, terribly angry, about losing. But the mark of the good loser [improve oneself even in defeat] is that he takes his anger out on himself [succeed at becoming a martyr, even if you do not succeed in the vulgar sense] and not on his victorious opponents or his team-mates [stand alone even in defeat, don't admit human needs, don't lean]."

It is this morality of demonstrated daily desert — this meritocracy, with active trading in merits and demerits — that lies behind heartland America's hatred of welfare and relief and the systematic alleviation of poverty. The deserving rise; if the undeserving are also helped, what happens to the scoring in this game of spiritual effort and merit badges? The free-market of virtue and soul-making is destroyed by such "controls," such interference with incentive. Emerson knew this: "Your miscellaneous popular charities; the education at colleges of fools, the building of meetinghouses to the vain end to which many now stand; alms to sots, and the thousand-fold relief societies; — though I confess with shame I sometimes succumb and give the dollar, it is a wicked dollar, which by and by I shall have the manhood to withhold."

. . . Every American is told that this land guarantees him "opportunity"; if he fails, it is his own fault — so he *must not fail.* Yet if he succeeds, it must be as a "common man," one who moved out from an equal starting place and who is not blocking an "equally equal start" for all those around him. He must start the race again every day, doubt past achievement, justify his success by repeating it. As Wilson put it, he must forsake "connections" and rely only on "character" for his moral credit.

Here, in active trading on this moral market, is energy generated for all other activities. This has been recognized by many critics, admirers or reformers of the American ethos. David Riesman says, "Americans have always sought that good opinion [of others] and have had to seek it in an unstable market, where quotations on the self could change without the price-pegging of a caste system or an aristocracy." Back in the Populist days, a reformer like Benjamin Flower could say that America must spiritually "keep the market open":

> Law-bulwarked privilege, possessing monopoly power, has always fattened off of productive industry . . . But baleful as is the influence of privilege in the realm of commercial activity, the evil dwarfs into insignificance when compared with its influence in fields that are largely speculative or theoretical; for here, while exerting the same impoverishing and demoralizing effects that mark it in the domain of material life, it encroaches on things intimately personal.

In that easy transition from "the material" to "the moral," in the attack on any "monopoly" of speculative ideas, in the praise of "productive industry," is the whole genius of America, our central conception of human achievement. Proving oneself in the free arena of competition is the test of manhood, truth, and political wisdom. And this is always, in the end, a way of proving oneself to *oneself*. The striver can never stop striving. It is because Nixon is so totally this sweaty moral self-doubting self-made bustling brooding type, that he represents the integral liberalism that once animated America and now tries to reassert itself.

The concept of the self-made man has been the key to America's liberalism. The central tenet of the great historical school of liberal thought has been a belief in self-regulation. . . . Self-regulation has been internalized in the American moral system; each man is a *self-made* man to the extent that the problem of control becomes irrelevant through individual restraint. Here is the only way of mastering one's fate: self-mastery. One must not only be industrious but self-denying— no "kid gloves." The code of the McGuffey Readers is a hard one; it opposes trivial culture and frills, the dilettantes, the "fancy-pants" — what Agnew, that resolutely McGuffeyized disciple of Nixon, calls the "effete" ways of intellectual "snobs." Handsome is as handsome does; and the doers are almost proud of ugliness in all but their handsome deeds. Our hero is the "snuff colored Ben" of D. H. Lawrence, moralizing Ben Franklin who cramped America's spirit with the calculations of self-improvement: "Absolutely got down by her own barbed wire of shalt-nots, and shut up fast in her own 'productive' machines, like millions of squirrels running in millions of cages."

"Self-government" is primarily a personal morality in America, not a political philosophy. If we do not "govern ourselves," we shall need a king to govern us, like recalcitrant ancient Israel. But if we do "govern ourselves" — our appetites, our desires — then Democracy is safe. Thus does our individualism reduce social problems, always, to the level of private morality, to things outside the scope of legislation. No one can make life better for others except those others themselves. A man can be self-made only by himself. Even when there are tasks that must be done by a communal effort, these should be left to "voluntarism." Turning the job over to government is a confession that one *needs* government, a confession of weakness, an admission that *self-government* has failed. As Nixon likes to put it, people do not become great by what the government does for them but by what they do for themselves.

Issue

The Price of Survival

Most Americans do not want to abolish poverty because they accept certain moral values.

Stanley Lebergott, 1976

There are probably in fairly prosperous years no less than 10,000,000 persons in poverty. . . . Something is known concerning these problems of poverty, and some of them at least are possible of remedy.

Robert Hunter, 1904

While successful Americans such as Lapham, Carnegie, or Nixon may have been pondering the price of their achievements, others were trying to fathom the causes for so much failure. Why did some "make it" while others did not? More importantly perhaps, who or what was defining the criteria for success or failure in the first place? Why did those criteria have to be followed? The explanations of *McGuffey's Readers* for one's failure would no longer suffice: no one could tell William Jennings Bryan and all those angry farmers that their economic plight was their own fault. And as agricultural organizations questioned the old ethic, so did others who were realizing that hard work, strong moral character and all the other virtues simply were not enough to survive in this industrial world.

If it was not a question of character that separated the poor from the prosperous, what, then, was it? Some observers (and protestors) pointed fingers at conspirators and evil persons who manipulated the nation's money supply or transportation network. Others dug deeper to try to understand "the system," whose assembly-line approach created a mind-set that ignored suffering. Frederick Howe and his family in Meadville, Pennsylvania, seemed blissfully ignorant of the squalor of the cities. How could that be? What does this reveal about success and failure?

The fundamental question confronting a student of success and survival is whether the *kind* of success that Americans valued *required* the extensive struggle for survival. To put it another way: Did the prosperous depend on the existence of the poor in order to maintain their position? For, after all, how can there be a "middle" class unless there is a "class" below as well as above it?

◆ DOCUMENTS ◆

Surviving the Urban System

JACOB RIIS

Riis was one of the first reporters to "tell it like it is" about life in the urban ghettos. Even though he is sympathetic to the plight of "the Bend," is he rendering a judgment nevertheless on their life styles? Also, who is responsible for the conditions in "the Bend"?

Where Mulberry Street crooks like an elbow within hail of the old depravity of the Five Points, is "the Bend," foul core of New York's slums. Long years ago the cows coming home from the pasture trod a path over this hill. Echoes of tinkling bells linger there still, but they do not call up memories of green meadows and summer fields; they proclaim the home-coming of the rag-picker's cart. In the memory of man the old cow-path has never been other than a vast human pig-sty. There is but one "Bend" in the world, and it is enough. The city authorities, moved by the angry protests of ten years of sanitary reform effort, have decided that it is too much and must come down. Another Paradise Park will take its place and let in sunlight and air to work such transformation as at the Five Points, around the corner of the next block. Never was change more urgently needed. Around "the Bend" cluster the bulk

From Jacob Riis, *How the Other Half Lives* (New York: Charles Scribner's Sons, 1929), pp. 55–58. Originally published in 1890.

of the tenements that are stamped as altogether bad, even by the optimists of the Health Department. Incessant raids cannot keep down the crowds that make them their home. In the scores of back alleys, of stable lanes and hidden byways, of which the rent collector alone can keep track, they share such shelter as the ramshackle structures afford with every kind of abomination rifled from the dumps and ash-barrels of the city. Here, too, shunning the light, skulks the unclean beast of dishonest idleness. "The Bend" is the home of the tramp as well as the rag-picker.

It is not much more than twenty years since a census of "the Bend" district returned only twenty-four of the six hundred and nine tenements as in decent condition. Three-fourths of the population of the "Bloody Sixth" Ward were then Irish. The army of tramps that grew up after the disbandment of the armies in the field, and has kept up its muster-roll, together with the inrush of the Italian tide, have ever since opposed a stubborn barrier to all efforts at permanent improvement. The more that has been done, the less it has seemed to accomplish in the way of real relief, until it has at last become clear that nothing short of entire demolition will ever prove of radical benefit. Corruption could not have chosen ground for its stand with better promise of success. The whole district is a maze of narrow, often unsuspected passageways — necessarily, for there is scarce a lot that has not two, three, or four tenements upon it, swarming with unwholesome crowds. What a bird's-eye view of "the Bend" would be like is a matter of bewildering conjecture. Its everyday appearance, as seen from the corner of Bayard Street on a sunny day, is one of the sights of New York.

Bayard Street is the high road to Jewtown across the Bowery, picketed from end to end with the outposts of Israel. Hebrew faces, Hebrew signs, and incessant chatter in the queer lingo that passes for Hebrew on the East Side attend the curious wanderer to the very corner of Mulberry Street. But the moment he turns the corner the scene changes abruptly. Before him lies spread out what might better be the market-place in some town in Southern Italy than a street in New York — all but the houses; they are still the same old tenements of the unromantic type. But for once they do not make the foreground in a slum picture from the American metropolis. The interest centres not in them, but in the crowd they shelter only when the street is not preferable, and that with the Italian is only when it rains or he is sick. When the sun shines the entire population seeks the street, carrying on its household work, its bargaining, its love-making on street or sidewalk, or idling there when it has nothing better to do, with the reverse of the impulse that makes the Polish Jew coop himself up in his den with the thermometer at stewing heat. Along the curb women sit in rows, young and old alike with the odd head-covering, pad or turban, that is their badge of servitude — her's to bear the burden as long as she lives — haggling over baskets of frowsy weeds, some sort of salad probably, stale tomatoes, and oranges not above suspicion. Ash-barrels serve them as counters, and not infrequently does the arrival of the official cart en route for the dump cause a temporary suspension of trade until the barrels have been emptied and restored. Hucksters and pedlars' carts make two rows of booths in the street itself, and along the houses is still another — a perpetual market doing a very lively trade in its own queer staples, found nowhere on American ground save in "the Bend." Two old hags, camping on the pavement, are dispensing stale bread, baked not in loaves, but in the shape of big wreaths like exaggerated crullers, out of bags of dirty bed-tick. There is no use disguising the fact: they look like and they probably are old mattresses mustered into service under the pressure of a rush of trade. Stale bread was the one article the health officers, after a raid on the market, once reported as "not unwholesome." It was only disgusting. Here is a brawny butcher, sleeves rolled up above the elbows and clay pipe in mouth, skinning a kid that hangs from his hook. They will tell you with a laugh at the Elizabeth Street police station that only a few days ago when a dead goat had been reported lying in Pell Street it was mysteriously missing by the time the offal-cart came to take it away. It turned out that an Italian had carried it off in his sack to a wake or feast of some sort in one of the back alleys.

Surviving the Rural System

HAMLIN GARLAND

The agricultural counterpart to Riis's urban story is presented here by Garland. In what ways are the farmers victimized as much by "the system" as by their particular landlord? Are there any essential similarities between the plight of Garland's farmers and Riis's immigrants?

" 'M, yes; 'm, yes; first-rate," said Butler, as his eye took in the neat garden, the pig-pen, and the well-filled barnyard. "You're gitt'n' quite a stock around yeh. Done well, eh?"

Haskins was showing Butler around the place. He had not seen it for a year, having spent the year in Washington and Boston with Ashley, his brother-in-law, who had been elected to Congress.

"Yes, I've laid out a good deal of money durin' the last three years. I've paid out three hundred dollars f'r fencin'."

"Um — h'm! I see, I see," said Butler, while Haskins went on:

"The kitchen there cost two hundred; the barn ain't cost much in money, but I've put a lot o' time on it. I've dug a new well, and I — "

From Hamlin Garland, *Main-Travelled Roads* (New York: Harper & Brothers, 1891), pp. 213–217.

"Yes, yes, I see. You've done well. Stock worth a thousand dollars," said Butler, picking his teeth with a straw.

"About that," said Haskins, modestly. "We begin to feel 's if we was gitt'n' a home f'r ourselves; but we've worked hard. I tell you we begin to feel it, Mr. Butler, and we're goin' t' begin to ease up purty soon. We've been kind o' plannin' a trip back t' *her* folks after the fall ploughin's done."

"*Eggs*-actly!" said Butler, who was evidently thinking of something else. "I suppose you've kind o' calc'lated on stayin' here three years more?"

"Well, yes. Fact is, I think I c'n buy the farm this fall, if you'll give me a reasonable show."

"Um — m! What do you call a reasonable show?"

"Well, say a quarter down and three years' time."

Butler looked at the huge stacks of wheat, which filled the yard, over which the chickens were fluttering and crawling, catching grasshoppers, and out of which the crickets were singing innumerably. He smiled in a peculiar way as he said, "Oh, I won't be hard on yeh. But what did you expect to pay f'r the place?"

"Why, about what you offered it for before, two thousand five hundred, or *possibly* three thousand dollars," he added quickly, as he saw the owner shake his head.

"This farm is worth five thousand and five hundred dollars," said Butler, in a careless and decided voice.

"*What!*" almost shrieked the astounded Haskins. "What's that? Five thousand? Why, that's double what you offered it for three years ago."

"Of course, and it's worth it. It was all run down then; now it's in good shape. You've laid out fifteen hundred dollars in improvements, according to your own story."

"But *you* had nothin' t' do about that. It's my work an' my money."

"You bet it was; but it's my land."

"But what's to pay me for all my — "

"Ain't you had the use of 'em?" replied Butler, smiling calmly into his face.

Haskins was like a man struck on the head with a sandbag; he couldn't think; he stammered as he tried to say: "But — I never'd git the use — You'd rob me! More'n that: you agreed — you promised that I could buy or rent at the end of three years at — "

"That's all right. But I didn't say I'd let you carry off the improvements, nor that I'd go on renting the farm at two-fifty. The land is doubled in value, it don't matter how; it don't enter into the question; an' now you can pay me five hundred dollars a year rent, or take it on your own terms at fifty-five hundred, or — git out."

He was turning away when Haskins, the sweat pouring from his face, fronted him, saying again:

"But *you've* done nothing to make it so. You hain't added a cent. I put it all there myself, expectin' to buy. I worked an' sweat to improve it. I was workin' for myself an' babes — "

"Well, why didn't you buy when I offered to sell? What y' kickin' about?"

"I'm kickin' about payin' you twice f'r my own things, — my own fences, my own kitchen, my own garden."

Butler laughed. "You're too green t' eat, young feller. *Your* improvements! The law will sing another tune."

"But I trusted your word."

"Never trust anybody, my friend. Besides, I didn't promise not to do this thing. Why, man, don't look at me like that. Don't take me for a thief. It's the law. The reg'lar thing. Everybody does it."

"I don't care if they do. It's stealin' jest the same. You take three thousand dollars of my money — the work o' my hands and my wife's." He broke down at this point. He was not a strong man mentally. He could face hardship, ceaseless toil, but he could not face the cold and sneering face of Butler.

"But I don't take it," said Butler, coolly. "All you've got to do is to go on jest as you've been a-doin', or give me a thousand dollars down, and a mortgage at ten per cent on the rest."

Haskins sat down blindly on a bundle of oats near by, and with staring eyes and drooping head went over the situation. He was under the lion's paw. He felt a horrible numbness in his heart and limbs. He was hid in a mist, and there was no path out.

Butler walked about, looking at the huge stacks of grain, and pulling now and again a few handfuls out, shelling the heads in his hands and blowing the chaff away. He hummed a little tune as he did so. He had an accommodating air of waiting.

Haskins was in the midst of the terrible toil of the last year. He was walking again in the rain and the mud behind his plough; he felt the dust and dirt of the threshing. The ferocious husking-time, with its cutting wind and biting, clinging snows, lay hard upon him. Then he thought of his wife, how she had cheerfully cooked and baked, without holiday and without rest.

"Well, what do you think of it?" inquired the cool, mocking, insinuating voice of Butler.

"I think you're a thief and a liar!" shouted Haskins, leaping up. "A black-hearted houn'!" Butler's smile maddened him; with a sudden leap he caught a fork in his hands, and whirled it in the air. "You'll never rob another man, damn ye!" he grated through his teeth, a look of pitiless ferocity in his accusing eyes.

Butler shrank and quivered, expecting the blow; stood, held hypnotized by the eyes of the man he had a moment before despised — a man transformed into an avenging demon. But in the deadly hush between the lift of the weapon and its fall there came a gush of faint, childish laughter and then across the range of his vision, far away and dim, he saw the sun-bright head of his baby girl, as, with the pretty, tottering run of a two-year-old, she moved across the grass of the dooryard. His hands relaxed: the fork fell to the ground; his head lowered.

"Make out y'r deed an' mor'gage, an' git off'n my land, an' don't ye never cross my line agin; if y' do, I'll kill ye."

Butler backed away from the man in wild haste, and climbing into his buggy with trembling limbs drove off down the road, leaving Haskins seated dumbly on the sunny pile of sheaves, his head sunk into his hands.

Targeting Threats to Survival
WILLIAM HARVEY

Why were some people successful while others were not? In the following selection, William Harvey creates the mythical "Coin's Financial School" as a way of explaining his argument that the manipulation of money — specifically the demonetization of silver in 1873 — prevented so many people from succeeding. Why would Harvey's arguments have such great emotional appeal?

The Money Unit

"In money there must be a unit. In arithmetic, as you are aware, you are taught what a unit is. Thus, I make here on the blackboard the figure 1. That, in arithmetic, is a unit. All countings are sums or multiples of that unit. A unit, therefore, in mathematics, was a necessity as a basis to start from. In making money it was equally as necessary to establish a unit. The constitution gave the power to Congress to 'coin money and regulate the value thereof.' Congress adopted silver and gold as money. It then proceeded to fix the unit.

"That is, it then fixed what should constitute one dollar, the same thing that the mathematician did when he fixed one figure from which all others should be counted. Congress fixed the monetary unit to consist of 37¼ grains of pure silver, and provided for a certain amount of alloy (baser metals) to be mixed with it to give it greater hardness and durability. This was in 1792, in the days of Washington and Jefferson and our revolutionary forefathers, who had a hatred of England, and an intimate knowledge of her designs on this country.

"They had fought eight long years for their independence from British domination in this country, and when they had seen the last red-coat leave our shores, they settled down to establish a permanent government, and among

From William H. Harvey, "Coin's Financial School," in George B. Tindall, ed., *A Populist Reader* (New York: Harper & Row, 1966), pp. 131–133, 137–138.

the first things they did was to make 371¼ grains of silver the unit of values. That much silver was to constitute a dollar. And each dollar was a unit. They then provided for all other money to be counted from this unit of a silver dollar. Hence, dimes, quarters and half-dollars were exact fractional parts of the dollar so fixed.

"Gold was made money, but its value was counted from these silver units or dollars. The ratio between silver and gold was fixed at 15 to 1, and afterward at 16 to 1. So that in making gold coins their relative weight was regulated by this ratio.

"This continued to be the law up to 1873. During that long period, the unit of values was never changed and always contained 371¼ grains of pure silver. While that was the law it was impossible for any one to say that the silver in a silver dollar was only worth 47 cents, or any other number of cents less than 100 cents, or a dollar. For it was itself the unit of values. While that was the law it would have been as absurd to say that the silver in a silver dollar was only worth 47 cents, as it would be to say that this figure 1 which I have on the blackboard is only forty-seven one-hundredths of one.

"When the ratio was changed from 15 to 1 to 16 to 1 the silver dollar or unit was left the same size and the gold dollar was made smaller. The latter was changed from 24.7 grains to 23.2 grains pure gold, thus making it smaller. This occurred in 1834. The silver dollar still remained the unit and continued so until 1873.

"Both were legal tender in the payment of all debts, and the mints were open to the coinage of all that came. So that up to 1873, we were on what was known as a bimetallic basis, but what was in fact a silver basis, with gold as a companion metal enjoying the same privileges as silver, except that silver fixed the unit, and the value of gold was regulated by it. This was bimetallism.

"Our forefathers showed much wisdom in selecting silver, of the two metals, out of which to make the unit. Much depended on this decision. For the one selected to represent the unit would thereafter be unchangeable in value. That is, the metal in it could never be worth less than a dollar, for it would be the unit of value itself. The demand for silver in the arts or for money by other nations might make the quantity of silver in a silver dollar sell for more than a dollar, but it could never be worth less than a dollar. Less than itself.

"In considering which of these two metals they would thus favor by making it the unit, they were led to adopt silver because it was the most reliable. It was the most favored as money by the people. It was scattered among all the people. Men having a design to injure business by making money scarce, could not so easily get hold of all the silver and hide it away, as they could gold. This was the principal reason that led them to the conclusion to select silver, the more stable of the two metals, upon which to fix the unit. It was so much handled by the people and preferred by them, that it was called the people's money.

"Gold was considered the money of the rich. It was owned principally by that class of people, and the poor people seldom handled it, and the very poor people seldom ever saw any of it." . . .

"I now think we understand," said Coin, "what the unit of value was prior to 1873. We had the silver dollar as the unit. And we had both gold and silver as money walking arm in arm into the United States mints.

The Crime of 1873

"We now come to the act of 1873," continued Coin. "On February 12, 1873, Congress passed an act purporting to be a revision of the coinage laws. This law covers 15 pages of our statutes. It repealed the *unit* clause in the law of 1792, and in its place substituted a law in the following language:

> That the gold coins of the United States shall be a one-dollar piece which at the standard weight of twenty-five and eight-tenths grains *shall be the unit of value.*

"It then deprived silver of its right to unrestricted free coinage, and destroyed it as legal tender money in the payment of debts, except to the amount of five dollars.

"At that time we were all using paper money. No one was handling silver and gold coins. It was when specie payments were about to be resumed that the country appeared to realize what had been done. The newspapers on the morning of February 13, 1873, and at no time in the vicinity of that period, had any account of the change. General Grant, who was President of the United States at that time, said afterwards, that he had no idea of it, and would not have signed the bill if he had known that it demonetized silver.

"In the language of Senator Daniel of Virginia, it seems to have gone through Congress 'like the silent tread of a cat.'

"An army of a half million of men invading our shores, the warships of the world bombarding our coasts, could not have made us surrender the money of the people and substitute in its place the money of the rich. A few words embraced in fifteen pages of statutes put through Congress in the rush of bills did it. The pen was mightier than the sword.

"But we are not here to deal with sentiment. We are here to learn facts. Plain, blunt facts.

"The law of 1873 made gold the *unit* of values. And that is the law to-day. When silver was the unit of value, gold enjoyed *free coinage,* and was legal tender in the payment of all debts. Now things have changed. Gold is the unit and silver does not enjoy free coinage. It is refused at the mints. We might get along with gold as the *unit,* if silver enjoyed the same right gold did prior to 1873. But that right is now denied to silver. When silver was the unit, the unlimited demand for gold to coin into money, made the demand as great as the supply, and this held up the value of gold bullion."

Organizing Agrarian Survival

WILLIAM JENNINGS BRYAN

After reading part of Bryan's "Cross of Gold" speech in this section, would you have voted for him? Do you think that Riis and Garland would have thought Bryan had solutions to the problems of the immigrant and the farmer? Note how Bryan turned "Coin" Harvey's economic arguments into a powerful political appeal.

And now, my friends, let me come to the paramount issue. If they ask us why it is that we say more on the money question than we say upon the tariff question, I reply that, if protection has slain its thousands, the gold standard has slain its tens of thousands. If they ask us why we do not embody in our platform all the things that we believe in, we reply that when we have restored the money of the Constitution all other necessary reforms will be possible; but that until this is done there is no other reform that can be accomplished.

Why is it that within three months such a change has come over the country? Three months ago, when it was confidently asserted that those who believe in the gold standard would frame our platform and nominate our candidates, even the advocates of the gold standard did not think that we could elect a president. And they had good reason for their doubt, because there is scarcely a State here today asking for the gold standard which is not in the absolute control of the Republican party. But note the change. Mr. McKinley was nominated at St. Louis upon a platform which declared for the maintenance of the gold standard until it can be changed into bimetallism by international agreement. Mr. McKinley was the most popular man among the Republicans, and three months ago everybody in the Republican party prophesied his election. How is today? Why, the man who was once pleased to think that he looked like Napoleon — that man shudders today when he remembers that he was nominated on the anniversary of the battle of Waterloo. Not only that, but as he listens he can hear with ever-increasing distinctness the sound of the waves as they beat upon the lonely shores of St. Helena.

Why this change? Ah, my friends, is not the reason for the change evident to any one who will look at the matter? No private character, however pure, no personal popularity, however great, can protect from the avenging wrath of an indignant people a man who will declare that he is in favor of fastening the gold standard upon this country, or who is willing to surrender the right

From William Jennings Bryan, *The First Battle* (Chicago: W. B. Conkey Co., 1897), pp. 204–206.

of self-government and place the legislative control of our affairs in the hands of foreign potentates and powers.

We go forth confident that we shall win. Why? Because upon the paramount issue of this campaign there is not a spot of ground upon which the enemy will dare to challenge battle. If they tell us that the gold standard is a good thing, we shall point to their platform and tell them that their platform pledges the party to get rid of the gold standard and substitute bimetallism. If the gold standard is a good thing, why try to get rid of it? I call your attention to the fact that some of the very people who are in this convention today and who tell us that we ought to declare in favor of international bimetallism — thereby declaring that the gold standard is wrong and that the principle of bimetallism is better — these very people four months ago were open and avowed advocates of the gold standard, and were then telling us that we could not legislate two metals together, even with the aid of all the world. If the gold standard is a good thing, we ought to declare in favor of its retention and not in favor of abandoning it; and if the gold standard is a bad thing why should we wait until other nations are willing to help us to let go? Here is the line of battle, and we care not upon which issue they force the fight; we are prepared to meet them on either issue or on both. If they tell us that the gold standard is the standard of civilization, we reply to them that this, the most enlightened of all the nations of the earth, has never declared for a gold standard and that both the great parties this year are declaring against it. If the gold standard is the standard of civilization, why, my friends, should we not have it? If they come to meet us on that issue we can present the history of our nation. More than that; we can tell them that they will search the pages of history in vain to find a single instance where the common people of any land have ever declared themselves in favor of the gold standard. They can find where the holders of fixed investments have declared for a gold standard, but not where the masses have.

Mr. Carlisle said in 1878 that this was a struggle between "the idle holders of idle capital" and "the struggling masses, who produce the wealth and pay the taxes of the country;" and, my friends, the question we are to decide is: Upon which side will the Democratic party fight; upon the side of the "idle holders of idle capital" or upon the side of "the struggling masses?" That is the question which the party must answer first, and then it must be answered by each individual hereafter. The sympathies of the Democratic party, as shown by the platform, are on the side of the struggling masses who have ever been the foundation of the Democratic party. There are two ideas of government. There are those who believe that, if you will only legislate to make the well-to-do prosperous, their prosperity will leak through on those below. The Democratic idea, however, has been that if you legislate to make the masses prosperous, their prosperity will find its way up through every class which rests upon them.

You come to us and tell us that the great cities are in favor of the gold standard; we reply that the great cities rest upon our broad and fertile prairies.

Burn down your cities and leave our farms, and your cities will spring up again as if by magic; but destroy our farms and the grass will grow in the streets of every city in the country.

My friends, we declare that this nation is able to legislate for its own people on every question, without waiting for the aid or consent of any other nation on earth; and upon that issue we expect to carry every State in the Union. I shall not slander the inhabitants of the fair State of Massachusetts nor the inhabitants of the State of New York by saying that, when they are confronted with the proposition, they will declare that this nation is not able to attend to its own business. It is the issue of 1776 over again. Our ancestors, when but three millions in number, had the courage to declare their political independence of every other nation; shall we, their descendants, when we have grown to seventy millions, declare that we are less independent than our forefathers? No, my friends, that will never be the verdict of our people. Therefore, we care not upon what lines the battle is fought. If they say bi-metallism is good, but that we cannot have it until other nations help us, we reply that, instead of having a gold standard because England has, we will restore bimetallism, and then let England have bimetallism because the United States has it. If they dare to come out in the open field and defend the gold standard as a good thing, we will fight them to the uttermost. Having behind us the producing masses of this nation and the world, supported by the commercial interests, and the toilers everywhere, we will answer their demand for a gold standard by saying to them: You shall not press down upon the brow of labor this crown of thorns, you shall not crucify mankind upon a cross of gold.

Poverty and Survival

ROBERT HUNTER

While Bryan was stirring hearts and consciences, others such as Robert Hunter were compiling data on the extent of poverty. Note Hunter's recommendations. Though he made them in 1904, do they not have a familiar ring about them? Why have we not been able to eradicate poverty?

There are probably in fairly prosperous years no less than 10,000,000 persons in poverty; that is to say, underfed, underclothed, and poorly housed. Of these about 4,000,000 persons are public paupers. Over 2,000,000 working-men are unemployed from four to six months in the year. About 500,000 male immigrants arrive yearly and seek work in the very districts where unemploy-

---

From Robert Hunter, *Poverty* (New York: Macmillan, 1904), pp. 337–339.

ment is greatest. Nearly half of the families in the country are propertyless. Over 1,700,000 little children are forced to become wage-earners when they should still be in school. About 5,000,000 women find it necessary to work and about 2,000,000 are employed in factories, mills, etc. Probably no less than 1,000,000 workers are injured or killed each year while doing their work, and about 10,000,000 of the persons now living will, if the present ratio is kept up, die of the preventable disease, tuberculosis. We know that many workmen are overworked and underpaid. We know in a general way that unnecessary disease is far too prevalent. We know some of the insanitary evils of tenements and factories; we know of the neglect of the street child, the aged, the infirm, the crippled. Furthermore, we are beginning to realize the monstrous injustice of compelling those who are unemployed, who are injured in industry, who have acquired diseases due to their occupation, or who have been made widows or orphans by industrial accidents, to become paupers in order that they may be housed, fed, and clothed. Something is known concerning these problems of poverty, and some of them at least are possible of remedy.

To deal with these specific problems, I have elsewhere mentioned some reforms which seem to me preventive in their nature. They contemplate mainly such legislative action as may enforce upon the entire country certain minimum standards of working and of living conditions. They would make all tenements and factories sanitary; they would regulate the hours of work, especially for women and children; they would regulate and thoroughly supervise dangerous trades; they would institute all necessary measures to stamp out unnecessary disease and to prevent unnecessary death; they would prohibit entirely child labor; they would institute all necessary educational and recreational institutions to replace the social and educational losses of the home and the domestic workshop; they would perfect, as far as possible, legislation and institutions to make industry pay the necessary and legitimate cost of producing and maintaining efficient laborers; they would institute, on the lines of foreign experience, measures to compensate labor for enforced seasons of idleness, due to sickness, old age, lack of work, or other causes beyond the control of the workman; they would prevent parasitism on the part of either the consumer or the producer and charge up the full costs of labor in production to the beneficiary, instead of compelling the worker at certain times to enforce his demand for maintenance through the tax rate and by becoming a pauper; they would restrict the power of employer and of ship-owner to stimulate for purely selfish ends an excessive immigration, and in this way to beat down wages and to increase unemployment.

Reforms such as these are not ones which will destroy incentive, but rather they will increase incentive by more nearly equalizing opportunity. They will make propertied interests less predatory, and sensuality, by contrast with misery, attractive to the poor.

Middle-Class Survivors

FREDERIC C. HOWE

Assuming that Howe represented much of white middle-class America in the late nineteenth century, how much resistance to the reforms of Bryan and Hunter would they have probably mounted? Are the Howes much different from many contemporary middle-class families when it comes to dealing with social problems?

There was nothing in my inheritance to make me want the world any different. None of my ancestors ever crusaded. They took no part in the Revolutionary War; they were not Abolitionists; they escaped service in the Civil War. My Mother's people were Quakers in a direct line of descent from the little band of settlers which Gustavus Adolphus sent out from Sweden in the early days of the seventeenth century to build a Swedish colony on the shores of Delaware Bay. There was no meeting-house in Meadville, and, like many Quakers, my mother's family had joined the Methodist church. Her grandparents were farmers who had drifted west till they came to rest in the very centre of what was later the town of Meadville, Pa. There my grandfather laid off a big city block and settled his five children around him.

My paternal ancestors came from the north of Ireland in the eighteenth century. They were what is known as Scotch-Irish, which means that they were Scotch Presbyterians who went over to Ireland and took the land away from the Irish and gave them their Scotch brand of religion in exchange. . . . My father came to Meadville as a young man and there he married my mother. There I was born and lived to my twenty-fifth year.

Neither of my parents had any interest in reform. They did not want the world changed. It was a comfortable little world, Republican in politics, careful in conduct, Methodist in religion. Religion to me was a matter of attending church, of listening to long and tedious sermons, of irritable, empty Sunday afternoons, church sociables, and Wednesday-evening prayer-meetings. To the older people it meant rivalry with Presbyterians and serious differences about the minister, the choir, and the power of a rich trustee who contributed generously to the church. Life revolved about our church, which was the finest in town. My father was president of its board of trustees. The neighbors whose opinions counted belonged mostly to it, although they might be Presbyterians. Unitarians were beyond some pale. Church activities and sectarian points of view bulked large in our lives, even though my mother had a gentle Quaker tolerance and kindliness and my father a quiet broadmindedness which was

From Frederic C. Howe, *The Confessions of a Reformer* (New York: Charles Scribner's Sons, 1925), pp. 9–12. Reprinted by permission of the publisher.

unusual in the community. Fellow churchmen did not understand his going across the public square on Sunday evenings to hear a Unitarian minister who had formerly been a Methodist and had renounced Methodism. The apostasy of Doctor Townsend had been in the nature of a public disgrace, hardly less than a crime. Lifelong friends shunned him. Yet my father, without discussion or defense of his action, forsook his own pew of a Sunday evening and went to hear strange doctrine.

My sisters and I were allowed to go to church or not, as we pleased. That was a rare departure from the Methodist pattern. I went to Sunday-school because I was in love with my Sunday-school teacher. I coveted the seat next to her during the Sunday-morning lesson and at parties which she arranged for us with the girls of Ida M. Tarbell's class, who sat near us in the big chapel.

I went to prayer-meetings on Wednesday evenings more often than to church on Sunday mornings. "Getting" religion, to my mind, was a catastrophic experience that changed a person in the twinkling of an eye. It should come young. It meant eternal damnation if it never came at all. Old people with quavering voices told about it at the Wednesday-evening meetings — told over and over again how it had happened to them. Repetition hardly staled the curious emotional appeal of their testimony. I wondered why my father never gave "testimony." As president of the board of trustees, it seemed to me that he ought to. I wondered if he had gotten religion. He never talked about it at home. In his consistent silence, when other brethren and sisters discussed their souls' salvation, he failed to live up to my conception of him, as he failed to live up to what the neighbors expected when he went to the Unitarian church. To experience religion seemed to me like a great climacteric; a tremendous personal drama that miraculously changed sinful nature. I drifted about the outskirts of the prayer-meetings getting hints of the drama, glimpses of the invisible scene where it was staged.

I escaped, more than my sisters, from the Methodist espionage of conduct. I went to the only dances in town, in the hall of the Taylor Hose Company. I played cards surreptitiously with a colored driver in the barn. And with my father's connivance I went to the theatre. That was a secret between the two males of the family. A smile and a meaning look at supper prefaced those happy evenings. I would meet my father casually in the yard when the meal was over. After a little banter he would say: "Like to go to the Opera House to-night to see Booth?" Or it might be Barrett, Joe Jefferson, Florence, Modjeska, or Lotta. I saw them all from inconspicuous seats in the top gallery. So much concession was made to "What will the neighbors think?"

These were purple spots of freedom, but what the neighbors might think seriously conditioned our lives. Watchful eyes observed us in all we did. There was a sense of being clamped down, stiff in a mould made for one. My mother was a neighborly person, ministering to the needs of every one on our street; but she was sensitive to their opinions and prejudices, deeply unwilling to have them flouted. And I rebelled against espionage, hated it, chafed under it. I sought ways of escape.

◆ MODERN ESSAY ◆

The Calculus of Economic Survival

STANLEY LEBERGOTT

The following selection does more than describe a society of haves and have-nots. The author is asking, in effect, whether we can afford not to have poverty. Note carefully the distinction between absolute and relative poverty. While we may move to wipe out absolute starvation or absolutely squalid living conditions, how serious are we about eliminating relative starvation or relatively bad living conditions? If relative poverty is abolished, what are the consequences for society? How powerful are certain industrial forces in shaping our goals, beliefs, and behavior? Does the author appear to be ironic in his approach?

There exist eight reliable ways to increase poverty. The United States now pursues seven of them. Should it continue to do so, poverty in America will continue. Now it is true that since 1936 the percent of American families below the official OEO poverty line has been cut, from 56 percent to less than 10 percent. And with our trillion-dollar GNP we have the wherewithal to cut that down to 1 percent by next Sunday. But it may be impossible to end poverty permanently without changing course on these seven ways. Yet doing so could change American capitalism beyond recognition.

We must begin from a truism: few Americans really want to end poverty. Is that truism contradicted by the strong speech of the young? by the Kennedy-Johnson poverty programs? or by the Nixon welfare program? Consider the following. America could immediately end the blinding poverty of India and Pakistan, if only it chose to do so. How? Rather simply, by dividing up the incomes of the three countries, share and share alike. By that single decisive action we could guarantee those nations against starvation. Naturally, U.S. incomes would have to fall, from about $4,000 a person to $600. How many Americans are prepared to take this step?

The typical *poverty* family today can buy as much food as the *average* U.S. worker could buy in our grandparents' time — plus better housing, more clothing, furniture, heat, and medical care.

Sensitive Americans are therefore exercised about something quite beyond ending starvation, providing a place to live, medical care, etc. They are

Selections from Stanley Lebergott, *The American Economy: Income, Wealth and Want* (copyright © 1976 by Princeton University Press), pp. 3–19. Reprinted by permission of Princeton University Press.

measuring not by any absolute standard, but by a relative one. Poverty is what afflicts Americans who fall behind today's here-and-now standard of living. As Harrington puts it: "The American poor are not poor . . . in the sixteenth century; they are poor here and now in the United States. They are dispossessed in terms of what the rest of the nation enjoys. . . . They watch the movies and read the magazines of affluent Americans, and these tell them that they are internal exiles. . . ." In an economy that bursts with productivity, that produces so fantastic a volume and variety of goods, poverty comes to be defined as relative to what the typical American enjoys.

I

The first way to increase poverty in the United States follows fairly obviously from that definition — namely, to increase the standard of living. Raise the consumption level of the typical American and you create poverty. Raise it again and you create more poverty. When Ford invented the auto he created poverty. When Zworykin invented TV he created more poverty. Raise the standard decade after decade and you create more and more (relative) poverty even while you are wiping out the old-fashioned (starvation) kind of poverty. "Solely as a result of growing affluence, a society will elevate its notions of what constitutes poverty." (So reports the President's Commission on Income Maintenance.)

Try as hard as it can, a nation cannot succeed in creating relative poverty unless it does three things.

1. It must use its workers more and more productively. And we know that American capitalism has become more productive with every passing decade.

2. It must pay those workers more and more. And we know the real wage of American workers has tripled since 1900.

3. Finally, it must prevent its workers from relapsing into the expenditure pattern of St. Simeon Stylites, or even of Thoreau. If American workers had devoted their increased incomes to the worship of God and nature, the "relative deprivation" kind of poverty could not have arisen.

But when higher wages are earned, and then devoted to raising the workers' standard of living, more poverty is produced. The narrow-visioned worker of 1900 might have been satisfied to ride a trolley to work. But his grandson — even his hippie grandson — requires a car or motorcycle. (Indeed 41 percent of our officially "poor" families own automobiles. Half a million own more than one car.) The 1900 housewife used a tin washboard. The 1975 housewife requires an electric washing machine and dryer (in the local laundromat or at home).

In 1900 15 percent of U.S. families had flush toilets; today 86 percent of our poor families do. In 1900 3 percent had electricity; today 99 percent of our poor do. In 1900 1 percent had central heating; today 62 percent of the poor do. In 1900 18 percent of our families had refrigeration, ice refrigeration; today 99 percent of our poor have refrigerators, virtually all mechanical.

The average American today works a third fewer hours than did his 1900 peer. Yet beyond food, rent, and clothing, his family spends ten times as much on all the other comforts and necessities of life as did the 1900 family (allowing for price change).

These spectacular increases could not, I would argue, have been achieved without heroic contributions by Madison Avenue. Keeping up with the Joneses — as they keep up with the TV ads — has become our normal way of life. Spirit and salesmanship, greed plus gab, produces a distinctive, an American, perspective. It was, after all, two American Marxists, Baran and Sweezy, who classified as poor those American families who could not regularly buy cans of "room air freshener." What homage to the advertising profession! What testimony to its success in expanding the American standard of necessity! Another American Marxist has written a text on *Radical Political Economy,* which devotes several pages to the $11-billion-yearly "waste" in "useless automobile model changes," excoriating such "fraudulent and trivial newness." But just as we nod in agreement, he goes on to define poverty. And he stipulates $5,900 a year as a "low absolute level of income" — in part because workers with such an income must "run a used car or use public transport." How terribly vulgar the used car! And how unfortunate those $10,000-income families who do not drive cars just off the show-room floor!

All this is not meant to ignore the ancient, decisive, and ubiquitous presence of envy. Long before the U.S.A. even existed, La Bruyere observed of another culture: "Life is brief and monotonous. It passes away in desire."

But surely one inference follows. If (a) American industry speeds productivity and pays higher wages, and if (b) advertising helps persuade American workers, to buy new, more elegant products, then American capitalism must continue to generate poverty.

II

A second way to increase poverty is to allow older people to live apart from their children. Perhaps young people today enjoy such close rapport with their parents that they wish to spend their entire lives with them. But an older generation had no such aspiration. The passage of the Social Security Act in 1936 began the process by which the state gave older people pensions which they could spend as they chose. Many of them promptly decided to live apart from their children: they valued their privacy and comfort. (So did their children and grandchildren.) But this move automatically increased the number of poverty families. And as we continue to allow old people to use their social security checks for living in homes of their own, we continue to increase the number of poor families.

III

There is a third force: the Men's Liberation Front. . . . Our national moral code includes the right of men to propagate children — and desert them. By doing so, of course, they increase poverty: mothers find it difficult to earn any income when they have young children. If they get a job, they must drop their work whenever the children fall ill. They therefore end up with less responsible jobs, at lower wage rates — and are paid for fewer hours. Is it surprising that the percent of families in poverty rises from 8 percent when the husband is present, to 32 percent when he is absent? For white families the rise is from 7 percent to 26 percent. For black families the rise is more than 30 percentage points, from 17 percent to 53 percent. . . .

IV

Paying old people not to work. Before Social Security old people simply had to work. In 1939 40 percent of men over 65 worked. But by 1973 only 24 percent were at work, though jobs were easier to locate and real wages far more attractive. Why so? It seems likely that the typical worker is quite ready to quit work after forty years of arduous and monotonous labor, and retire on social security. He sets a real value on leisure. But Harrington includes every older worker when he refers to "a misery that extends to 40 or 50 million people in the U.S. . . . that have remained impoverished in spite of increasing productivity and the welfare state." Indeed, those over 65 make up the largest single age group in his figure — as they do in most estimates of poverty. . . .

V

Raising our social standards. In the past many families kept out of poverty by sending their children to work. . . . Today very few do. We forbid families to use this method of getting out of poverty. We find the moral advance worth the resultant increase in poverty.

VI

A sixth method for increasing poverty is to keep the children of the poor alive. Every major advance in public health work and medical care has cut our death rates. . . . But the rich already received relatively good care. Hence that tremendous advance surely benefited poor families far more than the rich. . . . Hence more babies from poor families survived — to be heads of poor families in their turn. Americans rejected, and continue to reject, the older reality design in which the death rate kept down the poverty problem.

VII

A final force for increasing poverty is fecundity. . . . If a $5,000 income is divided among a husband, wife, and two children, they escape the poverty count — either by official government standards or those of the National Welfare

Rights Organization. But divide the same income among six children, and they cannot escape.

The faster Americans multiply their family size, and thereby divide their family income, the faster they create poverty. As the number of children per family increases from 2 to 9 or more, the proportion of families in poverty rises from 9 percent to 40 percent. . . . Our value system declares it desirable for the poor to have as many children as they please, however distraught some people may be by the resultant impact on the national poverty totals. Hence, even if every American worker were paid $10,000 a year we would still have poverty — among the families with five, six, or ten children.

What may we say in conclusion? That most Americans do not want to abolish poverty because they accept certain moral values. These include the desirability of not sharing equally with foreigners; the freedom of men to desert their families and of older people to live apart from their children; and the coercive wisdom of the state to forbid persons to double up in their housing, and to forbid children to work.

But even if these attitudes disappeared we could not expect that poverty in America would vanish. For poverty, as defined by either Harrington, or by President Nixon's Income Maintenance Commission, is measured by a changing consumption standard. And the central drive of American capitalism involves changing that standard. . . .

Hence, so long as Americans harken to the songs that Madison Avenue sings, judging their well-being by the expenditure of others, and so long as American workers are paid enough so that they can buy more and more "goods," the inevitable awaits us: the more successfully American capitalism operates, the more surely will poverty remain among us. It is only fair to add that Communist workers seem as efficient, as productive, and as greedy, as capitalist workers.

PART II

The Progressive Era

Introduction

The Progressive Era: Reform and Repression

At first, it may seem odd to equate political reform movements with instances of social repression during the early part of the twentieth century. To most people, "reform" conjures up images of rooting out corruption, bribery, and misuse of elective office, with the result that government becomes more democratic. "Repression," on the other hand, connotes the lynching of blacks, wiping out of Indians, denying freedom of speech, and illegal government spying on private citizens. Reform suggests the nobler impulses of the human race, while repression implies the baser instincts. How then can they be related, and how does such a relationship give us insight into our own time?

To begin with, both reformer and repressor have sought a more nearly perfect America. Political reformers — whether they were Andrew Jackson, William Jennings Bryan, Woodrow Wilson, or the Roosevelts — all had found something wrong with our political system, something that needed to be corrected, not only because of the specific ailment, but also because it was in keeping with the way in which we viewed our history. They saw history as a road map, directing us to America's golden age which was still to come. There was a mission to perform, a mission that demanded the continuing perfection of our government. Thus, many history books have portrayed our past as an unfolding drama, of a free people struggling to "form a more perfect union," a task that has not ended. Viewed in such a light, reform movements through the years are a periodic affirmation that we are staying on the path we intended to follow, even though we may have strayed at times. Thus we are maintaining the commitment of our historical destiny.

In their perverse ways, those who practiced repression were also concerned with perfecting American society. Just as the Massachusetts Puritans dealt harshly with religious dissenters who threatened to upset the "true faith," so did American settlers push aside the Indians because they stood in the way of "progress." Many southern whites feared the debasement of their race and society if blacks were given equal rights. Purity and perfection were of concern in the churches, too; religious conservatives who accepted a literal interpretation of the Bible branded as heretics those who suggested that humans evolved from lower forms of animal life. "Native" Americans — forgetting that *they* recently had been immigrants — were outraged at the swarms of eastern Europeans who invaded our shores, particularly between 1880 and 1920, because these newer arrivals had beliefs, customs, and religious practices that were alien to "the American Way" — and were therefore unacceptable. Not only individuals, but also institutions were scrutinized for signs of deviation from the norm. In a society that believed everyone could earn his or her own living through individual effort, why was it necessary to join a union? Why should unions turn against the employers who had given them jobs and who had supplied the energy and capital which built their great economy? Free enterprise, it was believed by many, was a cornerstone of our push toward perfection; and free enterprise did not need unions.

In each case, the black, the religious radical, the immigrant, the labor unionist was seen by another group — usually part of a dominant WASP majority — as being "less than perfect." Such "imperfection" either interfered with America's progress or else threatened her "purity." Obviously much depends upon who is defining such words as *purity, perfection,* and *progress.* The selections which illustrate *Demanding American Orthodoxy* in this section enable us to look at some of the "dominant majorities" in the United States, and to see what impelled them to believe that *they* had the key to perfection, that their destiny — in George Custer's words — should be given precedence over the destiny of the Indian. And lest we take too much comfort in the fact that minorities are no longer burned or their scalps lifted, that we no longer cut off the pigtails of Chinese immigrants or burn down Catholic convents, we might ask whether such repression is *essentially* different from the harassment and intimidation levied against certain groups who voiced their objections during the recent war in southeast Asia. Do we perhaps still repress groups, such as women, in order to secure a vision of the way our society should be?

There is another link binding reform to repression: change and diversity. "Nothing is nailed down, anymore," goes the old cry as people witness the rapid alteration of their cities, schools, factories, jobs, homes, and family relationships under the forces of industrialism, urbanization, and external and internal migration of people. Change and diversity were the two inescapable facts of American life around 1900; for many people, they were the only things that could be counted on. People could see for themselves what the growth of cities was doing to the small towns — and the changes brought to their way of life. Although change and diversity signalled great opportunities for many, it required equally great readjustments of attitudes as people were drawn together in new and different combinations of races and beliefs.

Many were frightened by what change and diversity meant and tried to deny it. Consequently, the movement of blacks from a position of slavery toward social and economic equality was met by segregation; the movement of whites to the plains meant annihilation for the Indian; the influx of new ideas about the origins of the earth was simply too much for people such as William Jennings Bryan to bear. "I am more interested in the Rock of Ages than in the age of rocks" was his retort to Clarence Darrow when asked his attitude about recent changes in geologic theories. In short, people repressed other people because they refused to accept the meaning of many of the changes that were destroying traditional modes of life and social strata.

But if change and diversity prompted socially repressive tactics from some, it forced others to consider seriously the need for political reform. It was clear, for example, that cities could not govern themselves as did small towns. The hallowed concept of the New England town meeting where everyone supposedly could show up to transact business was unworkable in a metropolitan setting. It also became clear that traditional theories of limited government were also outmoded. An article of political faith during the eighteenth and nineteenth centuries, limited government was founded on the belief that "that government which governs least, governs best," as Thomas Jefferson had put it. Military defense, protection of property, education of the young, some care for the poor (but not very much), and control of crime were the proper functions of government: keep taxes to a minimum and don't give very much power to our elected officials — since they will probably misuse it. Finally, argued proponents of limited government, do not try to solve every problem because it is impossible and it would create a bureaucracy that would bankrupt the treasury.

The cities, however, posed new and overwhelming challenges for the local governments, governments whose concepts and constitutions severely restricted their ability to respond. Population density created problems of housing codes and sanitation standards. The diversity of urban dwellers created language, economic, and social problems that could not be solved outside some kind of formal structure of government. The distance of workers from their jobs created transportation problems, as did the unpaved streets on which the horsecars ran. The breathtaking pace of urban construction confronted people with the choice whether they would allow any building to be placed anywhere, or whether there should be some kind of rational planning or zoning laws.

The failure of the city governments to respond to these crises helped produce the political boss. The boss offered answers to problems when City Hall could not: if a newly arrived immigant needed a job, if a constituent needed bail money to get out of jail, if a widow and her orphaned children needed a basket of coal, or if "one of the boys" was down on his luck and needed a loan, the boss could be counted on. All he asked in return was absolute allegiance on Election Day. "Vote early and often" was a familiar cry around political headquarters. Voters did not need to know how to read the candidates' names — they had merely to vote a straight ticket. And even the literate voters often felt obliged to repay the boss who had helped them when they needed help.

The political bosses did other favors as well. Because of their power they could decide which contractors received the jobs for municipal construction projects (in return for a kickback). It was the boss, such as George Washington Plunkitt, who got the inside information where a park might be built; thus he could buy the land and then quickly sell it to the city — for a handsome profit ("honest graft," Plunkitt called it). And the boss often decided on appointments to various boards and agencies, provided the candiate was loyal and contributed a percentage of his salary to the boss's "flower fund." And so it went for some 100 years, starting with the rise of Boss Tweed in New York City during the 1860s, and continuing well into the twentieth century. Indeed, many saw Mayor Richard Daley of Chicago as the last in a line of machine politicos.

Toward the end of the nineteenth century, outraged citizens began to ask a question that has perplexed reformers up to the present time: Can we not have government that is honest as well as effective? Behind this question lay another: Given the accelerating pace of change and the multiplying types of interest groups, nationalities, and ethnic blocs, by what standards do we define public honesty? (To be sure, robbing the public till for a vacation in Hawaii is a fairly obvious sin; but as government becomes more complex, so does the ethical dilemma of deciding what is "right.") Jane Addams was aware of that dilemma, as the selection by her demonstrates. By comparing the contemporary selections on Mayor Richard Daley of Chicago and Mayor Richard Lee of New Haven, Connecticut, one will see that the dilemma is as critical now as it was in Miss Addams's day. As an example, consider the mayor of a city who is willing to overlook a violation of a safety code by an important manufacturer, knowing that enforcement of that code would force plant shutdowns, putting hundreds of employees out of jobs and on the city welfare rolls. The mayor may justify his stand by insisting that his actions concerned a minor violation. The reaction should be harsh: minor by whose standards? That action is a violation of the law — and indicates just how loosely this mayor abides by the laws.

In addition to the search for perfection and the response to change and diversity, there is another element which complicates the paradox of reform and repression: the quest for power. In the musical play "1776," Benjamin Franklin half-humorously tells John Adams that "treason is a charge invented by the winners as an excuse to hang the losers." He meant, of course, that those who have the power can determine the rules of the game. Power is central to politics and to political reform because a great deal depends upon who governs and in what manner. Power is also the key to repression, because no matter whether the intimidation being exercised is violent or subtle, one group of people is forcing another to submit.

Indeed, the line between reform and repression can grow rather hazy. Was it reform or repression when the Congress passed, and the states ratified, the Eighteenth Amendment to the Constitution, banning the manufacture and sale of alcoholic beverages? Is it reform or repression to outlaw the use of marijuana? If the Progressives were so opposed to the behavior of the politically corrupt bosses, what kind of guarantee was there that their own moral concepts would be any less narrow? Many of the Progressives who supported such measures as direct election of senators, civil service reform, and the secret ballot also supported — in the name of reform — such measures as prohibition and immigration restriction. The champion of the Populists, William Jennings Bryan, who was the symbol of agrarian reform against the monied interests of the industrialist East, showed himself to be less than tolerant when religious liberals suggested that there might be more than one way to interpret the story of creation. And he was not hesitant to use the power of the State of Tennessee to repress such teachings as those of Charles Darwin.

The control of power was crucial to both reformer or repressor because it gave the means by which to dictate what was allowable conduct. The popularity of the reformer or the intimidation of the repressor also helped to decide how far that power could be exercised. In either case, the greater the crisis, usually the greater latitude enjoyed by the reformer or repressor. Thus, when municipal corruption became a national concern in the early twentieth century, the people were willing to grant more power to their mayors to clean up City Hall. Theodore Roosevelt and Woodrow Wilson, two presidents most closely associated with the Progressive reform movement, were also known as strong presidents who wielded more power than any of their predecessors since Lincoln. Ironically, it was under Wilson's administration that the Eighteenth Amendment was passed, that the United States invaded Mexico in order to try to influence the selection of a leader favorable to Wilson's concept of democracy, that the Marines were sent into Latin American countries to put down internal battles, that immigrants suspected of being radicals were arrested and deported without the right to a trial, and that people were jailed for peacefully speaking out against the growing American involvement in World War I.

The power then to reform can also become the power to repress; and the question of how far a dominant group — be it the government, a political party, or a particular race, class, or ethnic group — may go in the pursuit of its goals is one that bedevils contemporary society no less than it did the Progressive Era.

Jane Addams is an excellent example of a combination of idealistic reformer and street-wise politician. Her method in dealing with the likes of a George Washington Plunkitt or a Richard Daley would be to learn from them and use that learning to beat them at their own game. Fortunately, Addams was not a "repressor." She fought to give more and different people a bigger share in the system. Yet the influence and power that she wielded was considerable, and one might wonder what could have happened if she had used her power in ways other than she did.

Personalizing the Issues

Jane Addams:
The Gracious Radical of Hull House

In 1931 the Nobel Peace Prize was awarded to a seventy-one-year-old American woman, Jane Addams, founder of Chicago's famous Hull House. She accepted the award and promptly gave the $16,000 prize money to charity, a gesture that was characteristic of her renowned compassion and generosity.

Established in 1889, Hull House was the second settlement house in America, but it soon became the most famous. Its staff helped immigrants of Chicago's Nineteenth Ward adjust to American society, and worked to make local and state government more re-

sponsive to the needs of the urban poor. Its fame was due primarily to the greatness of its founder, but also to the dynamic women who shared Jane Addams's concern for the Greek, Italian, Sicilian, Russian, and German immigrants who lived in Chicago facing disease, vice, poverty, and premature death. The horrible conditions of the city are seen in the death rate of children at the time: babies born within the ward had about the same chance for survival as those born in sixteenth-century England.

Nothing in the first two decades of Jane Addams's life indicated that she would become the world's most famous social worker. Born in 1860 in Cedarville, Illinois, to Sarah and John Addams, she grew up in an environment typical of her social class. Her father, a prosperous Quaker businessman and politician, raised her after her mother's death in 1862 to respect his credo of honesty. As a state senator he gained fame as a man too honest even to attempt to bribe! Honesty was expected in his household. Once when Jane was seven, she lied to her father and could not sleep. She got up, went to the living room, and informed him of her poor behavior. Forgiveness was not asked, nor was it given. The expected had been done. The hug and kiss she received, however, enabled her to fall asleep immediately. Throughout her life John Addams's admonition that Jane "must always be honest with [herself] inside" controlled and directed her life.

That honesty was hard to come by, however, because John Addams was in no way the perfect father. For most of Jane's first twenty-five years, until she joined a Presbyterian church in Cedarville in 1885, she struggled with her conscience over the meaning and nature of Christianity. Instead of encouraging inquiries, her father thought that religion was to be accepted, not examined or challenged. Later she found many of the answers she sought in the humanism of Browning, Tennyson, and the Greek version of the Gospels, which she studied at the Rockford Female Seminary for Girls from 1877 to 1882.

The main purpose of Rockford Seminary (later Rockford College) was to train female missionaries. Recognizing Jane's talents immediately, the staff tried unsuccessfully to engage her in the missionary enterprise. Their efforts were so clever and tireless that the young student later commented that contesting their arguments was the best possible training one could have to be an independent thinker. Yet her teachers were not complete failures; Jane Addams left Rockford in 1882 full of the school's high-minded idealism, determined to study medicine and minister to the poor.

But her frail health jeopardized these goals. She could not complete her first year in medical school due to surgery for a chronic back ailment. For the next few years, as she recovered her health, she lived the life of the leisure class, although she resisted the entreaties of her stepmother to enjoy the whirl and excitement of society. Try as she might, the second Mrs. Addams never taught her stepdaughter to accept the frivolities of society.

While Jane resisted the temptation to marry and enjoy the so-called good life, she still had not developed a direction of her own until she toured Europe in 1888. She and a classmate, Ellen Starr, visited the poorer sections of Europe's capitals. In Madrid she witnessed the horror and brutality of a bullfight, which the rest of her companions enjoyed. She was shocked, and realized that many of the values of her class, particularly those of her stepmother, were false. Traveling around the world, visiting art museums, and attending bullfights suddenly seemed an empty life.

Fresh from her experience in Madrid, she went to London. Here, she and Ellen Starr visited Toynbee Hall, London's first settlement house. Established in 1884, its purpose was to alleviate the distress caused to the poor by rapid industrialization. The two idealists returned home determined to establish a similar institution in Chicago.

Back in Illinois in February of 1889, they found an enthusiastic audience for their idea. As Ellen Starr said, "the thing is in the air," for many other humanists wanted to prevent the economic, political, and social conflicts that were dividing America into two classes: the haves and the have-nots. Some historians have questioned Jane Addams's late start as a humanitarian, suggesting that the impetus came from some inner psychological weakness (particularly her inability to bear children due to a spinal operation), rather than to genuine concern for the poor. Since poverty and labor violence were not new in America, there is some basis for this contention. But this argument pales against the fact that when Hull House was established, it was only the second settlement house in America, social work was a thing of the future, and sociologists were a rare phenomenon. Until late in the nineteenth century most of the idealists who later became reformers erroneously assumed that the nation would adjust to industrialization as it had to other basic changes. Only when this concept was shown to be false was "the thing in the air."

To expedite their work, Jane Addams and Ellen Starr established Hull House in the heart of the Nineteenth Ward at the corner of Polk and Halstead streets. They found a decaying mansion that had been built by the wealthy Hull family, and from there they "virtually invented social work." Motivated by their concept that people cannot rise far above the level of their society unless they bring human compassion to it, the gentle radicals of Hull House brought about important changes in Chicago, Illinois, and the nation. Jane Addams and her associates worked to help people adjust to the changing concept of success in America and the rapid modernization of life.

Many people helped make Hull House an intellectual and social oasis, but the most important contributors to its success were three fascinating women: Florence Kelley, Julia Lathrop, and Alice Hamilton. The first to join the Hull House staff was Julia Lathrop. Like most of the other staff members, Julia Lathrop had roots deep in American history. Her first American ancestor, the Reverend John Lathrop, had arrived in America in 1634. As a nonconformist minister, he accepted exile from his homeland if that was the price of liberty. Nonconformity seemed to remain with the family. Julia's father, William Lathrop, was a champion of women's rights. He defended women in court, wrote the bill which permitted women to practice law, and trained the first woman lawyer in Illinois. Although Julia attended Vassar College, her home was in Rockford. Here she heard Jane Addams speak in 1889, and joined the crusade at Hull House. She shared more with Jane Addams than their mutual concern for the poor; both had been inculcated with the ideals of Abraham Lincoln from their Republican fathers.

Florence Kelley arrived at Hull House in 1891. When Jane Addams opened the door to greet her and a Kickapoo Indian named Henry Standing Bear, Miss Addams was carrying the cook's baby in one arm and the child of an Italian immigrant sweatshop worker in the other. This unusual introduction came as no shock to the experienced Miss Kelley. Her abolitionist family and her own flirting with socialism had conditioned her for the unexpected.

The last of the triumvirate to arrive was Dr. Alice Hamilton. Like Addams, Lathrop, and Kelley, she came from a leisure-class family that had lived in America for centuries. Like the others', her parents were also intellectually oriented idealists. Motivated by her mother's idea that there were two kinds of people — those who talk about wrongs and those who right them — she had studied medicine at the University of Michigan and the University of Leipzig, but positions for women doctors were rare, and she was among the unemployed when she arrived at Hull House six years after it was founded.

With the help of these three extraordinary women, Jane Addams turned Hull House into an intellectual and social center, constantly working toward her goal of reforming society and establishing a sense of community within the ward. The United States, as Carl Degler has noted, was never really a melting pot. National characteristics remained for centuries and many people were never allowed into the pot to be melted. America has been more like a salad bowl: the immigrant cultures retained their individual flavors, while the national culture was the dressing.

The Nineteenth Ward, however, was much more of a melting pot than the nation at large, basically because of the success of Hull House. Within a few years it was the center for forty clubs, a day nursery, a gymnasium, a playground, a dispensary, a school for adults, and a cooperative boarding house for working girls. Each week more than 2,000 people came to Hull House for one or more of these functions. Soon it was a cultural center as well, with its own art gallery, a little theater (which among other things gave performances of Greek tragedies in the original language), and a school of music. Guest speakers were of the highest caliber. John Dewey came to talk to illiterate immigrants about Greek philosophy, and a planned two-hour discussion lasted for five hours. Frank Lloyd Wright spoke on art and convinced the inhabitants of Hull House that their emphasis on handicrafts was outdated; the machine age was, he said, here to stay. Not all of the speakers were so illustrious or so well received. When one high-minded visitor told them they should enjoy the beauties of nature, particularly in the evening when they could walk to the river and enjoy the sweet smells of God's world, according to Ray Ginger, a German woman said, "Vell, all I can say is if dot woman say dot river smell good, den dere must be something do matter with dot woman's nose."

The immigrant woman was not being rude — she was merely expressing her views in the rampantly individualistic atmosphere of Hull House. No one was denied his or her say, and no one was turned away because of eccentricities. The inhabitants and visitors not only included Henry Standing Bear, but such diverse personalities as an elderly anarchist and a self-styled Hindu Mahatma who convinced the anarchist to look to Heaven, believe that he was divine, and eat nothing but popcorn and garlic.

The most formidable task facing Hull House was raising money. At first Jane Addams paid expenses out of her pocket, but as her program expanded, her modest income did not suffice. Thus she became a fund-raiser, using the same honesty, charm, and warmth to interest donors that had attracted talented people to work at Hull House. During most of the year she canvassed the midwest, and in the summer she went to resorts like Bar Harbor, Maine.

Her success in financing was no small accomplishment. Over the years her program expanded to include a public bath, a kindergarten, a penny savings bank for immigrants, an employment bureau, an orchestra; it also served as the headquarters for the various women's trade unions in the city. By 1920 the annual budget for all services was $100,000. Many of these services, including the kindergarten, public bath, and day nursery were eventually taken over by the city at Jane Addams's request. Although the services Chicago provided were inferior to those provided at Hull House, Jane Addams believed it was necessary to establish these as areas of public responsibilities.

Because the multifaceted programs at Hull House made the residents of the Nineteenth Ward aware of their own cultural heritage as well as the American culture, they had fewer problems adjusting to the nationalization of American life than most other immigrants. Furthermore, they learned how to make City Hall more responsive to their public needs. When the city took over many of the services once provided by Hull House, it established a precedent which the voters of the Nineteenth Ward would not let them forget.

Over the years, the gentle radicals of Hull House gained a degree of respectability, but it was not until the Nobel Peace Prize of 1931 was awarded that "society" accepted them. Their revolutionary ideas of social work were frightening; so too was their support of women's rights and labor unions. Although the so-called best people were slow in responding to them, the idealists of Hull House found ready acceptance in the world of reform.

Jane Addams wrote numerous books and articles and spoke for many worthy causes. Her colleagues worked in other ways. The reform governor of Illinois, John Peter Altgeld, appointed Florence Kelley to the position of State Factory Inspector. What she discovered in the state's factories was horrifying. Entrepreneurs who employed children were not legally responsible for the loss of life or limb by their employees, even when the accident occurred under circumstances that were in violation of the law. When Miss Kelley discovered that local lawyers would not institute law cases against the city's employers, she acquired a law degree from Northwestern and initiated her own cases. But she was not always successful: she promoted a law which established an eight-hour working day for women which was later ruled unconstitutional by the state Supreme Court.

Another staff member appointed by Governor Altgeld to an important position was Julia Lathrop. She accepted a position on the State Board of Charities. Her job was to investigate poorhouses to see that they were run efficiently. Her inspections included sliding down fire escapes to see if they were dependable.

Eventually Hull House's influence extended beyond Chicago as its staff shared, or led, many of the humanitarian crusades that led to the state's first factory inspection law and the first juvenile court in the United States. Most of their other crusades were successful, including a child labor law, improvement of welfare procedures, compulsory school attendance, and industrial safety. Their efforts on behalf of John Dewey's "learning by doing" helped progressive education get started. Education as the mere dissemination of knowledge was offensive to both Dewey and the ladies of Hull House. Such was their influence that the University of Chicago established a department of social research and courses in social work.

Their concern for education was not misplaced. Education was rightfully considered one of the new basic tools in the road to success. In early America, industry alone would bring success, but urbanism and industrialization changed the ground rules for success in America. Factory workers labored long hours at low pay and yet they were no better off at age forty than they had been at age thirty. Without education, there was little hope for significant advancement.

But whatever its accomplishments in education or in other fields, Hull House's primary goal was always to help immigrants adjust to the new American community, and its success was outstanding. In addition, life at Hull House was enjoyable. People who worked long hours in a sweatshop wanted a place to relax and have fun — Hull House was that place, mainly because the staff shared Jane Addams's concept that settlement work was more for the benefit of the doer than the recipient. They enjoyed their work and laughed more than they cried. Their professional endeavors, however, precluded marriage from their future, the reality most career women of the nineteenth century faced. Considering the happy home life Miss Addams and her associates had enjoyed as children, this was no small sacrifice. Fortunately, Hull House provided them with an even greater family. The "doers" received satisfaction by humanizing society, while the constantly changing status of the "recipients" demonstrated Jane Addams's basic premise that improving the environment improves the individual.

Before she died in 1935 at the age of seventy-four, Jane Addams had accomplished many things and received numerous awards. She was the first woman president of the National Conference of Charities and Correction, the first woman to receive an honorary degree from Yale, seconded Theodore Roosevelt's nomination at the Progressive Party Convention in 1912, served as an officer in the Woman's Suffrage Association, participated in Henry

Ford's Peace Crusade, helped found the American Civil Liberties Union, and lectured for Herbert Hoover's Food Administration during World War I.

Jane Addams's life was typified by the words of Julia Lathrop. After a strenuous day followed by a night spent delivering an illegitimate child whose mother had been shunned by the neighborhood, Jane Addams wearily mused to her companion that they could *not* care for the entire city; they had to stop somewhere. Julia Lathrop's response was that if "Hull House does not have its roots in human kindness, it is no good at all," and that unselfish attitude remained the basis of their operation.

Issue

The Quality of Urban Politics

Lee is what the politicians call a "doer"; he stands for something, and he and his program are inseparable.

Allan R. Talbot, 1970

Ethics as well as political opinions may be discussed and disseminated among the sophisticated by lectures and printed pages, but to the common people they can only come through example — through a personality which seizes the popular imagination.

Jane Addams, 1912

The Gilded Age had experienced problems of industrialization, urbanization, and immigration. The Progressive Era, extending roughly from the 1890s to World War I, witnessed efforts by reformers to develop solutions to those problems. While earlier reformers had addressed their concerns to farm problems, political honesty, or fiscal reform, the Progressive reformers concentrated their efforts to improve the quality of urban life through governmental reforms in the local city halls. They are also different in that they viewed the city as a kind of social, problem-solving laboratory, where different "solutions" could be tested in order to obtain the best "formula" for a better life.

Such an approach, however, assumed a number of things. First, the Progressives assumed that life under the old governmental styles — the political boss — was totally unsatisfactory to citizens. But some thoughtful Progressives began to ask themselves whether it was really that way. Second, Progressives assumed that a person's life could be improved by improving his or her environment. But is human nature that pliable? Would many people consider it an improvement of their environment if alcoholic beverages were banned? Would people be better off under Prohibition? In short, were the values of the Progressives representative of the values of the whole population?

Beneath these assumptions lay the question of what it was the Progressives themselves valued. While they had no doubt that their reforms reflected the "right kind" of value system — mainly, honesty and efficiency in government — others were not so sure. What did the Progressives mean by honesty and efficiency? Would those words improve city hall's delivery of social services? After all, the bosses did look out after their own and provided a personal element to government. In such a light, was it really asking so much to "vote early and vote often" on election day?

The Progressives essentially argued that the best way to reform city government was to run it more like a business. There should be expert administrators (the city manager); there should be a decentralization of power; patronage should be eliminated; and city jobs should be filled by the most qualified persons (through civil service examinations). But would such a government be any more representative of "the people" than were the machine bosses whom the Progressives battled?

The problem of effective city government is as crucial today as it was at the beginning of the twentieth century. Then, the urban population was approximately 45 percent of the total population; in 1975, it was over 70 percent. That fact, if no other, makes the solution even more compelling.

◆ DOCUMENTS ◆

Defining American Politics
JAMES BRYCE

Although James Bryce is an Englishman attempting to describe the American political system to a European audience, his approach allows us to ask: What were the strengths and weaknesses of our structures? Would it have been possible to have anything different yet equally democratic? How desirable is it to have "everyone" involved in politics? At one point Bryce refers to the professional politicians as "weeds." What does that tell us about Bryce's values?

Reprinted with permission of Macmillan Publishing Co., Inc. from *The American Commonwealth,* 2d ed., vol. 2, pp. 62–68, by James Bryce. Copyright 1910, 1914 by Macmillan Publishing Co., Inc., renewed 1938 by Elizabeth M. Bryce.

In America the Inner Circle, that is to say, the persons who make political work the chief business of life, for the time being, includes: —

First. All members of both Houses of Congress.

Secondly. All Federal office-holders except the judges, who are irremovable, and the "classified civil service."

Thirdly. A large part of the members of State legislatures. How large a part, it is impossible to determine, for it varies greatly from State to State. I should guess that in New York, Pennsylvania, New Jersey, California, Maryland, and Louisiana, half (or more) the members were professional politicians; in Connecticut, Ohio, Virginia, Illinois, Texas, perhaps less than half; in Georgia, Kentucky, Iowa, Minnesota, Oregon, not more than one-third; in Massachusetts, Vermont, and some other States, perhaps even less. But the line between a professional and non-professional politician is too indefinite to make any satisfactory estimate possible.

Fourthly. Nearly all State office-holders, excluding all judges in a very few States, and many of the judges in the rest.

Fifthly. Nearly all holders of paid offices in the greater and in many of the smaller cities, and many holders of paid offices in the counties. There are, however, great differences in this respect between different States, the New England States and the newer States of the North-west, as well as some Southern States, choosing many of their county officials from men who are not regularly employed on politics, although members of the dominant party.

Sixthly. A large number of people who hold no office but want to get one, or perhaps even who desire work under a municipality. This category includes, of course, many of the "workers" of the party which does not command the majority for the time being, in State and municipal affairs, and which has not, through the President, the patronage of Federal posts. It also includes many expectants belonging to the party for the time being dominant, who are earning their future places by serving the party in the meantime.

All the above may fairly be called professional or Inner Circle politicians, but of their number I can form no estimate, save that it must be counted by hundreds of thousands, inasmuch as it practically includes nearly all State and local and most Federal office-holders as well as most expectants of public office.

It must be remembered that the "work" of politics means in America the business of winning nominations (of which more anon) and elections, and that this work is incomparably heavier and more complex than in England, because: —

(1) The voters are a larger proportion of the population; (2) The government is more complex (Federal, State, and local), and the places filled by election are therefore far more numerous; (3) Elections come at shorter intervals; (4) The machinery of nominating candidates is far more complete and intricate; (5) The methods of fighting elections require more technical knowledge and skill; (6) Ordinary private citizens do less election work, seeing that they are busier than in England, and the professionals exist to do it for them.

I have observed that there are also plenty of men engaged in some trade or profession who interest themselves in politics and work for their party without any definite hope of office or other pecuniary aim. They correspond to what we have called the Outer Circle politicians of Europe. It is hard to draw a line between the two classes, because they shade off into one another, there being many farmers or lawyers or saloon-keepers, for instance, who, while pursuing their regular calling, bear a hand in politics, and look to be some time or other rewarded for doing so. When this expectation becomes a considerable part of the motive for exertion, such an one may fairly be called a professional, at least for the time being, for although he has other means of livelihood, he is apt to be impregnated with the habits and sentiments of the professional class.

The proportion between Outer Circle and Inner Circle men is in the United States a sort of ozonometer by which the purity and healthiness of the political atmosphere may be tested. Looking at the North only, for it is hard to obtain trustworthy data as to the South, and excluding congressmen, the proportion of men who exert themselves in politics without pecuniary motive is largest in New England, in the country parts of New York, in Northern Ohio, and the North-western States, while the professional politicians most abound in the great cities — New York, Philadelphia, Brooklyn, Boston, Baltimore, Buffalo, Cincinnati, Louisville, Chicago, St. Louis, New Orleans, San Francisco. This is because these cities have the largest masses of ignorant voters, and also because their municipal governments, handling vast revenues, offer the largest facilities for illicit gains.

I shall presently return to the Outer Circle men. Meantime let us examine the professionals somewhat more closely; and begin with those of the humbler type, whose eye is fixed on a municipal or other local office, and seldom ranges so high as a seat in Congress.

As there are weeds that follow human dwellings, so this species thrives best in cities, and even in the most crowded parts of cities. It is known to the Americans as the "ward politician," because the city ward is the chief sphere of its activity, and the ward meeting the first scene of its exploits. A statesman of this type usually begins as a saloon or barkeeper, an occupation which enables him to form a large circle of acquaintances, especially among the "loafer" class who have votes but no reason for using them one way more than another, and whose interest in political issues is therefore as limited as their stock of political knowledge. But he may have started as a lawyer of the lowest kind, or lodging-house keeper, or have taken to politics after failure in store-keeping. The education of this class is only that of the elementary schools: if they have come after boyhood from Europe, it is not even that. They have of course no comprehension of political questions or zeal for political principles; politics mean to them merely a scramble for places or jobs. They are usually vulgar, sometimes brutal, not so often criminal, or at least the associates of criminals. They it is who move about the populous quarters of the great cities, form groups through whom they can reach and control the ignorant voter, pack meetings with their creatures.

Their methods and their triumphs must be reserved for a later chapter. Those of them who are Irish, an appreciable though a diminishing proportion in great cities, have seldom Irish patriotism to redeem the mercenary quality of their politics. They are too strictly practical for that, being regardful of the wrongs of Ireland only so far as these furnish capital to be used with Irish voters. Their most conspicuous virtues are shrewdness, a sort of rough good-fellowship with one another, and loyalty to their chiefs, from whom they expect promotion in the ranks of the service. The plant thrives in the soil of any party, but its growth is more vigorous in whichever party is for the time dominant in a given city.

English critics, taking their cue from American pessimists, have often described these men as specimens of the whole class of politicians. This is misleading. The men are bad enough both as an actual force and as a symptom. But they are confined to a few great cities, those eleven or twelve I have already mentioned; it is their achievements there, and particularly in New York, where the mass of ignorant immigrants is largest, that have made them famous.

In the smaller cities, and in the country generally, the minor politicians are mostly native Americans, less ignorant and more respectable than these last-mentioned street vultures. The bar-keeping element is represented among them, but the bulk are petty lawyers, officials, Federal as well as State and county, and people who for want of a better occupation have turned office-seekers, with a fair sprinkling of store-keepers, farmers, and newspaper men. The great majority have some regular avocation, so that they are by no means wholly professionals. Law is of course the business which best fits in with politics. They are only a little below the level of the class to which they belong, which is what would be called in England the lower middle, or in France the *petite bourgeoisie,* and they often suppose themselves to be fighting for Republican or Democratic principles, even though in fact concerned chiefly with place hunting. It is not so much positive moral defects that are to be charged on them as a sordid and selfish view of politics and a laxity, sometimes amounting to fraud, in the use of electioneering methods.

These two classes do the local work and dirty work of politics. They are the rank and file. Above them stand the officers in the political army, the party managers, including the members of Congress and chief men in the State legislatures, and the editors of influential newspapers. Some of these have pushed their way up from the humbler ranks. Others are men of superior ability and education, often college graduates, lawyers who have had practice, less frequently merchants or manufacturers who have slipped into politics from business. There are all sorts among them, creatures clean and unclean, as in the sheet of St. Peter's vision, but that one may say of politicians in all countries. What characterizes them as compared with the corresponding class in Europe is that their whole time is more frequently given to political work, that most of them draw an income from politics and the rest hope to do so, that they come more largely from the poorer and less cultivated than from the higher ranks of society, and that they include but few men who have pursued any of those economical, social, or constitutional studies which form the basis of politics and legislation, although many are proficients in the arts of popular oratory, of electioneering, and of party management.

They show a high average level of practical cleverness and versatility, and often some legal knowledge. They are usually correct in life, for intoxication as well as sexual immorality is condemned by American more severely than by European opinion, but are often charged with a low tone, with laxity in pecuniary matters, with a propensity to commit or to excuse jobs, with a deficient sense of the dignity which public office confers and the responsibility it implies. I shall elsewhere discuss the validity of these charges, and need only observe here that even if the years since the Civil War have furnished some grounds for accusing the class as a whole, there are many brilliant exceptions, many leading politicians whose honour is as stainless and patriotism as pure as that of the best European statesmen. In this general description I am simply repeating what non-political Americans themselves say. It is possible that with their half-humorous tendency to exaggerate they dwell too much on the darker side of their public life. My own belief is that things are healthier than the newspapers and common talk lead a traveller to believe, and that the blackness of the worst men in the large cities has been allowed to darken the whole class of politicians as the smoke from a few factories will darken the sky over a whole town. However, the sentiment I have described is no doubt the general sentiment. "Politician" is a term of reproach, not merely among the "superfine philosophers" of New England colleges, but among the better sort of citizens over the whole Union. "How did such a job come to be perpetrated?" I remember once asking a casual acquaintance who had been pointing out some scandalous waste of public money. "Why, what can you expect from the politicians?" was the surprised answer.

Assuming these faults to exist, to what causes are they to be ascribed? Granted that politics has to become a gainful profession, may it not still be practised with as much integrity as other professions? Do not the higher qualities of intellect, the ripe fruits of experience and study, win for a man ascendancy here as in Europe? Does not the suspicion of dishonour blight his influence with a public which is itself as morally exacting as that of any European country? These are questions which can be better answered when the methods of party management have been described, the qualities they evoke appreciated, their reaction on men's character understood.

It remains to speak of the non-professional or Outer Circle politicians, those who work for their party without desiring office. These men were numerous and zealous shortly before and during the Civil War, when the great questions of the exclusion of slavery from the Territories and the preservation of the Union kindled the enthusiasm of the noblest spirits of the North, women as well as men. No country ever produced loftier types of dauntless courage and uncompromising devotion to principle than William Lloyd Garrison and his fellow-workers in the Abolitionist cause. Office came to Abraham Lincoln, but he would have served his party just as earnestly if there had been no office to reward him. Nor was there any want of high-souled patriotism in the South. The people gave their blood freely, and among the leaders there were many who offered up fine characters as well as brilliant talents on an altar which all but themselves deemed unhallowed. When these great issues were finally settled, and the generation whose manhood they filled began to pass away, there was less motive for ordinary citizens to trouble themselves about public affairs. Hence the professional politicians had the field left free; and as they were ready to take the troublesome work of organizing, the ordinary citizen was contented to be superseded, and thought he did enough when he went to the poll for his party. Still there are districts where a good deal of unpaid and disinterested political work is done. In some parts of New England, New York, and Ohio, for instance, citizens of position bestir themselves to rescue the control of local elections from the ward politicians. In the main, however, the action of the Outer Circle consists in voting, and this the ordinary native citizen does more steadily and intelligently than anywhere in Europe, unless perhaps in Switzerland. Doubtless much of the work which Outer Circle politicians do in Europe is in America done by professionals. But that lively interest in politics which the English Outer Circle feels, and which is not felt, save at exceptional moments, by the English public generally, is in America felt by the bulk of the nation, that is to say, by the large majority of native white Americans, and even by the better sort of immigrants, or, in other words, the American Outer Circle comes nearer to including the whole nation than does the Outer Circle of England. Thus the influence which counterworks that of professionals is the influence of public opinion expressing itself constantly through its countless voices in the press, and more distinctly at frequent intervals by the ballot-box. I say "counterworks," because, while in Europe the leaders and still more the average legislators share and help to make public opinion, in the United States the politician stands rather outside, and regards public opinion as a factor to be reckoned with, much as the sailor regards the winds and currents that affect his course. His primary aim, unless he be exceptionally disinterested, is place and income: and it is in this sense that he may be described as a member of a definite profession.

Privilege and Politics

TOM L. JOHNSON

Tom Johnson, a millionaire inventor and owner of a streetcar company in Indianapolis, later moved to Cleveland where he served as reform mayor from 1901 to 1909. Does Johnson's analysis of what was wrong with society have any bearing on what you see to be the problem today? What is the modern counterpart of "Privilege"?

The greatest movement in the world to-day may be characterized as the struggle of the people against Privilege.

On the one side the People — slow to wake up, slow to recognize their own interests, slow to realize their power, slow to invoke it. On the other, Privilege — always awake and quick to act, owning many of the newspapers, controlling the election and appointment of judges, dictating to city councils, influencing legislatures and writing our national laws.

What is Privilege?

Privilege is the advantage conferred on one by law of denying the competition of others. It matters not whether the advantage be bestowed upon a single individual, upon a partnership, or upon an aggregation of partnerships, a trust — the essence of the evil is the same. And just to the extent that the law imposes restrictions upon some men and not on others, just to the extent that it grants special favors to some to the exclusion of others, do the people suffer from this evil.

These law-made restrictions and benefits are many, but substantially all may be grouped, in the order of their importance, in the following five classes: land monopolies, taxation monopolies, transportation monopolies, municipal monopolies and patent monopolies.

The greatest of all governmental favors or special privileges is land monopoly, made possible by the exemption from taxation of land values.

The special privileges growing out of conditions created by our local, State and national tax systems are so far-reaching and disastrous in their effects that one might devote a volume to the discussion of this division of Privilege, and then not begin to compass the question.

Under transportation monopolies come the governmental favors to railroads and to those enterprises dependent upon the railroads, such as special freight lines, sleeping-car companies, express and telegraph companies.

Municipal monopolies consist of rights and special privileges in the public streets and highways which in the nature of the case cannot be possessed by all the people and can be enjoyed only by a few. Under this head come the

From Tom L. Johnson, *My Story* (New York: B. W. Huebsch, 1911), pp. xxxv–xl.

franchises which our cities grant to street railways, to water, gas, electric light and telephone companies, and in these lie the chief sources of corruption in municipal life.

Patent monopolies are the last distinct survival of a policy which once had a very much wider application and which in every other case has been abandoned because it was recognized to be unsound. At one time it was common enough to reward public service of almost any kind by the grant of a trade monopoly. Soldiers in war were tempted by the prospect of such a grant and often got it as the result of a victory. Statesmen were tempted and were often rewarded in the same way for services to the State, or services to their party. Now this is universally recognized to be an error.

Patent monopolies cut off from us the opportunity to take immediate advantage of the world's inventions. They exert upon many men an influence as baneful as the most corrupt lottery by tempting them from regular work and useful occupations. They interfere with the natural development of invention.

Useful inventions come naturally and almost inevitably as the next necessary step in industrial evolution. Most of them are never patented. The patents that are granted interfere with this natural development. If inventors must be rewarded it would be better to pay them a bounty than to continue a system productive of so much evil.

And so by securing in different ways "special privileges to some" and denying "equal rights to all," our governments, local, State and national, have precipitated the struggle of the people against Privilege.

It matters not what the question — whether a water or gas franchise, a street railway monopoly, a coal combination, an ordinary railroad charter, or the grabbing of the public domain — the issue between them is always the same.

Owners and managers of public-service corporations may change; so may their methods. They may respect public opinion or scorn it; they may show great consideration for their employees or treat them as machines; their policies may be liberal or the reverse; they may strive for all the traffic will bear, looking to dividends only, or they may share their profits with the public.

What of it?

So, too, political parties may change.

And what of that?

A Republican boss or a Democratic boss is equally useful to Privilege. It may seek legislative power through dealing directly with corrupt bosses, or it may find the control of party machinery by means of liberal campaign contributions the more effective; again it may divert the attention of the people from fundamental issues by getting them to squabbling over nonessentials.

This is often demonstrated when the contest is made to appear to be between two men, though in reality both are committed in advance to obey the wishes of Privilege. Superficial moral issues are especially serviceable in this particular line of attack.

But it is on the judiciary that Privilege exercises its most insidious and dangerous power. Lawyers whose employment has been entirely in its interests are selected for the bench. Their training, their environment, their self-interest, all combine to make them the most powerful allies of monopoly. Yet this may be, and often is, without any consciousness on the part of the judges themselves that their selection has been influenced by an interest opposed to the public good.

Thus unwittingly men, otherwise incorruptible, become the most pliable agents of Privilege and the most dangerous of public servants. No mere change of political names or of men can correct these evils. A political change will not affect judges with their judge-made laws, and so long as Privilege controls both parties, a political change will not affect the legislative bodies which create judges. An effective recall of judges would furnish the machinery to correct many abuses, and this step can be taken without waiting for the economic changes which must afford the final and fundamental relief.

For it is to *economic change,* and not to political change, that the people must look for the solution of this problem. Not *lawbreakers,* but *lawmakers* are responsible for bad economic conditions; and these only indirectly, for it is business interests controlling lawmakers that furnish the great motive force in the protection of Privilege.

The economic change that will correct these political abuses is one that must remove the prizes which Privilege now secures from the People. It must reserve to the public the ownership and management of public-service utilities so that they shall be regarded no longer as private loot, but as public rights to be safeguarded and protected.

That good, law-abiding corporations and good, well-meaning men cannot correct these wrongs without changing the economic conditions which produce them, has been proved times without number, and only serves to emphasize the fact that the real fight of the people is not to abolish lawbreaking, but to put an end to that lawmaking which is against the public good.

It is true that the contest looks like an unequal one; that the advantage seems to be entirely on the side of Privilege; that its position appears invulnerable.

Is there then no hope? Let us see.

The people's advance guard has been routed often, and will be time and time again. New recruits must come to the front. As the firing lines are decimated the discontented masses must rush forward to fill the gaps in the ranks. Finally, when *we are fighting all along the line,* public opinion will be strong enough to drive Privilege out of its last trench.

Agitation for the right, once set in motion, cannot be stopped. Truth can never lose its power. It presses forward gaining victories, suffering defeats, but losing nothing of momentum, augmenting its strength though seeming to expend it.

Newspapers controlled by the Interests cannot stop this forward movement, legislatures must yield to it, the courts finally see and respect it and political parties must go with it or be wrecked.

What more striking example could be cited than the disintegration of the Republican party as shown at the 1910 election, following so closely upon the almost unparalleled vote for its candidate for President?

Big Business, corrupt bosses, subservient courts, pliant legislatures and an Interest-controlled press may block, delay, apparently check its progress, but these are only surface indications. The deeper currents are all headed in the same direction, and once fairly started nothing can turn them back.

It is because I believe that the story of my part in this universal movement helps to illustrate the truth of this proposition that I have decided to tell it.

Politics and Corruption

CLAUDE H. WETMORE and LINCOLN STEFFENS

Wetmore and Steffens were two muckraking journalists who wrote a series of exposés about graft and corruption in several major cities. Not only did they detail the way in which bosses came to power, but they also showed how boss-ism could be rooted out. Yet did they foresee problems with the kind of re-form that Folk represented? Would it work everywhere? What are the chances today of a crusader cleaning out City Hall?

St. Louis, the fourth city in size in the United States, is making two announce-ments to the world: one that it is the worst governed city in the land; the other that it wishes all men to come and see it. It isn't our worst governed city; Philadelphia is that. But St. Louis is worth examining while we have it inside out.

There is a man at work there, one man, working all alone, but he is the Circuit (district or state) Attorney, and he is "doing his duty." That is what thousands of district attorneys and other public officials have promised to do and boasted of doing. This man has a literal sort of mind. He is a thin-lipped, firm-mouthed, dark little man, who never raises his voice, but goes ahead do-ing, with a smiling eye and a set jaw, the simple thing he said he would do. The politicians and reputable citizens who asked him to run, urged him when he declined. When he said that if elected he would have to do his duty, they said, "Of course." So he ran, they supported him, and he was elected. Now some of these politicians are sentenced to the penitentiary, some are in Mex-ico. The Circuit Attorney, finding that his "duty" was to catch and convict

From Claude H. Wetmore and Lincoln Steffens, "Tweed Days in St. Louis," *McClure's Magazine* (October 1902), XIX, 577, 580, 586.

criminals, and that the biggest criminals were some of these same politicians and leading citizens, went after them. It is magnificent, but the politicians declare it isn't politics.

The corruption of St. Louis came from the top. The best citizens — the merchants and big financiers — used to rule the town, and they ruled it well. They set out to outstrip Chicago. The commercial and industrial war between these two cities was at one time a picturesque and dramatic spectacle such as is witnessed only in our country. Business men were not mere merchants and the politicians were not mere grafters; the two kinds of citizens got together and wielded the power of banks, railroads, factories, the prestige of the city, and the spirit of its citizens to gain business and population. And it was a close race. Chicago, having the start, always led, but St. Louis had pluck, intelligence, and tremendous energy. It pressed Chicago hard. It excelled in a sense of civic beauty and good government; and there are those who think yet it might have won. But a change occurred. Public spirit became private spirit, public enterprise became private greed. . . .

Then the unexpected happened — an accident. There was no uprising of the people, but they were restive; and the opposition party leaders, thinking to gain some independent votes, decided to raise the cry "reform" and put up a ticket of candidates different enough from the usual offerings of political parties to give color to their platform. These leaders were not in earnest. There was little difference between the two parties in the city; but the Republican rascals had been getting the greater share of the spoils, and the Democrats wanted more than was given to them. "Boodle" was not the issue, no exposures were made or threatened, and the bosses expected to control their men if elected. Simply as part of the game, the Democrats raised the slogan, "reform" and "no more Ziegenheinism."

Mayor Ziegenhein, called "Uncle Henry," was a "good fellow," "one of the boys," and though it was during his administration that the city grew ripe and went to rot, his opponents talked only of incompetence and neglect, and repeated such stories as that of his famous reply to some citizens who complained because certain street lights were put out: "You have the moon yet — ain't it?"

When somebody mentioned Joseph W. Folk for Circuit Attorney the leaders were ready to accept him. They didn't know much about him. He was a young man from Tennessee; had been President of the Jefferson Club, and arbitrated the railroad strike of 1898. But Folk did not want the place. He was a civil lawyer, had had no practice in criminal law, cared little about it, and a lucrative practice as counsel for corporations was interesting him. He rejected the invitation. The committee called again and again, urging his duty to his party, and the city, etc.

"Very well," he said, at last, "I will accept the nomination, but if elected I will do my duty. There must be no attempt to influence my actions when I am called upon to punish lawbreakers."

The committeemen took such statements as the conventional platitudes of candidates. They nominated him, the Democratic ticket was elected, and Folk became Circuit Attorney for the Eighth Missouri District.

Three weeks after taking the oath of office his campaign pledges were put to the test. A number of arrests had been made in connection with the recent election, and charges of illegal registration were preferred against men of both parties. Mr. Folk took them up like routine cases of ordinary crime. Political bosses rushed to the rescue. Mr. Folk was reminded of his duty to his party, and was given to understand that he was expected to construe the law in such a manner that repeaters and other Election Day criminals who had hoisted Democracy's flag and helped elect him might be either discharged or receive the minimum punishment. The nature of the young lawyer's reply can best be inferred from the words of that veteran political leader, Edward R. Butler, Sr., who, after a visit to Mr. Folk, wrathfully exclaimed, "D—— Joe! he thinks he's the whole thing as Circuit Attorney."

The election cases were passed through the courts with astonishing rapidity; no more mercy was shown Democrats than Republicans, and before winter came a number of ward heelers and old-time party workers were behind the bars in Jefferson City. He next turned his attention to grafters and straw bondsmen with whom the courts were infested, and several of these leeches are in the penitentiary to-day, and the system is broken up because of his activity. But this was little more than the beginning.

St. Louis, indeed, in its disgrace, has a great advantage. It was exposed late; it has not been reformed and caught again and again, until its citizens are reconciled to corruption. But, best of all, the man who has turned St. Louis inside [out], turned it, as it were, upside down, too. In all cities, the better classes — the business men — are the sources of corruption; but they are so rarely pursued and caught that we do not fully realize whence the trouble comes. And so most cities blame the politicians and the ignorant and vicious poor. Mr. Folk has shown St. Louis that its bankers, brokers, corporation officers, its business men are the sources of evil, so that from the start it will know the municipal problem in its true light. With a tradition for public spirit, it may drop Butler and its runaway bankers, brokers, and brewers, and pushing aside the scruples of the hundreds of men down in blue book, and red book, and church register, who are lying hidden behind the statutes of limitations, the city may restore good government. Otherwise the exposures by Mr. Folk will result only in the perfection of the corrupt system. For the corrupt can learn a lesson when the good citizens cannot. The Tweed régime in New York taught Tammany to organize its boodle business; the police exposure taught it to improve its method of collecting blackmail. And both now are almost perfect and safe. The rascals of St. Louis will learn in like manner; they will concentrate the control of their bribery system, excluding from the profit sharing the great mass of weak rascals, and carrying on the business as a business in the interest of a trustworthy few. District Attorney Jerome cannot catch the Tammany men, and Circuit Attorney Folk will not be able another time to break the St. Louis ring. This is St. Louis's one great chance.

But, for the rest of us, it does not matter about St. Louis any more than it matters about Col. Butler et al. The point is, that what went on in St. Louis is going on in most of our cities, towns, and villages. The problem of municipal government in America has not been solved. The people may be tired of it, but they cannot give it up — not yet.

Politics as Business
WILLIAM RIORDAN

The narrator in this selection is George Washington Plunkitt, a successful and powerful boss who was kingpin of the New York City Democratic machine, otherwise known by the name of its headquarters, Tammany Hall. His view of reformers is easy to understand. Yet, do his views tell us something about why reform efforts are often unsuccessful in our time as well as his?

College professors and philosophers who go up in a balloon to think are always discussin' the question: "Why Reform Administrations Never Succeed Themselves!" The reason is plain to anybody who has learned the a, b, c of politics.

I can't tell just how many of these movements I've seen started in New York during my forty years in politics, but I can tell you how many have lasted more than a few years — none. There have been reform committees of fifty, of sixty, of seventy, of one hundred and all sorts of numbers that started out to do up the regular political organizations. They were mornin' glories — looked lovely in the mornin' and withered up in a short time, while the regular machines went on flourishin' forever, like fine old oaks. Say, that's the first poetry I ever worked off. Ain't it great?

Just look back a few years. You remember the People's Municipal League that nominated Frank Scott for mayor in 1890? Do you remember the reformers that got up that league? Have you ever heard of them since? I haven't. Scott himself survived because he had always been a first-rate politician, but you'd have to look in the newspaper almanacs of 1891 to find out who made up the People's Municipal League. Oh, yes! I remember one name: Ollie Teall; dear, pretty Ollie and his big dog. They're about all that's left of the League.

Now take the reform movement of 1894. A lot of good politicians joined in that — the Republicans, the State Democrats, the Stecklerites and the

From *Plunkitt of Tammany Hall* by William Riordan. Published by E. P. Dutton & Co., Inc., and reprinted with their permission. Pp. 17–20.

O'Brienites, and they gave us a lickin', but the real reform part of the affair, the Committee of Seventy that started the thing goin', what's become of those reformers? What's become of Charles Stewart Smith? Where's Bangs? Do you ever hear of Cornell, the iron man, in politics now? Could a search party find R. W. G. Welling? Have you seen the name of Fulton McMahon or McMahon Fulton — I ain't sure which — in the papers lately? Or Preble Tucker? Or — but it's no use to go through the list of the reformers who said they sounded in the death knell of Tammany in 1894. They're gone for good, and Tammany's pretty well, thank you. They did the talkin' and posin', and the politicians in the movement got all the plums. It's always the case.

The Citizens' Union has lasted a little bit longer than the reform crowd that went before them, but that's because they learned a thing or two from us. They learned how to put up a pretty good bluff — and bluff counts a lot in politics. With only a few thousand members, they had the nerve to run the whole Fusion movement, make the Republicans and other organizations come to their headquarters to select a ticket and dictate what every candidate must do or not do. I love nerve, and I've had a sort of respect for the Citizens' Union lately, but the Union can't last. Its people haven't been trained to politics, and whenever Tammany calls their bluff they lay right down. You'll never hear of the Union again after a year or two.

And, by the way, what's become of the good government clubs, the political nurseries of a few years ago? Do you ever hear of Good Government Club D and P and Q and Z any more? What's become of the infants who were to grow up and show us how to govern the city? I know what's become of the nursery that was started in my district. You can find pretty much the whole outfit over in my headquarters, Washington Hall.

The fact is that a reformer can't last in politics. He can make a show for a while, but he always comes down like a rocket. Politics is as much a regular business as the grocery or the dry-goods or the drug business. You've got to be trained up to it or you're sure to fail. Suppose a man who knew nothing about the grocery trade suddenly went into the business and tried to conduct it according to his own ideas. Wouldn't he make a mess of it? He might make a splurge for a while, as long as his money lasted, but his store would soon be empty. It's just the same with a reformer. He hasn't been brought up in the difficult business of politics and he makes a mess of it every time.

I've been studyin' the political game for forty-five years, and I don't know it all yet. I'm learnin' somethin' all the time. How, then, can you expect what they call "business men" to turn into politics all at once and make a success of it? It is just as if I went up to Columbia University and started to teach Greek. They usually last about as long in politics as I would last at Columbia.

You can't begin too early in politics if you want to succeed at the game. I began several years before I could vote, and so did every successful leader in Tammany Hall. When I was twelve years old I made myself useful around the district headquarters and did work at all the polls on election day. Later on, I hustled about gettin' out voters who had jags on or who were too lazy to come to the polls. There's a hundred ways that boys can help, and they get an experience that's the first real step in statesmanship. Show me a boy that hustles for the organization on election day, and I'll show you a comin' statesman.

That's the a, b, c of politics. It ain't easy work to get up to y and z. You have to give nearly all your time and attention to it. Of course, you may have some business or occupation on the side, but the great business of your life must be politics if you want to succeed in it. A few years ago Tammany tried to mix politics and business in equal quantities, by havin' two leaders for each district, a politician and a business man. They wouldn't mix. They were like oil and water. The politician looked after the politics of his district; the business man looked after his grocery store or his milk route, and whenever he appeared at an executive meeting, it was only to make trouble. The whole scheme turned out to be a farce and was abandoned mighty quick.

Do you understand now, why it is that a reformer goes down and out in the first or second round, while a politician answers to the gong every time? It is because the one has gone into the fight without trainin', while the other trains all the time and knows every fine point of the game.

The Limits of Political Reform

FINLEY PETER DUNNE

Dunne was a popular political commentator of the late-nineteenth century who exercised his satirical wit through two fictional characters, Mr. Dooley and Mr. Hennessy. Read this selection aloud. Why would Dunne use two "dumb Irishmen" to express his view? Do they provide additional insights into the nature of reformers and why reform may be short-lived? Do "the people" really want reform?

"Why is it," asked Mr. Hennessy, "that a rayform administhration always goes to th' bad?"

"I'll tell ye," said Mr. Dooley. "I tell ye ivrything an' I'll tell ye this. In th' first place 'tis a gr-reat mistake to think that annywan ra-aly wants to rayform. Ye niver heerd iv a man rayformin' himself. He'll rayform other people gladly. He likes to do it. But a healthy man'll niver rayform while he has th' strenth. A man doesn't rayform till his will has been impaired so he hasn't

From *Observations by Mr. Dooley* by Finley Peter Dunne. Used with the agreement of Greenwood Press, Inc., the reprint publisher. Pp. 167–170.

power to resist what th' pa-apers calls th' blandishments iv th' timpter. An' that's thruer in politics thin annywhere else.

"But a rayformer don't see it. A rayformer thinks he was ilicted because he was a rayformer, whin th' thruth iv th' matther is he was ilicted because no wan knew him. Ye can always ilict a man in this counthry on that platform. If I was runnin' f'r office, I'd change me name, an' have printed on me cards: 'Give him a chanst; he can't be worse.' He's ilicted because th' people don't know him an' do know th' other la-ad; because Mrs. Casey's oldest boy was clubbed be a polisman, because we cudden't get wather above th' third story wan day, because th' sthreet car didn't stop f'r us, because th' Flannigans bought a pianny, because we was near run over by a mail wagon, because th' saloons are open Sundah night, because they're not open all day, an' because we're tired seein' th' same face at th' window whin we go down to pay th' wather taxes. Th' rayformer don't know this. He thinks you an' me, Hinnissy, has been watchin' his spotless career f'r twenty years, that we've read all he had to say on th' evils iv pop'lar sufferage befure th' Society f'r the Bewildermint iv th' Poor, an' that we're achin' in ivry joint to have him dhrag us be th' hair iv th' head fr'm th' flowin' bowl an' th' short card game, make good citizens iv us an' sind us to th' pinitinchry. So th' minyit he gets into th' job he begins a furyous attimpt to convart us into what we've been thryin' not to be iver since we come into th' wurruld.

"In th' coorse iv th' twenty years that he spint attimptin' to get office, he managed to poke a few warrum laws conthrollin' th' pleasures iv th' poor into th' stachoo book, because no wan cared about thim or because they made business betther f'r th' polis, an' whin he's in office, he calls up th' Cap'n iv the polis an' says he: 'If these laws ar-re bad laws th' way to end thim is to enfoorce thim.' Somebody told him that, Hinnissy. It isn't thrue, d'ye mind. I don't care who said it, not if 'twas Willum Shakespere. It isn't thrue. Laws ar-re made to throuble people an' th' more throuble they make th' longer they stay on th' stachoo book. But th' polis don't ast anny questions. Says they: 'They'll be less money in th' job but we need some recreation,' an' that night a big copper comes down th' sthreet, sees me settin' out on th' front stoop with me countenance dhraped with a tin pail, fans me with his club an' runs me in. Th' woman nex' dure is locked up f'r sthringin' a clothes line on th' roof, Hannigan's boy Tim gets tin days f'r keepin' a goat, th' polis resarves are called out to protict th' vested rights iv property against th' haynyous pushcart man, th' stations is crowded with felons charged with maintainin' a hose conthrary to th' stachoos made an' provided, an' th' tindherline is all over town. A rayformer don't think annything has been accomplished if they'se a vacant bedroom in th' pinitinchry. His motto is 'Arrest that man.'

"Whin a rayformer is ilicted he promises ye a business administhration. Some people want that but I don't. Th' American business man is too fly. He's all right, d'ye mind. I don't say annything again' him. He is what Hogan calls th' boolwarks iv pro-gress, an' we cudden't get on without him even if his scales are a little too quick on th' dhrop. But he ought to be left to dale with his akels. 'Tis a shame to give him a place where he can put th' comether on millions iv people that has had no business thrainin' beyond occasionally handin' a piece iv debased money to a car conductor on a cold day. A reg'lar pollytician can't give away an alley without blushin', but a business man who is in pollytics jus' to see that th' civil sarvice law gets thurly enfoorced, will give Lincoln Park an' th' public libr'y to th' beef thrust, charge an admission price to th' lake front an' make it a felony f'r annywan to buy stove polish outside iv his store, an' have it all put down to public improvemints with a pitcher iv him in th' corner stone.

"Fortchnitly, Hinnissy, a rayformer is seldom a business man. He thinks he is, but business men know diff'rent. They know what he is. He thinks business an' honesty is th' same thing. He does, indeed. He's got thim mixed because they dhress alike. His idee is that all he has to do to make a business administhration is to have honest men ar-round him. Wrong. I'm not sayin', mind ye, that a man can't do good work an' be honest at th' same time. But whin I'm hirin' a la-ad I find out first whether he is onto his job, an' afther a few years I begin to suspect that he is honest, too. Manny a dishonest man can lay brick sthraight an' manny a man that wudden't steal ye'er spoons will break ye'er furniture. I don't want Father Kelly to hear me, but I'd rather have a competint man who wud steal if I give him a chanst, but I won't, do me plumbin' thin a person that wud scorn to help himsilf but didn't know how to wipe a joint. Ivry man ought to be honest to start with, but to give a man an office jus' because he's honest is like ilictin' him to Congress because he's a pathrite, because he don't bate his wife or because he always wears a right boot on th' right foot. A man ought to be honest to start with an' afther that he ought to be crafty. A pollytician who's on'y honest is jus' th' same as bein' out in a winther storm without anny clothes on."

Politics and Human Needs

JANE ADDAMS

As founder of the most famous settlement house in America, Jane Addams faced the problem of reconciling her idealism with the realities of Chicago politics. In so doing she came to understand something of the appeal of the bosses to their immigrant supporters. Does Addams betray a certain bias in her perceptions of the immigrants? Does she provide any clues as to how a reformer can be successful without becoming cynical?

From Jane Addams, *Democracy and Social Ethics* (New York: Macmillan, 1915), pp. 222–225, 228–229. Originally published in 1902.

It is difficult both to interpret sympathetically the motives and ideals of those who have acquired rules of conduct in experience widely different from our own, and also to take enough care in guarding the gains already made, and in valuing highly enough the imperfect good so painfully acquired and, at the best, so mixed with evil. This wide difference in daily experience exhibits itself in two distinct attitudes toward politics. The well-to-do men of the community think of politics as something off by itself; they may conscientiously recognize political duty as part of good citizenship, but political effort is not the expression of their moral or social life. As a result of this detachment, "reform movements," started by business men and the better element, are almost wholly occupied in the correction of political machinery and with a concern for the better method of administration, rather than with the ultimate purpose of securing the welfare of the people. They fix their attention so exclusively on methods that they fail to consider the final aims of city government. This accounts for the growing tendency to put more and more responsibility upon executive officers and appointed commissions at the expense of curtailing the power of the direct representatives of the voters. Reform movements tend to become negative and to lose their educational value for the mass of the people. The reformers take the rôle of the opposition. They give themselves largely to criticisms of the present state of affairs, to writing and talking of what the future must be and of certain results which should be obtained. In trying to better matters, however, they have in mind only political achievements which they detach in a curious way from the rest of life, and they speak and write of the purification of politics as of a thing set apart from daily life.

On the other hand, the real leaders of the people are part of the entire life of the community which they control, and so far as they are representative at all, are giving a social expression to democracy. They are often politically corrupt, but in spite of this they are proceeding upon a sounder theory. Although they would be totally unable to give it abstract expression, they are really acting upon a formulation made by a shrewd English observer; namely, that, "after the enfranchisement of the masses, social ideals enter into political programmes and they enter not as something which at best can be indirectly promoted by government, but as something which it is the chief business of government to advance directly."

Men living near to the masses of voters, and knowing them intimately, recognize this and act upon it; they minister directly to life and to social needs. They realize that the people as a whole are clamoring for social results, and they hold their power because they respond to that demand. They are corrupt and often do their work badly; but they at least avoid the mistake of a certain type of business men who are frightened by democracy, and have lost their faith in the people. The two standards are similar to those seen at a popular exhibition of pictures where the cultivated people care most for the technique of a given painting, the moving mass for a subject that shall be domestic and human. . . .

Ethics as well as political opinions may be discussed and disseminated among the sophisticated by lectures and printed pages, but to the common people they can only come through example — through a personality which seizes the popular imagination. The advantage of an unsophisticated neighborhood is, that the inhabitants do not keep their ideas as treasures — they are untouched by the notion of accumulating them, as they might knowledge or money, and they frankly act upon those they have. The personal example promptly rouses to emulation. In a neighborhood where political standards are plastic and undeveloped, and where there has been little previous experience in self-government, the office-holder himself sets the standard, and the ideas that cluster around him exercise a specific and permanent influence upon the political morality of his constituents.

Nothing is more certain than that the quality which a heterogeneous population, living in one of the less sophisticated wards, most admires is the quality of simple goodness; that the man who attracts them is the one whom they believe to be a good man. We all know that children long "to be good" with an intensity which they give to no other ambition. We can all remember that the earliest strivings of our childhood were in this direction, and that we venerated grown people because they had attained perfection.

Primitive people, such as the South Italian peasants, are still in this stage. They want to be good, and deep down in their hearts they admire nothing so much as the good man. Abstract virtues are too difficult for their untrained minds to apprehend, and many of them are still simple enough to believe that power and wealth come only to good people.

◆ MODERN ESSAY ◆

The Spectrum of Urban Politics

MIKE ROYKO and ALLAN R. TALBOT

Following are two selections that provide contrasting views of how to govern a city. How do you explain those differences in the light of the fact that both mayors were concerned with obtaining, keeping, and exercising power? Although Jane Addams probably could have gotten along with Mayor Daley, do you think she would have preferred Mayor Lee? Why or why not? For whom would Tom Johnson or "Mr. Dooley" have voted?

As you examine the internal workings of each mayor's administration, what would you say was each man's fundamental strength and weakness? How did each man view the locus of his power? While the document on Daley suggests several groups that might feel threatened by "hizzoner," who in New Haven might feel threatened by Mayor Lee's social engineering approach toward the remaking of neighborhoods?

[From *Boss: Richard J. Daley of Chicago*]

They [Mayor Richard J. Daley and Dr. Martin Luther King] had another meeting, the day after King led a giant Sunday rally and parade in the Loop, tacking a list of demands on the locked door of City Hall. Once again King told him that the housing market in the city had to be opened to blacks. Once again Daley produced a program that he said was in progress. King talked about jobs, and Daley produced another program. This went on for two hours.

Daley came out of the meeting shaking his head and saying, "They have no programs." What he meant was, they had no program that didn't include blacks moving into white neighborhoods.

Two days later, in hundred-degree temperatures, city workers began going through the West Side turning off fire hydrants that the residents had turned on for the kids to play in. For generations, fire hydrants had been turned on in the city's crowded neighborhoods to combat the humid heat of Chicago. Anybody who grew up in Chicago remembers playing in the gush of water. But Fire Chief Quinn had ordered them sealed on the West Side because he didn't want the city's water pressure to drop. Fighting broke out between some of the black residents and the police who were protecting the city crews. It spread, and the riot was on.

It was a big one. For the first time, snipers appeared, firing from the roofs and windows of the public housing projects. Two blacks, one a fourteen-year-old girl, were killed, and dozens more were injured. Five policemen were hurt. Looting spread over several square miles. On the second day, Wilson said the police couldn't handle it and the national guard was called in. On the third morning, Daley appeared on television and said:

"I think you can't charge it directly to Dr. Martin Luther King, but surely some of the people who came in here and have been talking for the last year of violence — they are on his staff. They are responsible in great measure for the instruction that has been given, for the training of these youngsters."

King's people, he seemed to be saying, were behind the hundreds of blacks who were smashing in the windows of white-owned stores that had been overcharging them for years, who were shooting at the police who had been bullying them for years.

Once again he had his "outsiders" to blame for the sores that for many years had been festering without treatment in his city.

But that afternoon he made a quick reverse when he sat down in his office with King, and other black leaders. The Urban League's Berry was there:

"On the Friday morning after the hydrant riots started we got together in an office downtown to see if we could get some fast action. Ray Simon from the mayor's office was with us, but he said he was there as an observer only. I told him that we wanted to see the mayor, that day, now, and I asked him to arrange it. He said he'd go to City Hall and see about it. I told him: 'There's a phone there, why don't you call?' He wouldn't do it, so we waited. Finally Simon called back and said he couldn't reach the mayor. So I called Daley's secretary and she said she didn't know where he was, so I said: 'We're coming over.' That was about three or four o'clock in the afternoon. When we got there, Daley came in.

"Now that morning, he had that press conference and he implied that Martin caused the riots, that Martin and some of his people had created the atmosphere for them. But in the afternoon, there were no newsmen or cameras in the meeting. It was private, in his office. So he seats Martin next to his desk, where he always puts the leaders of the groups he's seeing, and he says: 'Dr. King, I want to make one thing clear. We know you did nothing to cause the disorders and that you are a man of peace and love.'

"See? It was just the opposite of the statement he made that morning.

"He asked us what we thought could be done. We were worried about now, right now, so we didn't go back to the big problems. We told him to turn on the hydrants, put spray nozzles on them, and start giving black people safe passage to pools in white neighborhoods."

Now there was a program, and Daley liked it. Give them water. He had a whole lake right outside the door. Even before the riots ended a few days later, City Hall had embarked on a crusade to make Chicago's blacks the wettest in the country. Portable swimming pools were being trucked in. Sprinklers were attached to hundreds of hydrants, and water was gushing everywhere. The city's department of planning mobilized to launch a long-range program of black wetness. The Chicago Park District joined in. So did the Fire Department. Suddenly the entire city administration was thinking wet. One cynical civil rights worker said, "I think they're hoping we'll all grow gills and swim away."

Since the pools were an emergency measure, the city didn't have to bother with competitive bidding. So Daley's old Hamburg Club buddy, Fire Chief Quinn, brought a pool-builder friend down from Lake Geneva, Wisconsin, a popular weekend retreat, and cut him in on some of Chicago's pool business. Quinn's friend had built the pool on Quinn's Wisconsin farm.

When Daley emerged from that meeting with King he was finally able to announce that they had reached an agreement. He proudly outlined the wetness program and the headlines chorused: "Peace Plan! Daley-King Agreement Stirs Hope."

Unfortunately for Daley, the black man does not live by water alone. In a month King was marching again, and this time he had Daley worried and in a politically dangerous bind.

King announced that he was going to lead peaceful, nondisruptive marches into the city's white neighborhoods, the bungalow and blue-collar belt, to dramatize his plea for open housing. King had finally found the city's soft underbelly, and Daley knew it.

White Chicago could ignore the downtown marches. The riots didn't touch them directly either, since the blacks wrecked their own neighborhood. But white Chicago would react when the hated blacks and liberal white preachers and nuns showed up. Daley knew how they would react, too. . . . The city's racism, which he insisted wasn't there, would show itself. Daley knew that because if he didn't understand black Chicago, he knew the way white Chicago thought. He knew Bridgeport and that told him about every other neighborhood.

This time he was trapped. He couldn't arrest the marchers as he had done in Bridgeport, because this time they would be led by King, not by Gregory and some unknowns. If he arrested King for trying to lead a peaceful march, he'd be doing something even George Wallace hadn't done on the trek from Selma to Montgomery. He had to protect King and the marchers. To do that, there were bound to be some white heads split, which would be shown in living color on TV, and seen by the millions of white voters. And the fall elections were only ten weeks off. King had him.

The first march went into Gage Park, on the far Southwest Side. Many of the people in Gage Park had formerly lived in Englewood, Woodlawn, and other areas that had slowly turned black. They were Lithuanian, Polish, Italian in ancestry. They were blue collar in occupation, and they were haters. It was an ugly event. King was hit in the head with a rock. The bump was headlined around the world.

Daley pleaded publicly for King to come back to the conference table, to call off the marches. "There must be some way of resolving questions without marches," he said, looking plaintively into the camera.

Two days later, on a beautiful Sunday afternoon, the marchers went into Cragin, another bungalow section on the far Northwest Side. King had been taken ill, but the other civil rights leaders were there, along with a large turnout of priests and nuns. Cragin is a heavily Catholic area, with many Poles and Italians, but that didn't keep the nuns and priests from getting a face full of spit.

Once again it was nasty. The police kept the marchers on one side of the street, and the hecklers on the other, but many of the whites tried to break through. Others went in alleys behind the buildings and lofted rocks and bottles over the roofs. Their hearts weren't in it, but the police waded in, and that night the sight and sounds of clubs against a couple of white skulls, and white voices crying "brutality," poured out of the TV sets.

King's people said that was just the beginning. They were going to hold not one, but two, maybe three, marches a day, in different parts of town. Then they were going to march into the hard-nosed suburb of Cicero. When a Cicero politician heard their plan, he said simply, "Jesus, they won't make it. If they get in, they won't get out alive."

The white neighborhoods were furious, and much of their anger was directed at Daley. He had given the rioting blacks swimming pools, now the police were beating home-owning whites. The city's establishment was joining in, expressing disapproval of the new tactic. Even Archbishop Cody, who had earlier supported King's goals and demands, paying the price with sharply reduced Sunday collections in the backlash neighborhoods, now joined the chorus of those asking King to desist and get himself back to the good old conference table. James Bevel, one of King's men, snapped back: "When there's trouble, Daley sticks up his liberal bishop to say, 'You've gone far enough.' Well, we've got news for the man. If the archbishop doesn't have the courage to speak up for Christ, let him join the devil."

King had Daley reeling. If the marches increased in number the police couldn't possibly protect all the marchers. Blacks would be hurt, and the black neighborhoods might retaliate. . . .

Daley sent his legal department into court for an emergency injunction limiting the number of marches to one a day, requiring advance notice, and setting other ground rules. That cut off the immediate crisis, and if the blacks violated the court order the police could arrest them, which would look good on TV.

Then he called for a "summit conference," a mighty meeting of the city's business, religious, political, and civil rights leaders, to hammer out once and for all an agreement on housing, education, jobs, and the other weighty problems. Actually, all that was needed was for his administration to do its job, but with a "summit conference" there was always a chance he could talk his way out of it.

The conference, held in a Protestant church, found Daley and his group on the defensive. The civil rights groups laid out their demands — the same ones they had been making all summer. This time, however, Daley began giving ground, making concessions. He was calm, placating, even when the militants were sharp and argumentative. "At one point," Berry said, "Tom Keane leaned over and stage-whispered to Daley: 'Fuck 'em, Dick, we don't have to stay here and listen to this.' But Daley was friendly and controlled."

Daley got what he needed — a brief delay. A subcommittee was formed to work out the specifics of the "summit agreement." Between the injunction against mass marches and the subcommittee, Daley had time to breathe. Eight days later, the agreement was drafted and both sides met again at the summit and signed their names. There was great rejoicing.

King: "It is the first step in a thousand-mile journey, but an important step . . . one of the most significant programs ever conceived to make open housing a reality. . . . Never before have such far-reaching and creative concepts been made."

Daley: "I'm satisfied that the people of Chicago and the suburbs and the whole metropolitan area will accept this program in the light of the people who endorsed it. This program was worked out by the people of the Chicago Freedom Movement, labor unions, business groups and civic groups."

It was an impressive document, chock full of noble vows and promises. It was also without legal standing and wasn't worth the paper it was printed on. Only three months after it was signed, when the crisis was over, Alderman Keane said at a City Council meeting that "There is no Summit Agreement," and the people who took part in the meeting had merely agreed that open housing was "a goal to be reached," but there was no agreement beyond that.

He could say it then. The snow had fallen, Dr. King was back home in the South, the marches had faded into memory. Daley hadn't rejected Keane's suggestion to "fuck 'em." He just did it slowly.

[From *The Mayor's Game: Richard Lee of New Haven and the Politics of Change*]

Night and day separate the jubilation of election victory from the realization that one has finally arrived at the seat of power. Election Night for a victorious candidate is happily crowded with party well-wishers who quite naturally attribute success not to the appeal of the candidate but to the work of the party. In the minds of most party faithfuls, candidates do not win elections; they just lose them.

The morning after, the loneliness of public responsibility sets in, broken only by congratulatory calls and letters which have to be carefully answered. Now the candidate must face two interrelated questions.

The first is how to grasp the reins of power and exert influence and leadership. Elected executive posts in government offer no power transformers through which executive will may be automatically translated into public policy and then into government action. Rather, they offer varying legal powers, an important title, and some ceremonial trappings and the symbols of leadership. The impact a mayor makes and the power he exerts result from the blend of his personal convictions, his strength, and his skill with the built-in titular, ceremonial, and legal prerogatives of the job. But the quality of the man is much more important than the authority of the position. A man with strong convictions and effective powers of persuasion can take a so-called weak or even ceremonial mayoralty and make it the center of community action. Conversely, a man who avoids conflicts and is interested only in personal security or gain can be given the most potent legal authority and still be remembered only by his family and perhaps the Bureau of Internal Revenue.

The second question a new mayor must ask is what it is he wants to accomplish. Many mayors get excited about maintaining efficient city services, minding the tax rate, and maneuvering loyal party members and friends into available jobs. While all that is commendable or at least understandable, it has little bearing on the obvious problems that plague America's urban centers — the slums, the run-down schools, the choked streets, the filth, the human misery, the declining economic base, and the widespread ugliness.

Lee's answers to these questions had already been formed during his four-year waiting period, and perhaps even before that. "It may sound much too dramatic," he said recently, "but as I look back I think I was preparing for this job all my life. By 1951 I wanted it so bad I was like a rookie dying for the chance to show the manager that I was ready. Finally, when he sent me to the plate, it rained. But in 1953, after I finally made it, I was more ready than ever. I had a general idea of what I wanted to do. I felt I knew how to do it. The bat felt good in my hands."

Lee's background as a City Hall reporter and an alderman had given him a unique insight into the mayor's job and the personalities he would have to deal with. One long-time municipal employee, a maintenance man, offers this picture of an early trip of Lee's to City Hall after his victory:

"He was all fired up and in he comes through the front door. The place was suddenly full of noise, with Dick shaking hands with secretaries, the elevator men, and all. Everyone he greets with a smile, and he knew all our first names and we knew him. Dick was no stranger to City Hall."

Lee's knowledge of the personalities in city government included higher-level officials. One veteran city executive recalls his impression of Lee's victory in these terms:

"All of us knew Dick before he got elected, and I can't think of anyone who really disliked him. He was friendly, always had a smile. Of course everyone knew him from being an alderman and as a reporter. I suppose there was some uneasiness now that he was mayor, the same as there is whenever there's a new boss. But on a personal basis, he still seemed like the same Dick Lee."

Lee's grasp went beyond the first names and official titles of those in the city government. He had accumulated a formidable mental file on their strengths, weaknesses, and even some of their indiscretions. All this proved useful once he became mayor, as was his almost encyclopedic knowledge of the general lay of the city land. For instance, his personal secretary, Mrs. Robert Puckett, remembers that during the early days of the administration a request came in from Samuel Lubell, the voter analyst, for a profile on all New Haven wards, including the social and economic characteristics of the residents, election trends, and subleaders. Lee was interested in the request and took half an hour to dictate a memorandum so detailed it would have taken a Yale graduate student weeks of research to prepare. A staff should have an employee or a consultant with a thorough knowledge of its target area. The New Haven staff had Lee.

What lay under his knowledge, technique, and charm? "A simple, yet intense moral purpose," suggests Eugene Rostow, former Dean of the Yale Law School and now the Undersecretary for Political Affairs in the State Department. Rostow, no aloof observer of the New Haven scene, is a friend of Lee's and served as a co-chairman of the Citizens for Lee Committee in the 1953 campaign. "Very few of us at the University took any great interest in Dick's first two attempts to become mayor. He was a part of Yale, so we followed the campaigns, but they were really ordinary affairs with Dick hitting conventional themes of efficiency and honesty. But when he campaigned to rebuild the city, in 1953, he struck a responsive chord. He was attacking fundamental ills of our time, the moral, economic, and social injustice of the slum.

"Dick is no ordinary politician. He has successfully developed the skills of that trade, but he has used them to help others. I believe the reason he finally won in 1953 is that he abandoned the stock clichés of electioneering and allowed his morality to come through. Voters sense this in a candidate. From 1953 until now, the people have understood that Dick means it when he says that slums are evil and the city must be rebuilt. They sense his commitment and that's more important to them than any mistakes he might have made."

Some New Haveners might quarrel with Rostow's last comment, but it would be a matter of emphasis. One searches vainly in the papers, in the general political rhetoric, in the statements of opponents in New Haven from 1953 to the present for an attack on Lee's sincerity, his commitment, or the integrity of his program goals. Many disagree with him, some stress his mistakes, others patronize him with adjectives like "misguided," but no one attacks on grounds of a difference between what Lee has said he will do and what he tries to do. Lee is what the politicians call a "doer"; he stands for something, and he and his program are inseparable. . . .

The remarkable aspect of Lee's stewardship in New Haven is that urban renewal became the centerpiece of his administration and his personal and political reason for being. The process of public control of physical change intrigued and delighted him. It also lent itself to the undisciplined exaggerations of the Lee mind. As we shall see, he eventually began calling every improvement of his administration, from fire hydrants to sewers, "a product of our renewal program." A newcomer to New Haven, taken aback by these dramatic flourishes or Lee's personal color, might wonder how much substance, originality, or sincerity there is under his effervescent surface. Those who have spent time with him and have witnessed his interminable project tours, his angry notes to shoddy architects and landlords, and the great thrill he gets out of seeing models of new buildings can more easily discern the truth about him: he believes.

The renewal of any city requires strong, understanding leaders. It requires, as well, a good basic plan. It also needs vigorous day-to-day direction by someone who can make the plan a working blueprint, fight the battles a mayor cannot afford to fight, cement the agreements a mayor suggests, and produce the program results a mayor needs to get re-elected. New Haven had the plan and the leader. Now it needed a good doer. Finding such a man was a major preoccupation for Lee during the post-1953 election period.

A name which keeps popping up in the jammed Lee appointment book in the late fall of 1953 was Edward J. Logue, a man who over the years has been variously described as "a brilliant programmer," "the toughest man in the world," "a perfectly charming man," "an egotistical S.O.B.," "one of the best friends I ever had." He is, as one might deduce from those comments, a man for all occasions, fortified by a sense of drama second only to the man who was to be his boss in New Haven from 1953 until 1961, when he left for Boston, Massachusetts. Today, at the age of forty-five, Logue has risen to become one of the best-known and successful renewal chiefs in the nation by virtue of his work in New Haven and Boston. In December, 1965, *Life* in a special feature on the American city featured Logue as the "Bold Boston Gladiator." In the fall of 1953 his reputation was more modest. He was known mainly to Connecticut politicians as an energetic young lawyer who had worked as a special assistant to Governor Chester Bowles. Logue was a Bowles "bird dog." He carried out the Governor's orders on state reorganization, education, and labor problems. After Bowles lost to John Lodge in 1951, Logue became Bowles' special assistant in India, where he helped direct all phases of the Ambassador's activities and learned what Logue has described as "the great sense of urgency which should accompany public service — the feeling, as Chet once put it, that 'if the problem exists today, it should be dealt with today.' " Logue's drive has been his most salient characteristic in public service. It has given him the image of a tough, able, and often abrasive man of action. . . .

Lee and Logue approached the problems of New Haven with the fervor of a moral crusade and the pragmatism of practical politics. "Dick was often like a preacher," Logue has observed, "but the two-year term sometimes made it necessary to depart from the sermon and take some expedient action to show results." Each man staked his considerable ego on the outcome. Generally, it was Logue who proposed what should be done and Lee — the accepted boss — who decided what would be done and how, although everyone intimately connected with the program can recall at least one occasion when Lee did all three. Logue has never been happy with how writers have treated Lee in their descriptions of the relationship. "Somehow," he says, "it's implied, even stated, that I was the brains of the outfit, and Dick was the con man who got things done and served as a front. That's an enormous injustice to Dick. He percolates ideas, and he has a marvelous sense and appreciation for good planning. He also knows how to use people, and that's one of his great strengths.". . .

"[Logue was asked] 'What the hell are you guys trying to do?' I stopped for a minute, thought, and then replied, 'We're shooting the moon, that's what we're trying to do.' "

Issue

The Itch for Orthodoxy

> *The only thing I know for certain is that* this *time we women must seize control over our own lives. . . .*
>
> Robin Morgan, 1970

> *I believe in the protection of our pure womanhood.*
>
> Ku Klux Klan, 1924

Despite the assertion in the Pledge of Allegiance that we are to be "one nation, under God, indivisible . . . ." we have had great difficulty developing a national identity broad enough to include all Americans, yet tight enough to create a sense of community for each of us. Part of that difficulty stems from the continual and at times explosive growth in population, immigration, the size of our cities, our Pacific empire, our industrial productivity, and our scientific and cultural knowledge. Part of the difficulty also stemmed from the long heritage of racism that had manifested itself to most minorities, but particularly to Indians and blacks.

Throughout the nineteenth and twentieth centuries some Americans, trying to find a haven of stability in their cultural sea of change, sought to define "community" on narrow and specific grounds — race, creed, religious belief (or conformity). Although such an approach might be clear-cut, e.g., "Whites Only," it had the effect of isolating not only those who were being discriminated against but also those who were doing the discriminating. Other Americans, equally concerned about community, were perplexed by the question of how far a community could reasonably go in regulating the behavior of its citizens. Were certain kinds of behavior, such as freedom of speech, never to be regulated because of their importance? Or did the community, as part of its need to survive, have the right to curb even those basic freedoms under certain circumstances? If one examines present-day society from the same standpoint, we find it difficult to say when wiretapping in the name of "national security" (preservation of the community) becomes invasion of privacy, or when police enforcement becomes "police brutality."

Thus the question confronting us in this section is twofold: where does reasonable regulation of behavior end and outright repression begin, and what role do fear and uncertainty in the midst of change play in the repression that Americans visit upon one another?

• DOCUMENTS •

Defining the Orthodox American
GEORGE A. CUSTER

Custer did not accept the popular phrase that "the only good Indian is a dead Indian," and the selection by him suggests that he might have been less than enthusiastic in clearing them from the land. Even if he was willing to admit that Indians possessed certain admirable qualities, does that not make his conclusion all the more difficult to understand? What can impel us to repress people whom we may actually respect as individuals? What impelled Custer?

Inseparable from the Indian character, wherever he is to be met with, is [sic] his remarkable taciturnity, his deep dissimulation, the perseverance with which he follows his plans of revenge or conquest, his concealment and apparent lack of curiosity, his stoical courage when in the power of his enemies, his cunning, his caution, and last, but not least, the wonderful power and subtlety of his senses. Of this last I have had most interesting proof, one instance of which will be noted when describing the Washita campaign. In studying the Indian character, while shocked and disgusted by many of his traits and customs, I find much to be admired and still more of deep and unvarying interest. To me, Indian life, with its attendant ceremonies, mysteries, and forms, is a book of unceasing interest. Grant that some of its pages are frightful and, if possible, to be avoided, yet the attraction is none the weaker. Study him, fight him, civilize him if you can, he remains still the object of your curiosity, a type of man peculiar and undefined, subjecting himself to no known law of civilization, contending determinedly against all efforts to win him from his chosen mode of life. He stands in the group of nations solitary and reserved, seeking alliance with none, mistrusting and opposing the advances of all. Civilization may and should do much for him, but it can never civilize him. A few instances to the contrary may be quoted, but these are susceptible of explanation. No tribe enjoying its accustomed freedom has ever been induced

From George A. Custer, *My Life on the Plains, or Personal Experiences with the Indian* (New York: Sheldon & Co., 1874), pp. 19–23.

to adopt a civilized mode of life or, as they express it, to follow the white man's road. At various times certain tribes have forsaken the pleasures of the chase and the excitement of the warpath for the more quiet life to be found on the "reservation." Was this course adopted voluntarily and from preference? Was it because the Indian chose the ways of his white brother rather than those in which he had been born and bred?

In no single instance has this been true. What then, it may be asked, have been the reasons which influenced certain tribes to abandon their predatory, nomadic life, and today to influence others to pursue a similar course? The answer is clear, and as undeniable as it is clear. The gradual and steady decrease in numbers, strength, and influence, occasioned by wars both with other tribes and with the white man, as well as losses brought about by diseases partly attributable to contact with civilization, have so lowered the standing and diminished the available fighting force of the tribe as to render it unable to cope with the more powerful neighboring tribes with any prospect of success. The stronger tribes always assume an overbearing and dominant manner toward their weaker neighbors, forcing them to join in costly and bloody wars or themselves to be considered enemies. When a tribe falls from the position of a leading one, it is at the mercy of every tribe that chooses to make war, being forced to take sides, and at the termination of the war is generally sacrificed to the interests of the more powerful. To avoid these sacrifices, to avail itself of the protection of civilization and its armed forces, to escape from the ruining influences of its more warlike and powerful neighbors, it reluctantly accepts the situation, gives up its accustomed haunts, its wild mode of life, and nestles down under the protecting arm of its former enemy, the white man, and tries, however feebly, to adopt his manner of life. In making this change, the Indian has to sacrifice all that is dear to his heart; he abandons the only mode of life in which he can be a warrior and win triumphs and honors worthy to be sought after; and in taking up the pursuits of the white man, he does that which he has always been taught from his earliest infancy to regard as degrading to his manhood — to labor, to work for his daily bread, an avocation suitable only for squaws.

To those who advocate the application of the laws of civilization to the Indian, it might be a profitable study to investigate the effect which such application produces upon the strength of the tribe as expressed in numbers. Looking at him as the fearless hunter, the matchless horseman and warrior of the Plains, where Nature placed him, and contrasting him with the reservation Indian, who is supposed to be reveling in the delightful comforts and luxuries of an enlightened condition, but who in reality is groveling in beggary, bereft of many of the qualities which in his wild state tended to render him noble, and heir to a combination of vices partly his own, partly bequeathed to him from the paleface, one is forced, even against desire, to conclude that there is unending antagonism between the Indian nature and that with which his well-meaning white brother would endow him. Nature intended him for a savage state; every instinct, every impulse of his soul inclines him to it. The white race might fall into a barbarous state, and afterwards, subjected to the influence of civilization, be reclaimed and prosper. Not so the Indian. He cannot be himself and be civilized; he fades away and dies. Cultivation such as the white man would give him deprives him of his identity.

Education, strange as it may appear, seems to weaken rather than strengthen his intellect. Where do we find any specimens of educated Indian eloquence comparing with that of such native, untutored orators as Tecumseh, Osceola, Red Jacket, and Logan; or, to select from those of more recent fame, Red Cloud of the Sioux, or Satanta of the Kiowas? Unfortunately for the last-named chief, whose name has been such a terror to our frontier settlements, he will have to be judged for other qualities than that of eloquence. Attention has more recently been directed to him by his arrest by the military authorities near Fort Sill, Indian Territory, and his transportation to Texas for trial by civil court for various murders and depredations, alleged to have been committed by him near the Texas frontier. He has since had his trial, and, if public rumor is to be credited, has been sentenced to death. . . . His eloquence and able arguments upon the Indian question in various councils to which he was called won for him the deserved title of "Orator of the Plains." In his boasting harangue before the General of the Army, which furnished the evidences of his connection with the murders for which he has been tried and sentenced, he stated as a justification for such outrages, or rather as the occasion of them, that they were in retaliation for his arrest and imprisonment by me some three years ago. . . . One of the favorite remarks of Satanta in his orations, and one too which other chiefs often indulge in, being thrown out as a "glittering generality," meaning much or little as they may desire, but most often the latter, was that he was tired of making war and desired now "to follow the white man's road." It is scarcely to be presumed that he found the gratification of this oft-expressed desire in recently following the "white man's road" to Texas, under strong guard and heavily manacled, with hanging, to the Indian the most dreaded of all deaths, plainly in the perspective. Aside, however, from his character for restless barbarity, and activity in conducting merciless forays against our exposed frontiers, Satanta is a remarkable man — remarkable for his powers of oratory, his determined warfare against the advances of civilization, and his opposition to the abandonment of his accustomed mode of life, and its exchange for the quiet, unexciting, uneventful life of a reservation Indian.

If I were an Indian, I often think I would greatly prefer to cast my lot among those of my people adhered to the free open plains rather than submit to the confined limits of a reservation, there to be the recipient of the blessed benefits of civilization, with its vices thrown in without stint or measure. The Indian can never be permitted to view the question in this deliberate way. He is neither a luxury nor necessary of life. He can hunt, roam, and camp when and wheresoever he pleases, provided always that in so doing he does not run contrary to the requirements of civilization in its advancing tread. When the soil which he has claimed and hunted over for so long a time is demanded by this to him insatiable monster, there is no appeal; he must yield, or, like the car of Juggernaut, it will roll mercilessly over him, destroying as it advances. Destiny seems to have so willed it, and the world looks on and nods its approval. At best the history of our Indian tribes, no matter from what standpoint it is regarded, affords a melancholy picture of loss of life. Two hundred years ago it required millions to express in numbers the Indian population, while at the present time less than half the number of thousands will suffice for the purpose. Where and why have they gone? Ask the Saxon race, since whose introduction into and occupation of the country these vast changes have been effected.

But little idea can be formed of the terrible inroads which diseases before unknown to them have made upon their numbers. War has contributed its share, it is true, but disease alone has done much to depopulate many of the Indian tribes. It is stated that the smallpox was first introduced among them by the white man in 1837, and that in the short space of one month six tribes lost by this disease alone twelve thousand persons.

Enforcing American Orthodoxy

SPRINGFIELD WEEKLY REPUBLICAN

Our frequent exposure to violence in the communication media has made us less sensitive to the violence that people suffer because of their race. In this article a man is burned at the stake. What motivates the torturers? Fear? Depravity? Hatred? How satisfactory are their reasons for their actions?

NEWNAN, GA., Apr. 23 — Sam Holt, the murderer of Alfred Cranford and the ravisher of the latter's wife, was burned at the stake, near Newnan, Ga., this afternoon, in the presence of 2000 people. The black man was first tortured before being covered with oil and burned. An ex-governor of Georgia made a personal appeal to his townspeople to let the law take its course, but without the slightest avail.

Before the torch was applied to the pyre, the negro was deprived of his ears, fingers and genital parts of his body. He pleaded pitifully for his life while the mutilation was going on, but stood the ordeal of fire with surprising

---

From "Negro Burned Alive in Florida; Second Negro Then Hanged," *Springfield* (Mass.) *Weekly Republican*, April 28, 1899.

fortitude. Before the body was cool, it was cut to pieces, the bones were crushed into small bits, and even the tree upon which the wretch met his fate was torn up and disposed of as "souvenirs." The negro's heart was cut into several pieces, as was also his liver. Those unable to obtain the ghastly relics direct paid their more fortunate possessors extravagant sums for them. Small pieces of bones went for 25 cents, and a bit of the liver crisply cooked sold for 10 cents. As soon as the negro was seen to be dead there was a tremendous struggle among the crowd, which had witnessed his tragic end, to secure the souvenirs. A rush was made for the stake, and those near the body were forced against it and had to fight for their freedom. Knives were quickly produced and soon the body was dismembered.

One of the men who lifted the can of kerosene to the negro's head is said to be a native of Pennsylvania. His name is known to those who were with him, but they refuse to divulge it. The mob was composed of citizens of Newnan, Griffin, Palmetto and other little towns in the country round about Newnan, and of all the farmers who had received word that the burning was to take place.

W. Y. Atkinson, a former governor of Georgia, met the mob as he was returning from church and he appealed to them to let the law take its course. In addressing the mob he used these words: "Some of you are known to me and when this affair is finally settled in the courts, you may depend upon it that I will testify against you." A member of the mob was seen to draw a revolver and level it at Mr. Atkinson, but his arm was seized and the pistol taken from him. The mob was frantic with delays and would hear to nothing but burning at the stake.

Before being put to death, the negro is said to have confessed to killing Cranford, stating that he had been paid $20 by "Lige" Strickland, a negro preacher at Palmetto, for the deed.

Holt was located in the little cabin of his mother on the farm of the Jones brothers between Macon and Columbus and brought to jail.

Word was sent to Mrs. Cranford at Palmetto that it was believed Holt was under arrest and that her presence was necessary in Newnan to make sure of his identification. In some way the news of the arrest leaked out, and as the town has been on the alert for nearly two weeks, the intelligence spread rapidly.

From every house in the little city came its occupants, and a good-sized crowd had soon gathered about the jail. Sheriff Brown was importuned to give up the prisoner, and finally in order to avoid an assault on the jail and possible bloodshed, he turned the negro over to the waiting crowd.

A procession was quickly formed and the doomed negro was marched at the head of a yelling, shouting crowd through several streets of the town. Soon the public square was reached. Here ex-Gov. Atkinson of Georgia, who lives in Newnan, came hurriedly upon the scene, and standing up in a buggy importuned the crowd to let the law take its course.

Gov. Atkinson said: "My fellow citizens and friends: I beseech you to let this affair go no further. You are hurrying this negro on to death without an identification. Mrs. Cranford, whom he is said to have assaulted and whose husband he is said to have killed, is sick in bed and unable to be here to say whether this is her assailant. Let this negro be returned to jail. The law will take its course, and I promise you it will do so quickly and effectually. Do not stain the honor of the state with a crime such as you are about to perform." Judge A. D. Freeman of Newnan spoke in a similar strain and prayed the mob to return the prisoner to the custody of the sheriff and go home. The assemblage heard the words of the two speakers in silence, but the instant their voices had died away shouts of "On to Palmetto, burn him, think of his crime," arose, and the march was resumed.

Mrs. Cranford's mother and sister are residents of Newnan. The mob was headed in the direction of their house and in a short time reached the McElroy home. The negro was marched through the gate and Mrs. McElroy was called to the front door. She identified the African, and her verdict was agreed to by her daughter, who had often seen Holt about the Cranford place. "To the stake," was again the cry and several men wanted to burn the negro in Mrs. McElroy's yard. To this she objected strenuously, and the mob, complying with her wish, started for Palmetto. Just as they were leaving Newnan news was brought that the 1 o'clock train from Atlanta would bring 1000 people from Atlanta. This was taken to be a regiment of soldiers, and the mob decided to burn the prisoner at the first favorable place rather than be compelled to shoot him when the militia put in an appearance.

Leaving the little town, whose Sunday quiet had been so rudely disturbed, the mob, which now numbered nearly 1500 people, started on the road to Palmetto. A line of buggies and vehicles of all kinds, their drivers fighting for position in line, followed the procession, at the head of which, closely guarded, marched the negro. One and a half miles out of Newnan, a place believed to be favorable to the burning, was reached. A little to the side of the road was a strong pine tree. Up to this the negro was marched, his back placed to the tree and his face to the crowd, which jostled closely about him.

The clothes were torn from the negro in an instant. A heavy chain was produced and wound around his body. He said not a word to this proceeding, but at the sight of three or four knives slashing in the hands of several members of the crowd about him, which seemed to forecast the terrible ordeal he was about to be put to, he sent up a yell which could be heard for a mile. Instantly a hand grasping a knife shot out and one of the negro's ears dropped into a hand ready to receive it. He pleaded pitifully for mercy and begged his tormentors to let him die. His cries went unheeded.

PALMETTO, GA., Apr. 24 — The body of "Lije" Strickland, a negro preacher, who was implicated in the Cranford murder by "Sam" Holt, was found swinging to the limb of a persimmon tree within a mile and a quarter of Palmetto, Ga., early today. Before death was allowed to end the sufferings of the negro, his ears were cut off and the small finger of his left hand was severed at the second joint. These trophies were in Palmetto yesterday. On the chest of the negro was a piece of bloodstained paper, attached by an ordinary pin. On one side of this paper was written: —

— We must protect our ladies.

The other side of the paper contained a warning to the negroes of the neighborhood. It read as follows: —

Beware all darkies! You will be treated the same way.

Before being lynched, Strickland was given a chance to confess to the misdeeds of which the mob supposed him to be guilty, but he protested his innocence to the last. Three times the noose was placed around his neck and the negro was drawn up off the ground; three times he was let down with a warning that death was in store for him, should he fail to confess his complicity in the Cranford murder. Three times Strickland proclaimed his innocence, until weary of useless torturing, the mob pulled on the rope and tied the end around the slender trunk of the persimmon tree. Not a shot was fired. Strickland was strangled to death.

America's Imperial Orthodoxy
PHILIPPINE COMMISSION

The repression of minorities was not confined to American shores. When we acquired the Philippine Islands in 1898, we could not comprehend that in the eyes of Filipino patriots the United States had merely replaced Spain as the oppressor. Note that the following document promises many reforms to the Filipinos — but in what context and on whose terms?

At the time of the Commission's appointment peace existed in the islands. On the arrival of the civilian members in Manila hostilities had been in progress for a month. The Commission was not appointed as a "Peace Commission," as it has been often called. It was appointed as a civil Commission to accomplish the objects set forth in its instructions, one of which was to assist in the peaceful extension of American authority and the establishment of civil and

From *Report of the Philippine Commission to the President* (Washington: Government Printing Office, 1900), I, 3–5.

peaceful government among the people. . . . In pursuance of these instructions, and finding hostilities to exist, the Commission set to work to discover what it might do to help in bringing those hostilities to an end. Throughout its stay unremitting efforts in that direction were made along with its work on the other matters which had been intrusted to it. It early became convinced that the Tagalog rebellion was due to the ambitions of a few and the misunderstanding of the many. To clear away such misunderstanding, it issued, April 4, 1899, a proclamation to the people, as in its instructions it had been given power to do. In its English version the proclamation was as follows:

To the people of the Philippine Islands:
The treaty of peace between the United States and Spain, ratified several weeks ago by the former, having on March 20 been ratified by the latter, the cession to the United States, as stipulated by the treaty, of the sovereignty which Spain possessed and exercised over the Philippine Islands has now, in accordance with the laws of nations, received a complete and indefeasible consummation.

In order that the high responsibilities and obligations with which the United States has thus become definitively charged may be fulfilled in a way calculated to promote the best interests of the inhabitants of the Philippine Islands, His Excellency the President of the United States has appointed the undersigned a civil commission on Philippine affairs, clothing them with all the powers necessary for the exercise of that office.

The Commission desire to assure the people of the Philippine Islands of the cordial good will and fraternal feeling which is entertained for them by His Excellency the President of the United States and by the American people. The aim and object of the American Government, apart from the fulfillment of the solemn obligations it has assumed toward the family of nations by the acceptance of sovereignty over the Philippine Islands, is the well being, the prosperity, and the happiness of the Philippine people and their elevation and advancement to a position among the most civilized peoples of the world.

His Excellency the President of the United States believes that this felicity and perfection of the Philippine people is to be brought about by the assurance of peace and order; by the guaranty of civil and religious liberty; by the establishment of justice; by the cultivation of letters, science, and the liberal and practical arts; by the enlargement of intercourse with foreign nations; by the expansion of industrial pursuits, trade, and commerce; by the multiplication and improvement of the means of internal communication; by the development, with the aid of modern mechanical inventions, of the great natural resources of the archipelago; and, in a word, by the uninterrupted devotion of the people to the pursuit of those useful objects and the realization of those noble ideals which constitute the higher civilization of mankind.

Unfortunately, the pure aims and purposes of the American Government and people have been misinterpreted to some of the inhabitants of certain of the islands. As a consequence, the friendly American forces have, without provocation or cause, been openly attacked.

And why these hostilities? What do the best Filipinos desire? Can it be more than the United States is ready to give? They are patriots and want liberty, it is said. The Commission emphatically asserts that the United States is not only willing, but anxious, to establish in the Philippine Islands an enlightened system of government under which the Philippine people may enjoy the largest measure of home rule and the amplest liberty consonant with the supreme ends of government and compatible with those obligations which the United States has assumed toward the civilized nations of the world.

The United States striving earnestly for the welfare and advancement of the inhabitants of the Philippine Islands, there can be no real conflict between American sovereignty and the rights and liberties of the Philippine people. For, just as the United States stands ready to furnish armies, navies, and all the infinite resources of a great and powerful nation to maintain and support its rightful supremacy over the Philippine Islands, so it is even more solicitous to spread peace and happiness among the Philippine people; to guarantee them a rightful freedom; to protect them in their just privileges and immunities; to accustom them to free self-government in an ever-increasing measure; and to encourage them in those democratic aspirations, sentiments, and ideals which are the promise and potency of a fruitful national development.

It is the expectation of the commission to visit the Philippine peoples in their respective provinces, both for the purpose of cultivating a more intimate mutual acquaintance and also with a view to ascertaining from enlightened native opinion what form or forms of government seem best adapted to the Philippine peoples, most apt to conduce to their highest welfare, and most conformable to their customs, traditions, sentiments, and cherished ideals. Both in the establishment and maintenance of government in the Philippine Islands it will be the policy of the United States to consult the views and wishes, and to secure the advice, cooperation, and aid, of the Philippine people themselves.

In the meantime the attention of the Philippine people is invited to certain regulative principles by which the United States will be guided in its relations with them. The following are deemed of cardinal importance:

1. The supremacy of the United States must and will be enforced throughout every part of the Archipelago, and those who resist it can accomplish no end other than their own ruin.

2. The most ample liberty of self-government will be granted to the Philippine people which is reconcilable with the maintenance of a wise, just, stable, effective, and economical administration of public affairs, and compatible with the sovereign and international rights and obligations of the United States.

3. The civil rights of the Philippine people will be guaranteed and protected to the fullest extent; religious freedom assured, and all persons shall have an equal standing before the law.

4. Honor, justice, and friendship forbid the use of the Philippine people or islands as an object or means of exploitation. The purpose of the American Government is the welfare and advancement of the Philippine people.

5. There shall be guaranteed to the Philippine people an honest and effective civil service, in which, to the fullest extent practicable, natives shall be employed.

6. The collection and application of taxes and revenues will be put upon a sound, honest, and economical basis. Public funds, raised justly and collected honestly, will be applied only in defraying the regular and proper expenses incurred by and for the establishment and maintenance of the Philippine government, and for such general improvements as public interests may demand. Local funds, collected for local purposes, shall not be diverted to other ends. With such a prudent and honest fiscal administration, it is believed that the needs of the government will in short time become compatible with a considerable reduction in taxation.

7. A pure, speedy, and effective administration of justice will be established, whereby the evils of delay, corruption, and exploitation will be effectually eradicated.

8. The construction of roads, railroads, and other means of communication and transportation, as well as other public works of manifest advantage to the Philippine people, will be promoted.

9. Domestic and foreign trade and commerce, agriculture, and other industrial pursuits, and the general development of the country in the interest of its inhabitants will be constant objects of solicitude and fostering care.

10. Effective provision will be made for the establishment of elementary schools in which the children of the people shall be educated. Appropriate facilities will also be provided for higher education.

11. Reforms in all departments of the government, in all branches of the public service, and in all corporations closely touching the common life of the people must be undertaken without delay and effected, conformably to right and justice, in a way that will satisfy the well-founded demands and the highest sentiments and aspirations of the Philippine people.

Such is the spirit in which the United States comes to the people of the Philippine Islands. His Excellency, the President, has instructed the Commission to make it publicly known. And in obeying this behest the Commission desire to join with his Excellency, the President, in expressing their own good will toward the Philippine people, and to extend to their leading and representative men a cordial invitation to meet them for personal acquaintance and for the exchange of views and opinions.

MANILA, *April 4, 1899.*

Jacob Gould Schurman,
President of Commission.

George Dewey,
Admiral U. S. N.

Elwell S. Otis,
Major-General U. S. Volunteers.

Charles Denby
Dean C. Worcester.

John R. MacArthur,
Secretary of Commission.

Crusading American Orthodoxy

STANLEY FROST

The Ku Klux Klan, originally founded in 1868, was resurrected in 1915 and became so powerful a political force that it controlled state houses, influenced the Democratic national convention of 1924 , and could muster some 40,000 hooded marchers for a parade down Pennsylvania Avenue in Washington that same year. Does the following document provide some clues to its popularity? With how many of its beliefs would you agree?

A Klansman's Creed

I believe in God and the tenets of the Christian religion and that a godless nation can not long prosper.

I believe that a church that is not grounded on the principles of morality and justice is a mockery to God and to man.

I believe that a church that does not have the welfare of the common people at heart is unworthy.

I believe in the eternal separation of Church and State.

From Stanley Frost, *The Challenge of the Klan* (Indianapolis: Bobbs-Merrill, 1924), pp. 64–65. Reprinted by permission of the publisher.

I hold no allegiance to any foreign government, emperor, king, pope or any other foreign, political or religious power.

I hold my allegiance to the Stars and Stripes next to my allegiance to God alone.

I believe in just laws and liberty.

I believe in the upholding of the Constitution of these United States.

I believe that our Free Public School is the cornerstone of good government and that those who are seeking to destroy it are enemies of our Republic and are unworthy of citizenship.

I believe in freedom of speech.

I believe in a free press uncontrolled by political parties or by religious sects.

I believe in law and order.

I believe in the protection of our pure womanhood.

I do not believe in mob violence, but I do believe that laws should be enacted to prevent the causes of mob violence.

I believe in a closer relationship of capital and labor.

I believe in the prevention of unwarranted strikes by foreign labor agitators.

I believe in the limitation of foreign immigration.

I am a native-born American citizen and I believe my rights in this country are superior to those of foreigners.

Economic Orthodoxy

RALPH M. EASLEY

The bloody strikes between labor unions and employers during the last quarter of the nineteenth century raised the question: On whose terms would labor and American capital cooperate? Is Easley's praise of the "right kind" of labor leader an attempt to send a message to unions that they had better follow a certain type of leader — or else? What are Easley's assumptions?

From Ralph M. Easley, "What Organized Labor Has Learned," *McClure's Magazine* (April 1902), XIX, 483, 488, 490–492.

American capital has made conspicuous advancement in the methods and magnitude of its operation during the last ten years. All the world knows this. That labor has made equal or any progress in the same period seems not to be realized by the general public. I regard the advance of organized labor in the United States as one of the most remarkable developments of the last decade. Given a good deal more of stern, sound, knowing criticism, and I believe we shall escape the killing effects on industry charged to trades-unionism in England. For our labor is clearer-headed as well as bigger-muscled and shrewder-handed than foreign labor. It has its violence and its passions and its absurdities; but it can learn. It has learned. It has learned from England. I have heard the big leaders talk well about the evils of trades-unionism over there, and there is a sentiment well spread in the ranks that real dangers exist, which have already hurt business and reacted upon labor. It is all very well to say that all this is obvious. It is; but the present point is that unionism is learning it.

To be sure we often see labor acting as though it had learned nothing, and a large class of employers see only its ignorance and violence, and execrate unionism. This is such blind opposition as these same employers despise in the anti-trust fighters. The history of the organization of capital and of labor is a close parallel of crimes and mistakes, but that these are not essentials to either is proven by the progress, slow and hard though it be, which each is making.

The advance of organized labor is shown by a doubling in membership within the past three years; by the rise of new organizations and the revival of old organizations once crushed by the employers; by the confederation and mutual assistance of unions; by improved machinery of organization, bringing improved leadership and responsibility to the membership. But the best evidence of permanency is the improvement in the character of the unions, their broadening policies, the conservatism of their leaders, which have made possible the inauguration of joint conferences and agreements with employers based on mutual concessions. The increased use of these conferences and agreements during the past five years proves that some employers have come to look upon some unions as a good and permanent force.

. . . [T]he successful operation of the joint agreement has taught the unions the need of discipline and of conservative leadership. The stove makers have developed these. One of the most troublesome questions at the first conference was that of the union attitude toward the non-union men in the shops. It was finally agreed that the matter of the union or open shop should depend entirely upon whether a majority of the men in a given shop were union or non-union. If a shop had more than 50 percent union men, then union rules and regulations were to govern; the non-union men were not to be disturbed; all vacancies, however, were to be filled by unionists. In holding his men to this part of the contract, Martin Fox, president of the Iron Moulders' Union, during the first year or two, met many difficulties. He is a firm, quiet, reasoning man, and he explained patiently to his men that they were bound by the union agreement. When they hesitated, he forced them to submit by a threat of revoking the charter.

Union Discipline of Longshoremen

Another illustration is the history of the relations of the International Longshoremen's Association and the Dock Managers' Association, the latter being composed of representatives of all the larger shipping interests on the lakes, such as the Standard Oil, Carnegie's, M. A. Hanna and Co., Pickans, Mather and Co., and others. The longshoremen are pretty hard to handle; yet the chairman of the Dock Managers' Association told the writer recently that the discipline of the longshoremen's organization was so thorough, and their sense of honor so high, that when contracts were signed, the employers knew just what they could count on. Once in a while a new local union attempts to violate its contracts, but the national officers see to it that no inconvenience results to the employers.

A Union Leader Who Employed Non-Union Men

Last fall, for instance, trouble arose in Buffalo, and the longshoremen quit. Daniel Keefe, the president, hurried there. He is a big, brawny fighter. "Get back to work," he ordered the men at Buffalo. "You're under contract to negotiate first and strike afterward." They pleaded exception. He would not listen; there should be no discussion till the men resumed work. They refused, and Keefe gave them twelve hours to obey. When at the end of that time they still were out, Keefe revoked their charter, called on other unions to supply the places of the strikers, and when he could not get enough union men, *filled the strikers' places with non-union men* and broke the strike.

Walking Delegates not Agitators

I do not for a moment contend that organized labor as a whole has reached the stage where "its word is as good as its bond." I contend only that all the moral impetus that can be given the labor movement by its leaders is in that direction. I know that these leaders are frequently charged with being agitators and blatherskites, and with being for sale at all times to the highest bidder. There are corrupt men in labor's ranks, just as there are corrupt men in all other ranks of life, but the percentage is no greater. There are walking delegates who make nuisances of themselves by their officiousness and narrowness, and some who are even criminal, and have been suspected of calling strikes for the express purpose of demanding money from the employers before they would restore the *status quo*. This is nothing more or less than blackmail, and no union that I know of would permit such a rascal to remain in office after he was discovered. But if the acceptance of bribes by labor leaders argues the necessity for destroying the union, does not the offering of bribes by the employers argue the necessity for destroying organizations of capital?

Though valid objects frequently can be found to the methods of walking delegates, my observation has been that in labor controversies generally he has been the strongest advocate of peace. I have seen labor leaders placed in positions where it required courage of the highest order to stand for the right. In Chicago recently the Hod Carriers' Union made a contract with the master employers for an increase in wages, to take effect in sixty days. Some union in another craft had struck for an immediate raise in wages and got it, whereupon the hod carriers began clamoring for their advance to be made immediately. The contractors insisted upon the agreement standing, and the men called a mass meeting to take action. Herman Lillien, the business agent who had made the contract for the union, appeared at the meeting and begged the men to stand by their contracts, saying that he had spent five of the best years of his life in building up the organization; that now they proposed in one brief hour to wipe out all the result of his work; and that if they insisted upon such dishonorable conduct they should accept his resignation. The resignation was accepted, and the next moment a resolution to strike went through with a whoop. Not dismayed, Mr. Lillien issued an appeal, through the papers, to the men to ignore the action of the mass meeting, go back to work, and preserve their honor. Several hundred did so the next morning. Mr. Lillien kept at work and inside of two days he had the whole six thousand back at work, and was unanimously reinstated. And yet Mr. Lillien was one of those despised "walking delegates."

How Gompers Faced Contract Breakers

The big brewing concerns in Milwaukee had a contract with their men, which the men thought had been violated, and a boycott was placed upon all the products from those breweries. The brewers declared that they had not violated their contracts, and appealed to the Executive Committee of the American Federation of Labor. That committee carefully went through the matter, and decided that the union was wrong and should withdraw the boycott. The union was not willing to do this, and demanded that President Gompers should go to Milwaukee and face them. He went. There were something like three thousand men in the hall when Mr. Gompers arrived, and a gentleman who was present told me that he never saw a manlier fight made for the preservation of the integrity of contracts than Mr. Gompers made on that occasion. The temper of the men was hostile, yet Mr. Gompers unanimously carried his point, and the boycott was removed.

Passing of the Sympathetic Strike

That sympathetic strikes are illogical and generally react on the strikers, was clearly shown in the Boston sympathetic strike last spring, and the recent Chicago freight handlers' strike, both of them the first strikes of new organizations eager to try their newfound strength.

In Boston, all the master teamsters, an organization of three hundred members, had made a contract with the Teamsters' Union, but there was one member, a large contractor, who refused to be bound by the agreement. In order to whip him into line, the union proceeded to "pull out everybody," tying up all the master teamsters who had signed the contract, to the great advantage of the very firm they were fighting. This concern being the only one that could haul anything in Boston, not only made money out of the strike, but secured annual contracts from hundreds of firms, because it alone could guarantee to fill them.

Probably the occurrence which will have the greatest influence in directing the future policy of unions in this matter of sympathetic strikes is the recent action of the mine workers in refusing to strike in behalf of the anthracite workers. Said John Mitchell at that time, in his address to the Indianapolis convention:

> Sympathetic strikes have many adherents, and the efficacy of such meth-ods appeals strongly to those who, being directly involved in trouble, do not always recognize the effect of their action upon the public mind; but the past history of the labor movement teaches lessons that should not be forgotten-to-day. As far as my knowledge goes, I do not know of one solitary sympathetic strike of any magnitude which has been successful; on the contrary the most conspicuous among the sympathetic labor strug-gles have resulted in ignominious and crushing defeat, not only for the branch of industry originally involved, but also the divisions participating through sympathy.

Revised Creed of Organized Labor

Any one who watched closely the strikes and internal struggles of trades-unions ten years ago, must see progress in all this. For the rest let me set down in familiar, somewhat academic form, some of the things that, not the political economist, but the older, pace-setting labor organizations have learned and are teaching:

1. Strikes are bad, and should be a last resort.

2. Scales of wages should be determined by mutual concessions in con-ferences with employers rather than by a demand submitted by the union as an ultimatum.

3. When thus determined, this scale becomes a contract, which is not only as sacred as any business contract, but the violation of which by the union is also the most disastrous blow that can be struck at the principle of unionism.

4. Sympathetic strikes are unwise, because they violate contracts, bring injury to friendly employers and the friendly public, and arouse public opinion against the organization.

5. It is not essential to a contract that non-union men should be excluded from employment along with union men, provided they receive the same pay.

6. The union should attract the non-unionist by persuasion, not force, into membership.

7. Violence in conducting a strike alienates the public, brings the courts and the militia to the support of employers, and reacts disastrously upon the union.

8. Unionists should welcome new machinery.

9. Unions should abandon arbitrary restrictions on output, and direct their attention to questions of hours of labor and rates of pay.

Orthodoxy vs. Free Speech
U.S. v. SCHENCK

When the United States entered World War I, the Supreme Court had to decide how far antiwar protestors could go in exercising their right of free speech in urging opposition to the war effort. As you read the decision by Justice Oliver Wendell Holmes, do you accept his argument that free speech is reasonably subject to the circumstances in which society finds itself? Or is any regulation of such a fundamental right really a form of unjust repression?

Mr. Justice Holmes delivered the opinion of the court:

This is an indictment in three counts. The first charges a conspiracy to violate the Espionage Act of June 15, 1917, . . . by causing and attempting to cause insubordination, etc., in the military and naval forces of the United States, and to obstruct the recruiting and enlistment service of the United States, when the United States was at war with the German Empire; to wit, that the defendant wilfully conspired to have printed and circulated to men who had been called and accepted for military service under the Act of May 18, 1917 . . . a document set forth and alleged to be calculated to cause such insubordination and obstruction. The count alleges overt acts in pursuance of the conspiracy, ending in the distribution of the document set forth. The second count alleges a conspiracy to commit an offense against the United States; to wit, to use the mails for the transmission of matter declared to be nonmailable. . . . The third count charges an unlawful use of the mails for the transmission of the same matter and otherwise as above. The defendants were found guilty on all the counts. They set up the 1st Amendment to the Constitution, forbidding Congress to make any law abridging the freedom of speech or of the press, and, bringing the case here on that ground, have argued some other points also of which we must dispose.

U.S. v. Schenck, United States Reports, vol. 249, p. 48 (1918).

It is argued that the evidence, if admissible, was not sufficient to prove that the defendant Schenck was concerned in sending the documents. According to the testimony Schenck said he was general secretary of the Socialist party and had charge of the Socialist headquarters from which the documents were sent. He identified a book found there as the minutes of the executive committee of the party. The book showed a resolution of August 13, 1917, that 15,000 leaflets should be printed on the other side of one of them in use, to be mailed to men who had passed exemption boards, and for distribution. Schenck personally attended to the printing. On August 20 the general secretary's report said, "Obtained new leaflets from the printer and started work addressing envelopes," etc.; and there was a resolve that Comrade Schenck be allowed $125 for sending leaflets through the mail. He said that he had about fifteen or sixteen thousand printed. There were files of the circular in question in the inner office which he said were printed on the other side of the one-sided circular and were there for distribution. Other copies were proved to have been sent through the mails to drafted men. Without going into confirmatory details that were proved, no reasonable man could doubt that the defendant Schenck was largely instrumental in sending the circulars about. As to the defendant Baer, there was evidence that she was a member of the executive board and that the minutes of its transactions were hers. The argument as to the sufficiency of the evidence that the defendants conspired to send the documents only impairs the seriousness of the real defense. . . .

The document in question, upon its first printed side, recited the 1st section of the 13th Amendment, said that the idea embodied in it was violated by the Conscription Act, and that a conscript is little better than a convict. In impassioned language it intimated that conscription was despotism in its worst form and a monstrous wrong against humanity, in the interest of Wall street's chosen few. It said: "Do not submit to intimidation;" but in form at least confined itself to peaceful measures, such as a petition for the repeal of the act. The other and later printed side of the sheet was headed, "Assert Your Rights." It stated reasons for alleging that anyone violated the Constitution when he refused to recognize "your right to assert your opposition to the draft," and went on: "If you do not assert and support your rights, you are helping to deny or disparage rights which it is the solemn duty of all citizens and residents of the United States to retain." It described the arguments on the other side as coming from cunning politicians and a mercenary capitalist press, and even silent consent to the Conscription Law as helping to support an infamous conspiracy. It denied the power to send our citizens away to foreign shores to shoot up the people of other lands, and added that words could not express the condemnation such cold-blooded ruthlessness deserves, etc., etc., winding up, "You must do your share to maintain, support, and uphold the rights of the people of this country." Of course the document would not have been sent unless it had been intended to have some effect, and we do not see what effect it could be expected to have upon persons subject to the draft except to influence them to obstruct the carrying of it out. The defendants do not deny that the jury might find against them on this point.

But it is said, suppose that that was the tendency of this circular, it is protected by the 1st Amendment to the Constitution. . . . We admit that in many places and in ordinary times the defendants, in saying all that was said in the circular, would have been within their constitutional rights. But the character of every act depends upon the circumstances in which it is done. . . . The most stringent protection of free speech would not protect a man in falsely shouting fire in a theater, and causing a panic. It does not even protect a man from an injunction against uttering words that may have all the effect of force. . . . The question in every case is whether the words used are used in such circumstances and are of such a nature as to create a clear and present danger that they will bring about the substantive evils that Congress has a right to prevent. It is a question of proximity and degree. When a nation is at war many things that might be said in time of peace are such a hindrance to its effort that their utterance will not be endured so long as men fight, and that no court could regard them as protected by any constitutional right. It seems to be admitted that if an actual obstruction of the recruiting service were proved, liability for words that produced that effect might be enforced. The Statute of 1917, in § 4, punishes conspiracies to obstruct as well as actual obstruction. If the act (speaking, or circulating a paper), its tendency and the intent with which it is done, are the same, we perceive no ground for saying that success alone warrants making the act a crime.

Judgments affirmed.

Disciplining the Unorthodox

THE NEW YORK TIMES

The victory of communism in Russia in 1918 made federal and state officials in the United States so afraid that Bolshevism might triumph in this country that they were willing to go to extraordinary measures to stamp it out. But out of their zeal to rid the country of radicals, several perplexing questions emerge: Was there any difference essentially between their actions and reasons, and those of Justice Holmes (U.S. v. Schenck)? At what point does a community's legitimate desire to protect itself become an act of repression? In what ways can a newspaper's coverage of a sensitive political event contribute to a repressive mind-set?

From *The New York Times*, November 8, 1919, pp. 1, 3. © 1919 by The New York Times Company. Reprinted by permission.

73 RED CENTRES RAIDED HERE BY LUSK COMMITTEE

- Hundreds of Prisoners and Tons of Seditious Literature Taken to Headquarters

- 700 Policemen Take Part

- Chairman Lusk Tells of Admitted Determination to Seize the Government

- Palmer to Deport Reds

- More Than 200, Seized Friday, Must Leave Country — 80 More Taken in Bridgeport

Seventy-three radical headquarters in all five boroughs of this city were raided simultaneously last night for evidence of revolutionary propaganda by more than 700 policemen and various agents of the Federal and State Governments acting under the authority of search warrants issued by Chief Magistrate McAdoo to the Lusk Committee.

After lawyers for the committee had completed a canvass of some 500 prisoners at Police Headquarters at 1 o'clock this morning, they directed the police to hold about 100 men on charges of criminal anarchy and release the rest. Radical literature by the ton was confiscated by the police.

Among the places raided were editorial offices, meeting rooms, and printing shops, from which issued a large part of the revolutionary propaganda which has made its effect felt in Gary, Omaha, Seattle, and other centres of industrial disturbance, according to testimony before the Lusk Committee.

The places raided were all connected with the so-called "Communist Party," the group of radicals which has broken away from the Socialist Party and attempted to form a union of anarchists, I.W.W. syndicalists, and all other violent groups of radicals. The addresses of the seventy-three places, many of which are the editorial rooms of radical publications, were furnished by Associate Counsel Archibald E. Stevenson and Charles F. Donnelly of the Lusk Committee, who appeared yesterday morning before Magistrate McAdoo and obtained search warrants for the raids. Members of the New York Constabulary took part in the raids.

One of the first prisoners brought in by them was the famous "Jim" Larkin, the Irish labor agitator, who led the shipping strike in England in 1914. Larkin, who is regarded as one of the most dangerous of the agitators in this country, was arrested in McDougall Alley.

Simultaneous Raids in Five Boroughs

The plans for the raids were kept secret with great care, and shortly after 9 o'clock the raids started in all five boroughs. The raiders included members of the anarchist, narcotic and Italian squads, plainclothes men, 700 men in uniform, agents of the Department of Justice, inspectors of the Immigration Service, and the State Constabulary. The police were directed by Inspector

Faurot, and the entire movement was directed by State Senator Clayton R. Lusk, whose committee has been for months accumulating evidence on the radical propaganda in this State.

The Lusk Committee made public last night a list of the places raided, and the branches of the Communist Party described in the list include Lettish, Esthonian, Lithuanian, Ukranian, Jewish, Russian, Hungarian, German, Spanish, and Italian.

Fifty radical publications in various foreign languages, which are printed in this city, are the backbone of the Red movement in this country, according to Deputy Attorney General Berger, and many of these were raided last night. One of the purposes of th[e] raids was to gather evidence as to the future plans for causing outbreaks like those in Seattle and at Gary, which have been laid largely to inflammatory publications, printed in this city, with the aid, according to Mr. Berger, of wealthy parlor Bolsheviki of New York City.

After the raids started patrol wagons drove up to Police Headquarters and policemen began to stagger in under the weight of the Red literature which they were carrying. Prisoners were taken in droves, the dangerous Reds to be divided later from the innocent bystanders. . . .

Plans for Revolution Confessed

Senator Lusk, Chairman of the legislative committee investigating seditious activities, issued a statement last night in which he said that it was shown by the confession of leaders of the new Communist Party before the committee that they were aiming at the overthrow of the United States Government by revolution.

"It is the plain statement of the intention of the members of this organization to overthrow our established Government by force and unlawful means," said Senator Lusk. "The seventy-one local Communist organizations in New York City consisted of bodies of men and women openly and notoriously organized for the sole purpose of destroying our Government. They profess to believe and contend that the time has come when the Government is not strong enough to protect itself.

"These organizations are a direct public challenge to the authorities of the State and nation. A passive attitude on the part of the Government toward the disloyal agitators organizing its citizens against it has resulted in a constant growth of the movement, as has been clearly shown by the investigation made by this committee. It seems to me that the time has come to put into force stern measures to do away with this agitation and punish these disloyal leaders in the movement. The city and State officials are engaged in an effort to enforce the laws of the State.

"The committee considers that the result of this effort will be very helpful in preparing recommendations for action on the part of the Legislature, and regards it as a legitimate part of its work to do everything that it can to assist in this matter. It is perfectly willing to accept the onus of anything which may happen through its activity in an effort to protect our Government and citizens.

"It has been the policy of certain individuals and publications to furnish aid and assistance to the enemies of our country by criticising any efforts made by public officials to enforce the laws against sedition and protect our institutions.

"The time has come for the people of this country to take a definite stand on this question in order that we may know who our enemies are and deal with them as they deserve."

Hundreds of prisoners were landed at Police Headquarters in patrol wagons and automobiles of all descriptions. They were herded into the gymnasium, trial room, and all corners of the building, while the men considered to be the more important catches were questioned, generally through interpreters. One of the prisoners was a white-bearded man of 70 years. Several were carrying cases with musical instruments, protesting that they were merely taking their ease in their clubrooms when they had been arrested. One woman prisoner was taken to Police Headquarters by a plainclothes man.

The largest crowd of prisoners captured was taken at one of the Ukrainian branches at 222 East Fifth Street. The prisoners from this place, which had been raided some time previously, numbered 150. Thirty-five men were taken in a raid in East Broadway, near Rutgers Square, where the Communists were to have made their demonstration yesterday.

Several of the places raided were found locked and uninhabited, but membership books, records, and printed literature were carried away. Social functions were in progress at some of the resorts raided. A package party and dance was interrupted by the raiders at the Communist branch headquarters, 1,709 Pitkin Avenue, Brownsville, and thirty-eight merrymaking youths were arrested. The girls were detained for a time and then released.

The questioning of prisoners at Police Headquarters was done by counsel for the Lusk Committee, Major Archibald E. Stevenson, Frederick W. Rich, and Deputy Attorney General Berger. Scores of men judged to be innocent were turned loose with little delay. Some of them said that they had been attending benefits and parties with wives and children at the Communist halls when they had been arrested.

When Jim Larkin was questioned, he said that he claimed the protection of his Government, the Irish Republic. He was detained nevertheless.

QUICK DEPORTATION FOR RAIDED REDS

- Sixty-five Men and Women Caught in Radical Headquarters Taken to Ellis Island

- Soviet Rallies Broken Up

- Federal Agents Begin Work on Literature Seized — Sample Manifesto Given Out

Thirty-three men, most of them with bandaged heads, black eyes, or other marks of rough handling, and two women who had been arrested with the men in raids on radical headquarters in various parts of the city on Friday night, were taken to Ellis Island yesterday where an effort will be made to deport them as anarchists and revolutionaries.

About 150 other men who had been arrested by agents of the Department of Justice and members of the police anarchist squad in the raid on the Russian People's House were set free. Most of them also had blackened eyes and lacerated scalps as souvenirs of the new attitude of aggressiveness which has been assumed by the Federal agents against Reds and suspected Reds. Twelve of the men who were roughly handled and later released said they were soldiers. The others said they were teaching or attending classes at the People's House, where automobile repairing and the English language and other subjects were being taught.

After ordering the thirty-three men and two women sent to Ellis Island, Federal agents under Director William J. Flynn of the Bureau of Investigation of the Department of Justice, began work on the seized literature which was piled up in the Park Row Building in the offices of the Department of Justice. Most of the printed literature was in the Russian language, and will be a big job translating before the Federal authorities will know the value of their evidence.

Raid Followed Weeks of Work

Director William J. Flynn, who was in charge of the raids, refused to discuss them yesterday, saying that all information on the subject must come from Washington. Superintendent George F. Lamb of the New York Bureau of Investigation of the Department of Justice said the work of preparing for the raids and getting evidence against the persons to be arrested had covered weeks, and that the order to make the raids on Friday night had come from Washington.

The seizure of Red literature and records was expected to reveal proclamations in the Russian and other languages calling on radicals to observe the anniversary [of the Bolshevik Revolution] with a general strike or to rise against the Government. The Federal agents refused to say whether they had discovered anything yet of a violent character.

Seventy-five policemen patrolled Rutgers Square, which was to have been the scene of the Bolshevist rally today, but no meeting was attempted. Groups collected to see what might take place, but even these were broken up at word from the police to scatter.

The thirty-five alleged Reds who were sent to Ellis Island from this city last night were joined there by thirty of the same type who had been arrested in the northern district of New Jersey in raids directed by Federal Agent Frank

R. Stone of Newark. The entire sixty-five will be taken before a Federal Commissioner on Monday. Isaac Schoor, a lawyer, representing some of the arrested men, said he would attempt to free them all through habeas corpus proceedings.

The star prisoner was said to be Naum Stepauch, General Secretary and organizer of the Federation of Russian Workers. The two women were Dora Lipkin and Esther Bernstein. Other prisoners regarded as important are Marcus Oradowski, Treasurer of the Federation of Russian Workers; Peter Bianki, who is under indictment for criminal anarchy; Alexander Chernoff, Arthur Katjes, and John Vermanuk. Prisoners were taken in Brooklyn, Maspeth, L.I., and the Bronx, as well as in Manhattan.

Several of the prisoners told agents of the Department of Justice that they would be delighted if the Government would only deport them at once. They will probably be held in this country for some time, even if the courts order their deportation. Superintendent Lamb of the New York Bureau of Investigation of the Department of Justice said there was no way to send the men back to Bolshevist Russia, and that to send them to the anti-Bolshevist region in Southern Russia would be consigning them to execution by a firing squad, which the Government has so far refused to contemplate.

Defending Christian Orthodoxy

STATE OF TENNESSEE and THOMAS H. NELSON

What would prompt a state to pass a law forbidding the teaching of Darwinism? And why should Rev. Nelson react so angrily to Darwinian ideas? As in the previous selections, notice how the writer uses generally accepted truths as a basis on which to launch his attack.

[From the Tennessee anti-evolution act]

An act prohibiting the teaching of the Evolution Theory in all the Universities, Normals and all other public schools of Tennessee, which are supported in whole or in part by the public school funds of the State, and to provide penalties for the violations thereof.

From *Public Acts of Tennessee,* House Bill 185, chap. 27 and from Rev. Thomas H. Nelson, "The Real Issue in Tennessee," *Moody Bible Institute Monthly* (September 1925). Reprinted in Sheldon N. Griebstein, ed., *Monkey Trial: The State of Tennessee versus John Scopes* (Boston: Houghton Mifflin, 1960), pp. 3, 198–200. Reprinted by permission of the publisher.

SECTION 1.   BE IT ENACTED BY THE GENERAL ASSEMBLY OF THE STATE OF TENNESSEE, That it shall be unlawful for any teacher in any of the Universities, Normals and all other public schools of the State which are supported in whole or in part by the public school funds of the State, to teach any theory that denies the story of the Divine Creation of man as taught in the Bible, and to teach instead that man has descended from a lower order of animals.

SECTION 2.   BE IT FURTHER ENACTED, That any teacher found guilty of the violation of this Act, shall be guilty of a misdemeanor and upon conviction, shall be fined not less than One Hundred ($100.00) Dollars nor more than Five Hundred ($500.00) Dollars for each offense.

SECTION 3.   BE IT FURTHER ENACTED, That this Act take effect from and after its passage, the public welfare requiring it.

Passed March 13, 1925.
   W. F. Barry,
      Speaker of the House of Representatives.

   L. D. Hill,
      Speaker of the Senate.

Approved March 21, 1925.
   Austin Peay,
      Governor.

[From the *Moody Bible Institute Monthly*]

While in attendance at the Scopes trial at Dayton, Tenn., I came to the conclusion that the trial was misnamed.

It was God, our Father, Jesus Christ, our Saviour, Christianity and the true church, that was on trial there, while the whole world looked on.

With these mighty issues in the balance, it might well be, as the newspapers said, the greatest and most interesting subject ever discussed in this country, looked at from the angle of its having inspired more cablegrams, telegrams, telephones, and radiograms than were ever sent about any other subject.

Unitarian Propaganda

I concluded further, that Jews and Unitarians had joined forces to push this antichristian conflict. It was very fitting that Clarence Darrow, a criminal lawyer and an avowed agnostic, should lead in the defense of this evolution case, for the teaching of creative evolution is both criminal and atheistic.

While ignorant reporters were belittling this case, and belying and abusing William Jennings Bryan as the real nemesis of creative evolution. I consider it to be the mightiest issue that has ever been joined since the trial of Jesus Christ before Pontius Pilate.

The Son of God on Trial

His virgin birth, His vicarious death, His corporeal resurrection, His glorious ascension, His Spirit empowering of His people, were all on trial equally with the existence and activity of God our Father in creation.

The final outcome is not hard to forecast. The rabble, the thoughtless throng, are again crying, as of old, "Away with this man and release unto us Barabbas!"

The enthronement of the Antichrist, the great Apollyon of the last days, will be the final outcome.

Evolution Defined by Haeckel

No real Christian can swallow this atheistic, "theistic evolution" bait, without getting the hook and sinker also.

No true evolutionist can admit of a miracle or of the existence of God, either. Evolution is claimed by its proponents as "the non-miraculous origin and development of all things" or the "anti-Genesis origin of life and matter," *vide* Haeckel. This is the real issue.

We must not permit these word conjurers to confound evolution with natural growth. The development of the oak from the acorn is not evolution, but growth. The butterfly from the grub, is but natural development.

There must be an originative and biogenetic element in true evolution. That is, a super-added element of life or faculty must come into existence out of a previous non-existence, through a non-personal law or power called evolution.

Evolution a Rope of Sand

This unbridged gulf will yet form the tomb of evolution. The fact that geology can produce not one true fossil that shows one species changing into another, makes evolution a mere rope of sand, or, a chain whose every other link is missing. The natural atheism of the unregenerate heart is grasping quickly at the false claims of the pseudo-scientist who propagates this bunk. Thus the great apostasy of the last days will be given an impetus. God has said, "He is Antichrist who denieth both the Father and the Son." What the Romans have never done, apostate Protestants are now doing, under the leadership of Jews and Unitarians, deceived by the false claims of science.

The Scene of Battle Will Change

Those simple hill people in Tennessee are fighting a good fight, but the scene of conflict will be changed and all men will be forced to take sides, and that soon. It is Christ or Barabbas again. We need a new Protestantism. The real church must be purged of her apostate parasites. She will be small, but she will be clean enough to meet her coming Bridegroom. Let us as real Christians rally in prayer, faith, and sacrificial effort to combat this propaganda of the Devil and paid smoke screen of the so-called scientists. Let us organize to boycott every school, editor's chair, and pulpit that sanctions the same. We are false to our high Christian trust if we fail to do so. This fight must be carried into every corner of the country and into politics as well as into religion and education. It is purely an antichristian challenge to the church of Jesus Christ.

◆ MODERN ESSAY ◆

Attacking Orthodoxy at its Roots

ROBIN MORGAN

As several of the preceding documents have shown, Americans during the Progressive Era engaged in a repression of other Americans with a ferocity equalled only by its absurdity — at least it appears that way in retrospect. Yet was that repression so obvious at the time? Documents such as Justice Holmes's decision in the Schenk *case involving freedom of speech during World War I show that the issue of repression vs. regulation was not clearcut even at that time. As Mr. Holmes said, the right to freedom of speech is determined by the particular circumstances in which the speech occurs. And those circumstances change.*

How will future generations judge present-day attempts to regulate without repressing? How will they evaluate our struggles with issues such as abortion, gay rights, the treatment of prisoners, and censorship? Does the community have a right to set standards for our acceptance of these practices, or is any form of regulation unjustifiable repression?

Our modern essay concerns the issue of women's rights, and by implication, men's rights. No orthodoxy is so powerful as that defining sex roles. It pervades the way we speak, think, and behave. It tells us at the most basic level how we should treat each other, what it means to be a man or a woman. We punish people who violate this orthodoxy. We arrest people whose sex role behavior seems "unthinkable." We ridicule homosexuals, people with sex change operations, men who don't "wear the pants in their family," "effemi-

*nate men," "masculine women." The Equal Rights Amendment, proposing
equality before the law for both sexes, provokes bitter controversy. Antago-
nists picture the utter destruction of the social fabric should it pass. On the
other hand, feminists like Robin Morgan insist that "sexism is a repressive
orthodoxy that must be destroyed."*

*What are the similarities between the orthodoxy that is repressing women
today and that suffered in the earlier period? What are the differences? Does
the subtlety of sexism make it more repressive than overt forms of enforcing
orthodoxy? Does the pervasiveness of sexism suggest that this is an orthodoxy
that society needs to preserve?*

The Women's Liberation Movement is the only radical movement I know of
today which is dealing with the issue of class — *on a concrete as well as a
theoretical basis.* A number of people have written about the "caste and class"
analysis: that women could be class enemies but remain caste sisters. Women
function as a caste because we class-climb or class-descend *via* our men, and
because, in our inter-class and intra-class functions, we still take our definitions *from* men — and those definitions are always that of appendages. Thus
the ruling-class woman has no real power herself — she is merely the exqui-
sitely decorated property of a man rich enough to have one slave who does
absolutely nothing. Other people do things for her, and they are, of course,
poor black and brown and white women. Nevertheless, it is still the "job" of
the upper-class woman to "supervise" these tasks: the menu-planning, endless shopping, genteel hostess routine — which is just a diamond-studded vari-
ation of the usual female role. . . .

But what *do* we want? That's what they always ask us, as if they had
expected us, like tidy housekeepers, to come up in five short years with the
magic remedy cleanser that will wipe clean the unbelievable mess men have
created from their position of power during the past five thousand years.

We're beginning to grope toward some analyses that feel right. We know
that two evils clearly pre-date corporate capitalism, and have post-dated socialist revolutions: *sexism* and *racism* — so we know that a male-dominated
socialist revolution in economic and even cultural terms, were it to occur to-
morrow, would be *no* revolution, but only another coup d'état among men.
We know that many historians, scientists, and anthropologists (among them,
Briffault, Morgan, Mead, Levi-Strauss, Childe, Montague, Gorer, and Bene-
dict) note a connection between the concept of property-ownership (primitive
capitalism) and the oppression of women. Anthropology has also taught us
that women probably invented agriculture, were the first to domesticate animals, invented the concept of weaving and of pottery, and (according to Gor-
don Childe) invented language, which filled a need in their communal work
(rather than the necessary silence of the hunters). Anthropologists continue
to turn up examples which prove that competitive, aggressive, warlike cultures
are those in which sexual stereotypes are most polarized, while those social
structures allowing for an overlap of roles and functions between men and

women (in tasks, childrearing, decision-making, etc.) tend to be collectivist, cooperative, and peaceful. There are numerous theories about early matriarchal societies, and how and when they were overthrown.

One thing does seem clearer as time goes on: the nuclear family unit is oppressive to women (*and* children, *and* men). The woman is forced into a totally dependent position, paying for her keep with an enormous amount of emotional and physical labor which is not even considered work. As Margaret Benston points out, "In sheer quantity, household labor, including child care, constitutes a huge amount of socially necessary production. Nevertheless, in a society based on commodity production, it is not usually considered as 'real work' since it is outside of trade and the marketplace. . . . In a society in which money determines value, women are a group who work outside the money economy." In essence, women are still back in feudal times. We work outside capitalism, as unpaid labor — and it is the structure of the family that makes this possible, since the employer pays only the husband and, in fact, gets the rest of the family's services for free. (The word "family" comes from the Oscan *famel,* a servant, slave, or possession. The word "father" — *pater* — means owner, possessor, master. The Roman *pater familias* was thus an "owner of slaves." It is a phrase we use with affection even today.) Well over a hundred years ago, Alexis de Tocqueville, on visiting the United States, wrote that it seemed to him a "spermatic economy," revolving totally around its men and isolating its women to the functions of either ornament or workhorse. It's an apt description for [the 1970s].

But if the family as it now exists, with its paranoiac possessiveness of wife and of children, its isolation, and its plain unviability (one out of three American marriages ends in divorce), if this family disappears, what will it be replaced with, and who will determine that? It's obvious that when men think up alternatives (such as divorce or "just living together" or communal living) those alternatives have been known to royally louse women up, so that this time we must create the alternatives that *we* want, those we imagine to be in our self-interest. I, for one, think that some form of extended family structure (something like the old Jewish or Italian families, though not along blood lines, but living companions of choice) might be an answer. The way in which women have so far been used in "alternate culture" communes, however, has made me extremely wary. Instead of cooking Betty Crocker casseroles in Scarsdale, she's stirring brown rice in Arizona or on the Lower East Side, and instead of being the "property" of one man, she's now the "property" of all the men in the collective. It's a thoroughly terrifying subject to explore: what *are* our alternatives?

No one, clearly, has any answers yet, although a host of possibilities present themselves to confuse us all even further. Living alone? Living in mixed communes with men and women? Living in all-women communes? Having children? Not having children? Raising them collectively, or in the old family structure? The father and/or other men sharing equally in child care, or shouldering it entirely, or not being permitted any participation? Homosexuality as a viable political alternative which straight women must begin to recognize as such? More — homosexuality, or bisexuality, as a beautiful affirmation of human *sexuality,* without all those absurd prefixes? Test-tube births? Masturbation? Womb transplants? Gender control of the fetus? (*That* is an appalling idea in the context of a male-supremacist society such as our current one — in which everyone would prefer having boy babies, while females would be bred only to be further breeders!) Parthenogenesis? Why? Why not?

It has made me slightly dizzy trying to list them all — and I must have missed some — and there are others not even dreamed of yet. The only thing I know for certain is that *this* time we women must seize control over our own lives and try, in the process, to salvage the planet from the ecological disaster and nuclear threat created by male-oriented power nations. It is not a small job, and it does seem as if women's work is never done.

Meanwhile, a worldwide revolution is already taking place: Third World peoples, black and brown peoples, are rising up and demanding an end to their neo-colonial status under the economic empire of the United States. The blood of Vietnam, Laos, and Cambodia is mixing with the blood of Jackson, Watts, and Detroit. *How,* we are asked, *can you talk about the comparatively insignificant oppression of women, when set beside the issues of racism and imperialism?*

This is a male-supremacist question. Not only because of its arrogance, but because of its ignorance. First, it dares to weigh and compute human suffering, and it places oppressed groups in competition with each other (an old, and very capitalistic, trick: divide and conquer). Second, the question fails to even minimally grasp the profoundly radical analysis beginning to emerge from revolutionary feminism: that capitalism, imperialism, and racism are *symptoms* of male supremacy — sexism.

Racism as a major contradiction, for example, is surely based on the first "alienizing" act: the basic primary contradiction that occurred with the enslavement of half the human species by the other half. I think it no coincidence that all the myths of creation, in all religions, have to do with a "fall from grace" simultaneously with the emergence of set sexual roles.

It also seems obvious that half of all oppressed peoples, black, brown, and otherwise, are *women,* and that I, as a not-starving white American woman living in the very belly of the beast, must fight for those sisters to *survive* before we can even talk together as oppressed women. (Example: in Biafra, most of the millions who died of starvation were women and children. But men were well-fed, since the army needed them kept in good fighting health. That is the essence of male thinking at its most arrogant, *machismo,* militaristic, and *patri*otic. That is sexism.)

More and more, I begin to think of a worldwide Women's Revolution as the only hope for life on the planet. It follows, then, that where women's liberation is, *there* is, for me, the genuine radical movement; I can no more countenance the co-optive lip-service of the male-dominated Left which still stinks of male supremacy than I can countenance the class bias and racism of that male "Movement." I haven't the faintest notion what possible revolutionary role white heterosexual men could fulfill, since they are the very embodiment of reactionary-vested-interest-power. But then, I have great difficulty examining what men in general could possibly do about all this. In addition to doing the shitwork that women have been doing for generations, possibly not exist? No, I really don't mean that. Yes, I really do. Never mind, that's another whole book.

What I began to say earlier, though, was that the differences between "politico" and "feminist" women (as with other divisions of class, race, age, occupation, etc.) are possibly smokescreens, defenses from seeing a frightening truth, resistances to a consciousness that no matter what we are, say, do, or believe, there is no getting away from the shared, primary oppression of being female in a patriarchal world.

You, sister, reading this: I have no earthly way of knowing if you are already involved in women's liberation, and if so, how deeply; perhaps you have never yet been to one women's meeting, but only read and heard things about the movement in magazines and on TV; perhaps you find you have picked up the book out of anger, or defiance, or on a dare, or from genuine curiosity, or cynical amusement — or even as part of your job or your school course. I hope this book means something to you, makes some real change in your heart and head — and I take a terrific risk in saying such a corny thing, because I don't mean it as any sort of "hope you liked the book" statement. No, I mean it desperately, because if we who have put this together have failed you somehow, then we have failed ourselves seriously — because *you* are women's liberation. This is not a movement one "joins." There are no rigid structures or membership cards. The Women's Liberation Movement exists where three or four friends or neighbors decide to meet regularly over coffee and talk about their personal lives. It also exists in the cells of women's jails, on the welfare lines, in the supermarket, the factory, the convent, the farm, the maternity ward, the streetcorner, the old ladies' home, the kitchen, the steno pool, the bed. It exists in your mind, and in the political and personal insights that you can contribute to change and shape and help its growth. It is frightening. It is very exhilarating. It is creating history, or rather, *herstory.*

And anyway, you cannot escape it.

PART III

Prosperity and Depression

Introduction

Big Business, Big Government, and Little People

Although Americans like to be identified as rugged individualists, it is more accurate to portray them as people who organize to face those challenges insurmountable by individual effort. In our past, it was the community which carved out homes in the frontier, reformers who organized into parties or pressure groups to bring change, and workers who formed unions to counter the power of management.

At times the force being confronted in America was so massive that individual or even group actions were futile, making it necessary to enlist the authority of the state. An example is the attempt to shackle the giant corporations which began to emerge early in the twentieth century. Small businesses could not compete against the concentrated economic power these giants had. To restrain big business the American people employed big government, regardless of the danger that government, because of its bigness, could become isolated from the popular will and leave the individual as helpless as when the trusts operated unhindered. The antidote to that possibility was to put someone in the White House who would not forget even the most humble American. The president would make big government personal.

These are the problems this chapter addresses. Chronologically it covers the period from the election of 1912 to the depression-ridden New Deal years of Franklin Roosevelt a quarter-century later. Substantively it examines the controversy surrounding the governmental effort to regulate big business, and the problem of the alienation of big government from the people — two aspects of the larger problem concerning the relationship between individuals with limited power and organizations with massive power.

Government regulation of powerful economic interests began late in the nineteenth century with the Interstate Commerce Commission, expanded early in the twentieth century, exploded during the New Deal years, and today has become a way of life in America. Our economy and our daily life are influenced by the Interstate Commerce Commission, the Food and Drug Administration, the Federal Trade Commission, the Federal Power Commission, the Federal Aviation Administration, the Federal Reserve Board, the Civil Aeronautics Board, the Environmental Protection Agency, the Energy Research and Development Administration, the Federal Communications Commission, the U.S. Department of Agriculture, the National Highway Traffic Safety Administration, the Equal Employment Opportunity Commission, and many lesser known agencies.

Government regulation of corporate power was caused not just by the size of the corporate entities, but also by the public attitude toward them. For two decades following World War II corporations were viewed as benefactors, and public opposition was limited. A few social critics lamented the conformity the large corporations imposed on their employees and the number of college graduates who preferred to disappear into the ranks of the corporate executives rather than go into business for themselves. But such intellectual concerns were immaterial compared to the technological benefit brought about by the corporations. Americans were living better, and they believed that it was due to the research and development of the giant corporations. After all, General Electric and Ronald Reagan were telling them that GE's most important product was progress.

This mood began to change during the idealistic sixties when an increasing number of younger Americans challenged the maximization of profits as the primary motive of big business. Disillusionment with the role of multinational corporations and the role of the United States in world affairs further eroded popular support for the economic giants. From the sixties and into the seventies the anti-big business feeling has accelerated with the rise of environmentalists who have attacked business for its profit-first-ecology-second method of operation. Safety-oriented reformers have chastised business for failing to develop safer products. The energy shortage has led an increasing number of Americans to wonder if the major energy companies might be involved in a conspiracy. Finally, inflation and unemployment have created dissatisfaction with the status quo, and big business has received its share of the blame. It seems that once again we are on the edge of another movement in support of the "public interest" and against the "special interest."

Some of big business's critics argue that the problem is the size of the corporation. ITT is likened to a sovereign state, and its American counterpart, AT&T is so large that no one can find out what it is doing. The solution, some argue, is to dissolve such giant corporations. By breaking them up into more manageable units, the small businesses could compete — or so the theory goes.

Other reformers maintain the solution to be better regulation, not dissolution. For too long, they argue, government regulation has been the captive of the special interests, operating in secret and ignoring the public will. Their solution is more consumer involvement in the regulatory process.

This public disillusionment with big business has led the larger corporations to begin a campaign of public image-building. The oil companies have been most visible with their messages stating that the number of oil companies prevents a monopoly from existing. They explain that their profits are modest, that they are very concerned about the environment, and that they are constantly looking for ways to make life better for all of us. The Bell Telephone system urges us to realize it is not a faceless corporation, but rather a group of people working to bring loved ones together via long distance telephone; rates are not raised to make a greater profit for the corporation but to assure the first-class service Americans are due. This public image advertising is not intended to sell more products or services, but to gain our moral and political support.

What are we to believe? Are the reformers correct when they claim that special interests are served by government regulation, or are the corporations correct when they claim to be serving the public? Is increased competition in the public interest if it is less efficient and thus more costly to consumers? Even if there is such a thing as the public interest, can consumers maintain enough involvement to make regulatory agencies sensitive to their demands? Or is it possible that certain things are inevitable and the dominance of the economically powerful is one of them?

These questions which underlie today's debate were also present in 1912 when Woodrow Wilson and Theodore Roosevelt were locked in a contest for the presidency. Roosevelt believed large corporate powers were inevitable and thus opposed doing away with them. He favored strong government regulation. Wilson, on the other hand, preferred to dissolve the trusts, to reduce the size of business to a dimension more easily regulated. He won the election, yet never busted the trusts. Instead he established two regulatory agencies very much like those Roosevelt advocated — the Federal Reserve Board and the Federal Trade Commission.

Neither of these agencies was designed to break open the banking or manufacturing industries to the little people of America. They were intended to stop the wild speculation in banks which might cause a panic, and to prohibit the cutthroat industrial competition which led to instability in the economy. Since the major motive of the regulatory agencies was maintaining stability, it is not surprising that the Federal Reserve Board and the Federal Trade Commission soon came to be viewed as tools of finance and industry.

Even before these regulatory agencies had been established, leaders of the larger corporations (who had most to lose from cutthroat competition) sought to stabilize the economic situation by limiting such competition. In effect, the regulatory agencies gave the force of law to the type of control the corporations had desired. Such friendly regulation of the corporations by government, however, was not contrary to the public interest, for alternating periods of economic boom and bust struck as hard against the industrial worker as the industrial magnate. Nevertheless there was considerable ground for disagreement over what should be done and what could be done about regulating business. That debate from 1912 to 1929 is the focus of the first issue of this section.

If Americans felt helpless when confronting the economic giants of the 1920s, they felt totally powerless when confronted by the Great Depression after 1929. Corporate power had meant the loss of some small businesses, but the Great Depression meant unemployment for millions and a total lack of security for those who managed to hold onto jobs. In such extreme circumstances the American people once again turned to their government for help. What they wanted from their government was not clear — jobs would be nice; World War I veterans wanted "bonus" or cash benefits; whatever specific demand some had in mind, *all* wanted to be assured that they had not been forgotten by their government, especially not by their president.

Americans personify their government in the president: To many people the president *is* the government. If it does well, he receives the praise. If it fails to act, he receives the blame. When the people turn to the government for assurance that they have not been forgotten, it is the president's responsibility to reassure them. Herbert Hoover failed in that mission. He was never able to uplift the American people and restore their confidence. It was not that Hoover refused to talk to the nation — he did that and issued handfuls of press releases and pronouncements. It was not that he was unwilling to take any action; Hoover went farther than earlier presidents had to end the depression. The problem was that Hoover appeared isolated from the nation. When compared with his successor, Franklin D. Roosevelt, Hoover appeared almost unconcerned about the common people.

Some might argue that isolation is the nature of the presidency. Surrounded by secret service agents and top-level advisors, the president may seem isolated from the daily concerns of the people he is supposed to lead and serve. A direct contradiction to that image is Franklin D. Roosevelt: he won election in 1932, reelection in 1936, reelection to an unprecedented third term with a comfortable 54 percent of the votes, and then won an almost unthinkable fourth term in 1944. When he died, millions across the land wept sincere tears for a man who was loved. What did Roosevelt do that Hoover did not? Clearly Hoover failed to capture the imagination of the American people; just as clearly, FDR had. But how? Was it the New Deal, with its variety of contradicting agencies, its image of action, and moderately successful program of achieving a level of prosperity below which no American would fall? Or was it the Roosevelt style: the voice, the smile, the friendly manner?

What makes a president command such popular devotion — personality or program?

Critics of presidents such as Roosevelt and Lyndon Johnson complain that they employed the "bread and circuses" routine: they filled the stomachs of Americans and kept them entertained while foisting big government upon them. Every four years the Republicans argue that the Democrats want to spend, legislate, and regulate the country into a centralized big government state. The Democrats counter by claiming that the Republicans prefer to block progressive legislation and treat the unemployed as statistics rather than humans. Yet both parties produce similar candidates who try to show how close they are to the people. Shaking hands, eating hot dogs, and rubbing shoulders with the masses are part of the program. The Ford-Carter campaign of 1976 was a good example: Ford visited Yellowstone National Park to emphasize how he had worked for a living as a young man in the Depression, while Carter played softball, wore work clothes, and walked around Plains, Georgia, barefoot.

Every four years we go through the ritual of selecting a symbolic leader. In reality the president does not run the entire government, nor does he actually keep track of it. But it is important for the people of America to believe that the president is somebody they can trust. If the people believe that their president is honest, well-intentioned, and concerned about their welfare, they are at ease. But what makes the people attribute those traits to a person? In 1932 the people placed their faith in Franklin Delano Roosevelt and elected him. Clearly they found traits in him they liked so much as a symbol of the nation that they kept on electing him for as long as he lived. In the second issue in this section, we shall examine the personalities and programs of Hoover and Roosevelt to evaluate the relationship between the people and their president.

Franklin Roosevelt was not the only charismatic leader to capture the public imagination during the interwar years. Huey P. Long rose from obscurity to be "The Kingfish" of Louisiana, a United States Senator, and a potential candidate for the presidency before being gunned down by an assassin. Long's career illustrates how a dynamic personality and an attention-getting program can bring about political success. To some people he offered hope by doing battle with the special economic interests which dominated Lousiana, to others he represented the appearance of the gangster type in American politics. Huey P. Long introduces us to the issues covered in this section: dealing with the economically powerful, and what the people want in a leader.

Personalizing the Issues

Huey Long: "The Kingfish"

In the period between the two world wars, many Americans shared the frustration of being poor in the world's richest land. While they confined their protests to angry grumbling and emotional religious outbursts in the 1920s, the Great Depression gave them an opportunity to organize behind a variety of fascinating — if not altogether wholesome — leaders. The most fascinating of these, Huey Pierce Long, Jr., has been called a demagogue, a radical, a dictator, a fascist, and more recently, the "Messiah of the Rednecks." "Redneck" was originally a term used to describe the poor white

southern farmer whose fair skin turned red rather than brown when he worked in the sun. Huey Long rose to power in the twenties before the Depression; he achieved his greatest prominence in the thirties when the house of cards which had been the American business system fell down upon his so-called "redneck" followers.

Even Long's many detractors — and they are numerous — admit that Long rose to power in Louisiana because it had been misgoverned so long by the bayou state's businessmen, planters, utilities, railroads, and oil companies. They had formed a self-perpetuating political machine that cared only about power and profits. In the twenties, Louisiana was the most illiterate state in the union: 20 percent of its white population and nearly double that for its black were illiterate. The children of these illiterate farmers went over washed-out roads to run-down schools, or quit school to work long hours for wages they could barely survive on. Given a chance to protest, the average Louisiana voter swept Huey Long into power during the 1920s on a platform of Populist programs.

Much has been said about Huey Long's origins in radical Winn Parish where independent political action was often the rule. The delegate from Winn to the secession convention in 1860, for example, refused to vote for secession and thus the parish was jokingly referred to by other Southerners as the Free State of Winn. As Long said later, "My father and mother favored the Union. Why not? They didn't have slaves. They didn't even have decent land." Later the Populists and Socialists did well in Winn Parish. In 1912, Eugene Debs, the Socialist candidate for president, received more votes in the parish than the president of the United States, William Howard Taft. True, this was rural socialism, quite distinct from the ideology associated with the word "socialism" today, but it did create a political background for Long that gave him many political ideas and slogans. As a young man he debated two touring members of the Socialist Party on the relative merits of the Democratic party — understandably, Huey Long was influenced by Populism, Socialism, and the Democratic party.

No one ever doubted Long's mental brilliance or political ability. His father, although a man of only modest means, saw six of his nine children graduate from college. Huey was not one of the six, but the money would have been wasted — college would have only slowed his progress. As it was, he studied for eight months and passed the state bar exam, and at age twenty-one became a practicing attorney. Soon he was the epitome of a self-made man, first as a lawyer, then as a very successful Railroad Commissioner, and later as the Public Service Commissioner who yelled and screamed at the high cost of utilities in the state and thus forced many companies to lower their rates. This action was a great accomplishment in a state controlled by a political machine.

Long was so successful as Railroad Commissioner that he ran for governor in 1924, and tasted his first major defeat. Considering the fact that he was not a member of the machine and that he would not accept the support of the Ku Klux Klan (which was then a powerful force in Louisiana), he did amazingly well. He established a political name, a following, and a program. In the next election, at age thirty-five, he became Governor of Louisiana by borrowing the famous slogan of William Jennings Bryan, "Every Man a King."

Neither the people of Louisiana nor the established political machine was prepared for the shock waves that followed. Realizing that he could not expect members of the machine to support his policies, the new governor immediately cleaned house. All non-Long men who held political positions appointed by the governor were removed from office, and his supporters appointed to replace them. Like other politicians, he reportedly had taken bribes on the way to power, so the major corporations, the utilities, the railroads, and Standard Oil tried to bribe Long as they had nearly every other important state politician. But he was not to be bought at their price. He was out to smash the oligarchy and establish his own political dynasty; thus he needed power, not just money. As it was, there were other ways to become wealthy as Governor of Louisiana without selling out to the interests, and Long found them all.

Long wanted power, but he also wanted to achieve certain basic goals: better schools, free textbooks, crash programs on adult illiteracy, highways, bridges, hospitals, and lower tax and utility rates for the poor. Each of these goals was a calculated vote-getter. Amazingly he achieved them all. School appropriations were increased so that Louisiana could afford to keep the public schools open for the entire academic year for the first time in its history. Thousands of new students, who could not afford to attend school when they had to purchase their own books, entered school for the first time using books provided by the state, and 100,000 illiterate adults attended free night classes to get a basic education. Highways, bridges, and hospitals were built with dispatch. From 1928 to 1935 Louisiana increased its concrete roads from 296 to 2,446 miles, its asphalt roads from 35 to 1,308 miles, its gravel roads from 5,728 to 9,629 miles, and its number of major bridges from 3 to 40. This growth was achieved without increasing the taxes of the poor folk who had been supporting the state in the past. When taxes were increased they were levied on corporate interests — groups that had been untaxed before the Long era. Other finances were raised through a sound bond program.

As admirable as these goals were, Long found it impossible to achieve them through the normal democratic process. The machine fought each of them, including the tax on oil and the repeal of the poll tax. Long did not need the democratic process, however, because he used a variety of methods which included threats, bribes, and force. Separation of powers was ignored as the governor saw to it that bills were rammed through the legislature at a frightening rate — forty-four in twenty-two minutes on one occasion. He also saw to it that the appointive powers of the governor were increased so that he had control over mayors, teachers, and other state employees.

The boldness of Huey Long can be seen in his clash with Standard Oil.

As unbelievable as it might seem, until Long became governor oil companies had never been taxed in Louisiana. When he instituted a popular five-cents-a-barrel tax on oil, the machine decided it was time to impeach the "Messiah of the Rednecks." To do this they needed better than a two-thirds majority in the state senate, and they set out to purchase the necessary support. But to insure a defense against impeachment, Long had to bribe only one-third of the senate, which was cheaper and easier. And as he said, he could, and did, buy legislators like "sacks of potatoes." Thus impeachment died aborning. Later, one of the liberal opponents of the Long regime, journalist Hodding Carter, admitted the liberals had made a serious mistake when they joined forces with the most reactionary forces in Louisiana to oppose Long. Furthermore, Carter said, they failed to acknowledge any merits in the popular Long program, which made the electorate doubt the sincerity of Long's liberal opponents.

With the onset of the Great Depression, Long looked for greater power. Poor Southerners in other states looked to him and his programs as a panacea for their problems. Thus in 1930 Long was elected to the United States Senate. According to the state constitution, he had to resign as governor to run for the Senate, but Huey Long took no chances. He remained as governor until his election was insured. As his opponents said, he was by then the "state," or the state constitution, much more so than Louis XIV ever had been.

Shortly after he was elected, the new senator gained national fame when he granted an interview to two foreign dignitaries who were offended by the uncustomary uniform he wore during the interview: a red-and-blue dressing gown over green silk pajamas. The average American joined Long in his amusement, and supported him when he gallantly returned the call, in formal attire, to show that while American officials were unpretentious, they had good manners. Oddly enough, pajamas were his basic working uniform, as he loved to make decisions sitting in bed, surrounded by his henchmen. One of Long's detractors, who was allowed to witness this procedure, was amazed at how the governor discussed some twenty different problems in detail, and then reviewed each of the decisions without using any notes.

The pajama incident brought out an unusual side of Long's character. He was convinced that people loved a comic character, and he developed a façade which he thought would hide some of his more Machiavellian characteristics. When he answered the telephone, he did so à la Amos and Andy saying: "Hello dere, da Kingfish here." But, although he tried to create the impression of being a buffoon, he was a brilliant administrator. Unfortunately, he abused so many of his talents that Senator Alben Barkley of Kentucky told him he was "the smartest lunatic" he ever met. Thus his comic impudence was costly.

As a senator, Long had no more desire to play the game by the rules than he had as governor. He was in the Senate for power, and power came from his constituents, not his fellow senators. Therefore he violated all the rules of what has been called the "most exclusive private club" in the world, first by refusing to walk down the aisle with the senior senator from Louisiana, as all freshmen senators were supposed to do, simply because Long disliked the man. Later, Huey resigned all his committee positions because he thought the Senate was not really interested in helping poor people and denounced all but two of his new colleagues as "stuffed shirts."

If anyone was more popular with poor folks in the thirties than Huey Long, it was Franklin D. Roosevelt. Since they appealed to the same people, Long, a southern grass-roots Democrat, worked for the patrician Democrat from New York and even helped hold the southern delegates in line during the 1932 convention. But the Kingfish had no use for the conservatives and the intellectuals who formed part of FDR's team, and Long soon split with the New Deal. Once, when the conservative Raymond Moley was holding a meeting in a hotel room, Long kicked the door open and stood in the hall chomping on an apple, cursing the inhabitants of the room. When he left, Moley found one of the group cowering in the bathroom. Possibly the man had heard of Long's unorthodox methods of keeping his opponents in line in his home state.

Like his comic impudence, Long's opposition to Roosevelt was costly. His demand to force the New Deal to act more swiftly for the poor, and his labeling of the NRA as the "National Run Around" and "Nuts Running America" were popular, but his personal attacks upon the president were not. They created a groundswell of opposition just at the time the Kingfish got involved in a bizarre incident in a nightclub when the beer-guzzling senator somehow missed the urinal, but not a fellow occupant of the restroom. The man promptly belted him. The incident made national headlines as Long issued reports which constantly increased the number of assailants and called the attack, a "Wall Street plot."

Long's ridiculous extremes and his opposition to a popular president might have been fatal to a lesser man, but they hardly hindered the Louisiana dynamo. Despite the fact that Long was in the Senate, he had not relinquished control of the state government. His hand-picked successor fulfilled all of his demands immediately, and when the Kingfish needed additional support, he returned to the source of his strength, his constituents, and provided them with programs they needed, including the elimination of certain taxes and a debt moratorium.

What made Long popular throughout the entire South was his famous "Share our Wealth" program, in which he proposed that the government confiscate all income over $1,000,000 and all inheritances over $5,000,000, and distribute the money by giving each man $5,000 plus a guaranteed annual income of $2,000. Poor Southerners shared his belief that rich people created depressions while poor people endured them. Many of them also agreed with their "Redneck Robin Hood" that the only difference between the two major parties was that the Republicans skinned the voter from the ankles up, and the Democrats from the neck down.

The fact that the "Share our Wealth" program was economically and politically impossible had little impact upon Long's devoted followers. Their faith in him was unlimited. To a generation that was tired of "do-nothingism" government, Long's positive, "do-everythingism" government was exciting and refreshing. To a generation that was tired of the growing size and impersonality of government, Long's action-packed, personal government, responsive to popular demand, created the impression that the senator really was a political messiah. Even his critics recognized that "Huey kept the faith with the people" and that the hand of the Kingfish was felt throughout the land. He gave them something and let the corporations pay for it. Since he was one of the first government officials in America to wage a war on poverty openly, his constituents believed that his "Share our Wealth" program was the latest stage in Long's efforts on their behalf.

There was still another reason for the rural South to accept the viability of sharing the wealth. Long never sold his programs as a politician; he sold them as an evangelist. Although he was one of the most amoral politicians in America's history, he knew the importance of religion to his constituents. He had grown up in a home in which everyone attended all local religious ceremonies. On Sundays he attended church four times: Sunday school, religious services, youth meeting, and evening prayers. In addition to the midweek services the family attended every funeral within a ten-mile radius. There seems to be little reason to doubt his claim that most of the Long children read "the Scripture from cover to cover."

But Huey Long did more than read the Bible; he memorized huge portions of it and used them for political leverage. The basis for his "Share our Wealth" idea, for example, was the "Year of Jubilee" discussed in the twenty-fifth chapter of Leviticus. He was so effective that one historian has classed the senator with Father Charles E. Coughlin and Dr. Francis Townsend, two other rabble-rousers of the thirties, as "God's Angry Men." Coughlin and Townsend tried to develop some sort of economic analysis for their religious crusades, but not Long — he proudly proclaimed that he "never read a line of Marx or Henry George or any of them economists." His program was all based on "the law of God."

It was no accident that Huey campaigned like an evangelist or utilized ministers in his campaign. His chief assistant in his "Share Our Wealth Society" was another of "God's Angry Men," Gerald L. K. Smith, a fiery evangelist who openly flirted with fascism as a cure for the evils of the Depression. Smith's political rallies, like Long's, were "go to Jesus meetings," punctuated with "hymn singing, amen shouting, and numerous calls for deliverance." Both Smith and Long worked toward the deification of the Kingfish, because as the evangelist said, "No great movement has ever succeeded unless it deified one man." Little wonder that Long was known as the messiah. Long's angry critics were not far from the truth when they said his programs attempted to establish a "Hillbilly Heaven."

Another of Long's ideas that gained support was his contention that a third party would be more directly responsible to people than either of the existing parties. We will never know how far Huey Long might have gone because he was assassinated in the summer of 1935. Characteristically, the dying Kingfish pleaded that he did not want to leave this world since he had so many things left to accomplish.

A man who bribed, cheated, beat, kidnapped, and harassed his opponents, manipulated elections, cursed as if he had a corner on the market, and surrounded himself with dozens of brutal bodyguards is not exemplary of the American politician. Yet for all his brutal ways, Long gave Louisiana a government that for the first time met the needs of the people. Before his ascendency, state political plums usually fell to those who yelled "nigger" louder than anyone else, or to those who waved the Confederate flag and retold the glorious adventures of Robert E. Lee. In a state divided between black and white, Protestant and Catholic, Long never relied on racial or religious prejudice as a fulcrum to power. He let the racial, religious, and political past die, and forced his constituents to deal with contemporary issues. At a time when the Ku Klux Klan had great influence even in northern states, Long kept it out of state politics. When he heard that the Imperial Wizard of the Klan was to visit Louisiana, he said: "Quote me as saying that, that Imperial bastard will never set foot in Louisiana, and that when I call him a son of a bitch, I am not using profanity, but referring to the circumstances of his birth." Because of his refusal to play the bigot's game, many black voters shared his belief that he, not Abraham Lincoln, had freed the slaves in Louisiana.

Though Long may have been corrupt and a demagogue, the conflict in Louisiana was never one of corruption versus honesty, or demagoguery versus democracy; the conflict was between a corrupt, self-perpetuating oligarchy and a corrupt individual who did what the oligarchy never did — shared the state's wealth with others. Before Long, historians of the Pelican State could count the number of honest politicians in the state house on the fingers of one hand. Because democracy was neglected in Louisiana, the people were ready for a new leader who had a program that attacked the special interests and a charismatic personality that inspired confidence. Long had those traits and the skill to use them.

Issue

The Regulation of American Industry

> ... *Government regulation is fundamentally at variance with the philosophical assumptions underlying the American political system.*
>
> Peter H. Schuck, 1975

> *In the present day the limitation of governmental power, of governmental action, means the enslavement of the people by the great corporations who can only be held in check through the extension of governmental power.*
>
> Theodore Roosevelt, 1912

The twentieth century brought the rise of the billion dollar corporation and the demise of the "public be damned" image of business leaders. The new corporations with their new class of corporate managers seem less threatening than the "robber barons" of the nineteenth century. Yet many people wonder about the power which these corporate giants wield. In this section we confront the issue of how to control this concentrated economic power.

Woodrow Wilson favored breaking down the corporations into smaller and less powerful units, but never implemented his program. Instead, he increased government regulations. By the mid-1920s critics of government regulatory agencies were charging that the regulators were merely tools of the industries they were supposed to regulate. Defenders of the system asserted that the public interest was well served.

As you read the documents in this section, you will see that the writers favored the public interest but few, if any, were able to say what constituted the public interest. That is one of the major problems this section faces: What is the public interest and how is it served? Another problem addressed is whether government regulation of business can work. If government regulation inevitably leads to business dominating the regulatory agencies, regulation becomes impossible. Carried one step farther, if a particular industry can so dominate the sources of public information as to manipulate public opinion, does the public interest have any meaning at all?

◆ DOCUMENTS ◆

Regulation by Countervailing Power

THEODORE ROOSEVELT

Theodore Roosevelt describes his New Nationalism. What is the public interest he would have the government protect? Under Roosevelt's plan, who is going to determine what the public interest is? Given your study of American history, do you think a reform movement which pledged to secure social justice for the humble could be successful?

The key to Mr. Wilson's position is found in the statement . . . that "The history of liberty is a history of the limitation of governmental power, not the increase of it."

This is a bit of outworn academic doctrine which was kept in the schoolroom and the professorial study for a generation after it had been abandoned by all who had experience of actual life. It is simply the *laissez-faire* doctrine of the English political economists three-quarters of a century ago. It can be applied with profit, if anywhere at all, only in a primitive community under primitive conditions, in a community such as the United States at the end of the eighteenth century, a community before the days of Fulton, Morse, and Edison. To apply it now in the United States at the beginning of the twentieth century, with its highly organized industries, with its railways, telegraphs, and telephones, means literally and absolutely to refuse to make a single effort to better any one of our social or industrial conditions.

Moreover, Mr. Wilson is absolutely in error in his statement, from the historical standpoint.

So long as governmental power existed exclusively for the king and not at all for the people, then the history of liberty was a history of the limitation of governmental power. But now the governmental power rests in the people, and the kings who enjoy privilege are the kings of the financial and industrial world; and what they clamor for is the limitation of governmental power, and what the people sorely need is the extension of governmental power. . . .

The trouble with Mr. Wilson is that he is following an outworn philosophy and that the history of which he is thinking is the history of absolute monarchies and Oriental despotisms. He is thinking of government as embodied in an absolute king or in an oligarchy or aristocracy. He is not thinking of our government, which is a government by the people themselves.

From an address in San Francisco, September 14, 1912. Originally published in *Progressive Principles*, ed. Elmer H. Youngman (New York: Progressive National Service, 1913), pp. 419–427.

The only way in which our people can increase their power over the big corporation that does wrong, the only way in which they can protect the working man in his conditions of work and life, the only way in which the people can prevent children working in industry or secure women an eight-hour day in industry, or secure compensation for men killed or crippled in industry, is by extending, instead of limiting, the powers of government.

There is no analogy whatever, from the standpoint of real liberty, and of real popular need, between the limitations imposed by the people on the power of an irresponsible monarch or a dominant aristocracy, and the limitations sought to be imposed by big financiers, by big corporation lawyers, and by well-meaning students of a dead-and-gone system of political economy on the power of the people to right social wrongs and limit social abuses, and to secure for the humble what, unless there is an extension of the powers of government, the arrogant and the powerful will certainly take from the humble.

If Mr. Wilson really believes what he has said, then Mr. Wilson has no idea of our government in its actual working. He is not thinking of modern American history or of present-day American needs. He is thinking of *Magna Carta,* which limited the power of the English king, because his power over the people had before been absolute. He is thinking of the Bill of Rights, which limited the power of the governing class in the interest of the people, who could not control that governing class.

Our proposal is to increase the power of the people themselves and to make the people in reality the governing class. Therefore Mr. Wilson's proposal is really to limit the power of the people and thereby to leave unchecked the colossal embodied privileges of the present day.

Now, you can adopt one philosophy or the other. You can adopt the philosophy of *laissez-faire,* of the limitation of governmental power, and turn the industrial life of this country into a chaotic scramble of selfish interests, each bent on plundering the other and all bent on oppressing the wage-worker. This is precisely and exactly what Mr. Wilson's proposal means; and it can mean nothing else. Under such limitations of governmental power as he praises, every railroad must be left unchecked, every great industrial concern can do as it chooses with its employees and with the general public; women must be permitted to work as many hours a day as their taskmasters bid them; great corporations must be left unshackled to put down wages to a starvation limit and to raise the price of their products as high as monopolistic control will permit.

The reverse policy means an extension, instead of a limitation, of governmental power; and for that extension we Progressives stand.

We propose to handle the colossal industrial concerns engaged in interstate business as we are handling the great railways engaged in interstate business; and we propose to go forward in the control of both, doing justice to each but exacting justice from each; and we propose to work for justice to the farmer and the wage-worker in the same fashion.

Let me give you a concrete instance of what Mr. Wilson's policy, if applied, means as compared with ours. The Stanley Committee, the Democratic committee of the Democratic House of Representatives, has practically applied its interpretation of the Democratic platform about trusts, which is substantially the Republican platform, the Wilson-Taft platform. Some time previously under governmental suit the Standard Oil Trust was dissolved. Under the decree of the court the Standard Oil Company was split up into a lot of smaller companies, precisely as the Stanley Report proposes that similar trusts shall be split up. What has been the actual result? All the companies are still under the same control, or at least working in such close alliance that the effect is precisely the same. The price of the stock has gone up over one hundred per cent, so that Mr. Rockefeller and his associates have actually seen their fortunes doubled by the policy which Mr. Wilson advocates and which Mr. Taft defends. At the same time the price of oil to the consumer has gone up by leaps and bounds. No wonder that Wall Street's prayer now is: "Oh, Merciful Providence, give us another dissolution."

In short, the Taft-Wilson plan has actually resulted in enormously benefiting Mr. Rockefeller and his associates and in causing serious damage to all consumers.

The Progressive proposal is the direct reverse of all this. If we had our way, there would be an administrative body to deal radically and thoroughly with such a case as that of the Standard Oil Company. We would make any split-up of the company that was necessary real and not nominal. We would step in in such a case as this where the value of the stock was going up in such enormous proportion and forbid any increase of the price of the product. We would examine thoroughly and searchingly the books of the company and put a stop to every type of rebate and to every practice which would result in the swindling either of investors or competitors or wage-workers or of the general public.

Our plan — the plan to which Mr. Archbold of the Standard Oil Trust so feelingly objects as "Abyssinian treatment" — would result in preventing any increase of cost to the consumer and in exercising the kind of radical control over the corporation itself, which would prevent the stock-gambling antics which result in enormous profits to those on the inside, to those who, in the parlance of the street, know that "there is a melon to be cut."

Now, I have stated as fairly as I know how what Mr. Wilson's plan is, if his words mean anything, and what our plan is. And I ask every working man, every farmer, every professional and business man, to say for themselves which is best.

The people of the United States have but one instrument which they can efficiently use against the colossal combinations of business — and that instrument is the government of the United States (and of course in the several States the governments of the States where they can be utilized). Mr. Wilson's proposal is that the people of the United States shall throw away this, the one great instrument, the one great weapon they have with which to secure themselves against wrong. He proposes to limit the governmental action of the people and therefore to leave unlimited and unchecked the action of the great corporations whose enormous power constitutes so serious a problem in modern industrial life. Remember that it is absolutely impossible to limit the power of these great corporations whose enormous power constitutes so serious a problem in modern industrial life except by extending the power of the government. All that these great corporations ask is that the power of the government shall be limited. No wonder they are supporting Mr. Wilson, for he is advocating for them what they hardly dare venture to advocate for themselves. These great corporations rarely want anything from the government except to be let alone and to be permitted to work their will unchecked by the government. All that they really want is that governmental action shall be limited. In every great corporation suit the corporation lawyer will be found protesting against extension of governmental power. Every court decision favoring a corporation takes the form of declaring unconstitutional some extension of governmental power. Every corporation magnate in the country who is not dealing honestly and fairly by his fellows asks nothing better than that Mr. Wilson's programme be carried out and that there be stringent limitations of governmental power.

There once was a time in history when the limitation of governmental power meant increasing liberty for the people. In the present day the limitation of governmental power, of governmental action, means the enslavement of the people by the great corporations who can only be held in check through the extension of governmental power.

Free Enterprise vs. Industry

WOODROW WILSON

Woodrow Wilson argues against allowing the corporate giants to exist. How does Wilson's definition of freedom differ from Roosevelt's? Is Wilson's ideal of allowing every "man to exercise mastery over his own fortunes" likely to appeal to small business owners or blue-collar workers? Is Wilson's program a fanciful dream of returning to the nineteenth century, or a realistic appraisal of the power of the modern corporation?

Suppose you go to Washington and try to get at your government. You will always find that while you are politely listened to, the men really consulted

From Woodrow Wilson, *The New Freedom: A Call for the Emancipation of the Generous Energies of a People* (New York and Garden City: Doubleday, Page & Co., 1913), pp. 57–60, 194–207.

are the men who have the biggest stake, — the big bankers, the big manufacturers, the big masters of commerce, the heads of railroad corporations
and of steamship corporations. I have no objection to these men being consulted, because they also, though they do not themselves seem to admit it,
are part of the people of the United States. But I do very seriously object to
these gentlemen being *chiefly* consulted, and particularly to their being exclusively consulted, for, if the government of the United States is to do the
right thing by the people of the United States, it has got to do it directly and
not through the intermediation of these gentlemen. Every time it has come to
a critical question these gentlemen have been yielded to, and their demands
have been treated as the demands that should be followed as a matter of
course.

The government of the United States at present is a foster-child of the
special interests. It is not allowed to have a will of its own. It is told at every
move: "Don't do that; you will interfere with our prosperity." And when we
ask, "Where is our prosperity lodged?" a certain group of gentlemen say,
"With us." The government of the United States in recent years has not been
administered by the common people of the United States. You know just as
well as I do, — it is not an indictment against anybody, it is a mere statement
of the facts, — that the people have stood outside and looked on at their own
government and that all they have had to determine in past years has been
which crowd they would look on at; whether they would look on at this little
group or that little group who had managed to get the control of affairs in its
hands. Have you ever heard, for example, of any hearing before any great
committee of the Congress in which the people of the country as a whole were
represented, except it may be by the Congressmen themselves? The men who
appear at those meetings in order to argue for or against a schedule in the
tariff, for this measure or against that measure, are men who represent special
interests. They may represent them very honestly, they may intend no wrong
to their fellow-citizens, but they are speaking from the point of view always
of a small portion of the population. I have sometimes wondered why men,
particularly men of means, men who didn't have to work for their living,
shouldn't constitute themselves attorneys for the people, and every time a
hearing is held before a committee of Congress should not go and ask: "Gentlemen, in considering these things suppose you consider the whole country?
Suppose you consider the citizens of the United States?"

. . . . You know that Mr. Roosevelt long ago classified trusts for us as
good and bad, and he said that he was afraid only of the bad ones. Now he
does not desire that there should be any more bad ones, but proposes that
they should all be made good by discipline, directly applied by a commission
of executive appointment. All he explicitly complains of is lack of publicity
and lack of fairness; not the exercise of power, for throughout that plank the
power of the great corporations is accepted as the inevitable consequence of
the modern organization of industry. All that it is proposed to do is to take
them under control and regulation. The national administration having for

sixteen years been virtually under the regulation of the trusts, it would be merely a family matter were the parts reversed and were the other members of the family to exercise the regulation. And the trusts, apparently, which might, in such circumstances, comfortably continue to administer our affairs under the mollifying influences of the federal government, would then, if you please, be the instrumentalities by which all the humanistic, benevolent program of the rest of that interesting platform would be carried out!

I have read and reread that plank, so as to be sure that I get it right. All that it complains of is, — and the complaint is a just one, surely, — that these gentlemen exercise their power in a way that is secret. Therefore, we must have publicity. Sometimes they are arbitrary; therefore they need regulation. Sometimes they do not consult the general interests of the community; therefore they need to be reminded of those general interests by an industrial commission. But at every turn it is the trusts who are to do us good, and not we ourselves.

Again, I absolutely protest against being put into the hands of trustees. Mr. Roosevelt's conception of government is Mr. Taft's conception, that the Presidency of the United States is the presidency of a board of directors. I am willing to admit that if the people of the United States cannot get justice for themselves, then it is high time that they should join the third party and get it from somebody else. The justice proposed is very beautiful; it is very attractive; there were planks in that platform which stir all the sympathies of the heart; they proposed things that we all want to do; but the question is, Who is going to do them? Through whose instrumentality? Are Americans ready to ask the trusts to give us in pity what we ought, in justice, to take?

The third party says that the present system of our industry and trade has come to stay. Mind you, these artificially built up things, these things that can't maintain themselves in the market without monopoly, have come to stay, and the only thing that the government can do, the only thing that the third party proposes should be done, is to set up a commission to regulate them. It accepts them. It says: "We will not undertake, it were futile to undertake, to prevent monopoly, but we will go into an arrangement by which we will make these monopolies kind to you. We will guarantee that they shall be pitiful. We will guarantee that they shall pay the right wages. We will guarantee that they shall do everything kind and public-spirited, which they have never heretofore shown the least inclination to do."

Don't you realize that that is a blind alley? You can't find your way to liberty that way. You can't find your way to social reform through the forces that have made social reform necessary. . . .

I do not want to live under a philanthropy. I do not want to be taken care of by the government, either directly, or by any instruments through which the government is acting. I want only to have right and justice prevail, so far as I am concerned. Give me right and justice and I will undertake to take care of myself. If you enthrone the trusts as the means of the development of this country under the supervision of the government, then I shall pray the old Spanish proverb, "God save me from my friends, and I'll take care of my enemies." Because I want to be saved from these friends. Observe that I say these friends, for I am ready to admit that a great many men who believe that the development of industry in this country through monopolies is inevitable intend to be the friends of the people. Though they profess to be my friends, they are undertaking a way of friendship which renders it impossible that they should do me the fundamental service that I demand — namely, that I should be free and should have the same opportunities that everybody else has.

For I understand it to be the fundamental proposition of American liberty that we do not desire special privilege, because we know special privilege will never comprehend the general welfare. This is the fundamental, spiritual difference between adherents of the party now about to take charge of the government and those who have been in charge of it in recent years. They are so indoctrinated with the idea that only the big business interests of this country understand the United States and can make it prosperous that they cannot divorce their thoughts from that obsession. They have put the government into the hands of trustees, and Mr. Taft and Mr. Roosevelt were the rival candidates to preside over the board of trustees. They were candidates to serve the people, no doubt, to the best of their ability, but it was not their idea to serve them directly; they proposed to serve them indirectly through the enormous forces already set up, which are so great that there is almost an open question whether the government of the United States with the people back of it is strong enough to overcome and rule them.

Shall we try to get the grip of monopoly away from our lives, or shall we not? Shall we withhold our hand and say monopoly is inevitable, that all that we can do is to regulate it? Shall we say that all that we can do is to put government in competition with monopoly and try its strength against it? Shall we admit that the creature of our own hands is stronger than we are? We have been dreading all along the time when the combined power of high finance would be greater than the power of the government. Have we come to a time when the President of the United States or any man who wishes to be the President must doff his cap in the presence of this high finance, and say, "You are our inevitable master, but we will see how we can make the best of it?"

We are at the parting of the ways. We have, not one or two or three, but many, established and formidable monopolies in the United States. We have, not one or two, but many, fields of endeavor into which it is difficult, if not impossible, for the independent man to enter. We have restricted credit, we have restricted opportunity, we have controlled development, and we have come to be one of the worst ruled, one of the most completely controlled and dominated, governments in the civilized world — no longer a government by free opinion, no longer a government by conviction and the vote of the majority, but a government by the opinion and the duress of small groups of dominant men.

If the government is to tell big business men how to run their business, then don't you see that big business men have to get closer to the government even than they are now? Don't you see that they must capture the government, in order not to be restrained too much by it? Must capture the government? They have already captured it. Are you going to invite those inside to stay inside? They don't have to get there. They are there. Are you going to own your own premises, or are you not? That is your choice. Are you going to say: "You didn't get into the house the right way, but you are in there, God bless you; we will stand out here in the cold and you can hand us out something once in a while?"

At the least, under the plan I am opposing, there will be an avowed partnership between the government and the trusts. I take it that the firm will be ostensibly controlled by the senior member. For I take it that the government of the United States is at least the senior member, though the younger member has all along been running the business. But when all the momentum, when all the energy, when a great deal of the genius, as so often happens in partnerships the world over, is with the junior partner, I don't think that the superintendence of the senior partner is going to amount to very much. And I don't believe that benevolence can be read into the hearts of the trusts by the superintendence and suggestions of the federal government; because the government has never within my recollection had its suggestions accepted by the trusts. On the contrary, the suggestions of the trusts have been accepted by the government.

There is no hope to be seen for the people of the United States until the partnership is dissolved. . . .

The Roosevelt plan is that there shall be an industrial commission charged with the supervision of the great monopolistic combinations which have been formed under the protection of the tariff, and that the government of the United States shall see to it that these gentlemen who have conquered labor shall be kind to labor. I find, then, the proposition to be this: That there shall be two masters, the great corporation, and over it the government of the United States; and I ask who is going to be master of the government of the United States? It has a master now, — those who in combination control these monopolies. And if the government controlled by the monopolies in its turn controls the monopolies, the partnership is finally consummated.

I don't care how benevolent the master is going to be, I will not live under a master. That is not what America was created for. America was created in order that every man should have the same chance as every other man to exercise mastery over his own fortunes.

Industry and the Public Interest
GEORGE L. RECORD

According to George Record, is it possible to have elected officials who represent the public rather than special interests? Would a solution be the continued involvement of the public in the process of regulation? Does George Record think that there is anything which can compete with the economic power of the trusts? Is he correct?

We are at the end of a remarkable and historic experience in the endeavor to prevent and control monopoly in industry and transportation. After the Civil War thoughtful statesmen began to be apprehensive of the growth of what has since been called "big business." The astounding growth of the Standard Oil monopoly, with the corruption and scandals that accompanied it, first focused public opinion upon the question.

John Sherman sponsored a bill which became famous as the Sherman Act and which aimed to prevent monopoly in industry. The Interstate Commerce Commission was created to control the railroads in response to the same impulse. Then came the State public utility regulation idea to fix gas, electric light, water, and trolley rates by State commissions, advocated by Governor La Follette of Wisconsin and Governor Hughes of New York and finally adopted by every State in the Union. The Federal Trade Commission Act came along in President Wilson's time. It was a belated recognition of the fact that the industrial field required different machinery for administering the anti-trust idea and guarding against monopoly from the railroads and local public utilities.

In the past twenty years a large number of litigations and prosecutions, State and national, designed to prevent or to end monopolies in industry and unfair discriminations in railroad, electric light, and gas service, have been started and carried to a decision. But during all this period industrial monopolies, quasimonopolies, and combinations have steadily increased in number, size, wealth, and power, and financial syndicates have merged the railroads into a few great noncompetitive groups. We now have a few powerful and interrelated financial groups which dominate our staple fields of industry and control the light, power, and transportation facilities. Space permits only the mention of the more important of them.

The Standard Oil Company built up the control of the oil business. Five meat-packing concerns have secured a dominating position, if not a monopoly, in the meat trade and have reached out for the control of other lines. The

From George L. Record, "How Shall We Muzzle Monopoly?" *The Independent,* September 13, 1928, pp. 351–352, 361.

anthracite coal trust has created an absolute monopoly of that trade. The steel trust has a dominating position in the steel trade. There are other trusts which have been developed upon patents, such as the harvester trust, the General Electric and Westinghouse alliance, the great United Shoe Machinery concern, and the American Telephone Company. The development of allied trusts or combinations in the field of electric power and light is just now beginning to attract the attention of the country.

Most of these combinations have been built up and now operate in plain violation of our statute law, and in some instances in flat violation of the common law. Many of them have been brought before our courts in criminal and civil proceedings. Some of them have been ordered to dissolve and compete, as was the Standard Oil Company. But the dissolved parts continue to function as a trust exactly as they did before the dissolution decree. The anthracite coal trust has been declared guilty of illegal practices by the United States Supreme Court and the Interstate Commerce Commission. All of these trusts have been denounced in the halls of Congress during the whole long period of their development, and lawmakers have exhausted their ingenuity in framing statutes to destroy them or to limit their excessive prices or to put an end to their unfair trade practices. And yet all of these monopolies are admittedly stronger today than they ever were. . . .

The rewards of monopoly are so enormous, the stakes so vast that monopolists have a tremendous incentive to prevent regulating machinery being set up, and to control it after it is set up. The development of the modern political boss and his machine is in the public mind due to the control of patronage and contracts. As a matter of fact, this system has been developed principally with the money obtained from the privileged interests. These interests find that politicians in both parties can be subsidized so that they can procure the nomination of men for legislative and executive positions who can be trusted not to permit the passage of any laws affecting the privileges of the trusts. In case it is necessary to bow to public opinion and pass such laws, jokers are cleverly inserted which destroy or limit the effectiveness of the law, and the administration can put the execution of these laws in the hands of men friendly to the trusts. In the same way judgeships of our State and Federal courts are given to men who take the point of view of the trusts.

The La Follette Railroad Valuation Law provided that freight rates should be based upon the value of the railroad property and directed a valuation of such property based upon cost of construction, — the only basis upon which we can hope for just rates. The railroads fought this legislation for years and were finally defeated. But they got possession of the regulating machinery, and it now develops that after ten years of work and the expenditure of some $20,000,000 the whole plan of original cost has been abandoned. It further appears that even after exhaustive valuations have been made upon any basis, any finding will be taken to the Supreme Court.

In such litigation the reports of the valuation experts are not admissible as evidence, but the valuation details must be put in evidence all over again by witnesses, which will take years of time. When the decision is finally made by the court, prices and items will have materially changed, and the railroads can commence the trial all over again. The whole subject is so complicated by constitutional questions that the execution of the policy of regulation designed to curb monopoly is, under our political conditions, practically impossible.

This experience discloses the fact that, while you can put over with the public a policy such as regulation, after the policy triumphs in the law the great public sits back with a sigh of satisfaction, concludes that the job is finished, and can never be made to have any interest in the working of the machinery established to carry out the law. The execution of the law falls into the hands of the politicians, who, as I have shown, are controlled through political machines by the very interests which are to be regulated.

Co-opting the Regulators

GEORGE NORRIS

Senator George Norris was upset by the type of people President Calvin Coolidge was appointing to regulatory agencies. Based upon the evidence Norris presents and the arguments made by George Record in the preceding document, is it fair to conclude that an individual's advancement in the American political system depends upon how well he or she "plays the game" by giving the leaders what they want? What happens to those who show independence of action?

Laws enacted for the protection of life and property and for the regulation of transportation and business are of no value and of no effect if the executive department of government fails or neglects to enforce them. Recent executive appointments, made ostensibly for the purpose of giving effect to legislative acts of Congress, have raised a query in the minds of millions of law-abiding citizens as to whether a studied effort is not under way to put into office executive officials who are not honestly in sympathy with the enforcement of many of our regulatory laws. Appointments recently made to the Interstate Commerce Commission, to the Federal Trade Commission, and the action of the Executive with regard to the Tariff Commission, together with the appointment of Mr. Warren to be the head of the Department of Justice, all indicate that it is the intention of the present Administration to place representatives of so-called "big business" in charge of all the activities of the federal govern-

From George Norris, "Boring From Within," *The Nation*, September 16, 1925, pp. 297–299.

ment. I do not charge that any of the men appointed to the various positions are dishonest or incompetent, but without exception so far as I know every appointee has been some one who has no sympathy with the various acts of Congress passed for the purpose of regulating different activities but on the other hand believes that there should be practically no restraining hand placed upon trusts and monopolies.

The appointment of Mr. Warren as Attorney General would under ordinary circumstances have shocked the sensibilities of all our citizens. Virtually all his business life had been spent — very profitably spent — in carrying on the activities of the Sugar Trust. It stands uncontradicted that he, more than any other one man, was instrumental in organizing sugar factories in parts of the West in accordance with the wishes and the desires of Mr. Havemeyer, the head of the great Sugar Trust. These activities had ceased only a very short time before his appointment. It is fresh yet in the minds of all people that but a few years ago the Sugar Trust was engaged in a gigantic and stupendous scheme to deprive the government of millions of revenue. Both the producers of sugar beets and the consumers of sugar have been for many years more or less subject to the iniquities and the manipulations of this gigantic trust. The antitrust law was passed to save the people of the country, both producers and consumers, from the manipulations of such unholy organizations as this. To appoint one of the representatives of this gigantic monopoly as the head of the great Department of Justice, whose duty it is to protect the people from this wrong and to prosecute those who are guilty of violating the anti-trust laws, is, in every practical sense, a nullification of these laws, as effective as a repeal by act of Congress.

The appointment of Mr. Woodlock as a member of the Interstate Commerce Commission was another illustration of this scheme. Although the Senate had twice refused to confirm him, he was given a recess appointment and is now a member of that great commission. It is no secret that he is a railroad man. Everybody understands his viewpoint. His connection with the *Wall Street Journal* and his official connection with some of the great railroads of the country absolutely disqualify him in every moral sense from holding a position on the Interstate Commerce Commission. . . .

No charge of dishonesty is made against Mr. Woodlock. As far as I know he is able, and I presume he is perfectly conscientious, but his viewpoint disqualifies him for this position. He is put on a tribunal for the purpose of trying his own case, to regulate his own business. It would be like permitting a judge to try a case in which he was a party litigant. It would be the same as permitting the defendant in a law-suit to sit on the jury. The whole thing is contrary to the present-day civilization of justice and equality; and I submit that rather than turn the Interstate Commerce Commission over to railroad representatives, we ought to abolish the commission and permit the railroads to operate without a commission.

The same principle applies and the same course has been taken in the appointment of Mr. Humphrey as a member of the Federal Trade Commission.

He is a courageous and able executive officer. He has held public office for many years, and we are not left in doubt as to his attitude on public questions. During all his public service his viewpoint has stood out prominently, he has been a fearless advocate of big business in all lines. His record discloses that he can have no sympathy with the small business man who is protesting against unfair competition of trusts and monopolies. His appointment has changed the viewpoint of the commission. It now stands three to two in favor of the big-business idea.

What is the object of the Federal Trade Commission? The law was passed because it was thought that there was need of affording protection to the small business man against the monopoly and the machinations of trusts and combinations. Monopolistic concerns had, by unfair methods of competition, driven their competitors from the field, and the people of the country paid the expense in increased prices. Since Mr. Humphrey's advent this commission has decided that much of its business shall be transacted in secret. If the unfair business man goes before the commission and makes a secret promise that he will refrain from his illegal acts the entire matter is dismissed, no record is made, and the public gets no idea or knowledge of what actually transpired or happened. This means that a secret tribunal sits in judgment where the interests of all the people are involved and where millions of dollars are at stake.

Assuming, for the sake of argument, that the majority of the commission is perfectly honest and wants to do what is right, yet how long will it be until this secrecy brings fraud and corruption? The history of civilization demonstrates that one of the greatest evils of government is secrecy in governmental matters, and without exception history likewise demonstrates that no government has ever for any great length of time remained pure and just where the rights of men or property were subject to the adjudication of a tribunal whose deliberations took place in secret. Secret treaties have brought on many of the wars of the world. Secrecy in governmental affairs was one of the prime causes of the great World War. Secrecy in government through many years of struggle and hardship finally brought to ruin and degradation the great Russian government. Secrecy in a republic like ours is contrary to the very fundamental principles upon which our liberties rest. If the Federal Trade Commission, established for the purpose of protecting the small business man against the machinations of trusts and monopolies, is to be administered by men who believe that best results can be obtained by giving monopoly full sway, then why have the commission at all? If the men and corporations that are intended to be regulated by it are themselves to manage it and run it, then why not take the logical step — repeal the law and abolish the commission?

Another incident that illustrates the trend of the present Administration is the failure of the President to send the name of David J. Lewis, a member of the Tariff Commission, to the Senate, after he had given him a recess appointment. Again let us ask the question: What is the object of the Tariff Commission? It came after years of legislative struggle. Its object was to give the country as nearly as possible a scientific tariff — something that the country had never had. It was to establish a nonpartisan tribunal, a tribunal as free from prejudice and coercion as the Supreme Court itself, one that would gather the true facts necessary for the enactment of a tariff and lay these facts before the President and Congress. In order for the commission to accomplish any good or for its work to have any honest effect its investigations must be absolutely fair and its reports unshaded and untarnished, either by those opposed to any tariff or by those in favor of an unjustly high tariff. In the early part of the last Presidential campaign the commission was investigating the tariff on sugar. No one can deny the importance of such an investigation. Some wonderful disclosures came from that body. It appeared that there was at least one instance where members of the family of one of the commissioners, if not the commissioner himself, owned a large amount of stock the value of which was directly affected by the tariff. The term of office of Mr. Lewis, a member of the Tariff Commission, expired during this campaign. His ability, his honesty and integrity, and his courage have never been questioned. He was carrying out the spirit of the law in good faith. There were politicians who did not want this report on sugar made during the campaign. It would perhaps have been a political blunder to have refused a reappointment to Mr. Lewis at that particular time. The commission was nearly evenly divided. There were members who prior to their appointment had been known as lobbyists in favor of high-tariff schedules when tariff bills were pending before the committees of Congress. If a majority of the commission were composed of such men, then the work of the commission would be nullified. No one could have confidence in a report made by such a membership.

It seems to be the idea of those in control that the Tariff Commission should be composed of men whose whole lives disclose the fact that they have always advocated an exorbitantly high tariff. The action of the President would indicate that he is in sympathy with that idea. He reappointed Mr. Lewis during the campaign, but the appointment was only temporary; to become effective it required renewal when the Senate convened in December. By that time the campaign was over. The object of the temporary appointment had been accomplished, and the President declined to send the name of Mr. Lewis to the Senate, substituting someone else.

Thus one of the fairest and best men who ever sat on the commission was removed from office as soon as the campaign was over. But still the commission was not completely subject to the machinations of high-tariff barons. Mr. Culbertson and Mr. Costigan, members of that commission, who with Mr. Lewis had constituted a majority of it, were like him honestly and fearlessly carrying out the purpose of the law without fear or favor. Free traders on the one hand and high-tariff barons on the other had no effect upon their action. In order to further weaken the commission and to place it under the control of those who think the tariff ought to reach the sky Mr. Culbertson was given a diplomatic appointment. He was kicked upstairs in order to get him off the commission. I do not know what method can or will be taken to get rid of Mr. Costigan, if any. He still remains on the commission, standing there like a stone wall in the face of terrible opposition, striving to carry out the honest purposes of the act creating the commission. Let me in substance repeat my former question: Why have a tariff commission if we are to place it in control of tariff lobbyists and others interested in and believing in the mountain-high tariff? If the Tariff Commission is to become a one-sided tribunal, controlled by those who would use it only to bolster up a high tariff without regard to the truth, then why not let these people handle it directly instead of through the instrumentality of the commission? Why not after all abolish the commission and let those believing in special interests control the tariff directly? It would be much cheaper to let them have their way by simply enacting their ideas into law instead of going through expensive machinery of compelling the taxpayers to pay for a commission that, after all, has no other object than to carry out the ideas of its masters.

All of these commissions were established for a definite purpose. They came into existence in answer to an honest demand for the work which the law delegates to them. The anti-trust laws are likewise on the statute-books for the purpose of curing admitted evils. Are we now to nullify these laws? Are we to go back to the beginning and permit monopoly to have full sway, without any governmental curb? The effect of these appointments is to set the country back more than twenty-five years. It is an indirect but positive repeal of Congressional enactments, which no Administration, however powerful, would dare to bring about by any direct means. It is the nullification of federal law by a process of boring from within. If trusts, combinations, and big business are to run the government, why not permit them to do it directly rather than through this expensive machinery which was originally honestly established for the protection of the people of the country against monopoly and control?

The Ambiguity of Regulation
WILLIAM HUMPHREY

What are Federal Trade Commissioner Humphrey's complaints about the critics of the FTC? Is Humphrey's justification of secret deliberations by the FTC convincing? (Compare it to Norris's attack on secrecy in the preceding document.) How does Humphrey's view of the public interest differ from Record's or Norris's?

From William E. Humphrey, "Not Guilty Until Proved," *System, the Magazine of Business* (February 1927), pp. 153–155, 242.

Always, from earliest civilization, a great deal of talk has been heard about monopolies and unfair business practices. So today a great deal of agitation goes on about the practices of business, and especially about what is termed "big business."

Much loose talk flies about alleged violations of anti-trust laws. And most of it comes because between the white hemisphere of right and the black hemisphere of wrong is a gray middle zone in which even the wisest two men in the world cannot always agree on what is right and what is wrong.

Since the beginning of time a considerable part of humanity has been ever eager to serve as keeper for its brothers. Modern governments swarm with those who leap eagerly at the chance to point an accusing finger at their fellows. Crusading has since history began held its place as a king of sports.

Long public service has given me a profound distrust of the reformer. I feel a great public need is to make him see that a comparatively small proportion of folks need reforming — something we should all keep in mind.

Specifically when we think of business, we should not forget that the human element enters into the transaction of all business. Business represents a cross-section of the American people at its point of maximum diameter and accordingly possesses our average characteristics of failings and virtues.

From the vantage point of a position where the seamy side is constantly presented for my inspection it is nevertheless my conviction that 91% of the business of this nation is conducted honestly. And this is a most encouraging improvement from a few years ago. For this great change, most of the credit is due to business itself. Business has cleansed itself largely from two motives — honesty and selfishness. Business men are more and more realizing that it pays to be honest. It is the commissioners' belief that business does realize this which has caused most of the recent changes in the Federal Trade Commission's policy toward business.

The present majority is trying to make the chart and compass of the Commission that provision in the statute which says that the Commission shall proceed against any party it thinks guilty of violating the law, provided it believes it would be to the interest of the public so to do. I feel that the business men who have come in contact with the Commission during the last year realize this change in attitude, and I know that they fully indorse it.

Is this not the better way? Is it not better to proceed with caution in making our accusation? Should we not give the accused an opportunity to be heard before advertising him as a violator of law? Nowhere in this country, except in the Federal Trade Commission under the old rules, was it permitted to condemn a man first and try him afterwards; to convict first, and then hear the evidence.

Under the old rule the Commission was wrong in its accusations more than half the time. Certainly no citizen can "point with pride" to this record.

And the more clearly to illustrate just what an unjust accusation publicly handled can mean, let me cite a single case — leaving out, of course, the names.

The Commission issued a complaint against a corporation, charging it with having illegally acquired the stock of two of its competitors, in violation of the Clayton Act. To carry out this consolidation, the company had arranged to borrow some $40,000,000. When the case came to trial, it was found that the transaction was perfectly legitimate and would have been to the public interest. But, under the old rule, the Commission at the same time it filed the complaint issued a statement to the public purporting to give the facts.

The unfavorable publicity caused the bank to withdraw the loan, the credit of the company was destroyed, and it was driven into bankruptcy long before the hearing. Not only this company but also the two other companies with which it was to be consolidated were ruined. Some 3,000 workers were thrown out of employment. The innocent investors who owned the stocks and bonds of these concerns all lost their money. A great and legitimate industry was destroyed. The public and all others who were injured were entirely without redress.

When we changed the rule it was high time that governmental authorities should stop the practice of scourging a business first and ascertaining afterwards whether guilty or innocent.

The Federal Trade Commission's present policy is that we do not give out any facts on a case until we have tried it and know what the facts are. We have stopped convicting before the trial. . . .

The unfairness of proceeding at the outset to advertise the details of the accusations against those who are charged with violating the anti-trust law lies, among other things, in this: It is dishonest to say that there is a clear and distinct line of what is and what is not a violation of the anti-trust law; to claim that men always knowingly violate such laws; that men cannot in good faith sometimes be guilty of unfair practices.

Only a short time ago the Supreme Court of the United States, in two very important cases, divided four to five on whether a given set of facts constituted a violation of the anti-trust laws. If this great court with its eminent jurists cannot always agree on what facts constitute a violation of a given law, how can any one contend that business men — not learned in the law — can always know with certainty when they are guilty of violating the self-same law?

One thing for which the Commission is striving is the confidence of business and of the public. We cannot expect this confidence unless we deserve it. We cannot deserve it if we betray those who trust us. We want the business men of the country to know that the Commission will deal with them on the square. We want business to understand that any confidence given us will not be betrayed.

Then whence comes the violent opposition to the recent changes in the Federal Trade Commission procedure? It comes from that class — and that class only — which preaches the doctrine that success and dishonesty are synonymous in American business. The attitude of the majority of the Commission is expressed in what I call its "creed":

We do not believe that success is a crime.

We do not believe that failure is a virtue.

We do not believe that wealth is presumptively wrong.

We do not believe that poverty is presumptively right.

We do not believe that industry, economy, honesty, and brains should be penalized.

We do not believe that incompetency, extravagance, idleness, and inefficiency should be glorified.

We do not believe that big business and crooked business are synonymous. True, we will give closer scrutiny to big business than to small because of its greater power for good or evil.

We believe that 90% of American business is honest and anxious to obey the law. We want to help this 90% of honesty. We want to control or destroy the 10% that is crooked.

And the element that is helping us most in our work is business itself, which has needed but an intimation that ours was a constructive endeavor to insure maximum cooperation in the work it is ours to do.

Finessing the Regulators
C. H. PEASE

C. H. Pease, responding to an article by Ernest Greenwood, challenges what Pease views as propaganda. What is the answer to the question Pease raises: "If these corporations are permitted to dominate the sources of public information, what becomes of the individual citizen?"

Evidence before the [Federal Trade] commission indicates that the National Electric Light Association, known as the NELA, is made up of electric light and power companies; instructors, teachers, and practitioners of engineering and related sciences; companies or firms engaged in the manufacture of electric apparatus or equipment for the production or use of electric energy, and members and employees of those companies; firms of electrical jobbers, contractors, dealers, electrical or mechanical engineers; publishers' associations or others who are interested in advancing the use of electrical energy. It operates through twelve geographical divisions with headquarters throughout the country.

A joint committee organized during the war was revived and reorganized in 1927, and is made up of the representatives of the NELA, the American Gas Association, and the American Electric Railway Association, which to-

From C. H. Pease, "Facts *Are* Facts," *The Independent,* July 28, 1928, pp. 78–80.

gether control fifty per cent of the companies of the United States and more
than ninety per cent of the total output.

The NELA maintains a department known as the "Public Relations Service," which includes the Coöperation with Educational Institutions Committee, Customer Ownership Committee, Information Bureau Organizations Committee, Industrial Relations Committee, Manufacturers Advertising Committee,
Public Speaking Committee, Relations with Financial Institutions Committee, Woman's Committee, and Public Policy Committee. The latter is made
up of representative men, a number of whom have been past presidents of the
association itself.

There are in addition twenty-eight public-service information bureaus organized and operated within the States that are covered by the association.
These bureaus pass along to the public news material and information regarding the utilities, and assist the States and communities in building themselves
up, according to Paul S. Clapp, managing director of the NELA. The association maintains a director of publicity who acts as a sort of central head to
the various State publicity bureaus.

Says Mr. Clapp: "If I had something dealing with electrical matters that
I wished to have published in rural newspapers in a small town of say 5,000
to 10,000 people, I would send the material to the State director with the
suggestion that he have it published if possible." The NELA furnishes advertising copy to all member companies and all other electric light and power
companies in the country without cost. These advertisements quote the view-
points of prominent Americans on the great inefficiency of government in
business. The association sends out master plates from which matrices or elec-
trotypes can be made.

The State bureaus furnish a news service to the press in their territory
covering all questions dealing with public utilities, which includes articles and
reports of speeches opposing public ownership and legislation which is not
favored by the utilities. Local members are urged to advertise in local papers
and cultivate friendly relations with the papers, and if the paper does not use
the news service, the member is urged to call it to the attention of the editor
and urge that it be used. The local member becomes the local agent and representative of the bureau.

The Committee on Coöperation with Educational Institutions, among its
other activities, is making a national survey of the public schools and educational institutions to determine the character of instruction that is being given
on utility subjects, to examine all textbooks used, and if the instruction given
or the textbook used does not meet the approval of the committee, it seeks to
have both "corrected" so as to conform as nearly as possible to the views of
the private utilities. The various State publicity bureaus also furnish a regular
service to high schools and colleges, consisting of circulars and pamphlets giving utility information, and also expressing views and opinions dealing with
the economics of the utility industry and the advantages of private ownership.
Schools are encouraged to solicit and use this service in their classes. In some

instances special textbooks have been written under the direction and at the expense of the utilities to replace objectionable books in use.

The Public Speaking Committee trains speakers to present the utilities' point of view to women's clubs, luncheon clubs, chambers of commerce, and civic organizations. It employs college professors and well-known public men to give addresses throughout the country dealing with utility problems and legislative measures from the standpoint of private utilities. Many of these addresses are made without the connection of the utility companies with the speaker being disclosed. Reports of these speeches are furnished the Associated Press, and through the various State publicity bureaus are sent to the rural papers throughout the country. The Customer Ownership Committee attempts to interest customers in investing in preferred stock, without voting power, on the theory that a customer who has an investment in a utility company is not so liable to exhibit Bolshevist tendencies.

Here is the most perfectly organized, the best oiled, and the most effective machine for propaganda purposes that has ever been set up. Through this agency, backed by the pressure of millions of dollars of advertising annually expended through local papers and the large budgets raised for the support of its activities, the organized utilities are able to reach into practically every community and utilize the local press, to propagandize the public schools and colleges, to employ the best speaking talent in the country to present their point of view before practically every civic and commercial organization in the country.

The Joint Committee maintains a powerful lobby in Washington, but the testimony shows that it does not attempt to influence Congress directly. It operates indirectly through its far-flung propaganda organization to bring pressure from back home. This is a thousand times more effective than a direct approach. But it takes a tremendous organization like this to make it effective.

Admitted, says Mr. Greenwood to all this. What of it, and why not? Is it all right for John Jones to advocate his theories, but a crime for Sam Smith to do the same thing, merely because Sam Smith has laid up a little money for his old age?

But it is not quite so simple as that. Mr. Greenwood has missed an underlying factor that complicates the question. The private utilities enjoy special privileges, conferred upon them by the municipal governments. They are granted the use of public property and are given a complete monopoly to supply a service to the public which has become an absolute necessity. They are the beneficiaries of special privilege. In this capacity they must submit to certain restrictions and limitations which are not imposed on the other forms of private business that do not enjoy these special privileges.

For the protection of the public interest, the municipal government regulates the methods of doing business, the kind of service furnished, the rates that may be charged, and other important matters. If the public interest requires, other restrictions may also be applied. The purpose of the present inquiry is to ascertain whether it is safe to permit the unrestricted and unregulated right of these public-service corporations to propagandize on the tremendous scale that is now indicated. Will not the effect be to nullify the power of regulation by enabling the controlled to become the controller? If these corporations are permitted to dominate the sources of public information, what becomes of the individual citizen? So it is not so much a matter of whether a fact is a fact. The real question is, What is being done by the utilities, what does it mean, and what is the effect of it all?

I will not attempt to discuss the ethics of subsidizing nationally known writers to produce books, pamphlets, and magazine articles which appear to express the independent thought and views of the writers. Mr. Greenwood contends that the views of these writers are not affected thereby. Perhaps he is right. No one knows for certain except the writers themselves, and perhaps they do not. Still —

I am reminded of an acquaintance of mine who claimed to be a horticulturist and a soil expert. One day he received a proposition from a Texas real-estate promoter who proposed to subdivide a large cattle ranch and sell it out to "home-suckers." He wanted my horticultural friend to make an analysis and report as to whether it was good citrus soil or not. He said he would pay $25 and expenses for the report. However, he added, if it should turn out that it was really a good citrus soil, then he could well afford to pay $500.

"That man thinks he can buy me, but he is mistaken," commented the virtuous expert.

"Are you going to accept his proposition?" I asked.

"Oh, I might as well," was the reply. "But I am going to report exactly what I find," he added, and I have no doubt that this is exactly what took place. But — Upon his return I asked him what he found. "The finest citrus soil in the State," he said without a moment's hesitation.

◆ MODERN ESSAY ◆

Why Regulation Fails
PETER H. SCHUCK

The debate over regulation today is very much like it was a half century ago, except that today there is the additional question whether the economy is so complicated that it is beyond the control of any agency. In this essay, Peter

From Peter H. Schuck, "Why Regulation Fails," *Harper's Magazine*, September 1975, pp. 22–29. Copyright 1975 by Peter H. Schuck and reprinted by special permission of the author.

Schuck gives his views on why regulation fails. Are his views closer to Wilson's or Roosevelt's? How does Schuck define the public interest which the government should serve? The major concern in the 1920s was how to stop unfair business practices. Today, much government regulation concerns human safety rather than business competition. Is there a difference between regulating business competition and regulating a complete industry on environmental or safety issues? What is the best way to prevent regulation from being dominated by the regulated? How much regulation is enough?

. . . . Since the creation of the ICC in 1887, there have been four major waves of federal regulatory legislation. Regulation of meat, food, and drugs began in 1906. The Wilson Administration launched the Federal Reserve System and the Federal Trade Commission. Two decades later the economic havoc wreaked by the depression led to the creation of a plethora of new federal agencies to regulate, among other industries, investment banking and securities, airlines, natural gas and electric utilities, communications, agricultural production, and housing. During the last few years, economic regulation per se — the regulation of rates, entry, and standards of service — have been extended to the petroleum and petroleum products industry. Indeed, during the period of economic controls from 1971 to 1974, virtually the entire economy was subject to price regulation. Even more significant, however, was the dramatic expansion during the 1960s and 1970s of health and safety regulation in the fields of environmental protection, occupational conditions, intrastate meat and poultry inspection, food and drugs, radiation, and product safety, particularly auto safety. The economic distress of 1974 and 1975 has generated desperate calls for regulation of credit allocation and a restoration of wage and price controls. A system of national health insurance will require extensive regulation of health-care providers. Yet, just as the nation is preparing for a new spasm of regulation of enterprises previously governed largely by market forces, government is being urged — often by former advocates of regulation — to dismantle many of the existing regulatory systems. Because the outcome of these efforts will have profound implications for our politics and our economic life, it is important to understand what is at stake and what are the likely consequences of both approaches.

Much government regulation of business is widely accepted as necessary. Some businesses permitting dramatic economies of scale — generation of electricity is an example — supposedly require regulation because competition is not feasible. Yet when economist George Stigler tested this hypothesis by comparing rates and profits for regulated and unregulated electric utilities, he concluded that regulation made little difference. Stigler's explanation was twofold: even a monopoly utility faces competition from other energy sources, and what entrepreneurs do is simply beyond the control of even the most assiduous regulator. Another reason for regulation is "externality" — the effect of a transaction upon "innocent bystanders" or society as a whole (air pollution, for example). Many externalities, however, could be limited or eliminated with minimal regulation if effective compensation or cost-shifting mechanisms could be implemented — for example, effluent fees are imposed on polluters on the Ruhr River. Regulation may also be justified if serious market imperfections exist, such as monopolistic conditions, intractable consumer ignorance, or ineffective compensation mechanisms. Much health and safety regulation falls into this category. Even here, however, nonregulatory innovations, such as no-fault liability insurance, class actions, and cooperative purchasing by consumer aggregations, could reduce the need for much regulation. And some market imperfections, even when they persist, may be less inefficient or inequitable in their effects than the distortions inherent in the political-regulatory system.

The burden of justification lies heavy on the regulator. For government regulation is fundamentally at variance with the philosophical assumptions underlying the American political system. We are a liberal society, rooted in utilitarian ideas about the relation between citizen and state. The primary notion holds that the individual is the sole judge of his own interest and welfare and that individual satisfactions, be they "altruistic" or "selfish," are society's raison d'être. In this view, voluntary exchanges of value between individuals, as in a market transaction, are socially beneficial; by definition, such exchanges increase the welfare of both contracting individuals (else they would not engage in them), and, unless third parties are adversely affected, the welfare of society is thereby increased.

In addition to vindicating the liberal notion of *equity,* such voluntary exchanges between individuals promote *economic efficiency.* For all of these voluntary exchanges, when taken together, will tend to allocate the society's resources in ways that will maximize the satisfactions of the individuals in the society and thus put the resources to their best use.

Given these assumptions, government regulation will — except in the case of natural monopoly, externalities, or other market failure — always yield an inferior social result to free, voluntary exchanges between individuals. By specifying and limiting the terms under which transactions between individuals may take place, a regulation supplants their evaluations of their own interests and substitutes for these the judgment of the regulator. Individual and social welfare will be diminished thereby, particularly in the case of economic (i.e., rate and entry) regulation.

First. Certain transactions which both parties deem to be in their interests cannot be consummated because the regulation prohibits them. When an agency sets a rate, it prohibits all sales at a lower rate, even if both parties would gain by such a sale.

Second. Certain transactions which one or both parties deem to be contrary to their interests will nevertheless have to be consummated at the behest of the regulator, thus requiring either government coercion or a subsidy (whose cost will have to be borne by someone else). Companies are compelled by the Jones Act to engage high-cost American ships to carry cargo between American ports; consumers and shippers pay the compulsory surcharge.

Third. Regulation, by prescribing minimum standards which all must meet, will tend to limit entry and reduce diversity and consumer choice while increasing the costs of some, and perhaps all, sellers. Requiring that all television repair shops be licensed, for example, seems to have the effect of increasing repair costs and limiting competition, without apparent effect on the level of consumer fraud. Regulators have little use for the part-time electronics whiz who repairs TV sets in his garage during his spare time at low prices. If he does not obtain a license — either because obtaining one would be too costly or because he cannot meet the licensing requirements — he will either be driven out of business or will have to operate illegally; his customers will either be denied low-cost service or will have to pay some premium to compensate him for running the risk of detection. Similarly, regulation of taxicabs may assure consumers that no drug addict or alcoholic will drive a licensed cab and that such cabs are inspected three times a year. It will assure them of little else, however, other than fewer cabs on the streets and inflated fares. Even those who are fortunate enough to be picked up by gypsy cabs will be paying more than the free market price would be.

Fourth. Where it does not eliminate competition, regulation will tend to distort it, often in grotesque ways. The Federal Aviation Act frowns on price competition among the interstate airlines, and the CAB quickly pounces on any sign of rate-cutting. This results in competition being trivialized into "booze wars," "lounge wars," and fuselage decoration, with the passengers compelled to pay the bill.

Fifth. Where regulation appears to benefit one economic group, it usually does so by exacting a subsidy — often a hidden one — from other groups. Product safety regulation subsidizes those people who would have been injured by negligent manufacturers and would not have received compensation for their injuries. This subsidy occurs at the expense of the far larger number who would have been compensated for injury or escaped it entirely. Regulation of auto emissions primarily benefits residents of congested cities, whether or not they own cars, and the pollution-control industry; the costs are borne by all car owners, rich and poor, in Durango, Colorado, as well as in Los Angeles. Such regulatory cross-subsidies may or may not be justified on other noneconomic grounds, and they often reflect the will of Congress. Since regulation is necessarily a political process, it is not surprising that the groups exacting the subsidies are often those with the most political clout and that efficiency and equity considerations are usually ignored. Politically well-connected maritime interests, for example, extract vast sums annually from consumers because of federally authorized price fixing and other subsidies.

Sixth. Regulatory standards will tend to be either too high or too low to maximize social welfare; rarely will an agency strike the right balance or maintain it amid changing conditions. With regard to regulated rates, "too high" means that some or all producers will enjoy excessive profits, particularly if the regulated rates are floors or the agency prevents new competition from entering the industry. "Too low" means that incentives to producers will be insufficient to sustain adequate production. The Phase II price freeze in 1973, for example, caught the cattle industry in a squeeze between feed costs that were at a record high and moderate wholesale prices. Consumers paid dearly for the shortages that the freeze induced.

Seventh. The regulatory agency will rarely command the resources necessary to scrutinize the costs or behavior of each producer or firm that it regulates. Several years ago, the FCC, with an annual budget of $31 million, publicly acknowledged its inability to evaluate a proposed rate increase by ATT, with more than $31 *billion* in assets. Because of this chronic disparity and the costly "regulatory lag" that accompanies delay in agency decisions (the ICC took twelve years to approve the Chicago, Rock Island, and Pacific merger and before the decision could be made final, the line went bankrupt), regulators must take shortcuts which, while making their tasks manageable, also suppress the enormous variety and differentials between firms. When the Federal Power Commission in 1954 undertook regulation of producer rates for natural gas, it began by determining "just and reasonable" rates for each of the more than 3,000 individual producers. By 1960 the sheer number of backed-up rate proceedings had swamped the commission, and it was compelled to simplify the process drastically by lumping all producers together into fewer than a dozen "areas." Each producer in a given area was required to sell gas at or below the same "area rate," no matter what the cost-and-profit profile of the particular producer. Because even area data were difficult and expensive to compile, "area rates" were themselves determined by the commission on the basis of area or nationwide *averages*. The relationship between an area rate and the economic profile of any particular firm became further attenuated.

Even area-rate regulation, however, proved too complex for the commission; the Southern Louisiana area rate was not affirmed by the Supreme Court until 1974. In June 1974, the commission took the inevitable final step in this unhappy history, issuing a single "national rate" applicable to all but the smaller producers. Within six months, this "single" rate had been increased by almost 20 percent, had been repeatedly encumbered with exceptions, exclusions, and amendments, and had begun its long journey to the never-never land of judicial review. To an even greater extent than its predecessors, the national rate was an artificial construct, bearing about as much resemblance to the economic profiles of the individual producers as the "average American" does to the diverse society that he is said to exemplify.

The Federal Power Commission suggests another dilemma of regulation. In order to rationally regulate a market, one must regulate the *entire* market; if part of the market is unregulated, exchanges not permitted by the regulator will tend to flow into the unregulated sector, eluding control. Because only interstate sales are price-regulated by the FPC, an increasing quantity of natural gas has been sold and consumed in the states where the gas was produced, often for "inferior" uses and at prices four and five times the regulated prices. Similarly the Federal Reserve System has seen its control over the nation's money supply — and thus its regulatory influence — dwindle as more banks relinquish their membership for the more permissive environment of state regulation.

The obvious remedy for this regulatory impotence — expansion of the agency's authority to embrace the unregulated sector — only thrusts more intractable difficulties upon the regulator. As the number and diversity of transactions to be regulated grow arithmetically, the regulator's informational, coordinating, and political needs expand geometrically. The difference between the resources (staff, information, political influence) required by the ICC when it regulated only railroads and those that it requires today, when it must regulate motor carriers, water carriers, and freight forwarders as well, is a qualitative difference, a quantum leap in regulatory inadequacy. The ineluctable tendency of agencies to expand their activities spawns an equally immutable regulatory failure. The more it *may* regulate, the less it *can* regulate, relative to its responsibilities.

Regulation tends to reduce the incentives for technological or marketing innovation; often, it snuffs them out altogether. In 1974 the CAB flatly rejected a proposal by London-based Laker Airways to fly regular "no-frills" flights between New York and London for $125 each way. Professional licensing authorities have long used state regulatory power to maintain the status quo. Just as some medical societies, led by the AMA, stifled the development of innovative group health organizations, state bar associations have followed the lead of the American Bar Association, using their authority to thwart "closed panel" prepaid group legal service plans.

But for regulatory antediluvianism, the ICC leads the pack — backward. When the Southern Railway, a particularly well-managed and dynamic company, developed a larger and far more efficient freight car — the "Big John" — and sought to use it for the carriage of grain at vastly reduced rates, the ICC quickly stepped in to protect those carriers and shippers who would lose business to Southern. Only after four years and a successful appeal to the Supreme Court did Southern manage to introduce the innovation. In 1974 a major motor carrier, Pacific Intermountain Express Company, announced a stunning innovation. In an industry with adamantine resistance to change and an aversion to punctuality, PIE proposed to guarantee on-time delivery in exchange for a 10 percent premium; if PIE was late, *all* freight charges would be refunded. Over the vigorous protest of the Department of Transportation, the ICC ruled that this plan amounted to an offer of "free" transportation and was illegal.

Other agencies share the ICC's hostility to change. The FCC has stunted, perhaps irrevocably, the development of cable TV. The CAB labored long and mightily to arrest the growth of charter carriers offering low-cost transportation. The Forest Service has resisted multiple-use management and wilderness protection. The Federal Reserve Board has moved to squelch banking innovations which threatened to upset the existing competitive equilibrium.

While there is considerable agreement on the pernicious effects of government regulation, critics disagree about the root causes of regulatory failure and thus about appropriate remedies. One group, led by Ralph Nader, stresses the "capture" of regulatory agencies by the regulated industry, arguing that this process hopelessly compromises the integrity and independence of regulatory decisions. The "capture" hypothesis is particularly compelling at the state level, where the law often *requires* regulatory agencies, such as pollution-control authorities or pharmacy licensing boards, to be controlled by representatives of the regulated industry. Numerous federal agencies, from the Food and Drug Administration to the Federal Power Commission, have also been staffed at the highest levels with former and future industry members. Overt conflicts of interest occasionally surface. In 1974 the public learned that Robert C. Bowen, a former Phillips Petroleum executive, had helped write an obscure Federal Energy Office regulation that allowed crude oil producers, including Phillips, to count certain crude oil costs twice and to pass these extra costs — amounting to more than $300 million — on to consumers. At Congressional hearings called to investigate this "double dipping," it was revealed that then FEO head William Simon had repeatedly but unsuccessfully been urged to remove Bowen, but that Simon had demurred, feeling that Bowen was acting only in a technical "advisory" role. Even as these events were unfolding, the Ford Administration was attempting — unsuccessfully, as it turned out — to confirm Andrew Gibson as the new head of the same agency. Yet Gibson was then the president of a company deriving its revenues entirely from the oil and utilities industries, which was itself controlled by a major oil company and would be paying Gibson almost $1 million after his departure from the firm.

The "capture" of regulatory agencies often proceeds in subtler, less personalized ways. Industry-dominated advisory committees, such as the National Petroleum Council, channel ideas, data, priorities, and political support to regulators desperate for these resources, often behind closed doors. Typically, the agency cannot perform its regulatory duties without obtaining much economic and technical information, almost all of which must come from the regulated industry. Perhaps the most extreme case of agency dependence upon industry information is the Federal Power Commission's use of American Gas Association estimates of natural gas reserves to support its entire regulatory program. Although the AGA statistics had been demonstrated to be unreliable, self-serving, and compiled in possible violation of the antitrust laws, the FPC consistently failed to conduct an effective audit of natural gas reserves. When the Federal Trade Commission investigated the matter, the AGA estimates often turned out to be wildly inaccurate — understated by as much as 1,000 percent — and AGA reporting procedures were "tantamount to collusive price-rigging," according to the FTC staff study.

Certain reforms have commended themselves to those who see "capture" as the predominant obstacle to effective regulation: more rigorous conflict-of-interest laws; recruitment of consumer-oriented regulatory officials from sectors other than private industry; freedom-of-information reforms and "sunshine" laws; laws protecting whistle-blowers inside government agencies; financial assistance to consumer and environmental groups seeking to participate in the regulatory process; and the creation of a nonregulatory, federal-level Agency for Consumer Advocacy, empowered to represent consumer interests before regulatory agencies. These are essentially procedural reforms (although likely to have important policy consequences), and their efficacy presupposes that the problem with regulations is its proindustry bias.

To the Ash Council on Executive Organization, however, the difficulty of regulation lay elsewhere — in its lack of accountability, its glacial pace, and its rigid approach to problem solving. Those deficiencies, it believed, inhered in the formal "independence" of many regulatory agencies, their insulation from conventional political forces, particularly those emanating from the White House. To remedy this structural problem, the council proposed structural solutions. Most regulatory agencies would come under the direct control of the President (much as the Department of Transportation is now): an administrative court would be established to review agency decisions, and the organizational structure of the agencies would be streamlined.

Yet a third group of critics, led by economist Milton Friedman, regards these procedural and organizational reforms as essentially innocuous and of only marginal significance. To this group, the fundamental problem is the vast complexity and inter-relationship of the economic system and the inability of even the most well-intentioned, well-informed regulator to make even minimally "rational" decisions in the face of this complexity. This view holds that the regulatory actions of even a benign government will invariably produce unintended and unforeseen consequences which will dwarf the problem that regulation was designed to solve.

Such critics concede, as they must, that market imperfections often exist. They stress, however, that government intervention inevitably carries with it far more serious distortions of a political and bureaucratic nature. The political system is based upon majority rule and will tend to ignore the wishes of small minorities with special tastes; the economic market, however, usually enables even a tiny group — for example, those who wish to read pornographic literature or those who want to smoke low-nicotine cigarettes — to satisfy their desires if they are willing to pay for them. People tend to be far better informed about the products and services available in the economic market than about the issues and politicians available to them as voters in the political market; the selling of political candidates is at least as deceptive and banal as the selling of antiperspirants, and consumers know even less about the bureaucrats who will actually do the regulating. Moreover, the degree of concentration in economic markets is far less than the concentration of political power in the Democratic and Republican parties, and there is no Antitrust Division to police the political sphere. No seller of goods or services, except perhaps the rare monopolist, can long ignore the desires of its customers and still remain in business. The bureaucrat, however, in his own regulatory sphere has no competitor. Having no profit motive to guide his decisions, and no competitors to threaten him, he will respond to other motives, such as empire-building or buck-passing, which have nothing to do with consumer needs. He usually cannot be sued, cannot be fired, cannot even be identified.

Finally, regulation of private decisions by government inevitably increases the power of the state and reduces the autonomy of individual citizens. The centralization of power — the power to decide what products will or will not be produced and consumed, the power to prosecute for violations of innumerable regulations, the power to prescribe how people must treat one another in the most delicate human relationships — carries with it serious dangers to a democratic society: abuse of power, the sapping of private initiative and energy, the creation of a dependent and insecure citizenry.

To critics across the ideological spectrum from Milton Friedman to Ralph Nader, the remedy for these evils is to deregulate large sectors of the American economy. Abolition of rate regulation by the ICC, the CAB, and the Federal Maritime Commission are at the top of many reform agendas, while a substantial number would extend deregulation to the Federal Communications Commission, the oil and gas industry, and agricultural production as well. A few critics of regulation would even abolish the Food and Drug Administration, on the theory that it has retarded the introduction of drugs which could benefit consumers.

No Congress would go so far. But more limited regulatory reforms probably have far more public support than ever before. Certain political realities, however, remain inescapable — chiefly, the superior organization and political influence of those economic and bureaucratic interests served by regulation, compared to the diffuse and unorganized consumer interests with a stake in its reform. Which rural Congressman will be so suicidal as to advocate abandonment of subsidized rail, air, or trucking service to his district? Which Senator will be willing to say no to the politically hyperactive maritime unions and carriers seeking ever more generous subsidies in order to maintain jobs and profits? On the evidence so far, precious few.

Issue

Democracy and Presidential Leadership

To what our president represents, we react with passion.

Michael Novak, 1974

In a moment Roosevelt was gone. The audience stood in its tracks for quite some time, as if still under the spell, and then quietly began to leave.

Raymond Clapper, 1936

In this section we examine two presidents. One failed to provide the moral and symbolic leadership the people demanded and was consequently rejected. The other so captured the imagination and hearts of the American people that he was reelected as long as he lived. By comparing Herbert Hoover and Franklin Roosevelt, we begin to explore the issue of presidential leadership.

In the documents that follow, two aspects of presidential leadership are considered: the presidential program and the presidential style. Herbert Hoover's program, the New Individualism, was characterized by voluntarism and limited government action. Franklin Roosevelt's New Deal required compliance and extended government authority. Both programs had their defenders and enemies as well as their similarities and differences. Yet the New Deal captured the imagination of the American people while the New Individualism did not. Was it Roosevelt's program that led to his electoral triumphs?

In the case of Roosevelt and Hoover, however, one cannot separate the program from the personalities. Hoover did not inspire confidence. He appeared to be isolated from the public and lacked the human touch that people expect of their president. As Hoover could not inspire confidence in himself as a leader, his program was doomed to failure. Roosevelt, by contrast, was the ultimate politician who used the mass media to talk with the American people. His continued insistence that there would be no forgotten Americans and the ease with which he dealt with average Americans created a bond of friendship between the president and the people which assured continued popularity in spite of the shortcomings of the New Deal. And yet, there were those who worried about the power for evil as well as good in the willingness to shower such devotion on a single leader.

Hoover and Roosevelt demonstrate the importance of both style and program to successful presidential leadership. They also raise questions about what Americans need in a president.

◆ DOCUMENTS ◆

Desperation and Democracy

TIME

In 1932 World War I veterans marched on Washington to plead for government relief from their economic distress. While in Washington, the veterans clashed with federal troops sent to remove them from the city. Given the extent of the violence, did Hoover have an alternative to the use of federal troops?

When War came in 1917 William Hushka, 22-year-old Lithuanian, sold his St. Louis butcher shop, gave the proceeds to his wife, joined the Army. He was sent to Camp Funston, Kan. where he was naturalized. Honorably discharged in 1919, he drifted to Chicago, worked as a butcher, seemed unable to hold a steady job. His wife divorced him, kept their small daughter. Long jobless, in June he joined a band of veterans marching to Washington to fuse with the Bonus Expeditionary Force. "I might as well starve there as here," he told his brother. At the capital he was billeted in a Government-owned building on Pennsylvania Avenue. One of thousands, he took part in the demonstration at the Capitol the day Congress adjourned without voting immediate cashing of the Bonus.

Last week William Hushka's Bonus for $528 suddenly became payable in full when a police bullet drilled him dead in the worst public disorder the capital has known in years.

Prelude to Washington's bloody battle was a third march toward the White House by some 200 Reds, led by Communist John Pace, Michigan contractor. It was a routine performance which the police efficiently squelched with much pate-thwacking and nine arrests. One veteran climbed a tree, kept shouting "We want our Bonus!" until police dragged him down, gagged him. This radical demonstration, outlawed by the regular B. E. F., was important only in that it gave Administration officials the idea of blaming Communists for all that followed.

From *Time Magazine,* August 8, 1932, pp. 5–6.

More serious trouble was presented by the Treasury's attempt to repossess Government property on the south side of Pennsylvania Avenue, three blocks west of the Capitol. Wholesale warehouses, a cheap hotel, automobile showrooms, a Chinese restaurant and an undertaking shop occupied the row of old ugly brick buildings on this site. The U. S. had bought up the land as part of its plan to beautify the Federal City. The plot was to be converted into a park. Wreckers had knocked the walls out of the buildings when the B. E. F. began to arrive last May. Brigadier General Pelham Glassford, Washington's long-legged, kindly police chief, arranged to halt demolition, have veterans quartered in the skeletonized buildings. With Congress gone and the Bonus fight over, the Treasury sought to evict the veterans and start work again. Four times 200-odd veterans were ordered out. Four times they refused to budge.

One morning last week General Glassford finally persuaded Walter W. Waters, the B. E. F.'s curly-headed commander, to evacuate his men on the promise of new quarters elsewhere. Treasury agents arrived at 10 a. m. to clear the buildings. Most of the veterans refused to leave. Police helped the Federal men do their job. Hundreds of veterans swelled to thousands as men flocked from other B. E. F. camps to the scene to watch the eviction. By noon the buildings had been practically cleared when a trio of veterans carrying a U. S. flag tried to march back in. Police blocked them. Somebody tossed a brick. "There's a fight!" went up the cry. More bricks flew.

"Give the cops hell!" a veteran shouted. His massed companions pressed in upon the police, now flailing with their clubs. The fighting spread with quick contagion. One policeman had his head bashed in. Veterans trampled him. Blood streamed down others' faces. Veterans swung scrap iron, hunks of concrete, old boards. General Glassford rushed into the mêlée, was knocked flat by a brick. Before he could get up, a veteran snatched off his gold police badge. A riot call brought 800 extra police to battle several thousand of the B. E. F.

"Be peaceful, men! Be calm!" shouted General Glassford. "Let's not throw any more bricks. They're mighty hard and hurt. You've probably killed one of my best officers."

"Hell, that's nothing," a veteran flung back. "Lots of us were killed in France."

Meanwhile hot-headed veterans had seeped back into their old quarters to tussle with police amid the rubble. Officers George Shinault and Miles Zamanezck were cornered on the second floor. "Let's get 'em!" someone shouted. The two policemen pulled their revolvers. A half dozen shots banged out. William Hushka keeled over with a bullet in his heart (1:25 p. m.). Two other veterans were wounded. One of them, Eric Carlson, 38, of Oakland, Cal., died later.

The street fighting gradually subsided. A legless veteran inside the Government building loudly challenged the police to remove him. He was ignored. General Glassford withdrew his forces. The B. E. F. cooled off, recovered its head. Commander Waters, who had kept out of the fray, nervously declared: "The men got out of control. There's nothing I can do."

But there was something the three District of Columbia Commissioners governing the city could do and they did it. President Hoover was lunching when the Commissioners called to ask him for Federal troops. "Tell them to put their request in writing," said the President. They wrote:

"A serious riot occurred. . . . This area contains thousands of brickbats and these were used by the rioters in their attack upon the police. . . . It will be impossible to maintain law & order except by the free use of firearms which will make the situation a dangerous one. The presence of Federal troops will result in far less violence and bloodshed."

Without declaring martial law (he did not have to because Washington is Federal territory), President Hoover ordered Secretary of War Hurley to call out the Army from Fort Myer in nearby Virginia. Secretary Hurley passed the command along to handsome, well-tailored General Douglas MacArthur, Chief of Staff, in the following crisp dispatch (2:55 p. m.):

"You will have United States troops proceed immediately to the scene of the disorder. Surround the affected area and clear it without delay. . . . Any women and children should be accorded every consideration and kindness. Use all humanity consistent with the execution of this order."

Six minutes later cavalry and infantry, to the number of 1,000 men began moving into Washington for an encounter with the B. E. F. for which the War Department had long been preparing. In their wake came five small tanks, a fleet of trucks. Bayonets glittered in the sun, equipment clanked over the pavement as the force marched slowly up Pennsylvania Avenue. Reaching the "affected area" (4:45 p. m.) troopers rode straight into the hooting, booing ranks of the B. E. F. Veterans scrambled out of the way of swinging sabres, trampling hoofs. Steel-helmeted infantrymen with drawn revolvers advanced 20 abreast. Behind them came others with rifles lowered, bayonets prodding.

Suddenly tear gas bombs began to pop on the street. The soldiers put on their masks, pushed slowly on while the heavy grey fumes cut great gaps in the retreating throng of veterans. Citizen spectators tangled with the soldiers, were ordered to "get the hell out of the way." The Government buildings were methodically gassed. A huge Negro sat in a crotch of a tree, waving a U. S. flag and sonorously chanting: "God that gave us this h'yar country, h'ep us now."

The unarmed B. E. F. did not give the troopers a real fight. They were too stunned and surprised that men wearing their old uniform should be turned against them. Here & there veterans would toss back gas bombs with half-forgotten skill, kick the troopers' horses, throw a few bricks, swear bitter oaths at the impassive regulars, most of them youngsters. But resistance was wholly unorganized.

General MacArthur directed the military operation, tears streaming down his cheeks, not from emotion but from the fumes of the bombs. When his cavalry rode down a group of veterans with a U. S. flag, a spectator sang out:

"The American flag means nothing to me after this." General MacArthur snapped: "Put that man under arrest if he opens his mouth again."

The rout of the B. E. F. from Pennsylvania Avenue broke its back. But the military was not yet through. It "gassed" small scattered camps in the vicinity of the Capitol, shoved out their occupants, left smoking ruins behind. By 9 p. m. the troopers had advanced to the Anacostia bridge, beyond which on the mudflats lay Bonus City, the B. E. F.'s main encampment. The camp commander rushed out waving a white shirt for a truce, asked for time to evacuate the several hundred women and children. He got an hour's grace.

As the infantry moved into Bonus City (10:14 p. m.) gassing each wretched shack and shanty, veterans by the thousands trudged off into the night. Some carried their belongings wrapped in bundles on their backs. One drunk went lurching away bearing only a large oil lamp. A few sang old War songs. Women carried babies in their arms. Huts and lean-tos were set afire, partly by the departing veterans, partly by the soldiers. By midnight Bonus City, once the home of 10,000 jobless hungry men & women, was a field of roaring bonfires. President Hoover could see its fiery glow on the Eastern sky from his White House window. At dawn the place was a charred & blackened ruin. The B. E. F. was gone. Not a shot had been fired by the victorious Army.

The Day's Toll: Dead, 2; injured, 55; arrested, 135, including Charles P. Ruby, D. S. C., first to greet the President at the New Year's day reception at the White House in 1931 (TIME, Jan. 12, 1931).

In France Joe Angelo of Camden, N. J., was decorated for saving the life of Major George O. Patton. At Anacostia Major Patton headed the cavalry that drove Joe Angelo out of his B. E. F. quarters.

Repressing Democratic Disorder

HERBERT HOOVER

Is Hoover correct when he asserts order and civil tranquillity to be the first requisites of economic reconstruction? What threat does Hoover see in the B.E.F.? Does presidential leadership require the use of force?

The President said:

A challenge to the authority of the United States Government has been met, swiftly and firmly.

After months of patient indulgence, the Government met overt lawlessness

From Herbert Hoover's press conference statement, July 29, 1932.

as it always must be met if the cherished processes of self-government are to be preserved. We cannot tolerate the abuse of Constitutional rights by those who would destroy all government, no matter who they may be. Government cannot be coerced by mob rule.

The Department of Justice is pressing its investigation into the violence which forced the call for Army detachments, and it is my sincere hope that those agitators who inspired yesterday's attack upon the Federal authority may be brought speedily to trial in the civil courts. There can be no safe harbor in the United States of America for violence.

Order and civil tranquillity are the first requisites in the great task of economic reconstruction to which our whole people now are devoting their heroic and noble energies. This national effort must not be retarded in even the slightest degree by organized lawlessness. The first obligation of my office is to uphold and defend the Constitution and the authority of the law. This I propose always to do.

The Sources of Democratic Revolution
WALTER WATERS

Is Walter Waters' view of the men in the B.E.F. similar to Herbert Hoover's view? What was the "new American system" Waters says the nation needs?

You, who may never have been forced through actual hunger to accept charity or even loans that are given with faint hope of repayment, do not know the double damage that poverty works. It affects the body but, worse, it wrecks self-respect. Charity does keep the body alive after a fashion, but it reduces to a minimum any satisfaction in living; it prevents actual physical suffering but at the expense of mental torture. In time, taken in regular doses, it can have but one ending, the complete annihilation of a man's faith in himself and the complete rout of the desire that every decent man should have, to improve himself and his position in society. I found that a large percentage of these men in Portland were, like myself, ex-service men. They had fought, so they had been told a few years before, "to save the nation"; they had fought, it now seemed, only in order to have a place in which to starve.

Among these men there was profound discontent with conditions. There was a ravaging desire to change them but a complete and leaden ignorance of the way to do it. Yet, among these men, hungry, desperate, downcast, there

From Walter W. Waters, *B.E.F.: The Whole Story of the Bonus Army* (New York, 1933 and reprinted by AMS press, 1970), pp. 7–13, 101–102, 255.

was little or no talk of the need for violent action. It was every man for himself. One can merge one's individuality in the mass when active, even in wartime when death taps at the shoulders of men, one by one; but starving makes a man think of himself first and foremost. Yet these men were just as loyal to the nation as they had ever been. They were just as patriotic, just as law-abiding as their more fortunate neighbors who had jobs. In other nations similar conditions might lead to revolution. Among these men the very thought, let alone the desire, was never in their minds.

These men did think and talk a great deal about the so-called Bonus. The name "Bonus" is unfortunate. It is not a gift, as that word implies. It is a payment of money to *compensate* those men who served in the Army for the difference in pay between that of service men and non-service men in 1918. The bill, asking payment in full of the adjusted compensation for wartime service, was introduced by Representative Patman of Texas and, during the early winter of 1931, was pending in Congress. The majority of veterans were hoping that it would pass.

These men had fallen far down into the valley of despair. Some push was necessary to start them out and up over the hill. Jobs would have provided the best sort of impetus but there were no jobs. The Bonus, a lump sum of money, could act in the same fashion. Debts could be met, doctors' bills paid, a fast fraying credit renewed, and one man could look another in the eye once more. It mattered not that the Bonus was not due, legally, until 1945. What man, having a promise to pay at a later date would not ask his debtor for it in advance if he believed that the debtor could afford the money and if his own need was not only great but critical? These men felt that the Government had the money. Newspapers, which can always be picked out of trash cans in the parks and public places, published stories of extensions of credit to foreign nations. Headlines told of loans to railroads and to large corporations.

This is not the place to argue the justice or the fallacy of the demand for the immediate payment of the Bonus. The point, continually forgotten, is that the Bonus in these men's minds became a substitute or a symbol for that long dreamt of new start, a job. These men had nothing to which to look forward except to the shiny shoulders of the man in front of them in the breadline. Whenever I asked these men which they would rather have, the Bonus or a job, the reply was nearly always the same: "A job, of course. But where's a job coming from? I've looked every day for over a year and haven't found one."

When asked what they would do with the Bonus, their answers were alike: "First, I'd buy the kids some clothes, then I'd pay the rent, then the grocery bill. And believe me, we'd have at least one good Sunday dinner." Frequently one heard, "Well, I could at least pay my debts and then maybe my credit would hold up until I do get a job."

All this could not fail to impress me because it conformed exactly to my own condition and viewpoint.

During this time I was anxiously watching reports in the newspapers of the progress of Bonus legislation. Having been originally reported for consideration in December, the bill was continually being postponed to some future date. . . .

I noticed, too, that the highly organized lobbies in Washington for special industries were producing results; loans were being granted to their special interests and these lobbies seemed to justify their existence. Personal lobbying paid, regardless of the justice or injustice of the demand. . . .

My interest in all this was not inspired through pure curiosity or altruistic benevolence. I was broke, and was unable to pay the rent on the two small rooms we were occupying in one of the poorer sections of the city. The man who managed the building was a veteran and only his kindness and sympathy prevented our being moved out on the street. For food we were forced to depend solely on friends or on the municipal charity organizations.

Yet, in my pocket was an obligation of the Government promising to pay me at a later date a sum of money. Now, perhaps, it is clear why I and a hundred thousand more wanted that money if it could possibly be secured. . . .

Here, then, is the origin of the Bonus Expeditionary Force. . . .

The Bonus, incidentally, meant to these men "a break." It was a bit of capital to be used for a start. It was a new start which these men wanted — that was the only "break" that would do them any good. The expenditure of large sums of money for relief was only a temporary measure, to keep men alive through hunger and hardship. That was no new start.

There will be no great growth of radicalism in America so long as men repeat, "Jeeze — if only I had one more chance," or "If only I got a break . . ." Radicalism flourishes only when men come to believe that there is no longer any chance for a "break." When men say: "There ain't no such things as breaks possible for us. We're down and we'll stay there unless we do something about it," then radicalism thrives.

And it thrives when a Government so far forgets the temper of the men who made it as to call out troops to chase them out of their capital city.

I can testify that the Communists did not inspire nor direct the B.E.F. nor make many converts before the eviction. I cannot speak of the number of the B.E.F. who are today "Reds." Their conversion to radicalism, however, was not the work of the few Communists in Washington. Their conversion to Communism was due to Mr. Hoover and his Administration, to whom hungry men seemed to be radicals and not Americans, typical optimists, hoping for "the break." . . .

The B.E.F. was broken up, the first active organ of economic protest in America. The men returned to some city or other, home or otherwise, there to roam the streets hopelessly seeking work or to shuffle in breadlines, despondently accepting food.

There they remain, crying examples, not of the need for the Bonus, but of the need for a new American system.

The Presidency of the People

SHERWOOD ANDERSON

How could one tell whether Sherwood Anderson's perspective of the presidency was correct? Does the "Battle of Washington" indicate that Hoover was out of touch with the reality of America? How seriously should Anderson's solution be taken? Is there a solution to the isolated presidency?

Norfolk, Virginia, August 11

Mr. Herbert Hoover
President of the United States
Washington, D. C.

Dear Mr. President: I am an ex-soldier, an ex-laboring man, a native American, now a professional writer. Yesterday I came to Washington with a group of writers to protest the treatment given the bonus army in Washington. Coming to a President of my country to voice such a protest isn't a thing I like to do. With me it is like this: I am intensely interested in the lives of the common everyday people, laborers, mill hands, soldiers, stenographers, or whatever they may be. It may be because I, myself, come out of the laboring class. I was born in a poor family, I am still poor. I understand that you also were once poor.

Being a writer I am inclined to lead a quiet life, going about and peering into the corners of life. It happens that for the last four or five years I have spent most of my time in a cheap car going about to factory towns in America, going into the homes of poor farmers, into the houses of workers in mill villages. I haven't been doing any kind of propaganda. I have been looking, watching, finding out what I could about American life.

I came yesterday to Washington to speak to you, came as a delegate from a group of American writers and intellectuals. I did not want to come. I had no desire to make you uncomfortable. It was your birthday. You were receiving friends. You were preparing your speech of acceptance of renomination as President. Political advisers were, I dare say, flocking about. That is your life — perhaps it has to be your life. I am not criticizing it. I came with the other writers because I was myself uncomfortable.

Mr. President, I've been seeing at first hand the condition of men out of work in America. I have been walking with them, talking with them, sitting with them. To me, although they are men and women out of work, they re-

---

From Sherwood Anderson, "Listen Mr. President," *The Nation,* August 31, 1932, pp. 191–193.

main fellow-Americans. I have been seeing things with my own eyes: men who are heads of families creeping through streets of American cities eating from garbage cans; men turned out of houses and sleeping week after week on park benches, on the ground in parks, in the mud under bridges. The great majority of these men are eager enough to work. Our streets are filled with beggars, with men new to the art of begging.

I came to you with the other writers because I was ashamed not to come. When men are starving I am ashamed not to speak up. When men are trying to assert their rights to live decently in America, trying to organize to assert more effectually their human rights — when these men are brutally put down by police or soldiers — bear in mind I have seen these things with my own eyes — when that happens something within me hurts and bleeds.

What I am trying to say to you is that men like me do not want to be radicals. I am, myself, a story-teller. I would like to give all my time and thought and energy to story-telling. I can't.

I am wondering, Mr. President, if men like you, men now high in our public life, captains of industry, financiers — the kind of men who seem always to be closest now to our public men — I am wondering if all of you are not nowadays too much separated from the actuality of life. Everything has been very highly organized and centralized in America. Perhaps *you* have been organized and centralized out of our common lives.

I have an idea. It may amuse you. I think we Americans ought to elect two Presidents. For example, let you and Mr. Roosevelt both be President for the next four years. They may prove to be eventful years. Let you serve, say for three months, and then let Mr. Roosevelt have his term. In the interval you come out of your White House and away from your political advisers, industrial magnates, and bankers, and spend the time with me. We will get into my cheap car and live for a time as millions of Americans live now. Together we will walk at night in city streets, into houses of workers, into parks and camps where the unemployed gather, into a thousand places you have never seen. When you go back into your Presidency.I will then take Mr. Roosevelt for his turn. It will be educational to you both. I swear it. Incidentally it may turn out to be the most interesting three months of your life.

As it happens, Mr. President, not all of my friends are poor or unemployed. I know personally a good many rich and powerful Americans, and I know that something quite dreadful does happen to all of you rich and powerful men. You do get horribly separated from actuality. I guess you can't help it. Recently I was staying in the house of a rich man, a friend — as kind-hearted a man as I.know. One evening I heard him talking. Do you know, Mr. President, that he did not think the present depression was so bad. He spoke of it as a passing thing, not of really great importance. I remember how I felt as he talked. There was no personal dislike of the man. I love him, but he did not know, does not himself feel what life has made me feel. Several times I went out of his house to walk alone, and often within a few blocks I saw men, often young men, eating from garbage cans, sleeping on benches, always tired, always hungry. Seeing nothing in the future but more of the same.

I have seen and talked to many poor farmers who are now losing their little bits of land, who are now poor, destitute, and discouraged. There are little things that happen to a man. I spoke of my heart being made to bleed. Your heart would be made to bleed also, seeing what I have seen. Recently, within the year, I was walking one day in a wood. It had rained. The ground was wet. I went silently. Suddenly I heard a voice. I crept forward. There was a little Virginia farmer kneeling by a fence at the edge of the wood and praying. Tears ran from his old eyes. I crept away without being seen, but afterward I inquired. He was just a hard-working poor American farmer who had a big family and who had got into debt, and whose little farm was to be sold. He did not know where to turn. He was frightened, hurt, and perplexed, kneeling there and crying to God. He is not an isolated figure. He represents, as I have pictured him here, millions of Americans now.

You, Mr. President, and myself have a good deal in common. We were once both poor boys, both came from poor families. You went the road of money-making, of power-getting, and I went another road. Just the same, if I know anything at all, I know that we are both perplexed. When the group of American writers of whom I was one went recently to Washington to try to speak to you personally of all these things, it is true that we made a point of the treatment recently given to the perplexed soldiers who have been camped down there. That is what they were — perplexed men. Think of the promises we Americans made those men but a few years ago.

This is my own attitude. Before going on this fruitless mission to Washington to try to see and talk to you personally, hoping, perhaps to take to you a little cry out of the masses of people, I went to see some of the Communist leaders. The idea that they had any effect on the mass of soldiers in Washington is absurd. It is a joke, Mr. President. It is true that some of them went to Washington to try to work there among the soldiers, but they, themselves, told me that they could do nothing. "We couldn't touch those men." I think they told me the truth. Newspapermen and many citizens of Washington have told me how, all the time they were there, they went about flag-waving and begging. They demanded so little from their government, after all the things that had been promised them, that the situation was laughable.

When we writers came to Washington you would not see us. A Mr. Theodore G. Joslin, one of your secretaries, I believe, did finally see us. He told us firmly and finally at once that you would not bother to see us. Then an amusing thing happened. He was a bit nervous and pale. He said he did not speak to us for you or as your secretary, but as a fellow-American and a fellow-writer. He seemed to me a rather pathetic figure at that moment. He lectured us like a lot of schoolboys. The import of what he said was that the trouble at Washington, in regard to the bonus army, was that the men weren't soldiers. We were given the idea that the distraught men that had come to Washington were really Huns. They went about attacking police and trying to tear down government. They threw stones at harmless soldiers. You would have thought that the soldiers and police were unarmed rather than these distraught, puzzled men out of work — the same men who but so short a time ago were our national heroes.

Mr. President, after this absurd incident in Washington, on your birthday, we writers separated. I went to see a friend. We had a talk. He is not an unsuccessful man as I am, but is very successful. He said that, even in Washington, you were utterly separated from the reality of life in America now, so surrounded by yes-sayers that nothing touched you. He suggested to me an idea. He said that when you were in the Far East, when you were making your fortune, you handled coolies. He said that you had come to think of most of us here in America, who happen to be poor or out of work, as coolies. He thought you believed in the whip. That is what we came to Washington to protest against, Mr. President — the whip. Its lash is falling across the backs of millions of Americans. It is the lash that is making radicals in America.

I return to my suggestion. If my notion that we elect both you and Mr. Roosevelt is absurd and you are reelected I suggest that you take that vacation. Sneak out of the back door at the White House some evening. Let me take you with me for a few weeks so that you may see with your own eyes what is happening to millions of Americans, what American life is becoming.

Sherwood Anderson

The Limits of Presidential Leadership
HERBERT HOOVER

What is the function of government as seen by Hoover? What does Hoover believe to be the real danger to the nation? If Hoover was going to be popular with the people, was it necessary for him to act in a way he would term demagoguery? Can a program of self-help rather than government help ever be a popular program? Given the size of the Depression, was self-help alone a realistic program? Can government action promote self-help?

... I wish to say something of my conception of the relation of our government to the people and of the responsibilities of both, particularly as applied to these times. The spirit and devising of this government by the people was to sustain a dual purpose — on the one hand to protect our people amongst

---

From Herbert Hoover's address to the 1932 Republican National Convention.

nations and in domestic emergencies by great national power, and on the other to preserve individual liberty and freedom through local government.

The function of the Federal Government in these times is to use its reserve powers and its strength for the protection of citizens and local governments by support to our institutions against forces beyond their control. It is not the function of the Government to relieve individuals of their responsibilities to their neighbors, or to relieve private institutions of their responsibilities to the public, or of local government to the states, or of state governments to the Federal Government. In giving that protection and that aid the Federal Government must insist that all of them exert their responsibilities in full. It is vital that the programs of the Government shall not compete with or replace any of them but shall add to their initiative and their strength. It is vital that by the use of public revenues and public credit in emergency the Nation shall be strengthened and not weakened.

And in all these emergencies and crises and in all our future policies we must also preserve the fundamental principles of our social and economic system. That system is founded upon a conception of ordered freedom. The test of that freedom is that there should be maintained equality of opportunity to every individual so that he may achieve for himself the best to which his character, ability, and ambition entitle him. It is only by this release of initiative, this insistence upon individual responsibility, that there accrue the great sums of individual accomplishment which carry this Nation forward. This is not an individualism which permits men to run riot in selfishness or to override equality of opportunity for others. It permits no violation of ordered liberty. In the race after the false gods of materialism men and groups have forgotten their country. Equality of opportunity contains no conception of exploitation by any selfish, ruthless, class-minded men or groups. They have no place in the American system. As against these stand the guiding ideals and concepts of our Nation. I propose to maintain them.

The solution of our many problems which arise from the shifting scene of national life is not to be found in haphazard experimentation or by revolution. It must be through organic development of our national life under these ideals. It must secure that coöperative action which builds initiative and strength outside of government. It does not follow, because our difficulties are stupendous, because there are some souls timorous enough to doubt the validity and effectiveness of our ideals and our system, that we must turn to a State controlled or State directed social or economic system in order to cure our troubles. That is not liberalism; it is tyranny. It is the regimentation of men under autocratic bureaucracy with all its extinction of liberty, of hope, and of opportunity. Of course, no man of understanding says that our system works perfectly. It does not. The human race is not perfect. Nevertheless, the movement of a true civilization is toward freedom rather than regimentation. This is our ideal.

Ofttimes the tendency of democracy in presence of National danger is to strike blindly, to listen to demagogues and slogans, all of which would destroy and would not save. We have refused to be stampeded into such courses. Ofttimes democracy elsewhere in the world has been unable to move fast enough to save itself in emergency. There have been disheartening delays and failures in legislation and private action which have added to the losses of our people, yet this democracy of ours has proved its ability to act.

II

Our emergency measures of the past three years form a definite strategy dominated in the background by these American principles and ideals, forming a continuous campaign waged against the forces of destruction on an ever widening or constantly shifting front.

Thus we have held that the Federal Government should in the presence of great national danger use its powers to give leadership to the initiative, the courage, and the fortitude of the people themselves; but it must insist upon individual, community, and state responsibility. That it should furnish leadership to assure the coördination and unity of all existing agencies, governmental and private, for economic and humanitarian action. That where it becomes necessary to meet emergencies beyond the power of these agencies by the creation of new Government instrumentalities, they should be of such character as not to supplant or weaken, but rather to supplement and strengthen, the initiative and enterprise of the people. That they must, directly or indirectly, serve all the people. Above all, that they should be set up in such form that once the emergency is passed they can and must be demobilized and withdrawn, leaving our governmental, economic, and social structure strong and whole.

We have not feared boldly to adopt unprecedented measures to meet the unprecedented violence of the storm. But, because we have kept ever before us these eternal principles of our Nation, the American Government in its ideals is the same as it was when the people gave the Presidency into my trust. We shall keep it so. We have resolutely rejected the temptation, under pressure of immediate events, to resort to those panaceas and short cuts which, even if temporarily successful, would ultimately undermine and weaken what has slowly been built and molded by experience and effort throughout these hundred and fifty years.

It was in accordance with these principles that in the first stage of the depression I called the leaders of business and of labor and agriculture to meet with me and induced them, by their own initiative, to organize against panic with all its devastating destruction; to uphold wages until the cost of living was adjusted; to spread existing employment through shortened hours; and to advance construction work, public and private, against future need.

In pursuance of that same policy, I each winter thereafter assumed the leadership in mobilizing all the voluntary and official organizations throughout the country to prevent suffering from hunger and cold, and to protect the million families stricken by drought. When it became advisable to strengthen the states who could not longer carry the full burden of relief to distress, I held that the Federal Government should do so through loans to the states and thus maintain the fundamental responsibility of the states. We stopped the attempt to turn this effort to the politics of selfish sectional demands. We kept it based upon human need.

It is in accordance with these principles that, in aid to unemployment, we are expending some six hundred millions in Federal construction of such public works as can be justified as bringing early and definite returns. We have opposed the distortion of these needed works into pork-barrel nonproductive works which impoverish the Nation.

It is in accord with these principles and purposes that we have made provision for one billion five hundred millions of loans to self-supporting works so that we may increase employment in productive labor. We rejected projects of wasteful nonproductive works allocated for the purpose of attracting votes instead of affording relief. Thereby instead of wasteful drain upon the taxpayer we secure the return of their cost to Government agencies and at the same time we increase the wealth of the Nation.

It was in accordance with these principles that we have strengthened the capital of the Federal land banks — that on the one hand confidence in their securities should not be impaired, and on the other that farmers indebted to them should not be unduly deprived of their homes. The Farm Board by emergency loans to the farmers' coöperatives served to stem panics in agricultural prices and saved hundreds of thousands of farmers and their creditors from bankruptcy. We have created agencies to prevent bankruptcy and failure of their coöperative organizations, and we are erecting new instrumentalities to give credit facilities for livestock growers and the orderly marketing of farm products.

It was in accordance with these principles that in the face of the looming European crises we sought to change the trend of European economic degeneration by my proposal of the German moratorium and the standstill agreements as to German private debts. We stemmed the tide of collapse in Germany and the consequent ruin of its people, with its repercussion on all other nations of the world. In furtherance of world stability we have made proposals to reduce the cost of world armaments by a billion dollars a year.

It was in accordance with these principles that I first secured the creation by private initiative of the National Credit Association, whose efforts prevented the failure of hundreds of banks, and loss to countless thousands of depositors who had loaned all their savings to them.

As the storm grew in intensity we created the Reconstruction Finance Corporation with a capital of two billions to uphold the credit structure of the Nation, and by thus raising the shield of Government credit we prevented the wholesale failure of banks, of insurance companies, of building and loan associations, of farm-mortgage associations, of livestock-loan associations, and of railroads in all of which the public interest is paramount. This disaster has been averted through the saving of more than 5,000 institutions and the knowledge that adequate assistance was available to tide others over the stress. This was done not to save a few stockholders, but to save twenty-five millions of American families, every one of whose very savings and employment might have been wiped out and whose whole future would have been blighted had those institutions gone down.

It was in accordance with these principles that we expanded the functions and powers of the Federal reserve banks that they might counteract the stupendous shrinkage of credit due to fear, to hoarding, and to foreign withdrawals.

It is in accordance with these principles that we are now in process of establishing a new system of home-loan banks so that through added strength by coöperation in the building and loan associations, the savings banks, and the insurance companies we may relax the pressure of forfeiture upon home owners, and procure the release of new resources for the construction of more homes and the employment of more men.

It was in accordance with these principles that we have insisted upon a reduction of Governmental expense, for no country can squander itself to prosperity on the ruins of its taxpayers, and it was in accordance with these purposes that we have sought new revenues to equalize the diminishing income of the Government in order that the power of the Federal Government to meet the emergency should be impregnable.

It is in accordance with these principles that we have joined in the development of a world economic conference to bulwark the whole international fabric of finance, monetary values, and the expansion of world commerce.

It is in accordance with these principles that I am today organizing the private industrial and financial resources of the country to coöperate effectively with the vast Governmental instrumentalities which we have in motion, so that through their united and coördinated efforts we may move from defense to powerful attack upon the depression along the whole national front.

These programs, unparalleled in the history of depressions in any country and in any time, to care for distress, to provide employment, to aid agriculture, to maintain the financial stability of the country, to safeguard the savings of the people, to protect their homes, are not in the past tense — they are in action. I shall propose such other measures, public and private, as may be necessary from time to time to meet the changing situations and to further speed economic recovery. That recovery may be slow, but we will succeed.

And come what may, I shall maintain through all these measures the sanctity of the great principles under which the Republic over a period of 150 years has grown to be the greatest nation on earth.

The Demand for Presidential Leadership

FRANKLIN D. ROOSEVELT

How do the actions of Roosevelt differ from those taken by Hoover? What is there in Roosevelt's plan that would inspire popular confidence, while Hoover's would not?

The legislation which has been passed or is in the process of enactment can properly be considered as part of a well-grounded plan.

First, we are giving opportunity of employment to one-quarter of a million of the unemployed, especially the young men who have dependents, to go into the forestry and flood-prevention work. This is a big task because it means feeding, clothing and caring for nearly twice as many men as we have in the regular army itself. In creating this civilian conservation corps we are killing two birds with one stone. We are clearly enhancing the value of our natural resources, and we are relieving an appreciable amount of actual distress. This great group of men has entered upon its work on a purely voluntary basis; no military training is involved and we are conserving not only our natural resources, but our human resources. One of the great values to this work is the fact that it is direct and requires the intervention of very little machinery.

Second, I have requested the Congress and have secured action upon a proposal to put the great properties owned by our Government at Muscle Shoals to work after long years of wasteful inaction, and with this a broad plan for the improvement of a vast area in the Tennessee Valley. It will add to the comfort and happiness of hundreds of thousands of people and the incident benefits will reach the entire Nation.

Next, the Congress is about to pass legislation that will greatly ease the mortgage distress among the farmers and the home owners of the Nation, by providing for the easing of the burden of debt now bearing so heavily upon millions of our people.

Our next step in seeking immediate relief is a grant of half a billion dollars to help the States, counties and municipalities in their duty to care for those who need direct and immediate relief.

The Congress also passed legislation authorizing the sale of beer in such States as desired it. This has already resulted in considerable reemployment and incidentally has provided much-needed tax revenue.

From Franklin D. Roosevelt's second fireside chat, May 7, 1933.

We are planning to ask the Congress for legislation to enable the Government to undertake public works, thus stimulating directly and indirectly the employment of many others in well-considered projects.

Further legislation has been taken up which goes much more fundamentally into our economic problems. The Farm Relief Bill seeks by the use of several methods, alone or together, to bring about an increased return to farmers for their major farm products, seeking at the same time to prevent in the days to come disastrous overproduction which so often in the past has kept farm commodity prices far below a reasonable return. This measure provides wide powers for emergencies. The extent of its use will depend entirely upon what the future has in store.

Well-considered and conservative measures will likewise be proposed which will attempt to give to the industrial workers of the country a more fair wage return, prevent cut-throat competition and unduly long hours for labor, and at the same time encourage each industry to prevent overproduction.

Our Railroad Bill falls into the same class because it seeks to provide and make certain definite planning by the railroads themselves, and the assistance of the Government, to eliminate the duplication and waste that is now resulting in railroad receiverships and continuing operating deficits.

It is wholly wrong to call the measures that we have taken Government control of farming, industry, and transportation. It is rather a partnership between Government and farming and industry and transportation, not partnership in profits, for the profits still go to the citizens, but rather a partnership in planning, and a partnership to see that the plans are carried out.

The Duties of Presidential Leadership

FRANKLIN D. ROOSEVELT

Unlike the fireside chats, the following Roosevelt statements were made in the closed meetings of the National Emergency Council. Are there any forgotten Americans in FDR's program for recovery? How does Roosevelt's response to the bottom 40,000,000 differ from the way Hoover would have responded? What does Roosevelt's view of the purposes of the TVA reveal about his philosophy of government?

From the minutes of the December 11, 1934, meeting of the National Emergency Council.

... We have a great many people working, and no one person knows what the other person is doing, except myself — right here, nowhere else in the government — as to the coordination of the public works program, the relief program, and the housing program, insofar as new legislation goes; and nobody knows exactly what is going to be done until the third of January. We are seeking to cut down relief in this sense; there are only two schools of thought, one school represented by a number of very worthy persons who believe we should adopt the dole system in this country because it would cost less. We have somewhere around five million people on relief in the United States today, on a subsistence basis; we can save a great deal of money by just giving them cash or market baskets on Saturday night, thereby destroying morale at the saving of a large sum of money. That is out of the window; we are not going to adopt that policy. The policy is going to be to eliminate that form of relief all we possibly can. That means the adoption of the alternative, which is furnishing work instead of the dole. We are working on that at the present time.

As a part of that work program we come to the question of the housing program. The easiest way is to explain it, once more, in words of one syllable. There are in this country about 120,000,000 people. The government is doing something for three groups of that 120,000,000 people in the way of housing. The richest group for whom we are doing something are people who have borrowing capacity. That is to say, they have either jobs with incomes that go with jobs, or at least form a class of sufficient wealth in the community for banks and other lending agencies to lend money to them. For various reasons, banks and other lending agencies have shown a disinclination to come forward as fast as we hoped they would. We, therefore, have tried to stimulate lending by private agencies through the establishment of the Housing Administration. The Housing Administration has made very great progress — excellent progress. It has operated through the system of the guaranteeing of a percentage of the loan; in other words, the insurance method. They have been lending money so far under Title I of the Housing Act to people — I think I am right, Jim and Dan — with average income of about $2,750 a year. In almost every case, those people already have their own homes and they are borrowing money to improve their existing homes. People in this country with an average of $2,750 a year income are rich people. They are far above the average in respect to income; and we are doing a fine job for them.

Next come the people a little lower down the scale, but people who still have borrowing capacity — some form of security to offer to private capital. Those are the people who already had their homes or their farms. Bill Myers and John Fahey are looking after their wants. In other words, the Farm Credit Administration is extending government credit or the credit of the federal farm banks or federal home loan banks is being extended to people who already have property. They are extending it in the form of loans or in the form of reduced interest rates in existing mortgages. Those people come into a lower income group in almost all cases than the people who go to Jim Moffett. There may be 10,000,000 men, women, and children who have taken advantage of the Housing Administration; there might be another 10,000,000 people, or possibly 15,000,000 — perhaps 20,000,000 people — who would take advantage of the Farm Credit Administration or the Home Owners' Loan organization. That is about 30,000,000 people in this country.

Below them is the largest mass of the American population — people who have not got enough, either in earning capacity or in security in the form of tangibles, to go either to Moffett or Fahey or Myers. Those are the people who are living — most of them — in un-American surroundings and conditions. They cannot be helped by the Housing, the Farm Credit, or the Home Loan; they are too poor. They cannot go to a bank or a building and loan association or to a private money lender and get money to improve their living conditions. The question comes up, are we licked in trying to help them in their living conditions? A good many real estate people consider we are; and they say the government should not help them. We say, "Will private capital help them?" They say, "No, it can't, but we don't want the government to help them." Are we licked in trying to help these people — forty million of them, men, women, and children? Their answer is, "Yes, we are licked; we must not do anything to help them, because we might interfere with private capital." The answer is, "No, we are not licked! We are going to help them!" I am telling you quite a lot about policies; we are going to help those forty million people by giving them better houses — a great many of them, all we possibly can. Hence, there is no conflict whatsoever in the government's housing program — never was. They fall into entirely different social groups. The program of building houses has nothing to do with the Housing Administration, nothing to do with the Farm Credit, nothing to do with the Home Owners' Loan. It is an entirely separate proposition and will have entirely separate handling. And, incidentally, we will kill two birds with one stone; we are going to provide better housing, and put a lot of people to work.

I think it is clear to everybody and there will be no further question about any conflict, because there is no conflict. Then we come down to another thing — TVA and electric power. There have been two confusions of thought, perhaps among some members of the administration and certainly in the public mind. I will also set it out in words of one syllable. TVA is not an agency of the government. It was not initiated or organized for the purpose of selling electricity. That is a side function. . . .

There is a much bigger situation behind the Tennessee Valley Authority. If you will read the message on which the legislation was based you will realize that we are conducting a social experiment that is the first of its kind in the world, as far as I know, covering a convenient geographical area — in other words, the watershed of a great river. The work proceeds along two lines, both of which are intimately connected — the physical land and water and soil end of it, and the human side of it. It proceeds on the assumption that we are going to the highest mountain peak of the Tennessee Watershed and we are going to take an acre of land up there and say, "What should this land be used for, and is it being badly used at the present time?" And a few feet farther down we are going to come to a shack on the side of the mountain where there is a white man of about as fine stock as we have in this country who, with his family of children, is completely uneducated — never had a chance, never sees twenty-five or fifty dollars in cash in a year, but just keeps body and soul together — manages to do that — and is the progenitor of a large line of children for many generations to come. He certainly has been forgotten, not by the Administration, but by the American people. They are going to see that he and his children have a chance, and they are going to see that the farm he is using is classified, and if it is not proper for him to farm it, we are going to give him a chance on better land. If he should use it, we are going to try to bring him some of the things he needs, like schools, electric lights, and so on. We are going to try to prevent soil erosion, and grow trees, and try to bring in industries. It is a tremendous effort with a very great objective. As an incident to that it is necessary to build some dams. And when you build a dam as an incident to this entire program, you get probably a certain amount of water power development out of it. We are going to try to use that water power to its best advantage.

Insofar as competition goes with other companies — private companies — it comes down to a very simple proposition. There has been, again, a confusion of thought. The power people — not the people who are running the operating companies but the people who have cornered the control of those operating companies in large financial groups called holding companies — have been talking about the attack on utility securities. There is a perfectly clear distinction well expressed by an effort made the other day in New York to get the insurance company to join with the holding companies in opposing the government program. I think it was Mr. Ecker of the Metropolitan who, on being asked to join in the attack, was told that the security bonds — the utility bonds — of the Metropolitan would be jeopardized, made the perfectly simple answer that the larger insurance companies, like the savings banks, if you go through their portfolios of securities that make up their resources against policies, those portfolios will show a very large number of utility bonds; but in every case of the larger companies and the savings banks those bonds are bonds of operating companies. In other words, they represent money that was put into the actual development. It is a pretty fair guess that ninety-nine and a half per cent of the bonds of all the operating company utilities in the United States are worth at least a hundred cents on the dollar today. They are absolutely all right. The only utility securities which are all wrong are the securities of holding companies, which securities represent no cash invested in electrical development itself. They represent merely financial transactions, and therefore, it is a perfectly safe position for anybody to take that the government program does not jeopardize in any way the securities of honest operating companies. If every operating utility company was concerned only with making the interest on its bonds and a reasonable profit on its stock, they could reduce their rates per kilowatt hour to the household users of power throughout the United States and survive, making a good living and an honest profit.

Personal Charisma and Democratic Leadership

RAYMOND CLAPPER

Raymond Clapper writes about the Roosevelt style. Could Roosevelt's style have won Roosevelt his popularity without the New Deal program? Could the program have been popular without the Roosevelt style to sell it? Is there any contradiction between the New Deal programs as described by the two Roosevelt documents and the Roosevelt style described here?

3/37

Surely you know him, this man who found a nation ridden with fear and brought it through to new confidence;

Who summons courage equal to the hour, either to close the banks or to cross good souls by offering beer to thirsty White House guests; who lashes out at his enemies with hard scorn yet whose heart melts when he sees a lonely young girl at her first East Room party and tells her, by his order, to command the most handsome young man on the adjoining terrace to waltz with her;

Who speaks before throngs with such seeming assurance yet whose hand, we see, trembles while he waits out the long applause; who stands with dignity before the world, yet who as a kindly host draws a familiar, crumpled pack of cigarettes from his pocket and, with apologies, offers them to the lady on his left, even as you and I;

Who lives with human warmth in a thousand flashing moments, on and off the national stage, as scenes come tumbling into memory . . . visiting, on the eve of his first inauguration, an obscure shop in New York to ask an old Negro to come with him to Hyde Park and pack his beloved ship prints for the journey to Washington . . . winding through crowds which press about his slowly moving automobile with their echoing murmur, "I almost touched him" . . . back from a Pacific cruise, leaning, tanned and smiling, on the bridge of the cruiser *Houston* as it warps to dock at Portland, Ore., sighting on shore a Harvard classmate of 30 years ago and calling out as one old grad to an-

From Raymond Clapper, *Raymond Clapper: Watching the World,* ed. Mrs. Raymond Clapper (New York: McGraw-Hill, 1944), pp. 86–90.

other, "Hello, Curtis. Class of 1904" . . . pausing during a speech from the rear platform of his train to explain, "I'll have to wait a minute; there's a grand kid fight going on down here" . . . reluctantly revealing his election guesses in which he grossly underestimates his own popularity . . . laughingly arguing with his staff that he could make a better campaign against himself than his opponent does, because he knows his own weaknesses . . . driving for hours in an open automobile under a drenching rain and dismissing it as a trifle with the remark, "I don't mind having my shoes full of water, but I don't like to sit in a bath tub with my clothes on" . . . solicitous over the poor, careworn fellow on the curb in Philadelphia who, in a gesture of gratitude, tosses his watch into the automobile; imploring the police to find the man and return it . . . moving, day after day, in the East and in the West, in the North and in the South, always through seas of countless, unknown thousands, a living symbol of democracy;

Who, born in luxury, linked by family to ten Presidents, has made himself the champion of forgotten men and women, using his talents as was said of Benjamin Franklin, in an attempt to subdue the ugly facts of society to some more rational scheme of things; at peace with himself and at ease in his job; fixed in purpose, flexible in method; concerned not so much that the rich shall sleep peacefully in their beds but that everyone shall have a bed in which to sleep;

Who, afflicted so that he is unable to move a step without support, is yet a man of action; who has traveled more, been seen and heard by more, been voted for by more free men and women than anyone else before him;

Who wants to bring about in his time a world which shall venture some few paces on into the vistas of hope which science and man's ingenuity have opened to us, to write in the pages of time his small message, as a friend who is with us for a few bright hours before he travels on.

6/29/36

No one who was at the Philadelphia convention will easily forget the night at Franklin Field, which revealed Roosevelt, not merely the good political showman, but a master ripened into the fullness of his powers. It is not probable that many of us who were there shall experience anything like it again.

After a week of cheap, tinhorn ballyhoo which never rose above the level of a shoddy political war dance, a new spirit of dignity seemed to settle over the convention scene as it moved from the turbulent hall out into the evening calmness under the open sky.

Probably 100,000 persons were there, undoubtedly the largest political audience ever assembled in this country. In nearly 20 years of political reporting, I have never in any political meeting observed quite the atmosphere which dominated this night. The audience was not noisy, wild, nor hysterical, but it was sympathetic — deeply so, I should say. It listened. It seemed to understand.

Undoubtedly the arrangements contributed toward creating this mood. Instead of a brassy band blaring out "Hail, Hail, the Gang's All Here," the Philadelphia Symphony Orchestra played the final movement of a Tschaikowsky symphony. Imagine warming up a political meeting with a symphony concert. At first it seemed a foolish mistake. You can't pep up a political audience on Tschaikowsky.

Then beside the director's stand a small, white, doll-like figure appeared, Lily Pons, the Metropolitan Opera Company's little songbird. She bared her tiny throat to that vast crowd, to whom she must have appeared no larger than a snowflake, and sang the "Song of the Lark." One hundred thousand people sat in breathless enchantment. In that vast ocean of people gathered for a political hurrah, there was not the faintest stirring, not a sound save the muffled clicking of telegraph instruments in the press box. When she finished, dozens of political writers were on their feet joining in the deafening applause. Something had happened to that audience. It had been lifted, not to a cheap political emotional pitch, but to something finer. It was ready for Roosevelt.

He entered the arena, not to some raucous thumping air, but to the symphony orchestra's stately stringing of "Pomp and Circumstance."

Preliminaries were dispatched quickly and then Roosevelt spoke. It was his moment. It was now or never. This was the flood tide of his opportunity.

With a voice never more confident, never more commanding, never warmer in its sympathy, Roosevelt played upon his audience with one of the most skillful political addresses of our time. It was more than a feat of showmanship. It was a work of art which all of the political instincts of the Roosevelt dynasty were summoned to aid.

Economic royalists . . . We have conquered fear. . . . Privileged princes of new economic dynasties . . . The spirit of 1776 . . . The flag and the Constitution stand for democracy, not tyranny; for freedom, not subjection; and against dictatorship by mob rule and the overprivileged alike. . . . The enemy within our gates . . . We cannot afford to accumulate a deficit in the books of human fortitude. . . . Divine justice weighs the sins of the cold-blooded and the sins of the warm-hearted in different scales. . . . This generation of Americans has a rendezvous with destiny. . . . It is a war for the survival of democracy. I am enlisted for the duration.

Each word was loaded with the subtle power of suggestion, designed to sap the force of every attack from his opponents. Like the fathers of 1776, he was fighting not political royalists but economic royalists. Memories of his battle against fear and panic in March, 1933, were awakened as if to recapture once more the mood in which the nation hailed him as its deliverer. The Republican Party promises to restore the people's liberties. Roosevelt declares war for the survival of democracy. His mistakes are those of a warm heart. They will be judged leniently.

But the master's superb touch was still to come. As he finished, standing there with his mother and family around him, the strains of "Auld Lang Syne" floated out over the audience. There was a pause. "I'd like to hear 'Auld

Lang Syne' again," the President said. The audience joined in, these thousands and Roosevelt, as old friends who had fought through the crisis together. Still a third time it was repeated. As a political theme song, it will be a hard one to beat.

In a moment Roosevelt was gone. The audience stood in its tracks for quite some time, as if still under the spell, and then quietly began to leave.

10/1/36

President Roosevelt and Governor Lehman were riding back from the armory to the railroad station in an open automobile. As they arrived at the station, the driveway was blocked by a uniformed men's chorus of the American Legion, which sang several songs. The last one was the President's favorite, "Home on the Range." The White House warbler, Secretary McIntyre, joined in but the rendition would have been superb even without Mac's assistance.

"That's fine," said the President. "I think I'll have some pictures taken."

So he and Governor Lehman got out of the car and took their stance in the front line of the chorus. Legion hats were placed on their heads. Cameras lined up and the chorus began singing the old wartime favorite, "Pack Up Your Troubles in Your Old Kit Bag." Roosevelt sang with them, and at the end, he threw his head over close to the singer next to him and twisted his mouth in a barber-shop-baritone finish.

A trivial incident to you and me because it was all done so simply and naturally, just as you might act at the end of a good party. Yet imagine Hoover doing it, or Coolidge or Wilson. And I don't think Governor Landon sings either, at least his Republican friends insist that he is not a radio crooner. Roosevelt had reason to be tired. He might have been bored at being delayed in reaching his train where rest and isolation awaited. There also was his dignity to consider. Presidents just don't sing in public. He might have politely thanked the Legion chorus for its effort and gone on.

You say it was good politics for him to do what he did. It was. But the reason he is a good politician is that such things come naturally and instinctively to him. You say a duck swims well, but that is because swimming comes naturally to a duck. It doesn't have to take lessons.

The distinguishing thing about Roosevelt as a politician is his acute sixth sense. He needs less prompting, less coaching, less hunching by idea men than the average candidate. His best speeches are not the ones prepared for him but the ones he writes himself, when he dispenses with tiresome facts and swings out gaily with satirical references to angry old gentlemen who have lost their silk hats. He liked that touch in his Syracuse speech.

All of this suggests why Roosevelt functions on the campaign trail with such smooth efficiency, with the natural athlete's work. Roosevelt's whole week has been made merry by a story which he retells to his visitors. A Republican candidate, being driven through crowds in a certain city, heard shouts for Roosevelt. Showing some annoyance, a lady politician riding in his automobile sought to reassure him. "Don't pay any attention to them," she said, "they are only working people."

Roosevelt the candidate passes by no opportunity. He lays a cornerstone of a new medical unit at Syracuse University and remarks pointedly, "I have laid many cornerstones and as far as I know, none of the buildings has tumbled down yet."

This is a P.W.A. project, one of the many for educational purposes, so in a few words Roosevelt seizes this opportunity to say that such expenditures of Federal money have permitted educational facilities to expand during the depression without loading heavier tax burdens on local communities.

Thus everything is grist for Roosevelt's mill. He snatches ideas for his speeches out of casual conversations, out of everything he sees, out of the removal of railroad tracks from the main street of Syracuse, out of what 10,000 years of wear and tear will do to the face of Jefferson carved on the side of Mt. Rushmore, out of the rainbow that appears over his shoulder in North Carolina. When Roosevelt is out campaigning, he "finds tongues in trees, books in the running brooks, sermons in stones," and vote fodder in everything.

Republicans may charge, as Colonel Knox did the other night, that Roosevelt is a waster at Washington. Be that as it may. But when the President puts on his battered dusty-colored campaign hat, when he hooks up the loudspeakers to the rear of the presidential train, when he goes off of the Government official expense account and on the Democratic National Committee account, all boondoggling ceases. Roosevelt the politician wastes nothing, not even — unlike the Chicago packers — the squeal.

• MODERN ESSAY •

Crowning the Democratic King
MICHAEL NOVAK

Michael Novak maintains that our president is our king, priest, and prophet. By making him such, are we forcing him to be isolated from the American people? Is there a line between charisma and demagoguery? How do the conclusions of Novak help in understanding the public reaction to Hoover and Roosevelt?

Reprinted with permission of Macmillan Publishing Co., Inc. from *Choosing Our King: Powerful Symbols in Presidential Politics* by Michael Novak. Copyright © 1974 by Michael Novak. Pp. 3–5, 41–47.

Every four years, Americans elect a king — but not only a king, also a high priest and a prophet. It does not matter that we are a practical and sophisticated people, no longer (we think) influenced by symbols, myths, or rituals. To what our president represents, we react with passion.

The president of the United States is no mere manager of an insurance firm. The way he lives affects our image of ourselves. His style and his tastes weigh upon our spirits. Eisenhower encouraged a "silent" generation, Kennedy an "activist" decade. Nixon at first made some feel solid and appreciative and others, even in the beginning, heavy and ashamed. Intimate and personal feelings are affected by our experience of various presidents.

The symbolic power of the president is real. Ten million police officers, heads of boards of education, lawyers, judges, realtors, union leaders, and local officials calibrate their daily decisions according to the support or the resistance they expect from the White House. What will the Justice Department do, or fail to do? The president is able to make his own views felt in every town and village of the nation, by compulsion and enforcement, by imitation and antipathy. On the local level, if ultimately one expects support far up the line, great risks can be taken. If one is left to one's own resources merely, one must confront the local balance of powers.

Some speak of the "moral leadership" of the presidency as though what we need is a moral man out in front, like a cavalry officer lowering his saber. Yet moral leadership in the presidency is not something habitually "out in front" of us, but something that infiltrates our imaginations and our hearts. The president, whoever he is, affects our *internal* images of authority, legitimacy, leadership, concern. By his actions, he establishes a limit to national realism. What he *is* drives us away from America and makes us feel like exiles — or attracts our cooperation. Cumulatively, the presidents under whom we happen to live influence our innermost attitudes. . . .

The psychic power inherent in the president's office derives directly from the people. The president is obliged to make ritual pilgrimages among them — to touch them, to "press the flesh" as Lyndon Johnson put it — to complete the electric circuit of his symbolic connection with them. At least every four years, the campaign pilgrimage reopens this fundamental symbolism. The people get to "know" their president, and he them. Their approval, at the crowning symbolic conclusion of the campaign, "legitimizes" his later economic and administrative decisions.

A campaign is a symbolic "long march," a *rite de passage,* not practical in dollars-and-cents, perhaps not even practical as an "education in the issues," but symbolically indispensable. If the people cannot see the president's personality torn and tested, how can they trust their lives, fortunes, and honor to his decisions? A presidential campaign is an *agon.* How do the candidates bear up under its tortures? It is a blood rite. The candidate suffers *for the people's sake.* They select which candidate has most united himself to them.

In a column in the *New York Post,* Max Lerner caught a glimpse of the underlying realities:

> The whole thing becomes an elaborate exercise in what Irving Goffman
> has called "ritual face" — the way a man must appear in public, whatever
> his interior confrontation with himself — the tortured process of acquiring,
> losing, and saving some image of political salvation. . . . Running for
> President . . . has become a punishing ordeal . . . compounded of . . . polit-
> ical hoopla, commercial greed, personal megalo-mania, and national
> bread-and-circuses. . . . The Presidential office is itself an ordeal. . . . A
> man has to be stretched on a rack, tempered in a fiery furnace, to see if
> he has the stuff of survival in him.
>
> Give the voter some reflective chance to assess and reassess each mad-
> man who offers himself for the sacrificial ordeal. And pray for the health
> and sanity, as well as the survival power, of the men who make it.

Say, if you will, that electoral campaigns are "merely" symbolic. Something powerful is going on. A single word may destroy a man (Romney's
"brainwashed"). The big spenders don't necessarily win (Lindsay in Florida).
A man's personality may crack (Muskie's tears in New Hampshire; Nixon's
outburst in 1962). Symbolic violations may exclude a healthy, popular, and
able candidate (Kennedy at Chappaquiddick). Assassination may intervene
(the attempt upon Wallace in 1972). The underdog may surprise virtually
everybody (McCarthy in 1968; McGovern in 1972). "Intangibles" are many.

To run for president, a person must show great capacity to raise money.
Still, despite the amounts of money involved, we spend less every four years
to determine who will fill the most powerful office in the world than we spend
annually to determine which team will win the national football championship.
(The religions of football and of politics meld more profoundly in our national psyche than the exchange of metaphors suggests: game plan, campaign,
field general. Even their financial base is more parallel than meets the eye:
corporate profiteers, regional events, fan participation.)

To run for president, a person must show great organizational capacities.
But "organization" is a matter of morale and motivation as well as of bureaucratic charts, funds, and lines of command. The organization must have symbolic access to a wide range of voters. Committed workers cannot win if their
plans encounter indifference or hostility among the people.

So, not least among prerequisites is a sound instinct for the current expectations of the national self-understanding. Required is not only a reading
of the "popular mood," but also of the symbolic structures underlying that
mood. One might read the mood correctly but violate certain expectations,
taboos, or forms, and thus forfeit the public's trust. These expectations, taboos, and forms may not seem "rational," but there is no denying their
effectiveness. One might have many millions of dollars in a campaign chest,
a splendid organization, vulnerable opposition, and nevertheless forfeit all
advantage.

The landscape and the laws of America's symbolic life are so little defined
that practical politicians usually discover them the hard way and by accident.
So oriented are they to what is "practical" that they often speak sheepishly

and even defensively about symbolic realities. They seem to feel that symbolic realities are "emotional" or "irrational." In fact, these symbolic realities are the interpretive structures according to which people understand their own experience. What is more "real" than that? Or more closely related to understanding? Symbolic realities are rational and reasonable and intelligent. *All* thinking is symbolic. *All* acting is symbolic. *All* language is symbolic. It is part of our peculiar rationalism that we find it awkward to bow to this humble but universal demand of human intelligence and morality.

Not all symbolic attempts to interpret experience are equally accurate or acceptable. Like hypotheses, symbols may be tested against the experience they seek to interpret. They may be criticized, modified, or rejected. If we approach symbolic realities in a quasi-scientific, practical way, perhaps they will not seem so threatening.

Politicians with long experience on the national scene learn how to work with the civil religion and its variants. Thus, Ray Price, an experienced adviser to Richard Nixon, wrote a revealing memorandum for the Nixon staff in 1967. In this remarkable document, Price seems apologetic and embarrassed about so unpragmatic a matter as a national symbol system. He gives the issue a "practical" edge by suggesting how image-makers and public-relations persons might make use of it.

"Politics is much more emotional than it is rational," Price begins. It would be more accurate to say "more symbolic than pragmatic." "And this is much more true of presidential politics." He continues:

> People identify with a President in a way they do with no other public figure. Potential presidents are measured against an ideal that's a combination of leading man, God, father, hero, pope, king, with maybe just a touch of the avenging Furies thrown in. They want him to be larger than life, a living legend, and yet quintessentially human; someone to be held up to their children as a model; someone to be cherished by themselves as a revered member of the family, in somewhat the same way in which peasant families pray to the icon in the corner. Reverence goes where power is.

But sometimes power goes where reverence is. As Lyndon Johnson felt reverence slip away in 1968, he felt his power slipping too.

We shouldn't credit the press, Price continues, with a greater leaven of reason than the general public shares: "The press may be better at rationalizing their prejudices, but the basic response remains an emotional one." "Prejudices"? Merely "emotional"? To look at the matter as Price does is to be embarrassed that humans have moral needs, that the feeling of commitment and dedication is as necessary as air, that humans require a sense of purpose. People expect more of a president than practical skills. One may "manipulate" that expectation and treat it as a weakness to be exploited. It is also a strength in the people, ultimately prompting them in revulsion to spew out the demagogue. To treat with contempt the longings of a people for a measure of self-transcendence is to invite their bitterness. They do not like to be "taken."

Of course, Price is trying to break through the merely practical biases of his readers, to get them to take symbolic matters seriously:

> Selection of a President has to be an act of faith. It becomes increasingly so as the business of government becomes ever more incomprehensible to the average voter. This faith isn't achived by reason; it's achieved by charisma, by a feeling of trust that can't be argued or reasoned, but that comes across in those silences that surround the words. The words are important—but less for what they actually say than for the sense they convey, for the impression they give of the man himself, his hopes, his standards, his competence, his intelligence, his essential humanness, and the directions of history he represents.

But how do the people judge a candidate, his "standards," his "essential humanness," or harder still "the directions of history he represents"? In the light of standards they themselves share, through an image of what a good human being is as they see it, by the direction of history as they feel it coursing in their own lives and plans. All these inclinations of theirs are socially shaped, socially inculcated.

The image of what a "good" president is is shaped by experiences with past presidents. The people have "a presidential instinct." They may admire a person for many qualities. But a good president? That's a farther, more narrow gate to enter.

The American president functions as king, prophet, and priest because America functions as a secular religion. Being an American is a state of soul. Yet it is not easy to define what this "being American" is. We are far from being all alike. To speak about "Americans," without noting how many disparate groups there are among us, is to be isolated from reality. There is not some vast mass of "Middle Americans." There is no homogeneous majority of "Silent Americans." Go and see — this people is enormously diverse.

Yet no member of any minority is unaffected by the experience of America. Two men may be "black brothers," but the one from Ethiopia or Nigeria will be the first to note that the other — from Atlanta or Cleveland or New York — is utterly American, not African. A Polish-American may not feel he has been recognized for his true value in America, may feel in some respects like an "outsider," but a visit to Poland will soon assure him that he is no longer simply Polish. A white Southerner may feel every day the contempt of the white Northern liberal, yet in England discover acutely that he is without doubt a "Yank." Italo-Americans born in Brooklyn distinguish themselves sharply from those thousands of Italian-Americans who continue to immigrate to Brooklyn each year, and who come as literate persons, secure in their cultural and political identity.

America is a corporate experience. We come into this experience from different locations and at different times, with different perceptions and different preparation. Each of us knows a different America. Yet that corporate experience in which we all participate is unlike any other on the face of the earth.

A nation from its inception undergoing traumatic experiences of loneliness, revolution, slavery, depression, global adventure, assassination, guilt, space exploration, defeat — such a nation is a crucible of vivid experience which none escape. We are, each in our different ways, American *because* we have been through these things together. In their light, we are prepared to evaluate "the directions of history" our presidential candidates represent.

At every turn in our national life, the symbols and images of our national self-understanding are invoked. In the light of our civil self-conceptions, investors fan out around the world, troops are dispatched, national interests are weighed.

A contest for the presidency is a contest for several symbolic centers of America. It is a contest for the souls, imaginations, and aspirations of Americans as much as for the nation's levers of power. It is also a contest between national self-images. Not infrequently citizens will vote against their self-interests, coldly and economically defined, for the sake of symbols more important to them. To call such behavior irrational may be to miss the fact that humans do not live by bread alone. And it is possible, of course, that in reaching for bread they may receive instead a stone. Fundamentally, in choosing a president people choose — now more pragmatically, now more symbolically — what satisfies themselves. Criteria for what is necessary to satisfy them are supplied by an instinct learned and nourished by the history of the national self-understandings active among us.

The Price memo of 1967 continues:

> Most countries divide the functions of head of government (prime minister) and chief of state (king or president). We don't. The traditional "issues" type debates center on the role of the head of government, but I'm convinced that people vote more for a chief of state—and this is primarily an emotional identification, embracing both a man himself and a particular vision of the nation's ideals and its destiny.
>
> All this is a roundabout way of getting at the point that we should be concentrating on building a received image of RN as the kind of man proud parents would ideally want their sons to grow up to be: a man who embodies the national ideal, its aspirations, its dreams, a man whose image the people want in their homes as a source of inspiration, and whose voice they want as the representative of their nation in the councils of the world, and of their generation in the pages of history.

Winning the loyalty of hundreds of thousands of volunteers, workers, and doorbell-ringers is beyond the competence of the candidate as mere manager or mere executive. It is a task for the candidate as symbol-maker. The presidential candidate must evoke a huge symbolic response, issue significant symbolic rewards. People must feel that what they are doing is good, worthy, and important. . . .

PART IV

An Insecure World

Introduction

Modern America

Since World War II we have been the richest and most powerful nation in the world. In spite of this fact, or perhaps because of it, we have found life in the post-war world more troublesome than in earlier days when we were neither so rich nor so powerful. World War II altered the balance of power: Germany, Italy, Japan, France, and Britain fell from the ranks of major military powers, leaving only the two superpowers to face each other. The Soviet Union and the United States abandoned their wartime alliance and entered into a form of hostility known as the Cold War. How the Cold War began is a major topic of historiography: some scholars maintain that unreasonable American demands threatened legitimate Soviet interests, prompting the Soviets to retaliate. Other scholars argue that the Americans responded to Soviet expansion, and that the Soviets were the aggressors, not we. However it began, the Cold War created great tension both internationally and within the United States.

At the same time, the political face of the world underwent radical change. The European imperial powers found it impossible to continue their hold over what has since become known as the Third World. China rejected the West; India gained its independence from Great Britain; Indonesia emerged from colonial status; the Vietnamese fought and defeated first the French and then the Americans to rid themselves of western domination. In the Middle East,

211

Arab nationalists were successful in driving out French and British influence. More slowly, black Africa began to fall away from European control. Britain, Portugal, Belgium, and France had to abandon their African colonies. Even in Latin America, where the "colonies" were economic more than territorial, states began to assert themselves. Cuba was successful; Guatemala was not.

Americans viewed this changing world with great apprehension. We perceived ourselves as a nation besieged, a nation at war. Indeed, we were besieged and at war, but not as we had been before. There was no line on a map which the American people could watch to see who was winning. We could not send George Patton's tanks into an area, nor could we order a carrier strike force to bombard a target. Instead, we used economic aid, political deals, military alliances, and secret intelligence units to defeat the enemy.

In two other ways this Cold War differed from earlier wars. Abroad, our foreign policy goal was to preserve the nation's preeminent world position. Success was measured by the absence of change, and our foreign policy became reactionary. At home we were not sure who the enemy was. Certainly the enemy included the Soviets, or at least the Soviet leaders. But did it also include Americans who were sympathetic to the ideals the Soviets espoused? What of those Americans who preferred a more socialistic state, were they also the enemy? Were those Americans who were good capitalists but who objected to some aspects of American foreign policy also the enemy? During wartime, it was easy to make decisions on who was friendly and who was the enemy: anyone who did anything to harm the war effort was the enemy. During World War II, thousands of Americans of Japanese ancestry were incarcerated in relocation centers, an action which had financial and psychological consequences of an incalculable nature. During wartime, the government can perform such arbitrary actions in the name of national self-preservation. But what about during peacetime? What are the limits of government action when there is no war or when there is a Cold War?

We have been facing that question for more than three decades, and we seem to be no nearer an answer now than we were in 1947. In fact, in the few years since Watergate directed public attention to the intelligence community, there have been a series of revelations concerning the abuses committed by the Central Intelligence Agency and the Federal Bureau of Investigation. It is clear that in the name of national security, the CIA has been acting domestically (which is illegal) and in a rather arbitrary manner. Similarly, the FBI has, upon occasion, acted outside of the law in gathering information on people through burglaries, illegal wiretaps, and opening of mail. The Bureau has compiled dossiers on law-abiding citizens, disrupted dissident groups it considered undesirable, and used its influence to harm the careers of individuals the Bureau thought particularly undesirable.

Critics charge that such direct action against a suspect who could not be convicted in a court of law is tantamount to a state run not by laws but by a secret police. To this charge others respond that the excesses have been few in number and that one cannot tell who is potentially disloyal without performing some surveillance. Because the FBI and the CIA are run by humans, they argue, there will be mistakes, but that is the price we must pay for living in a hostile world.

Once again Americans must examine how and where to draw a line between the rights of the individual and the right of the state to protect itself. Where one would draw that line depends upon two factors: the nature of the threat confronting the nation and the importance of diversity in one's value system. Those who see the United States locked in a death struggle with a foreign power are likely to condone actions which infringe the liberties of the citizenry. During the Watergate hearings, former presidential aide John Ehrlichman justified the burglarizing of the office of Daniel Ellsberg's psychiatrist on grounds of national security. Ehrlichman insisted that it was necessary to keep such actions in the perspective of the times. He went so far as to say that in cases of extreme danger to the nation's security even murder would be justified. But who is to decide what the national security justifies? How can anyone be sure that some clandestine government action was motivated out of a pure sense of national security and not out of hatred for the individual or group being acted upon? Some people would believe that there was a greater threat from the arbitrary and illegal actions of the Nixon administration or J. Edgar Hoover than from any foreign power.

Where and how to draw a line between the rights of the individual to be free from police harassment and the right of the state to protect itself is a most difficult problem. The first issue in this section chronicles the early years of the Cold War during which the issue was debated.

At the same time that the nation was worrying about its internal security, it was facing the problem of its relationship to the Third World. The issue entered the arena of public debate in the 1960s, a time of much controversy over foreign aid and programs such as the Peace Corps. Some critics accused the United States of ignoring the needs of the poor nations. Still harsher critics maintain that rather than neglecting the Third World, the United States has sought to keep it in a subservient position to the industrialized world. As part of its program to remain the dominant economic power in the world, these critics charge, the United States aligned with the old imperial powers against the rising nationalist movements which threatened the traditional role of private enterprise. Whatever the motive, it is true that the United States worked to overthrow governments which challenged the preferred position of American economic interests in their countries: in Iran the CIA successfully displaced the premier, Mohammed Mossadegh; in Guatemala the leftist government of Jacobo Arbenz Guzman attacked the giant American-owned United Fruit company and was subsequently overthrown by a CIA-backed military intervention; the Guatemala coup served as a model for the CIA-backed Bay of Pigs operation against Fidel Castro in 1961, a notably unsuccessful effort. As recently as 1973, the CIA appears to have intervened in Chile to get rid of the Marxist government of Salvadore Allende after Allende had nationalized the American-owned copper companies.

By the 1970s it had become clear that the Third World nations could not long be held in line by the industrialized West. We could no longer use nineteenth-century tactics of sending gunboats to chastise an erring state, nor could we use the style of the 1950s, when political rulers could be bought by rich nations. Increasingly, the nationalist leaders have asserted themselves and demanded a greater share of the wealth of the world. Today, these articulate Third World leaders are using international conferences, the United Nations, and direct diplomatic channels to ask the United States what it is going to do about the economic problems which face most of the people of the world.

They turn to the United States because we are among the richest of nations. Since the 1950s we have been living the life of the consumer society. We have even become a nation of conspicuous consumers, leading the world in consumption for the sake of consumption. Although we constitute 5 percent of the world's population, we consume a disproportionate amount of the world's resources and energy: we live in a splendor of which most of the world cannot dream. More than one third of our households have more than one automobile. We are so wealthy we can send half of our high school graduates to college (when they get there, a major problem is where to park their cars). The average student eats more meat in a week at college than millions of Third World people consume in a year. While the world worries about starvation, Americans spend millions trying to cope with obesity.

Within our affluent society there are pockets of poverty in which Americans live in substandard housing, eat poorly, suffer from disease, crime, and a loss of hope. But our society is so affluent that our definition of poverty is far above what the Third World poor can dream of achieving. For example, in the United States housing is substandard if it is structurally dilapidated or lacks hot running water, a private bath, or a private toilet. By that definition there has been a constant decline in such housing until we currently have roughly 5 percent substandard homes. By contrast, in many sections of the Third World, 75 percent of the homes have no piped water inside or outside of the home. Though the poor still exist in the United States, we have placed a bottom level under most of them which is still far above that level at which the Third World poor live. American affluence has brought free education, free (though frequently inferior) health care, improved housing, and a welfare program which, for all its shortcomings, means that the American poor can survive.

We Americans enjoy our affluent society and isolate ourselves from the reality of world poverty to such an extent that we cannot imagine how the majority live. The world's poor will no longer be ignored, and the United States must develop a policy to cope with the problem of rich and poor sharing the same planet. When doing this, three points need to be kept in mind.

First, the prosperity of the United States rests upon the continued supply of adequate raw materials to feed American industry. Many of those raw materials come from Third World countries which have begun to organize to fix prices at a level more advantageous to themselves. Since 1940 we have consumed more minerals than all of humanity prior to 1940. By the end of the 1960s the United States (though only about 5 percent of the world's population) consumed 40 percent of the aluminum, 32 percent of the petroleum, and 29 percent of the world's production of nickel, sulfur and tin — to name just the leading minerals. In contrast, the Third World consumed only 7 percent of the world aluminum production, 15 percent of the petroleum, and even less of the other commodities. How much longer we can continue consuming minerals at that rate without doing ecological or economic damage remains to be seen.

A second factor is the proliferation of nuclear weapons into Third World countries. That development means that any conflict between "have" and "have not" nations could have frightening consequences. Even if a First World nation should never become involved in a war with the Third World, any regional war over food or mineral resources would cause extensive environmental and economic dislocation.

Finally there is an unquantifiable factor. Are we as a nation willing to lower our standard of living so non-Americans can live better? If we are not, if we should sit by and watch disease, starvation, and war reduce the excess population by millions of people, what impact will that have on our self-image? The second issue discussed in this section presents some of the thoughts of those who have analyzed these questions during the 1960s and into the 1970s. It is the final issue in this book, and is the most complicated and potentially the most deadly we have to face.

One person who spoke out for bringing the Third World into partnership with the First World was the black athlete, lawyer, scholar, singer, and actor, Paul Robeson. Robeson disagreed with the direction his country was going. During the peak of the Cold War he called for an end to the American foreign policy he believed to be imperialist and racist. As a result, Paul Robeson suffered the consequences of being labeled a loyalty risk.

Personalizing the Issues

Paul Robeson: The American Othello

He has always been referred to as a "giant of a man," but on this particular autumn day in 1915 he did not look much like a giant. His six-foot-three-inch frame was broken and battered amid the other bodies at the bottom of a football pile-up. For the next ten days he lay in bed recuperating from a dislocated shoulder, a broken nose, and numerous cuts and bruises. Other seventeen-year-old freshmen might have quit after such a mauling, but not Paul Robeson. His father had often told him that a black always represents his race, thus it was his responsibility to prove that blacks were not

"quitters." He did not quit; he went on to a dazzling academic career at Rutgers that included election to Phi Beta Kappa — the national honorary scholastic fraternity — and selection as an end on Walter Camp's All-American football team in 1917 and 1918.

All-American and Phi Beta Kappa were just two of the many honors Robeson achieved while in college. He was also a member of the Student Council, valedictorian of his class, a star debater, and the recipient of twelve letters in athletics. Although his voice was later called the "greatest musical instrument in the world," Robeson did not sing with the Glee Club: concerts were always followed by dances, and Robeson understood that his presence was not welcome at those social events.

Graduating in 1919, Robeson moved to Harlem and entered Columbia Law School. He helped finance his law school training by playing professional football with the barn-storming Milwaukee Badgers. In 1923 Robeson graduated first in his class and took a position with a leading New York law firm. He soon learned to hate his job because he was the only black in the office and the color line was firmly established in both personal and professional relations. Robeson prepared brilliant briefs, but others had to argue them in court; black lawyers were not allowable in an era of all-white juries.

Robeson rapidly came to the conclusion that there was little future for him in law. Knowing he had to find an outlet for his enormous talents, his wife, Eslanda Cardoza Goode Robeson, introduced him to her intellectual friends in New York's Greenwich Village. Here he occasionally did dramatic readings at small parties. His rich bass voice, which soon became famous throughout the world, opened theatrical doors for him. In 1924 he starred in Eugene O'Neill's *All God's Chillun Got Wings,* a play about a racially mixed marriage. *All God's Chillun* was a controversial beginning for an even more controversial career. As O'Neill's character faced the ugliness of a world in which he was evaluated on the color of his skin, so too did Robeson.

In the remaining years of the twenties, Robeson appeared on stage and in concert in the United States and Europe. When he sang "Old Man River" in the 1928 London production of *Showboat,* he established a level of achievement that frustrated many black artists who tried the role. His performances at the Drury Theater excited British audiences. Their reaction drastically altered the future of the world's most famous black artist. An exponent of positive thinking, Robeson had never admitted the frightening nature of many of the indignities he and his race had suffered in America. He had endured them, hoping they were transitory. But when he arrived in London and discovered that he no longer had to ride the freight elevator to attend his own concert, nor had to sit in the back of the bus, nor had to eat or sleep at someone's home because hotels and restaurants did not want his patronage, thirty-one years of suffered indignities created an internal explosion.

In London, Robeson met George Bernard Shaw and discovered socialism; he met Africans and discovered his cultural heritage; and he met English workers and discovered his purpose in life. All three encounters produced a new man, an idealist who believed that all oppressed people should be relieved of the burden of oppression. While later critics were to call him a "commie," "pinko," or "leftist," the crucial turning point in his life occurred when he was accepted in London and Moscow as a man, and not an "uppity nigger," or a "talented Negro artist." He came to believe that socialism and communism would save humanity, yet neither of these concepts made the lasting impression upon the great artist as did the lack of racial prejudice he found in Europe. This discovery excited him, and helped him achieve the highest level of artistic achievement during his sojourn in Europe from 1929 to 1939.

Influenced by European intellectuals, he made his first trip to the Soviet Union in 1934 and was impressed with the lack of prejudice within the communist nation. He noted that minorities, particularly those east of the Ural Mountains, were treated with compassion and understanding by the government. Like many humanists of the era, he misunderstood the character of Joseph Stalin, but it is not surprising that the great athlete who was not allowed to play in the National Football League, the great lawyer who could not argue his own cases in court, and the great actor who was often unemployed because there were so few roles available for blacks, enthusiastically embraced a people who appeared to have eliminated discrimination from their way of life. And the love was mutual. Long before he became a propaganda weapon in the Soviet arsenal, the Russians loved and admired this American artist who sang for them in their native language.

In the decade that Robeson spent in Europe, the world changed as drastically as did the artist. The inferno which engulfed the continent in war reinforced Robeson's belief that people must always resist the oppressor. In 1939, as fascist forces appeared to be engulfing Europe, Robeson returned to the United States. Here, during the next six years, he achieved many great artistic triumphs, both as a concert artist and an actor. As always, he gave concerts to help raise funds for charities, particularly those which helped refugees fleeing from Nazi domination. During the war years he earned great fame through constant participation in war bond drives, entertaining at USO shows, and open participation in any cause that would improve the condition of mankind. All of these earned him numerous honors: awards from high schools, honorary degrees from colleges, and the title of the "Troubadour of Freedom." But while his patriotism made him famous, it was his artistry that gave him his greatest personal satisfaction, particularly his revival of Shakespeare's *Othello* on Broadway in 1943.

In 1944 he was honored by an invitation to speak with Vice President Henry A. Wallace at a Lincoln's birthday celebration. At his own birthday in the same year, 8,500 guests donated thousands of dollars to the African Affairs Council.

In the early forties Robeson became the most famous black in America.

Had he wanted to divorce himself from the plight of the black American and colonial peoples around the world, fame and fortune could have been his. But this was an impossible stand for a man of Robeson's convictions. He hated fascism and sang for leftist troops fighting against fascism in the Spanish Civil War; he hated imperialism and walked out of one of his movies when he discovered its blatant proimperialist bias; he hated racism and turned down several Hollywood offers because the movies portrayed blacks as "plantation hallelujah shouters" who solved their problems by "singing their way to glory."

As an outspoken champion of black equality in America, Robeson was a popular civil rights leader. In October 1945 the NAACP gave him the thirteenth annual Spingard Award for "distinguished achievement and concern for the rights of all." Robeson was acknowledged as the kind of person needed to end racism in America. However, this popularity declined during the late 1940s because the times changed and Robeson did not. He traveled abroad and denounced the counterrevolutionary forces in the United States which allowed racism to flourish. He criticized an American foreign policy which supported European control of black Africa. He inflamed American public opinion when he announced that the American black would never fight against the Soviet Union, that President Truman would have to establish a dictatorship in the South to protect blacks, and that Americans should try communism. When the House Un-American Activities Committee said Robeson belonged to thirty-four communist front organizations, and the Soviet newspaper *Pravda* called him a friend of the Soviet Union, Robeson was cast out from the circle of leaders acceptable to the black bourgeoisie. He thus served as a lightning rod for the attacks of the forces of intolerance while other black leaders preferred to move to safer ground.

Robeson the singer found it increasingly difficult to perform. The city council of Peoria, Illinois, ordered the cancellation of a Robeson concert and in 1947 Albany, New York, tried to do the same. Only a court injunction saved that concert for Robeson. The Albany concert coincided with the beginning of the Truman administration's loyalty review of 2 million government employees. The origins of the Cold War and the fear that communists were infiltrating America created a massive intolerance of those people who espoused "wrong" beliefs. It is not surprising then that in 1949 a Robeson concert in Westchester, New York, was turned into a riot by anti-Robeson demonstrators.

The 1950, McCarran Internal Security Act required communists to register with the Attorney General as agents of a foreign power. In order to obtain a passport, the applicant was required by the State Department to sign an affidavit of nonmembership in the Communist Party. Robeson refused to sign the affidavit because he considered it unconstitutional and degrading. He went to court. From 1950 until his court case was decided in his favor in 1958, Robeson lived in the United States unable to perform and deprived of the passport that would permit him to travel abroad. Robeson could have gone to

Europe through Canada since no passport was required to cross that border, but the government informed him that if he did so he would be prosecuted upon his return. The United States was his home and he did not want to become an exile. Thus the American Othello who was unwanted in the United States was kept from performing abroad where audiences loved him. His only performance prior to 1958 was to a British audience through a transoceanic telephone connection. Unable to perform, Robeson's income fell from $104,000 in 1947 to only $2,000 in 1950. No recording company would deal with him. When he wrote a new song, one that he thought particularly powerful, he was forced to record it in his own apartment in New York City.

Robeson's statements that black Americans would not fight the Soviet Union and that the Russians had a superior society to that of the United States would be enough to bring on the type of persecution he experienced during the era of McCarthyism. Yet Robeson's problems with his government sprang not from such simple things as love of the Soviet Union and civil rights. Robeson was an anticolonialist in an era when the world seemed very unsteady. Nationalist revolutions, many supported by communists, were sweeping through the world. Robeson denounced the industrial powers which sought to preserve their imperial hold over African, Asian, and Latin American peoples.

Robeson studied African culture while he was in Europe. He learned several African languages and familiarized himself with the philosophy and poetry of Africa. He came away from his studies confident "that along with the towering achievements of the cultures of ancient Greece and China there stood the culture of Africa, unseen and denied by the imperialist looters of Africa's material wealth." Most Americans looked upon Africa and the rest of what we now call the Third World as backward, if not barbarian. Robeson saw a culture as great as that of ancient Venice, and denounced the foreign policy of the industrialized West which sought to keep the Third World in a subservient position. Paul Robeson was a proud Afro-American. Long before it was fashionable, Robeson maintained that "the colonial peoples — the colored peoples of the world — are going to be free and equal no matter whose 'best interests' are in the way."

The State Department never claimed it had denied Robeson his passport *because* he would have gone abroad and urged the colonial peoples to assert their independence. The Department did claim, however, that it had the legal right to deny a passport on those grounds if it so desired. Robeson's statements were seen as interference in the foreign policy of the United States, and during the Cold War, that had to be stopped.

Robeson's struggle with the government was not limited to the State Department. In 1952, Robeson was awarded the Stalin Peace Prize, which carried with it a $25,000 grant. The Internal Revenue Service insisted that the income was taxable; Robeson insisted that it, like the Pulitzer and Nobel prizes, was tax-free. Not until 1959 did the IRS give up its position.

In the meantime the Supreme Court used a technicality to strike down the State Department's authority to withhold passports. The Court did not rule that withholding a passport to keep a citizen from traveling abroad was unconstitutional; it simply ruled that Congress had not been specific enough in authorizing the State Department as the agency to do the withholding. It was hardly a victory, but Robeson did receive his passport and spent the next five years traveling in Europe, often in poor health. In 1959 he was invited to star in the opening production of the Stratford-on-Avon Shakespeare Memorial Theater commemorating its hundredth season. Britons who waited in line all night to get tickets for the opening performance were not disappointed. The famous Shakespearean critic W. A. Darlington called Robeson's Othello the second best he had ever seen, and the most powerful.

But his English triumph only underscored the tragedy of his life. From age sixty on, his life was a constant battle with poor health. Robeson died in January, 1976, after spending his last years removed from the public eye and too ill to receive the many long-overdue awards then being given to him. In 1970, for example, the New York Chapter of the Association for the Study of Negro History and Life gave him the coveted Ira Aldrige Award for his service to humanity. In that same year he was inducted into the Hall of Fame of the Black Academy of Arts and Letters for his notable sustained contributions.

A third honor was bestowed in 1970, showing the changing temper of the times. During the forties and fifties, some Rutgers alumni had wanted Robeson's name taken from the rolls of the college. Cooler heads prevailed, however, and two decades later the university dedicated an arts and music lounge in the student union to its most famous black alumnus, Paul Robeson. But like most awards it came too late.

In his last American concert in 1958, Robeson spoke of the Othello he had so often played and seemed to be talking of himself: "Othello came from a culture as great as that of ancient Venice. He came from an Africa of equal status and he felt he was betrayed, his honor was betrayed and his human dignity was betrayed."

Issue

Loyalty and International Security

*The danger to democracy is that official observation, even at its best,
is intimidating to most people . . . .*

Edgar Ericson, 1976

*The federal government of the United States is entitled to take what-
ever measures are necessary to secure its continued existence.*

Thomas J. Brown, 1949

How many civil liberties must we surrender to preserve our freedom? How
many civil liberties can we surrender without sacrificing our freedom? During
wartime the answer may be most easily resolved in favor of restricting liberty
to secure survival. When actual conflict rages, the danger to the nation is often
"clear and present," as Justice Holmes put it. During times of peace, we would
be more likely to allow the fullest possible range for civil liberties, perhaps
even erring on the side of what one commentator calls "permissiveness." But
what is the proper balance between national security and individual liberty in
the twilight zone between war and peace during a cold war?

To make such a decision, one must first determine the nature of the threat.
Most Americans in 1947 perceived the Soviet Union to be an aggressive nation seeking to overthrow the American government. Was there really a threat
from the Soviet Union? Was the Cold War the result of Soviet aggressiveness,
or was it the result of American hostility toward the Soviet Union? If what
appeared as Soviet hostility was only a response to arbitrary and threatening
American actions, was there a need to examine the loyalty of American citizens?

As you examine the documents in this section, you will see that the question of the proper balance between individual liberty and national security is
only part of the issue. The more difficult question is how the proper balance
can be maintained. If Truman's 1947 loyalty review program was within the
bounds of propriety, how could one be sure that it would not be used to enforce conformity on issues unrelated to national security or grow into the un-
restrained persecution which characterized McCarthyism? A quarter century
after Harry Truman and Joe McCarthy, we again face the same issue.

◆ DOCUMENTS ◆

The Sources of National Insecurity

HENRY A. WALLACE

Henry A. Wallace discusses with various people in Washington the emerging Cold War. Why does Wallace think the United States is provoking the Soviet Union? Why do the others think the Soviet Union is the aggressor? How influential was recent history in the arguments used?

January 2, 1946

. . . The dinner at Joe Alsop's was most interesting. There were present Ben Cohen, Justice Black, Grace Tully, and Mr. and Mrs. Gaud. The Gauds come from South Carolina but are now living in New York. Apparently Gaud was in China for a time, I suppose with the Army. He is a lawyer and violently anti-Russian.

Immediately after we left the ladies the Russian subject opened up. Alsop and Gaud were vigorous proponents of the thesis of getting tough with the Russians. Justice Black and I took the other side. Gaud said we ought to "kick the Russians in the balls." He said we ought to check them at every opportunity. I said I thought the Russians were entitled to free access through the Dardanelles; that they had been promised this in World War I. Gaud said this was "crap"; I replied that his statements were "crap." He said, "Well, then, we are even." Alsop said we ought to know what the Russian intentions were. He said as to Russia we had no intentions. He said that a democracy like ours never had any intentions. Nobody else knew where we were going and we didn't know ourselves. I said to Joe, "In other words, you look on Russia as a young man and think that he ought to declare his intentions regarding the young lady. You assume that the young lady has no intentions of her own at all." Ben Cohen took somewhat the same slant as Justice Black and myself and Alsop called his statements "a barrel of horse-shit." Alsop's point of view was that the Russians had a government just like Germany's; that they were expanding just like Germany, and that the situation was just like that of Germany when Germany moved into Austria. He said he was one who believed that we should have gotten into the war when Germany moved into Poland. I said it was apparent to me that both Alsop and Gaud belonged

---

From John Morton Blum, ed., *The Price of Vision: The Diary of Henry A. Wallace, 1942–1946*, pp. 536–537, 546–548, 556–557, 560–561. Copyright © 1973 by the Estate of Henry A. Wallace and John Morton Blum. Reprinted by permission of Houghton Mifflin Company.

to that group who believed that war with Russia was inevitable and the quicker it came the better. I described that group as consisting of certain Chinese, the London Poles, the more well-to-do people in all the countries immediately surrounding Russia, certain reactionary business groups in the United States, certain generals in the United States, et al. I didn't include any mention of the Catholic church as I had in my thinking of yesterday. I did include the Tory English and said that it seemed to me that what Alsop and Gaud proposed was really pulling chestnuts out of the fire for Britain. I said it seemed to me that the cost of a war with Russia was so infinitely greater than the value of any oil in the Near East that we should not consider getting into war with Russia over Azerbaijan, access to the Dardanelles, or Rumania. Alsop began to shift ground because he did not want to be accused of wanting war with Russia. He finally centered on the thesis that we had to know the Russian intentions. Justice Black made the point that we had no more business messing in Rumania and Bulgaria than Russia had messing in Mexico and Cuba. He said that we would no more tolerate an unfriendly government in Mexico than Russia would tolerate an unfriendly government in Rumania. I advocated that the proper way to handle the situation was to raise the standards of living of the people in the Near East; that from the standpoint of the peace of the world and the welfare of humanity water for irrigation for the people in the East was more important than oil for the navies and the war machines.

February 12, 1946

... I had a very interesting luncheon with Bill Bullitt, who is very anti-Russian and who obviously had me in to try to make me anti-Russian also. Of course Bullitt's attitude toward Russia has been obvious for the last seven or eight years ...

Bill ... proceeded to get down to the business of attacking Russia with the greatest speed possible. He said he was a good Democrat and he felt my domestic policies were marvelous. He thought my foreign policy was pretty bad. He said he thought I shared some of the ideas of Joseph Davies; I said I certainly did. I told him my foreign policy was based fundamentally on the idea of avoiding World War III and doing our part towards raising the standard of living in the backward areas of the world. He was very critical of Stalin's recent speech. I told him that I thought this was accounted for in some measure by the fact that it was obvious to Stalin that our military was getting ready for war with Russia; that they were setting up bases all the way from Greenland, Iceland, northern Canada, and Alaska to Okinawa, with Russia in mind. I said that Stalin obviously knew what these bases meant and also knew the attitude of many of our people through our press. We were challenging him and his speech was taking up the challenge.

Bill described the Communist Party as a privileged, persecuting minority group of the same type as the Spanish Inquisition. He described the Russian people as perfectly lovely people for whom he had the greatest admiration. He said that while he was Ambassador to Russia he had taught the Russian army to play polo and the Russian factory workers to play baseball. He just loved the Russian people but, unfortunately for the Russian people, they were held completely in subjection by this privileged, persecuting group known as the Communist Party . . .

He said these Bolsheviks are charming people. He spoke of Stalin as a man of extraordinary intelligence. He says he has brown eyes with a bluish film over them. He says he has extraordinary intuition; that when you talk with him he seems to be reaching out all over the room with his mind in a dozen different directions; that he can follow half a dozen different conversations simultaneously. He said, "Stalin at one time was very affectionate toward me. At one time when he had had a little too much to drink he kissed me full on the mouth — what a horrible experience that was!" He spoke about the different people whom Stalin had shot — people who at one time were close to him. He said the Russians were like an amoeba, sending out pseudopods, surrounding that which they could digest and avoiding that which they could not digest. He then proclaimed that the proper policy of the United States was to put indigestible particles in their path. He said because of the fact that the United States had the atomic bomb we could come down firm with Russia and get away with it. I said I thought that was where the trouble had begun; that after we got the atomic bomb and acted the way we did, the Russians felt it necessary to enter upon an armaments race with us; that since we proposed to have bases clearly aimed at Russia, a large number of atomic bombs, and a large Navy, the Russians could feel that we were aiming the whole thing directly at them. . . .

March 5, 1946

The most significant event of March 5 was the dinner given by Dean Acheson at which were present Dick Casey, the Australian minister to the United States, and his wife, Walter Lippmann and his wife, and Chip Bohlen and his wife. Before we sat down to eat the subject for discussion was Winston Churchill's speech. Mrs. Acheson spoke in lyrical terms about it. She has always admired Churchill and never more than yesterday. I asked what he had said and she said he advocated a military alliance between the United States and England against Russia. Mr. and Mrs. Casey became glowing in their comments. I promptly interjected that the United States was not going to enter into any military alliance with England against Russia; that it was not a primary objective of the United States to save the British Empire. At this point Mrs. Casey became almost fanatical, perhaps I should say frenzied. She said it was to save the world, not the British Empire. Casey spoke of the Russians as being beasts. I said instead of talking about military alliances it was high time to talk about an effective method of disarmament. I said it would destroy the United Nations to have two of the chief members of the United Nations ganging up against a third member. I said what we ought to have would be effective disarmament with complete inspection on both sides, including inspection of all atomic bomb facilities and supplies. Casey interjected very brusquely, "We might as well talk about a trip to the moon." Then suddenly everyone became very polite and the matter did not come up again until after dinner . . .

We then got to talking about Russia again and it was apparent that Bohlen, Acheson, and Casey all think that the United States and England should run the risk of immediate war with Russia by taking a very hard-boiled stand and being willing to use force if Russia should go beyond a certain point. Bohlen part of the time claimed that Russia was resuming the tactics she had used in the 17th century and part of the time that she was using the tactics advocated by Lenin. I asked him what were the tactics used by Lenin. He said to drive a wedge between the capitalistic countries and then pick on the weaker ones of the capitalistic countries. I advocated as a program that we have an agreement on disarmament and that the United States and Britain then proceed to show backward peoples of the world that their system would give them a higher standard of living than the Russian system. I said that what Russia feared was encirclement by the United States and England; that she saw us busily setting up military and naval bases whose only object could be to attack Russia. Bohlen made fun of this idea and said that it was not the United States which was on the offensive; that it was Russia. I said it was very unfortunate that Churchill had made the kind of speech he was reported to have made, because he was the one who back in 1919 was calling the Bolsheviks such names and doing everything he could to assemble an Allied force to destroy the Bolsheviks. I said I didn't see how these warlike words of Churchill now could have any more real influence on the Russians than his warlike attitude toward the Bolsheviks had in 1919. I said the American people were not willing to send American boys anywhere to fight now; that certainly the Russians did not want to fight anybody now; that in all probability the situation would finally work out on a basis that would cause the Russians completely and utterly to distrust us; that it would cause the Russians to engage in a race with us in the making of atomic bombs; that while they might be a long way behind us at the present time they would have enough bombs to destroy us fifteen years hence; that with the Russians completely distrusting us because of the way we had handled them they would not scruple fifteen years hence to drop bombs on us without warning; that they would have no hesitation in continuing their fifth column activities in all the nations of the world; that they could use these fifth columnists effectively to destroy our form of government.

March 13, 1946

The only significant event of the day was the speech made by Averell Harriman to the BAC [Business Advisory Council]. It was a strictly anti-Russian speech. Harriman made it clear that he was in accord with Winston Churchill and that we should be tough with the Russians, even though by so doing we were running the risk of war. He said the communists in every country in the world were simply stooges for Stalin and that they were out to overthrow our form of government. It was mostly old, old stuff of the kind we have heard for the last 25 years. Harriman said he had great hopes that the Russians were going to come along all right until the time of the Yalta Conference in March of 1945. At that time he became convinced that they would not reform.

Harriman said he spoke only for himself and not for the State Department. Chip Bohlen and Elbridge Durbrow were present at the meeting. Every so often Harriman would stop and turn to them for confirmation. The BAC found it very impressive and were in enthusiastic accord with Harriman. They will now go out over the country and spread the word that we are going to get tough with Russia even though it means war. Harriman made the point, however, that he was sure Stalin did not want war, and that he was going to do everything he could to expand territorially without war. Harriman thinks we are in the same position relative to Russia in 1946 that we were relative to Germany in 1933; that the important thing is to stop Russia before she expands any further.

Hoffman of Studebaker got up after Harriman had completed and said that he thought the talk was perfectly marvelous; that it ought to be given in every town in the United States, and asked Harriman why he didn't go on a speaking tour carrying the banner. Harriman replied, saying that he couldn't consider going on a speaking tour; that if he said what he had said there he would be immediately subject to attack. He said all the commies in the CIO would be after him.

There was considerable discussion then on how important it was to fight any organization that had any commies in it. It was obvious to me as I listened to Harriman and those in the discussion afterwards, that these businessmen don't have the slightest idea of what is going on in the world or what is going to happen. It was also obvious to me that Harriman in spite of the fact that he has been in Russia for several years, never really found out what the score was. He is a nice fellow whom I like personally but I don't think he understands either Russia or the world situation. He and his kind if they have their way will bring on a war which will result in the United States eventually becoming a dictatorship either to the left or the right.

Internal Disloyalty and National Security

WILLIAM C. BULLITT

In this statement, former Ambassador William C. Bullitt shows he has learned several lessons. Is it fair to compare the Soviet Union to Nazi Germany? In what ways does Bullitt believe the Soviet Union threatens the United States?

The United States, without question, today is in danger, as President Truman very clearly brought out in his statement asking for support for Greece and Turkey. He said that the national security of the United States was involved. I believe those were his exact words. Perhaps I have not quoted him correctly, but that was the sense of some of his words. The safety of the United States is involved because the gradual taking over of countries, the gradual taking over of areas, while possible future victims are lulled into a false sense of security, is the essence of the Soviet tactics, just as it was the essence of Hitler's tactics.

And I make this observation, realizing that it is one that it will be difficult, perhaps, to believe: The situation of the United States today very greatly resembles the situation of the French Republic in the year 1936. At that time France had the largest air force in the world, by far the most powerful army in the world, and a navy which was vastly superior to the German Navy. Nevertheless, at that moment Hitler dared start on his career of conquest by marching his troops into the Rhineland on the 7th day of March 1936. The French could have crushed him with extreme ease. They had every right to, as it was a flagrant violation of the Treaty of Versailles, and they had a right to march to Berlin, if they chose, and take over Germany and impose whatever terms they pleased.

But France wanted to balance its budget. Mobilization of the army was extremely unpopular, as it always is, because it tears men away from their homes and their affairs, and furthermore Hitler constantly was saying that he bore no ill will toward France, and that he had no intention of ever attacking France. In consequence, there were a lot of perfectly good Frenchmen of good intention and weak heads who believed that Hitler would never attack France — like certain star-gazers in the United States, who believe that the Soviet Union will never attack the United States. So what did the French do? They did nothing. Hitler consolidated his position in the Rhineland, built the Siegfried Line and by it locked France out of central and eastern Europe entirely,

---

From U.S., Congress, House, Committee on Un-American Activities, *Bills to Curb or Outlaw the Communist Party of the United States: Hearings on H.R. 1884 and H.R. 2122,* 80th Cong., 1st sess., March 24, 1947, pt. 1, pp. 5–6. Testimony of William C. Bullitt.

successfully seized the countries who were France's allies in eastern Europe, made his deal with Stalin, divided Poland with Stalin, and finally attacked France. The only thing that France had gained by not marching and smashing Hitler, as she could have very easily in 1936 — in fact, we even have the document in which Hitler ordered his troops to leave the Rhineland if the French should mobilize — the only thing they acquired by their quiescence was to be crushed completely 4 years later.

At the present time the United States is far stronger than the Soviet Union. We are as much stronger than the Soviet Union today as France was stronger than Germany in 1936 — and Stalin knows it.

When we took a strong stand on Turkey last year, when we took a strong stand on Iran this year, the Soviet Union did not dare to move. But time is running against us, exactly as it ran against France after 1936. The Russian Army and Air Force are growing stronger every day. They are still turning their major energies into the production for war and not into consumer goods. They are consolidating their hold on the hundred million people they have taken over in eastern Europe and could use them all today, or almost all of them, for war purposes. Their aggression in China is progressing, although at the moment Chiang Kai-shek's armies are advancing, for behind his lines there is such economic difficulty that the whole Chinese Government position is threatened. Communists trained in Moscow have achieved leadership of the Indochinese independence movement, an entirely genuine movement at bottom, but now in the hands of the Communists.

In South America the Communists are increasingly infiltrating the trade-unions and have control of the trade-unions in many countries. There are three Communist members today of the Government of Chile. The Communists have grown so strong in both Cuba and Venezuela that democratic government is threatened in both countries, and in Brazil recently, after an election, the country woke up to discover that the Communists had become the largest party in the city council of its capital, Rio de Janeiro.

Now, under these circumstances the existence in the United States of an enormous fifth column of the national Communist dictator is an even greater threat to the United States than was ever the fifth column of the National Socialist dictatorship of Hitler, and, therefore, I think that you have brought up this question at an extremely appropriate moment.

Security vs. Loyalty

HENRY STEELE COMMAGER

Henry Steele Commager examines the abuses of loyalty review programs.
Is it possible for a government to accept Commager's intellectualized defini-
tion of loyalty? If Bullitt is correct in his assessment of the Soviet threat, is
Commager asking for too much leniency?

On May 6 a Russian-born girl, Mrs. Shura Lewis, gave a talk to the students
of the Western High School of Washington, D. C. She talked about Russia —
its school system, its public health program, the position of women, of the
aged, of the workers, the farmers, and the professional classes — and compared, superficially and uncritically, some American and Russian social institutions. The most careful examination of the speech — happily reprinted
for us in the *Congressional Record* — does not disclose a single disparagement
of anything American unless it is a quasi-humorous reference to the cost of
having a baby and of dental treatment in this country. Mrs. Lewis said nothing
that had not been said a thousand times, in speeches, in newspapers, magazines, and books. She said nothing that any normal person could find objectionable.

Her speech, however, created a sensation. A few students walked out on
it. Others improvised placards proclaiming their devotion to Americanism. Indignant mothers telephoned their protests. Newspapers took a strong stand
against the outrage. Congress, rarely concerned for the political or economic
welfare of the citizens of the capital city, reacted sharply when its intellectual
welfare was at stake. Congressmen Rankin and Dirksen thundered and light-
ened; the District of Columbia Committee went into a huddle; there were demands for housecleaning in the whole school system, which was obviously shot
through and through with Communism.

All this might be ignored, for we have learned not to expect either intelligence or understanding of Americanism from this element in our Congress.
More ominous was the reaction of the educators entrusted with the high responsibility of guiding and guarding the intellectual welfare of our boys and
girls. Did they stand up for intellectual freedom? Did they insist that high-
school children had the right and the duty to learn about other countries? Did
they protest that students were to be trusted to use intelligence and common
sense? Did they affirm that the Americanism of their students was staunch

From Henry Steele Commager, "Who Is Loyal to America?" *Harper's Magazine,* September 1947, pp. 192–199. Copyright 1947 by Henry Steele Commager and reprinted
with his permission.

enough to resist propaganda? Did they perform even the elementary task, expected of educators above all, of analyzing the much-criticized speech?

Not at all. The District Superintendent of Schools, Dr. Hobart Corning, hastened to agree with the animadversions of Representatives Rankin and Dirksen. The whole thing was, he confessed, "a very unfortunate occurrence," and had "shocked the whole school system." What Mrs. Lewis said, he added gratuitously, was "repugnant to all who are working with youth in the Washington schools," and "the entire affair contrary to the philosophy of education under which we operate." Mr. Danowsky, the hapless principal of the Western High School, was "the most shocked and regretful of all." The District of Columbia Committee would be happy to know that though he was innocent in the matter, he had been properly reprimanded!

It is the reaction of the educators that makes this episode more than a tempest in a teapot. We expect hysteria from Mr. Rankin and some newspapers; we are shocked when we see educators, timid before criticism and confused about first principles, betray their trust. And we wonder what can be that "philosophy of education" which believes that young people can be trained to the duties of citizenship by wrapping their minds in cotton-wool.

Merely by talking about Russia Mrs. Lewis was thought to be attacking Americanism. It is indicative of the seriousness of the situation that during this same week the House found it necessary to take time out from the discussion of the labor bill, the tax bill, the International Trade Organization, and the world famine, to meet assaults upon Americanism from a new quarter. This time it was the artists who were undermining the American system, and members of the House spent some hours passing around reproductions of the paintings which the State Department had sent abroad as part of its program for advertising American culture. We need not pause over the exquisite humor which congressmen displayed in their comments on modern art: weary statesmen must have their fun. But we may profitably remark the major criticism which was directed against this unfortunate collection of paintings. What was wrong with these paintings, it shortly appeared, was that they were un-American. "No American drew those crazy pictures," said Mr. Rankin. Perhaps he was right. The copious files of the Committee on Un-American Activities were levied upon to prove that of the forty-five artists represented "no less than twenty were definitely New Deal in various shades of Communism." The damning facts are specified for each of the pernicious twenty; we can content ourselves with the first of them, Ben-Zion. What is the evidence here? "Ben-Zion was one of the signers of a letter sent to President Roosevelt by the United American Artists which urged help to the USSR and Britain after Hitler attacked Russia." He was, in short, a fellow-traveler of Churchill and Roosevelt.

The same day that Mr. Dirksen was denouncing the Washington school authorities for allowing students to hear about Russia ("In Russia equal right is granted to each nationality. There is no discrimination. Nobody says, you are a Negro, you are a Jew") Representative Williams of Mississippi rose to denounce the *Survey-Graphic* magazine and to add further to our understanding of Americanism. The *Survey-Graphic,* he said, "contained 129 pages of outrageously vile and nauseating anti-Southern, anti-Christian, un-American, and pro-Communist tripe, ostensibly directed toward the elimination of the custom of racial segregation in the South." It was written by "meddling un-American purveyors of hate and indecency."

All in all, a busy week for the House. Yet those who make a practice of reading their *Record* will agree that it was a typical week. For increasingly Congress is concerned with the eradication of disloyalty and the defense of Americanism, and scarcely a day passes that some congressman does not treat us to exhortations and admonitions, impassioned appeals and eloquent declamations, similar to those inspired by Mrs. Lewis, Mr. Ben-Zion, and the editors of the *Survey-Graphic.* And scarcely a day passes that the outlines of the new loyalty and the new Americanism are not etched more sharply in public policy.

And this is what is significant — the emergence of new patterns of Americanism and of loyalty, patterns radically different from those which have long been traditional. It is not only the Congress that is busy designing the new patterns. They are outlined in President Truman's recent disloyalty order; in similar orders formulated by the New York City Council and by state and local authorities throughout the country; in the programs of the D.A.R., the American Legion, and similar patriotic organizations; in the editorials of the Hearst and the McCormick-Patterson papers; and in an elaborate series of advertisements sponsored by large corporations and business organizations. In the making is a revival of the red hysteria of the early 1920's, one of the shabbiest chapters in the history of American democracy; and more than a revival, for the new crusade is designed not merely to frustrate Communism but to formulate a positive definition of Americanism, and a positive concept of loyalty.

What is the new loyalty? It is, above all, conformity. It is the uncritical and unquestioning acceptance of America as it is — the political institutions, the social relationships, the economic practices. It rejects inquiry into the race question or socialized medicine, or public housing, or into the wisdom or validity of our foreign policy. It regards as particularly heinous any challenge to what is called "the system of private enterprise," identifying that system with Americanism. It abandons evolution, repudiates the once popular concept of progress, and regards America as a finished product, perfect and complete.

It is, it must be added, easily satisfied. For it wants not intellectual conviction nor spiritual conquest, but mere outward conformity. In matters of loyalty it takes the word for the deed, the gesture for the principle. It is content with the flag salute, and does not pause to consider the warning of our Supreme Court that "a person gets from a symbol the meaning he puts into it, and what is one man's comfort and inspiration is another's jest and scorn." It is satisfied with membership in respectable organizations and, as it assumes that every member of a liberal organization is a Communist, concludes that every member of a conservative one is a true American. It has not yet learned that not everyone who saith Lord, Lord, shall enter into the kingdom of Heaven. It is designed neither to discover real disloyalty nor to foster true loyalty.

II

What is wrong with this new concept of loyalty? What, fundamentally, is wrong with the pusillanimous retreat of the Washington educators, the barbarous antics of Washington legislators, the hysterical outbursts of the D.A.R., the gross and vulgar appeals of business corporations? It is not merely that these things are offensive. It is rather that they are wrong — morally, socially, and politically.

The concept of loyalty as conformity is a false one. It is narrow and restrictive, denies freedom of thought and of conscience, and is irremediably stained by private and selfish considerations. "Enlightened loyalty," wrote Josiah Royce, who made loyalty the very core of his philosophy,

> means harm to no man's loyalty. It is at war only with disloyalty, and its warfare, unless necessity constrains, is only a spiritual warfare. It does not foster class hatreds; it knows of nothing reasonable about race prejudices; and it regards all races of men as one in their need of loyalty. It ignores mutual misunderstandings. It loves its own wherever upon earth its own, namely loyalty itself, is to be found.

Justice, charity, wisdom, spirituality, he added, were all definable in terms of loyalty, and we may properly ask which of these qualities our contemporary champions of loyalty display.

Above all, loyalty must be to something larger than oneself, untainted by private purposes or selfish ends. But what are we to say of the attempts by the NAM and by individual corporations to identify loyalty with the system of private enterprise? Is it not as if officeholders should attempt to identify loyalty with their own party, their own political careers? Do not those corporations which pay for full-page advertisements associating Americanism with the competitive system expect, ultimately, to profit from that association? Do not those organizations that deplore, in the name of patriotism, the extension of government operation of hydro-electric power expect to profit from their campaign?

Certainly it is a gross perversion not only of the concept of loyalty but of the concept of Americanism to identify it with a particular economic system. This precise question, interestingly enough, came before the Supreme Court in the Schneiderman case not so long ago — and it was Wendell Willkie who was counsel for Schneiderman. Said the Court:

> Throughout our history many sincere people whose attachment to the general Constitutional scheme cannot be doubted have, for various and even divergent reasons, urged differing degrees of governmental owner-

ship and control of natural resources, basic means of production, and banks and the media of exchange, either with or without compensation. And something once regarded as a species of private property was abolished without compensating the owners when the institution of slavery was forbidden. Can it be said that the author of the Emancipation Proclamation and the supporters of the Thirteenth Amendment were not attached to the Constitution?

There is, it should be added, a further danger in the willful identification of Americanism with a particular body of economic practices. Many learned economists predict for the near future an economic crash similar to that of 1929. If Americanism is equated with competitive capitalism, what happens to it if competitive capitalism comes a cropper? If loyalty and private enterprise are inextricably associated, what is to preserve loyalty if private enterprise fails? Those who associate Americanism with a particular program of economic practices have a grave responsibility, for if their program should fail, they expose Americanism itself to disrepute.

The effort to equate loyalty with conformity is misguided because it assumes that there is a fixed content to loyalty and that this can be determined and defined. But loyalty is a principle, and eludes definition except in its own terms. It is devotion to the best interests of the commonwealth, and may require hostility to the particular policies which the government pursues, the particular practices which the economy undertakes, the particular institutions which society maintains. "If there is any fixed star in our Constitutional constellation," said the Supreme Court in the Barnette case, "it is that no official, high or petty, can prescribe what shall be orthodox in politics, nationalism, religion, or other matters of opinion, or force citizens to confess by word or act their faith therein. If there are any circumstances which permit an exception they do not now occur to us."

True loyalty may require, in fact, what appears to the naïve to be disloyalty. It may require hostility to certain provisions of the Constitution itself, and historians have not concluded that those who subscribed to the "Higher Law" were lacking in patriotism. We should not forget that our tradition is one of protest and revolt, and it is stultifying to celebrate the rebels of the past — Jefferson and Paine, Emerson and Thoreau — while we silence the rebels of the present. "We are a rebellious nation," said Theodore Parker, known in his day as the Great American Preacher, and went on:

> Our whole history is treason; our blood was attainted before we were born; our creeds are infidelity to the mother church; our constitution, treason to our fatherland. What of that? Though all the governors in the world bid us commit treason against man, and set the example, let us never submit.

Those who would impose upon us a new concept of loyalty not only assume that this is possible, but have the presumption to believe that they are competent to write the definition. We are reminded of Whitman's defiance of the "never-ending audacity of elected persons." Who are those who would set the standards of loyalty? They are Rankins and Bilbos, officials of the D.A.R. and the Legion and the NAM, Hearsts and McCormicks. May we not say of Rankin's harangues on loyalty what Emerson said of Webster at the time of the Seventh of March speech: "The word honor in the mouth of Mr. Webster is like the word love in the mouth of a whore."

What do men know of loyalty who make a mockery of the Declaration of Independence and the Bill of Rights, whose energies are dedicated to stirring up race and class hatreds, who would straitjacket the American spirit? What indeed do they know of America — the America of Sam Adams and Tom Paine, of Jackson's defiance of the Court and Lincoln's celebration of labor, of Thoreau's essay on Civil Disobedience and Emerson's championship of John Brown, of the America of the Fourierists and the Come-Outers, of cranks and fanatics, of socialists and anarchists? Who among American heroes could meet their tests, who would be cleared by their committees? Not Washington, who was a rebel. Not Jefferson, who wrote that all men are created equal and whose motto was "rebellion to tyrants is obedience to God." Not Garrison, who publicly burned the Constitution; or Wendell Phillips, who spoke for the underprivileged everywhere and counted himself a philosophical anarchist; not Seward of the Higher Law or Sumner of racial equality. Not Lincoln, who admonished us to have malice toward none, charity for all; or Wilson, who warned that our flag was "a flag of liberty of opinion as well as of political liberty"; or Justice Holmes, who said that our Constitution is an experiment and that while that experiment is being made "we should be eternally vigilant against attempts to check the expression of opinions that we loathe and believe to be fraught with death."

III

There are further and more practical objections against the imposition of fixed concepts of loyalty or tests of disloyalty. The effort is itself a confession of fear, a declaration of insolvency. Those who are sure of themselves do not need reassurance, and those who have confidence in the strength and the virtue of America do not need to fear either criticism or competition. The effort is bound to miscarry. It will not apprehend those who are really disloyal, it will not even frighten them; it will affect only those who can be labeled "radical." It is sobering to recall that though the Japanese relocation program, carried through at such incalculable cost in misery and tragedy, was justified to us on the ground that the Japanese were potentially disloyal, the record does not disclose a single case of Japanese disloyalty or sabotage during the whole war. The warning sounded by the Supreme Court in the Barnette flag-salute case is a timely one:

> Ultimate futility of such attempts to compel obedience is the lesson of every such effort from the Roman drive to stamp out Christianity as a disturber of pagan unity, the Inquisition as a means to religious and dy-

nastic unity, the Siberian exiles as a means to Russian unity, down to the fast-failing efforts of our present totalitarian enemies. Those who begin coercive elimination of dissent soon find themselves exterminating dissenters. Compulsory unification of opinion achieves only the unanimity of the graveyard.

Nor are we left to idle conjecture in this matter; we have had experience enough. Let us limit ourselves to a single example, one that is wonderfully relevant. Back in 1943 the House Un-American Activities Committee, deeply disturbed by alleged disloyalty among government employees, wrote a definition of subversive activities and proceeded to apply it. The definition was admirable, and no one could challenge its logic or its symmetry:

> Subversive activity derives from conduct intentionally destructive of or inimical to the Government of the United States—that which seeks to undermine its institutions, or to distort its functions, or to impede its projects, or to lessen its efforts, the ultimate end being to overturn it all.

Surely anyone guilty of activities so defined deserved not only dismissal but punishment. But how was the test applied? It was applied to two distinguished scholars, Robert Morss Lovett and Goodwin Watson, and to one able young historian, William E. Dodd, Jr., son of our former Ambassador to Germany. Of almost three million persons employed by the government, these were the three whose subversive activities were deemed the most pernicious, and the House cut them off the payroll. The sequel is familiar. The Senate concurred only to save a wartime appropriation; the President signed the bill under protest for the same reason. The Supreme Court declared the whole business a "bill of attainder" and therefore unconstitutional. Who was it, in the end, who engaged in "subversive activities" — Lovett, Dodd, and Watson, or the Congress which flagrantly violated Article One of the Constitution?

Finally, disloyalty tests are not only futile in application, they are pernicious in their consequences. They distract attention from activities that are really disloyal, and silence criticism inspired by true loyalty. That there are disloyal elements in America will not be denied, but there is no reason to suppose that any of the tests now formulated will ever be applied to them. It is relevant to remember that when Rankin was asked why his Committee did not investigate the Ku Klux Klan he replied that the Klan was not un-American, it was American!

Who are those who are really disloyal? Those who inflame racial hatreds, who sow religious and class dissensions. Those who subvert the Constitution by violating the freedom of the ballot box. Those who make a mockery of majority rule by the use of the filibuster. Those who impair democracy by denying equal educational facilities. Those who frustrate justice by lynch law or by making a farce of jury trials. Those who deny freedom of speech and of the press and of assembly. Those who press for special favors against the interest of the commonwealth. Those who regard public office as a source of private gain. Those who would exalt the military over the civil. Those who for selfish and private purposes stir up national antagonisms and expose the world to the ruin of war.

Will the House Committee on Un-American Activities interfere with the activities of these? Will Mr. Truman's disloyalty proclamation reach these? Will the current campaigns for Americanism convert these? If past experience is any guide, they will not. What they will do, if they are successful, is to silence criticism, stamp out dissent — or drive it underground. But if our democracy is to flourish it must have criticism, if our government is to function it must have dissent. Only totalitarian governments insist upon conformity and they — as we know — do so at their peril. Without criticism abuses will go unrebuked; without dissent our dynamic system will become static. The American people have a stake in the maintenance of the most thorough-going inquisition into American institutions. They have a stake in nonconformity, for they know that the American genius is nonconformist. They have a stake in experimentation of the most radical character, for they know that only those who prove all things can hold fast that which is good.

IV

It is easier to say what loyalty is not than to say what it is. It is not conformity. It is not passive acquiescence in the status quo. It is not preference for everything American over everything foreign. It is not an ostrich-like ignorance of other countries and other institutions. It is not the indulgence in ceremony — a flag salute, an oath of allegiance, a fervid verbal declaration. It is not a particular creed, a particular version of history, a particular body of economic practices, a particular philosophy.

It is a tradition, an ideal, and a principle. It is a willingness to subordinate every private advantage for the larger good. It is an appreciation of the rich and diverse contributions that can come from the most varied sources. It is allegiance to the traditions that have guided our greatest statesmen and inspired our most eloquent poets — the traditions of freedom, equality, democracy, tolerance, the tradition of the higher law, of experimentation, co-operation, and pluralism. It is a realization that America was born of revolt, flourished on dissent, became great through experimentation.

Independence was an act of revolution; republicanism was something new under the sun; the federal system was a vast experimental laboratory. Physically Americans were pioneers; in the realm of social and economic institutions, too, their tradition has been one of pioneering. From the beginning, intellectual and spiritual diversity have been as characteristic of America as racial and linguistic. The most distinctively American philosophies have been transcendentalism — which is the philosophy of the Higher Law — and pragmatism — which is the philosophy of experimentation and pluralism. These two principles are the very core of Americanism: the principle of the Higher Law, or of obedience to the dictates of conscience rather than of statutes, and the principle of pragmatism, or the rejection of a single good and of the notion of a finished universe. From the beginning Americans have known that there were new worlds to conquer, new truths to be discovered. Every effort to confine Americanism to a single pattern, to constrain it to a single pattern, to constrain it to a single formula, is disloyalty to everything that is valid in Americanism.

The Triumph of Security

THOMAS J. BROWN

Thomas J. Brown argues that the loyalty program is justified. Is Brown correct when he claims that the government may do anything to survive because its survival is the only protection of human liberty? If so, what becomes of the concept of inalienable rights? What criteria should be used to determine a person's loyalty? Were they being used in the Truman program? How many people may be denied "justice" in the name of national security before there is an abuse of power?

On March 21, 1947, a federal loyalty program was instituted by order of President Truman (Executive Order 9835) prescribing procedures for the administration of an "employees' " loyalty program in the executive branch of the government. The order was a partial answer to a hostile Congress determined to find Communists in the Democratic administration. It was also the outgrowth of a very real fear of Communist infiltration into the federal administration.

This first service-wide loyalty check in the federal ranks was actually the development of a more limited loyalty concept expressed in the 1939 Hatch Act. The terms of this Act made membership in any organization advocating the overthrow of the constitutional government of the United States grounds for removal from federal office. Following the enactment of the Hatch Act, the Civil Service Commission in 1940 announced that it would not certify for employment any member of the Communist Party, the German American Bund, or any other Communist or Nazi organization. Appropriation acts after 1940 forbade expenditures for salaries of such persons. The Federal Bureau of Investigation stepped into the picture in 1941, after Congress appropriated $100,000 to investigate federal workers charged with being "members of subversive organizations or to advocate the overthrow of the Federal Government." The investigations which followed revealed some of the weaknesses of the

From Thomas J. Brown, "Is the Loyalty Program Justified? YES!" *Forum,* January 1949, pp. 38, 40–43.

program. First of all, there was considerable vagueness surrounding the meaning of the word "subversive." In the absence of a congressional definition, Attorney General Biddle included as "subversive organizations" those with Communist backgrounds or affiliations and American Fascist, Nazi, Italian, and Japanese organizations. A differentiation was made between organizations frankly Communist or Nazi, and those which were misleading "front" organizations. Experience proved to the satisfaction of the F.B.I., but not to Congress, that the investigation of members of "front" organizations had results utterly disproportionate to resources expended," and that the "futility and harmful character of a broad personnel inquiry have been too amply demonstrated." It was recommended that future checks be limited to subjects "clearly pertinent to the vital problem of internal security."

Statutory provisions forbidding the employment of "subversive persons" remained on the books and an appropriation of 1942 required a similar investigation. Between July 1, 1942, and June 30, 1945, 6,193 cases were referred to the F.B.I., resulting in 101 dismissals, 75 other administrative actions, and 21 resignations.

The Civil Service Commission was able to refuse to certify applicants on broader grounds, if it found a "reasonable doubt" as to the loyalty of the applicant. Between July, 1940, and March 31, 1947, there were 1,313 civil service rulings of ineligibility where loyalty was a major factor, out of a total of 43,811 ratings. It must be remembered that the Commission had insufficient funds for a complete check and investigated less than 400,000 out of 7,000,000 placements.

Dissatisfaction in Congress with the conducting of the investigations led to the setting up of the President's Temporary Commission of Employee Loyalty in November, 1946. This Commission made a thorough study of previous investigations and concluded that they had been "ineffective in dealing with subversive activities which employ subterfuge, propaganda, infiltration and deception." It acknowledged that there were some subversive and disloyal persons in the employ of the federal government and asserted that "whatever their number, the internal security of the government demands continuous screening . . . of present and prospective employees. The presence . . . of *any* disloyal . . . persons . . . presents a problem of such importance that it must be dealt with vigorously and effectively."

Executive Order 9835 grew out of the recommendations of this temporary commission. It stated that the twofold objective of the loyalty program was to afford "maximum protection . . . [to] the United States against infiltration of disloyal persons into the ranks of its employees" and to give "equal protection from unfounded accusations . . . [to] the loyal employees of the Government."

A six-point standard of disloyalty is outlined in the order, with the general provision that "on all the evidence, reasonable grounds exist for belief that the person involved is disloyal to the government of the United States. The six "activities and associations" to be considered are: (1) sabotage and espionage; (2) treason or sedition or advocacy thereof; (3) support of the forceful overthrow of the constitutional government of the United States; (4) disloyal, intentional disclosure of confidential documents; (5) acting to serve the interests of another government in preference to the interests of the United States; (6) "membership in, affiliation with, or sympathetic association with any foreign or domestic organization, association . . . designated by the Attorney General as totalitarian, fascist, communist, or subversive. . . ."

After much criticism of point six in the order, the Attorney General finally submitted the list of "subversive" organizations for publication, and the list was published on December 4, 1947. It included 80 groups and 11 schools, and was necessarily incomplete.

The program was begun in August, 1947, with the routine finger-printing of 2 million federal employees. A short questionnaire was designed for identification purposes, and all federal employees were required to fill it in. All names were then sent to the F.B.I. for clearance, and unless "derogatory information" was found in the F.B.I. files, the names were cleared. A "full field investigation" followed only if derogatory information was found.

The results of a field investigation are reviewed within the F.B.I. and then sent to a loyalty board in the appropriate agency, composed of not less than three persons. An adverse finding at this level occasions a letter of charges to the employee, including the factual details of the charges "so far as security determinations will permit." The employee may answer the charges in writing and may call for an administrative hearing, where he may present evidence and be represented by counsel. The hearing is private.

Suspension follows an adverse hearing, but provision is made for appeal to the agency head and, if this appeal is denied, to the central Loyalty Review Board. This central Review Board is made up of 23 private citizens serving without compensation, representative of a broad cross-section of the American public. Similar procedure may be followed by an applicant for a federal position ruled "ineligible" for security reasons by the Civil Service Commission.

Of the 2 million names sent to the F.B.I., over half had been cleared according to an announcement of March 16, 1948, and 777 full investigations had resulted. Of these, 170 had been completed, with 94 adverse findings resulting.

Justification

The protection given to federal employees under the loyalty program does not extend to employees of the Departments of State and Defense or to the Atomic Energy Commission. These departments have statutory authority to remove summarily any employee "in the interest of national security." Dismissal from these departments as a "security risk" carries with it no right of appeal, although there are indications that in some cases appeal to the Loyalty Board will be allowed.

The Federal Loyalty Program as outlined above is vital to the internal security of the United States today. There are those who still close their eyes to the fundamental conflict between the United States and the Soviet Union, but they are dwindling in number. The Loyalty Program can be defended on four broad grounds: (1) a sovereign state has an inherent and inalienable right of self-defense; (2) Communist infiltration menaces the safety of our sovereign government today; (3) in most cases, fair procedures have been instituted for appealing disloyalty rulings; (4) there is no inherent right of any employee to federal employment.

Every sovereign state must defend itself from its enemies both external and internal. Self-preservation is a "primary and essential right." Any government unwilling or unable to defend itself soon loses its independence altogether. This is no less true of a democracy than of a dictatorship. The preservation of the state, therefore, is paramount to the rights of its individual citizens, who would have no rights at all should the state disintegrate.

The "moral right of revolution," further, cannot be recognized by the constitutional and sovereign state. The right of revolution is diametrically opposed to the preservation of the state and must always be countered by the state if possible.

Thus the exclusion from the country of aliens believing in the forceful overthrow of the United States government is completely justified. So is the exclusion of such persons, citizens or not, from any type of federal employment. Today, as we shall see below, the peculiar type of offensive adopted by the avowed enemies of the United States necessitates even more stringent measures for the preservation of our constitutional government.

The leaders of the Soviet Union have repeatedly and publically declared their enmity to the principles for which this country stands. Although they modify their stand for reasons of expediency from time to time, there can be no doubt that they are working for the establishment of Communist regimes in every country of the world. This would mean the end of the government of the United States as we know it. Communism unquestionably menaces our safety as a democratic, freedom-loving people.

Although many Americans have a nodding familiarity with the so-called "Red menace," few of us have a real understanding of its character. Through the Cominform, successor to the Comintern, the leaders of the Soviet Union direct the party line in every country of the world. American Communists are not, and cannot be, exceptions to this rule, for communism allows no exceptions. Communist Party members in the United States, and everywhere else, take their orders in the last analysis from Moscow.

The complications of the problem are twofold. First, it is extremely difficult to detect Communists because they are trained to conceal their identity by fair means or foul. Basic Communist precepts invalidate rules of democratic morality, and no obligation is felt by a Communist to confess his political connection. Unfortunately, this difficulty means that "fellow-travelers" and muddle-headed liberals are often the only frank supporters of Soviet Communist policy. Consequently, they pay high penalties for their mistaken support of an unpatriotic cause. But they do not pay altogether unfairly. This needs strong emphasis. However well-meaning the Soviet-sympathizers may be, their presence in important positions in the federal government represents a potential danger to the United States. Communists must be removed because of their fundamental disloyalty. Fellow-travelers and Left-wing sympathizers must be removed because of their incredible stupidity.

Individual Freedom

Second, it is extremely difficult to deal with the disloyal or potentially disloyal because of our high standards of individual freedom. In pure democratic theory, no man should be made to suffer, least of all by the government, for his own opinions. Freedom of opinion has always been one of our most cherished rights. In its effort to ferret out disloyalty, the Loyalty Program frankly and openly limits this freedom. It is, therefore, challenged as unconstitutional and dictatorial, as a harbinger of the very totalitarianism we fear. This is not so. Because of the danger faced by our government, it has the inalienable right of self-preservation. But the provisions and the operations of the Loyalty Act guard individual rights as much as possible.

Very, very few employees of the federal government have ever been subjected to more than a cursory investigation. Of the present employees, over a million have already been "cleared" after fingerprinting and identification without any further questioning. When they realize that the Loyalty Program protects their government and their jobs, they appreciate its purpose.

Of those employees whose records have led to a field investigation, comparatively few have been discharged. This fact has led the ignorant to proclaim the uselessness of the Loyalty Program; it leads the informed to marvel at its discrimination.

Executive Order 9835 prescribes the methods of appeal after field investigation, leaving nothing to the chance prejudices of department or other agency heads. As we have noted above, the defendant may have counsel, he may appear at hearings, he may appeal his case not once but twice.

Because of the rather special nature of loyalty cases, the defendant unfortunately may not have all the appurtenances of a court trial. When the evidence against him has been gathered by the F.B.I. from sources they do not want to disclose for security reasons, then those sources are not disclosed to the defendant. Cross examination is not permitted. These are admitted drawbacks to a fair trial. Yet when the nature of the charges and the danger to the government is considered, they do not appear to be major drawbacks to the program as a whole.

Employees of the Departments of State and Defense are obviously in a weaker position if their loyalty comes under investigation. Because these departments represent "sensitive areas" of the government, where disloyalty would be extremely and perhaps immediately dangerous, summary dismissal is allowed by law. In most cases, it appears that the provisions for review made by Executive Order 9835 will be extended to employees of "sensitive areas." But in some cases, there will be no right of appeal or review.

It is well for us all to remember that no citizen of the United States holds an inherent right to a federal job, although many federal job-holders think they do. An employee of the federal government has a heavy and solemn obligation to that government. His loyalty must be unquestioning and un-questionable. Americans have an inalienable right to their own opinions. They are welcome to question the precepts of this government and every other government. They are free to sympathize with Soviet Russia and, today, to join the Communist Party she sponsors in this country. They may even, under our more than liberal laws, put a foreign country's welfare before that of their own country. BUT, and this is a very important "but," — they have no right, and they commit a grave moral wrong, when they accept federal employment under conditions such as these.

Out and out Communists — party members — are more completely aware of these truths than any other Americans. No Communist accepts federal employment without complete awareness of his disloyalty. To such persons in the federal employ the government owes less than nothing.

What does it owe to the Left-wing liberals and Communist sympathizers who more frequently are sifted out in the Loyalty Program? To them, we believe, it owes a fair and unprejudiced hearing, and no more than that. This hearing all suspects may have on appeal to the Loyalty Board. It owes them, perhaps, the opportunity of resignation from the federal service before the investigation is publicized. This opportunity they usually get also.

Mass Hysteria

And what does the government owe its millions of loyal employees? An explanation of the reason for the Loyalty Program and an assurance that for most of them, fingerprinting and a brief questionnaire will be routine and nothing more. This unfortunately the government has not yet succeeded in getting across to many of its employees. Partly because the Left-wing has stirred up mass hysteria, many government employees are more fearful for their jobs than they need be. According to the Left-wing press, anyone who has ever ridden in a car-pool with a Left-winger, or bought the *Nation* or the *New Republic,* or joined a radical student group, or contributed to a doubtful charity, is in imminent danger of unemployment.

The facts belie these cries of alarm. From personal experience, I feel sure that the number of federal employees who have ever done any of these "dangerous" things is many, many times greater than the number being investigated by the F.B.I. and the Civil Service Commission. Statistics on the number of discharges testify to the fairness of the Program and the level-headedness of the F.B.I.

Naturally, the Program is not perfect. Mistakes, grave mistakes, have been made, and innocent persons have suffered. This is part of the price the American people must pay for the Cold War, for Yalta, Cairo, and Moscow, for their long appeasement of Fascism and Naziism which in turn allowed communism to flourish in Europe. This is part of the price that every federal employee must pay for his employment under present conditions.

And this is no secret. The Loyalty Program is no undercover program. Everyone who remains in or enters federal employment is well aware that he must be willing and able to stand thorough investigation. If his present views, or his past activities, are such that he fears for his federal job, he should resign.

These are harsh words. But we live in a harsh world and struggle against an ideology for which "harsh" is a kind word. The federal government of the United States is entitled to take whatever measures are necessary to secure its continued existence. For — and this is a truth almost always overlooked by the "liberals" — the continued existence of the United States is our only guarantee of the continuing existence of liberal democracy. It may be, in the last analysis, our only guarantee of our own individual existence. Let the "liberals" ask themselves the whereabouts of their brothers in Czechoslovakia, in Austria, in Russian-occupied Germany! Let them face the nature of our enemy, the danger to our country! If they will do this honestly, they will agree with all patriotic and intelligent Americans that the federal loyalty program is justified today.

"Disloyalty" on Trial
PAUL ROBESON

Paul Robeson testifies before the House Un-American Activities Committee in 1956. On what basis does the Committee question Robeson's loyalty? Were Robeson's statements about the United States and the Soviet Union harmful to the security of the United States? Did his statements justify questioning of his loyalty? What is the atmosphere which permeates the hearing?

Mr. Robeson: Could I say that for the reason that I am here today, you know, from the mouth of the State Department itself, is because I should not be allowed to travel because I have struggled for years for the independence of the colonial peoples of Africa, and for many years I have so labored and I can say modestly that my name is very much honored in South Africa and all over Africa in my struggles for their independence. That is the kind of independence like Sukarno got in Indonesia. Unless we are double-talking, then these efforts in the interest of Africa would be in the same context. The other reason that I am here today is again from the

From U.S., Congress, House, Committee on Un-American Activities, *Investigation of the Unauthorized Use of United States Passports,* 82d Cong., 2d sess., June 12, 1956, pt. 3, pp. 4499 ff. Testimony of Paul Robeson.

State Department and from the court record of the court of appeals, that when I am abroad I speak out against the injustices against the Negro people of this land. I sent a message to the Bandung Conference and so forth. That is why I am here. This is the basis and I am not being tried for whether I am a Communist, I am being tried for fighting for the rights of my people who are still second-class citizens in this United States of America. My mother was born in your State, Mr. Walter, and my mother was a Quaker, and my ancestors in the time of Washington baked bread for George Washington's troops when they crossed the Delaware, and my own father was a slave. I stand here struggling for the rights of my people to be full citizens in this country and they are not. They are not in Mississippi and they are not in Montgomery, Ala., and they are not in Washington, and they are nowhere, and that is why I am here today. You want to shut up every Negro who has the courage to stand up and fight for the rights of his people, for the rights of workers and I have been on many a picket line for the steelworkers too. And that is why I am here today. . . .

Mr. Arens: Did you make a trip to Europe in 1949 and to the Soviet Union?

Mr. Robeson: Yes; I made a trip to England and I sang. . . .

Mr. Arens: Did you go to Paris on that trip?

Mr. Robeson: I went to Paris.

Mr. Arens: And while you were in Paris, did you tell an audience there that the American Negro would never go to war against the Soviet Government?

Mr. Robeson: May I say that is slightly out of context? May I explain to you what I did say? I remember the speech very well, and the night before in London, and do not take the newspaper, take me, I made the speech, gentlemen, Mr. So and So. It happened that the night before in London before I went to Paris, and will you please listen?

Mr. Arens: We are listening.

Mr. Robeson: That 2,000 students from various parts of the colonial world, students who since then have become very important in their governments and in places like Indonesia and India, and in many parts of Africa; 2,000 students asked me and Dr. Dadoo, a leader of the Indian people in South Africa, when we addressed this specific conference, and remember I was speaking to a peace conference, a conference devoted to peace, they asked me and Dr. Dadoo to say there that they were struggling for peace, that they did not want war against anybody. It was 2,000 students who came from populations that would range to six or seven hundred million people, and not just 15 million.

Mr. Kearney: Do you know anybody who wants war?

Mr. Robeson: They asked me to address this conference and say in their name that they did not want war. That is what I said. There is no part of my speech made in Paris which says that I said that 15 million American Negroes would do anything. I said it was my feeling that the American people would struggle for peace and that has since been underscored by the President of these United States. Now, in passing, I said ——

Mr. Kearney: Do you know of any people who want war?

Mr. Robeson: Listen to me, I said it was unthinkable to me that any people would take up arms in the name of an Eastland to go against anybody, and gentlemen, I still say that. What should happen would be that this United States Government should go down to Mississippi and protect my people. That is what should happen.

The Chairman: Did you say what was attributed to you?

Mr. Robeson: I did not say it in that context.

Mr. Arens: I lay before you a document, containing an article, I Am Looking for Full Freedom, by Paul Robeson, in which is recited a quotation of Paul Robeson.

Mr. Robeson: That is fine.

Mr. Arens: This article appears in a publication called the Worker dated July 3, 1949.

Mr. Robeson: That is right.

Mr. Arens (reading):

> At the Paris Conference I said it was unthinkable that the Negro people of America or elsewhere in the world could be drawn into war with the Soviet Union.

Mr. Robeson: Is that saying the Negro people would do anything? I said it is unthinkable. I did not say it there; I did not say that there. I said that in the Worker.

Mr. Arens (reading):

> I repeat it with hundredfold emphasis: They will not.

Did you say that?

Mr. Robeson: I did not say that in Paris; no.

Mr. Arens: Did you say that in this article?

Mr. Robeson: I said that in America. And, gentlemen, they have not yet done so, and it is quite clear that no Americans or no people in the world probably are going to war with the Soviet Union, so I was rather prophetic, was I not, and rather prophetic. We want peace today and not war.

Mr. Arens: On that trip to Europe, did you go to Stockholm?

Mr. Robeson: I certainly did and I understand that some people in the American Embassy tried to break up my concert, and they were not successful.

Mr. Arens: While you were in Stockholm, did you make a little speech?

Mr. Robeson: I made all kinds of speeches; yes.

Mr. Arens: Let me read you a quotation of one of your speeches, and see if it comes to your mind.

Mr. Robeson: Let me listen.

Mr. Arens: Do so, please.

Mr. Robeson: I am a lawyer.

Mr. Kearney: It would be a revelation if you would listen to counsel.

Mr. Robeson: In good company I usually listen, but you know people wander around in such fancy places, you know, and would you please let me read my statement at some point?

The Chairman: We will consider your statement.

Mr. Arens (reading):

> I do not hesitate 1 second to state clearly and unmistakably: I belong to the American resistance movement which fights against American imperialism, just as the resistance movement fought against Hitler.

Mr. Robeson: Just like Frederick Douglass and Harry Tubman were underground railroaders, and fighting for our freedom; you bet your life.

The Chairman: I am going to have to insist that you listen to these questions.

Mr. Robeson: I am listening.

Mr. Arens (reading):

> If the American warmongers fancy that they could win America's millions of Negroes for a war against those countries (i.e., the Soviet Union and the peoples' democracies) then they ought to understand that this will never be the case. Why should the Negroes ever fight against the only nations of the world where racial discrimination is prohibited, and where the people can live freely? Never! I can assure you, they will never fight against either the Soviet Union or the peoples' democracies.

Did you make that statement?

Mr. Robeson: I do not remember that. But what is perfectly clear today is that 900 million other colored people have told you that they will not, is that not so? 400 million in India and millions everywhere have told you precisely that the colored people are not going to die for anybody and they are going to die for their independence. We are dealing not with 15 million colored people. We are dealing with hundreds of millions.

Mr. Kearney: The witness has answered the question and he does not have to make a speech.

Mr. Arens: Did you say in effect that Stalin was a great man and Stalin had done much for the Russian people, for all of the nations of the world, for all working people of the earth? Did you say something to that effect about Stalin when you were in Moscow?

Mr. Robeson: I cannot remember.

Mr. Arens: Do you have a recollection of praising Stalin?

Mr. Robeson: I can certainly know that I said a lot about Soviet people, fighting for the peoples of the earth.

Mr. Arens: Did you praise Stalin?

Mr. Robeson: I do not remember.

Mr. Arens: Have you recently changed your mind about Stalin?

Mr. Robeson: Whatever has happened to Stalin, gentlemen, is a question for the Soviet Union and I would not argue with a representative of the people who, in building America wasted 60 to 100 million lives of my people, black people drawn from Africa on the plantations. You are responsible and your forebears for 60 million to 100 million black people dying in the slave ships and on the plantations, and don't you ask me about anybody, please.

Mr. Arens: I am glad you called our attention to that slave problem. While you were in Soviet Russia, did you ask them there to show you the slave labor camps?

The Chairman: You have been so greatly interested in slaves, I should think that you would want to see that.

Mr. Robeson: The slaves I see are still as a kind of semiserfdom, and I am interested in the place I am and in the country that can do something about it. As far as I know about the slave camps, they were Fascist prisoners who had murdered millions of the Jewish people and who would have wiped out millions of the Negro people could they have gotten a hold of them. That is all I know about that. . . .

Mr. Arens (reading):

> Now, the Soviet Union is the only country I have ever been in where I have felt completely at ease. I have lived in England and America, and I have almost circled the globe but for myself, wife, and son, the Soviet Union is our future home.

Mr. Robeson: If it were so we would be there. My wife is here and my son is here, and we have come back here.

Mr. Arens: Let me complete this paragraph and see if it helps explain why it is not your future home.

> For a while, however, I would not feel right going there to live. By singing its praises wherever I go I think that I can be of the most value to it. It is too easy to go to the Soviet Union, breathe the free air, and live happily ever afterward.

Were those your sentiments?

Mr. Robeson: I came back to America to fight for my people here, and they are still second- and third-class citizens, gentlemen, and I was born here of the Negro people and of working people and I am back here to help them struggle.

Mr. Scherer: Did you say that?

Mr. Robeson: I have said that many times.

Mr. Scherer: Did you say what he read to you?

Mr. Robeson: I do not even know what he is reading from, really, and I do not mind. It is like the statement that I was supposed to make in Paris. Now, this was not in context, but I thought it was healthy for Americans to consider whether or not Negroes should fight for people who kick them around, and when they took a vote up North they got very nervous because a lot of white Americans said, "I do not see why the hell they would."

Mr. Arens: Did you, while you were in Moscow, make this statement:

> Yes, the Communists march at the front of the struggle for stable peace and popular democracy. But they are not alone. With them are all of the progressive people of America, Wallace's party, and the Negroes of the South, and workers of the North.

Mr. Robeson: Now you are making it up, brother. I would have to get my own copy of the speech.

Mr. Arens: I put it to you as a fact and ask you, while you are under oath, to deny the fact that you made that statement.

Mr. Robeson: I am not denying, but do not just read anything into something. How could I say what Wallace's party would do, or what somebody else would do? That is nonsense.

Mr. Arens: While you are under oath, why do you not deny it?

Mr. Robeson: The Soviet Union and the People's Democracy in China are in the forefront of the struggle for peace, and so is our President, thank goodness, and let us hope we will have some peace, if committees like yours do not upset the applecart and destroy all of humanity. Now can I read my speech?

The Chairman: You have made it without reading it. . . .

Mr. Arens: Let me quote from an article appearing in a paper, and see if you recall this speech:

> I have the greatest contempt for the democratic press and there is something within me which keeps me from breaking your cameras over your heads.

Did you say that to the press people in New York City about the time you were addressing this rally in June of 1949?

Mr. Robeson: It is sort of out of context.

Mr. Arens: That was out of context?

Mr. Robeson: I am afraid it is.

Mr. Arens: Would you want to refresh your recollection by looking at the article?

Mr. Robeson: Yes. That was not at a meeting. Why do you not say what it was? When my son married the woman of his choice, some very wild press men were there to make a sensation out of it, and this thing was at his wedding, and I did not say "democratic press," I said "a certain kind of press," and I was reaching for a camera to break it, you are quite right.

Mr. Arens: That was a misquotation?

Mr. Robeson: It was not at a meeting. It was when I came out of my son's wedding, and why do you not be honest about this? There is nothing about a meeting, it was a wedding of my son.

Mr. Arens: Does not this article say, "Paul Robeson Addressing a Welcome Home Rally"?

Mr. Robeson: I do not care what it says.

Mr. Arens: That is wrong, too, is it?

Now I would invite your attention, if you please, to the Daily Worker of
June 29, 1949, with reference to a get-together with you and Ben Davis.
Do you know Ben Davis?

Mr. Robeson: One of my dearest friends, one of the finest Americans you can
imagine, born of a fine family, who went to Amherst and was a great man.

The Chairman: The answer is "Yes"?

Mr. Robeson: And a very great friend and nothing could make me prouder
than to know him.

The Chairman: That answers the question.

Mr. Arens: Did I understand you to laud his patriotism?

Mr. Robeson: I say that he is as patriotic an American as there can be, and
you gentlemen belong with the Alien and Sedition Acts, and you are the
nonpatriots, and you are the un-Americans and you ought to be ashamed
of yourselves.

The Chairman: Just a minute, the hearing is now adjourned.

Mr. Robeson: I should think it would be.

The Chairman: I have endured all of this that I can.

Mr. Robeson: Can I read my statement?

The Chairman: No, you cannot read it. The meeting is adjourned.

Mr. Robeson: I think it should be and you should adjourn this forever, that
is what I would say.

◆ MODERN ESSAY ◆

The Limits of Security
EDGAR ERICSON

*Edgar Ericson's essay shows that the security problem confronting American
society has not thawed along with the Cold War. Ericson writes that what is
objectionable about the CIA surveillance is that it was done contrary to law.
Could we solve the problem by legalizing the actions of the FBI and CIA
which Ericson describes, or is the problem not one just of statute law but the
balance between the concepts of individual liberty and national security? Ericson raises questions he cannot answer: How do you permit police authorities
ample latitude to decide if someone is a danger to the state without permitting
them to abuse that latitude? Who is to determine what person, what action,
what thought is a danger to the State?*

From Edgar Ericson, "The CIA and the Crisis of Democracy," pp. 26–27. This article
first appeared in *The Humanist* January/February 1976 and is reprinted by permission.

While on a recent visit to Washington, D.C., I had a glimpse into an unlawful operation of our government that few Americans have had at first hand. I examined the CIA file on myself, surrendered under the Freedom of Information Act. It contained a selection of my speeches and publications as Leader of the Washington Ethical Society during the years of the Vietnam conflict. Comparatively few Americans have had this experience because this operation of the Central Intelligence Agency was strictly a violation of law and has only recently come to light. In disclosing the CIA's unlawful intrusion into domestic dissent during the Vietnam war, President Ford last June characterized the agency's action as "regrettable" and assured the nation that steps had been taken to safeguard against a recurrence of such abuses by the government. A committee of Congress continues to examine the record of these violations for the purpose of strengthening congressional oversight of potentially dangerous intelligence operations.

As I leafed through a file containing about an inch and a half of material on the Washington Ethical Society — consisting primarily of copies of my addresses and the Leader's page from the monthly newsletter, plus an assortment of routine announcements of social activities and coming events — my personal feeling was a mixture of astonishment and amusement. If it were not for the sinister potential of such domestic surveillance, one might dismiss it as something akin to a Marx Brothers comedy. There I had been during the middle and late 1960s, using all the wits and talents I had to shout from the housetops my moral objections to America's pursuit of the war in Vietnam, airing my views by radio and television at every opportunity, helping to organize public rallies, speaking at every assembly and teach-in to which I gained an invitation, testifying before committees of the House and Senate, and appearing before the Director of Selective Service and the Presidential Appeal Board on behalf of a liberalized provision for conscientious objectors — in short, living in a virtual goldfish bowl in an effort to put every resource I had into public witness against the war — only to learn this year that the CIA was paying an informer to observe the organization I served and to collect my utterances. While I appreciate all this attention, the CIA could have secured a much more complete record by simply getting on the mailing list and subscribing to my speeches.

We might be inclined to dismiss such business as an expensive joke — a waste of public resources that could be better used — if more ominous abuses were not coming to light day by day. A Senate report has documented the involvement of the CIA in assassination plots in foreign countries, and a congressional hearing has disclosed how another agency, the FBI, under J. Edgar Hoover's aegis, had engaged in a six-year campaign to disrupt and defame the career of Martin Luther King — at one point sending King a letter that he understood as a demand to commit suicide or face unknown dire consequences. The late Director Hoover, by the admission of his own agents, pursued Dr. King in order to settle a personal score. King had committed the crime of daring to criticize the director of the FBI, and Mr. Hoover's actions have all the earmarks of a personal vendetta.

Thus, we are forced to reevaluate another idol of the American childhood — the fearless, incorruptible director of the FBI, protector of the innocent and scourge of the underworld. Better to be the ringleader of a crime syndicate or a dope smuggler than a nonviolent reformer who shows insufficient reverence for the Chief.

These disclosures, following a cascade of evidence since Watergate, have awakened thoughtful Americans to a realization of how close we have come to the subversion of the democratic system by our own government. Some say we have lost democracy already and that the loss is beyond remedy, but I reject this view. I believe that the events that resulted from Watergate, forcing the resignation of a grossly erring president and exposing police-state practices by federal agencies, have given the American nation a second chance, a chance to cleanse our government, to arrest the growth of lawless police power, and to restore the vitality of our republican structures and constitutional freedoms.

I do not wish to be interpreted as an opponent of legitimate law-enforcement and intelligence work. We recognize that there *are* violent and lawless people at large and a democratic society must be prepared to cope with those who violate the public peace. When terrorists attempt to bomb bus stations and public and private buildings, we must give law-enforcement agencies the power to investigate their conspiracies and intercept their crimes. It does not dismay me to learn that the organization I served as religious leader while I was engaged in anti-war and civil-rights activities was investigated. Police and investigative agencies must have reasonable latitude to determine by observation whether a particular group or individual is engaged in lawful dissent or in criminal activity. What does disturb me is that this surveillance, like many other CIA operations, was done unlawfully.

Since I was one of the first and most outspoken of Washington's religious leaders to oppose the Vietnam war — as I had earlier criticized our interventions in Cuba and other Latin American states — it seemed to me only reasonable to assume that an agency responsible for the security of the United States would examine my motives and associations. There is nothing objectionable in this precaution if it is done within the prescriptions of law and with scrupulous regard for the rights of free speech and freedom of association.

The danger to democracy is that official observation, even at its best, is intimidating to most people, having what the Supreme Court has described as a chilling effect on free expression. It is therefore essential that investigative agencies be limited to necessary operations as defined and controlled by statute.

What is objectionable in the CIA's surveillance of sixteen Washington-area organizations — including the Washington Ethical Society, the Urban League, and other moderate civil-rights and antiwar groups — is that, as President Ford confirmed, it was done contrary to law by an agency explicitly prohibited by its congressional charter from engaging in domestic activity. By separating the functions of the CIA from those of the FBI and other investigative agencies, Congress had sought to provide a defense against the growth of a superagency with runaway powers. Experience has shown how feeble these protections were.

A free people must establish beyond question that investigative and police agencies are not authorized to prosecute, punish, or defame anyone. Ever! They are not headmasters, censors, intimidators, or assassins. Their sole function is to apprehend lawbreakers and provide evidence to the Justice Department, which is responsible for prosecution in the courts.

The abuse of police powers is worldwide. Americans who cherish their freedom share a common cause with dissenters like Andrei Sakharov and Roy Medyedev in the Soviet Union. When we read Alexander Solzhenitsyn's account of his experiences with the Soviet police during the months prior to his expulsion, including the interrogation and suicide of a friend who had hidden a manuscript for him, we see a preview of our common fate, if we should ever fail to curb the power of a politically directed police force. The world is our Gulag if we relax our vigil.

These thoughts were very much in my mind as I sat down to review the CIA file. One document in the dossier was an address entitled "Keeping the Person in the Picture," which I had delivered at a Sunday morning meeting of the Washington Ethical Society on December 5, 1965. A CIA agent had dutifully underlined certain key passages in the text. I admit that I find his choices intriguing, especially one paragraph which he had boldly underlined and where he had added a double stroke down the margin to make certain its significance was not missed. I am indebted to this unknown CIA operative for paying special heed to this passage and would like to show my gratitude by resurrecting it for our consideration today as an appropriate text for our present topic — almost ten years to the day after it was first delivered as part of a discourse on the moral basis of freedom.

I had said, and the agent carefully underlined: "A chief worry of many thoughtful Americans is the development of the many new techniques and devices for controlling human beings, spying upon their lives and opinions, regulating their dissent through economic and governmental reprisals, attitude testing, security checks, and the like — which invade areas of personal privacy and which the framers of the Bill of Rights never dreamed of. Despite our proud heritage and personal liberty, we may be in the process of degenerating from a community of persons into a mere collectivity, made up of docile and manipulated masses."

Another underlined passage on the same page: "Man is a being of moral concerns and perception who cannot surrender his ethical interest without losing his humanity; his universe of values has at its center a perception of his own worth, and the worth of all other persons who share his humanity. This is the generating principle of our moral realities."

Still another passage which attracted the CIA agent's pencil: "A free culture — or what we would recognize as a free culture — must acknowledge a wide area of choice to the individual; that a choice — if it is to be meaningful — cannot be restricted arbitrarily to what happens to be popularly received at the moment. As long as the dissenter is not overtly overthrowing the freedoms of his neighbors, his opinions and tastes must be left to his conscience."

I cannot know, of course, what logic guided the CIA reviewer to mark these and other passages. Everything that appears to have caught his eye is of such a general philosophical and spiritual character that I suspect he was only meditating — engaging in a kind of Sunday School reverie at government expense. There may be an issue of church-state separation hidden somewhere in this. But without knowing his reasoning, I am willing to praise his sense of discrimination; for if his purpose was to evaluate my motives, to distill the essence of my ethical philosophy and social conscience, he chose the very passages I would select as a guide to my actions. He even underlined a portion of a sentence that reads: "Non-conformity is not an end in itself but an inner discipline which has as its object the discovery and release of those qualities and attributes which cannot be mass produced or mass supported, values which are uniquely individual and must be created anew in each human life which is to possess them."

Perhaps the agent's motive in marking these particular selections was to exonerate me of suspicion, to give me a clean bill of health, having found that my objection to the war in Vietnam was based on loyalty to democratic and humanistic principles — as I always insisted it to be. I will give the agent the benefit of the doubt and assume this to be the fact. But the larger issue remains. No matter how well-intentioned and discriminating my wartime guardian angel at CIA headquarters may have been, he was nevertheless engaged in a nefarious practice violating a law designed to protect the civil liberties of the people that clearly mandated that the CIA should not engage in just such domestic spying.

Other addresses that I delivered in that period, including some that the CIA apparently missed, took the position that the government, under both Democratic and Republican presidents, had usurped powers denied to them by the Constitution and by moral law and that citizens in strict loyalty to the democratic tradition must be prepared, when necessary, to resist that usurpation of their consciences by all appropriate nonviolent means. Nonviolent resistance is an arduous discipline, requiring complete openness, without resort to deception or double-dealing in any form or degree. A nonviolent conspiracy or intrigue would be a contradiction in terms. This position, eloquently developed by Martin Luther King and his associates in the civil-rights struggle, prompted Mr. Hoover to unleash his brutal vendetta of harassment and vilification that tormented Dr. King to the end of his life. In America we have had a taste of the kind of police work that the Soviet KGB and other authoritarian police agencies are accustomed to use with deadly effectiveness against dissenters in their countries.

I planned here to compare the growing abuses in our system that resemble denials of human rights in the Communist nations, and specifically in the

Soviet Union. I wished to show that Americans and Soviet dissenters, such as Sakharov, have a common cause. Disclosures of FBI abuses against Martin Luther King and Andrew Young, of the Southern Christian Leadership Conference, further documentation of CIA lawlessness abroad, and my personal examination of the CIA file improperly gathered on the Ethical Society, which I served as leader, have caused me to focus on abuses in American society, with little time to develop the very serious breaches of human rights in the Soviet Union. But I do not want the brevity of my comments on Soviet denials of human rights to be interpreted as minimizing them. Whatever deficiencies we confront in our structure of personal liberties, the Soviets suffer a hundredfold. I would not be able to publish this article in the Soviet Union.

World public opinion must not for a moment take its eyes off the courageous Soviet dissenters who are pressing for human rights in that nation. World public opinion — our awareness of their struggle — is the only protection they have. The current refusal of the Soviet government to allow the distinguished physicist Andrei Sakharov to travel to Oslo to receive the Nobel Peace Prize is a manifestation of that government's continuing suppression of everyday personal freedoms.

At a great risk to themselves, a number of Soviet dissenters have smuggled manuscripts abroad for publication in the West, in an effort to tell their story to the world. (For those interested, I would suggest a short, readily available paperback, *My Country and the World,* written by Andrei Sakharov.)

These voices of dissent warn us that détente can be a trap if it makes us indifferent to the human struggle for civil liberties in either the capitalist West or the Communist East. The struggle for human rights is indivisible, and we are reminded that powerful systems of control in both East and West tend to narrow or to deny our liberties.

Democracy is not simply a political system. It fundamentally expresses a moral conception of human life.

The democratic ethic imposes upon us a twofold obligation: to restore the health of our democracy at home as a beacon of decency and hope, and to reach out with moral support to all our brothers and sisters who strive to be free. This requires of us that we practice the freedom we have.

Issue

The Have and Have-Not Nations

We are entering a period in which rapid population growth, the presence of obliterative weapons, and dwindling resources will bring international tensions to dangerous levels for an extended period.

Robert Heilbroner, 1974

. . . the first, overriding, frighteningly pressing task of this year and this century is to feed, clothe and unleash from fear the millions who, through no fault of their own, live in such desolation.

Peggy and Pierre Streit, 1961

The contrast between affluent America and the poverty-ridden Third World is usually ignored in the United States. Americans touring abroad avoid slums, peasant hovels, and areas of disease or starvation. Occasionally, however, a news report brings a bit of reality into our lives. When confronted with the abject poverty that pervades so much of the world, how do Americans respond?

Some are shocked and lament a world in which the rich live in affluence and disregard the poor. Other defend the status quo with the justification that there is not enough wealth in the lands of the rich to lift the poor out of their misery. Still others have maintained we are doing all we can.

Though Americans have preferred to ignore rather than confront the issue of the gulf between rich and poor, the nation has taken some action. Foreign aid has been distributed to the Third World states in limited quantities except in the case of Vietnam where massive economic resources and technical skills were employed. In the 1960s impressive numbers of Americans volunteered for the Peace Corps as a personal commitment to help the world's needy.

In spite of these efforts, the gap between rich and poor has remained wide. Starvation haunts millions of people and the resulting moral, political, and economic considerations force us to face the problem. What have we done? What can we do? What should we do?

◆ DOCUMENTS ◆

Comparing the Haves and Have-Nots
PEGGY and PIERRE STREIT

In 1961 Peggy and Pierre Streit suggested that the Cold War could be useful if it opened the eyes of America to the conditions of the poor people of the world. Has this happened? What explanation do you have or have you heard for the disparity between the wealth of America and the poverty of the Third World?

SHIRAZ, Iran

"Eighty-eight per cent of the people in America own television sets." There it is, the shortest of items in today's local English-language newspaper — there, amid the news about Iran, the cold war, and world crisis. "Eighty-eight per cent of the people in America own television sets" — the mere tick of a statistic, addressed, as it were, to whom it may concern. And our thoughts turn back to seven years of travel in the Middle East and Asia.

We think of India and the daily drive we made to New Delhi from our home on the outskirts of the city. On the way there was a small refugee village and in it a dump heap. Each day, as we passed, we watched the village dogs and the village women, side by side, clawing through the refuse with unnerving intensity for scraps of food.

And we remember Kabul, Afghanistan, its newly paved streets dusted with a thin coat of sand blown in from the plains. Roaming those streets was a band of dirty, barefoot scavenger boys — all 7 or 8 years old, each with a square metal can strapped to his back. They followed the carriages, searching for horse droppings, and when they found some they scooped up the manure with their small hands and, with a deft, practiced motion, tossed it over their shoulders into the cans, to be sold later to Afghan farmers.

We remember, a few winters ago, a little girl on the sleet-covered streets of South Teheran. Her head was bent into a wind that blew her cotton dress against her legs. She was barefoot. As she walked the flesh of her heels, cracked by the cold, left little arcs of blood in the snow.

And so, this morning, as we read that 88 per cent of all Americans own television sets, we ask ourselves, as we have so often before, what we and what our countrymen have done to merit the bounty and the comfort with which we live, and what so much of the world has done to warrant its destitution.

Why is it that we can look forward this evening to the quiet comfort of an ample meal while, not two miles away, thousands of drought-driven Iranian nomads are on their weary way south in search of food for themselves and their gaunt animals? Why is it that we can buy new clothes — clothes we don't really need — while in Calcutta thousands of men, women and children who sleep under bridges and in doorways lack even a piece of cloth to put between themselves and the pavement?

Why are we permitted to look to tomorrow without fear of want, when for so many in this world, tomorrow may well bring flood, famine or disease to destroy all that they cherish? Why are we permitted to enjoy the blessings of freedom and security, knowing that well-established democratic institutions in the United States have peacefully elected a new President, while in most of the under-developed world there is no freedom, there are no democratic institutions — or even much understanding of them or hope that they may soon provide the blessings enjoyed in the West?

Why have we been so fortunate? It would be pleasant to believe we have earned our good fortune because we have worked harder than the millions of people we see toiling on barren land. But we know better.

We have seen too many Indian farmers trudging behind primitive, wooden plows under a searing sun; we have seen too many Nepalese women bent double in their rice fields, their legs covered with leeches; we have seen too many Iranian children hunched over their ill-lit carpet looms, to have any such illusions. We know that never in our lives have we worked, one day, as hard as most of the people of the world work each day. We cannot lay claim to our comfortable lives because of diligence.

Perhaps we have been luckier than most because we are wiser, and wisdom brings its just rewards. But we are mindful of the many thoughtful, stimulating evenings spent under thatched roofs discussing the problems of the world with illiterate Indian or Afghan or Iranian farmers. It has been made abundantly clear to us that a man may be uneducated, but he may also be wise; he may be poor, but he may also have dignity; he may be hard-pressed but he may also maintain his pride. Thus, we cannot believe that we or our countrymen are more fortunate than others because we have a monopoly on intelligence.

Perhaps we are blessed above others because we are more generous, more honest or more dedicated. But this is not a point we would care to have to defend against the hungry peasants who have insisted on sharing their meals with us; against impoverished farmers who have gone to great lengths to return to us things we left in their villages; against the hundreds of young people we have met whose work for their young, struggling countries demands a kind of personal sacrifice we have never known.

We ask ourselves, then, if perhaps our good fortune is not due to our system of government, to our freedom and democracy, and if these are not our just inheritance from the men who won them in the United States—from George Washington, Thomas Jefferson and Abraham Lincoln. But this, too, we must reject. For, we ask, what have *we personally* ever done, more than most of the other people of the world, to earn or merit these blessings?

We can find no satisfactory reason, in short, to explain why, in a world that now has the capability of caring for *all* its people, there are so many poor and so few rich. And we feel very strongly that in this fact — in the very magnitude of the disparity of living standards, in the very number of people involved, in the very enormity of the injustice — a self-evident truth emerges: that apart from preserving the peace, the first, overriding, frighteningly pressing task of this year and this century is to feed, clothe and unleash from fear the millions who, through no fault of their own, live in such desolation.

This is a massive and urgent undertaking. It is no longer one for a few missionaries or teachers but one requiring the marshaling of the intellectual, material and spiritual resources of nations — nations rich enough to provide 88 per cent of their people with television sets. Whatever contributes to this mobilization, whatever speeds this process must be welcomed.

What *could* speed this process? To date, the greatest — one might almost say the only — impetus to this mobilization has been the cold war.

In the past fifteen years the tremendous job of bridging the gap between the affluence of the West and the poverty of the East has begun. In the seven years we have been traveling in this part of the world we have seen enormous accomplishment. Much of it has been due to Western aid. But a big part has also been played by the Russians.

Honesty compels us to admit, however, that the principal reason the United States has undertaken to help raise the world's standard of living is not that there are poor people who rightfully should be sharing more equally the good things of the earth; but that Americans are afraid that if they do not do something about their misery, the miserable will turn to the Communists in desperation. And undoubtedly the forces that motivate the Communists are very similar. The Soviets have undertaken a share of the burden, not because the welfare of the people is a primary concern, but because they want their ideology to prevail and aid is one means to that end.

It would be pleasant to believe that were East and West not embroiled in a cold war both the United States and the Soviet Union would continue their help to the underdeveloped world. But, regretfully, we haven't that much faith. If the cold war ended tomorrow, so, we fear, would the bulk of the efforts being made to help the earth's unfortunates.

We wonder, actually, whether when the history of these days is written a century from now the cold war may not emerge as one of the greatest boons that mankind has ever known. Certainly, it seems to have been the one force powerful enough to marshal the intellectual and material resources of the United States on a national scale in behalf of the underprivileged, and to cause other countries to follow the American lead with aid programs of their own.

But we wonder if the cold war may not also emerge as a boon to the overprivileged — the 88 per centers. One can hope that it may prove to be a force that, carrying Americans to the far corners of the earth and opening their front pages, their eyes and their hearts to the needs around them, will finally transform a response based on fear and self-preservation into a true concern for justice and the welfare of all men.

Assessing Have-Not Claims

JOHN FISCHER

John Fischer has a different perspective of the world than the Streits show in the preceeding essay. What does Fischer see as inevitable? When he urges action in accordance with the "clearly defined interests of the United States," what does he mean? How does Fischer's view of the world and American interests differ from the views of Peggy and Pierre Streit?

> *Why should we pay taxes when we can always get more money from the Americans?*
>
> A wealthy landowner of Nepal,
> quoted in *Time*, February 3, 1961

Dear Fowler:

As a taxpayer, I was delighted to hear that you will be taking over the job of running our foreign-aid program.

For one thing, I know you are a hard man. When we started working together on that intelligence operation back during the war, I found that a certain gaiety of manner was, in your case, the cover for a streak of tungsten-carbide ruthlessness. It was useful then, and it will be even more welcome now. Like a lot of other bled-pale taxpayers, I need a hard man to protect me — from that non-taxpayer in Nepal and millions of leeches like him all over the world. . . .

What makes me really cheerful about your appointment is the fact that

---

you have had a good deal of experience in economic warfare. You will know how to use foreign aid as a weapon.

So long as you use it that way — as the best weapon we have in the not-so-cold war that we'll be fighting for so long as anybody can see into the future — then I'm pretty sure that most taxpayers will be willing to give you whatever money you need, for as long as you need it. But if you fritter it away for other purposes — to prop up shaky dictators, for example, or in a heartwarming effort to abolish poverty where poverty is inevitable — then you will have an eruption on your hands. If I read the seismograph correctly, the public's annoyance with that kind of waste has just about reached the explosion point.

For some of your predecessors didn't know just what they were meant to accomplish with all that money. Buy friendship? Strengthen allies? Feed everybody who is hungry? Undermine the Soviet empire? Carry out a Senator's pet project? Industrialize Africa? Arm Vietnamese guerrillas? Clinch a few doubtful votes in the United Nations? Since in recent years the White House seldom specified precise objectives, the poor administrators tended to dribble out the cash for a little of everything. Usually with no strings attached. That has been the No. 1 fetish — for we were never, never meant to "interfere with the internal affairs" of the countries who got our money. Even when everybody knew that El Presidente was a thief, we dared not insult him by asking for a look at the books.

From your past performance, I'm fairly certain you won't operate that way. Wall Street people tell me you are a tough negotiator. And I know you are sophisticated enough to realize that everything America does (or doesn't do) in the way of foreign aid is going to interfere with somebody's internal affairs. So I trust you will abandon our traditional hypocrisy, tie a chain on every dime — and yank hard if it isn't spent in the clearly defined interests of the United States. . . .

For example, when Cheddi Jagan was elected prime minister of British Guiana a few weeks ago, he announced that he would condescend to accept our money. He is against "Yankee imperialism," of course. After all, he is an acknowledged Marxist, who plans to follow "a policy of neutralism like Nehru and Nasser." But since Tito, Nehru, and Poland get American aid, he wants his share of the gravy.

Perhaps Dr. Jagan should be told these facts of life:

1. There isn't enough gravy to go around. Even if the United States — and Russia, and Western Europe — cut off their own economic growth and poured *all* of their savings into the underdeveloped countries, they still couldn't provide enough capital to industrialize all of those nations as fast as they demand. The aid which actually will be available, from all sources, East and West, won't begin to meet the expectations of Dr. Jagan and his sixty-odd rival claimants. Some will have to do without; none will get all he wants.

2. Many of the underdeveloped countries will always be poor. They just don't have the resources to support a modern industrial society — nor the

land to feed their already hungry and fast-growing populations. (D. W. Brogan has estimated that at least half of the new nations created in the last decade can never hope to be self-supporting.)

3. Latin America, in particular, is going to be disappointed. Most Latins apparently expect the Kennedy Administration's Alliance for Progress program to solve all their woes. It cannot — simply because the Latin American population is growing 3 per cent a year. There is virtually no prospect that the continent as a whole can increase its production of food and manufactured goods at a rate much faster than that, no matter how much Yankee money it gets. The luckier countries — Brazil, perhaps, and Argentina, Venezuela and a few others — may achieve a slow improvement in their living standards. The others will have to run their fastest just to stay in the same place.

4. What the Latins (and most other underdeveloped areas) need more than money — or anything else — is birth control. But for domestic political reasons, on this problem we can offer no help.

5. Given these facts, it makes sense for us to concentrate our help in those countries where it is likely to produce really worthwhile results — both economic and political. (India may be the prime case. It has a fighting chance to build both a stable economy and a democratic government; and its race with China may well determine the future of all Asia. Annoying as Nehru may be from time to time, this looks like a good place to put our blue chips.) But the hopeless cases will have to go to the end of the queue. Can Dr. Jagan prove his case isn't hopeless?

Your big trouble — as I'm sure you know — will not come from the young rebels like Jagan. It will come from men who look just as respectable as you — the bankers, generals, and landowners who have long formed the traditional ruling class in much of Latin America.

They are the rich Guatemalans who won't let their Congress pass an income tax — even though social injustice in their country is so flagrant that they had to be rescued from a Marxist regime only a few years ago, and may soon be threatened by another. They are the Brazilian millionaires who put their money into real-estate speculation (and Swiss banks) instead of industrial development. They are the twelve families who own El Salvador, and don't believe in either education or shoes for their peasants.

You will meet them soon enough, because President Kennedy has warned them that they will have to mend their ways if they hope to see any of that Alliance for Progress cash. So they will promise you anything you ask — and deliver nothing.

For any real reform would mean the end of them, their families, and the delightful way of life they have enjoyed for the last three hundred years. Like Winston Churchill, they have no intention of presiding over the liquidation of their empires.

The smart ones realize, of course, that such empires can't last much longer. They have seen them crumble already, in Mexico, Venezuela, Costa Rica, Cuba. They are likely therefore to steal all they can — from their countrymen, and from your aid funds — and then to skip out just before the revolution pops. After all, that plan worked fine for Perón, Batista, Jiménez, Patiño, most of the Trujillo family, and plenty of other strong men who are now living it up in St. Tropez and Miami Beach.

The only way you can beat their game is to side with The Good Revolutionists — the democratic ones like Figueres, Muñoz-Marín, Gallegos, and Betancourt. In the long run, such men are the only workable alternative to the other kind of revolutionists, of the Castro, Jagan, Arbenz, and Guevara variety.

For genuine social revolution — as contrasted with the old-fashioned palace coup, which changed nothing but the hand in the till — is probably inevitable in most of Latin America. It offers the only hope for even those modest gains, in living standards and human dignity, which the Alliance for Progress can honestly promise. Your job is to preside over that revolution — to guide it, nudge it along, and make it work. If you can't do it, the Kremlin has plenty of trained men ready and eager to take it over.

A strange assignment for a Wall Street lawyer? Indeed it is — especially since some of your friends are bound to get hurt. Certain big American corporations aren't going to like it — United Fruit, for example, and some (though not all) of the oil and mining companies which have enjoyed privileged positions in a number of Latin countries. Often they have been silent partners of the old ruling group. Lots of Latins suspect they can block any real change — until a local Castro comes along.

I suspect you are plenty durable enough to handle that kind of pressure, even if it comes from solid businessmen you have known for years, and who may have been valued customers of your old firm. But it won't be any fun.

If it is any comfort, you can look forward to dealing simultaneously with a different kind of pressure: blackmail. Your new clients are expert at it, because most of them have been using it on us for years. All they have had to say is: "Give me what I want" — it may be a hydroelectric project, or a flock of tanks to keep the army happy, or a few million to replace what The Boys stole out of the last budget — "or I will go to Moscow."

Nearly always they have been getting away with this kind of bluff. The one memorable exception was Nasser; when John Foster Dulles refused to give him his Aswan Dam, he did turn to Moscow, and he did get it there. But curiously enough, Egypt has not yet been gobbled up. In fact, Nasser has outlawed the local Communist party, and he is, if anything, a bit more respectful to Americans than he used to be. He still calls us monsters, of course, but we are only one-headed monsters now.

At some point, you too will have to say "No" — simply because you won't have enough money to pay off all the blackmailers who will be calling on you. When some sheik or generalissimo wants another $39 million to build a palace for his latest mistress, you will have to tell him to send the bill to Mr. Khrushchev.

But not always. For sometime that sheik actually will be gobbled up if he goes to the Kremlin; and he may hold a chunk of real estate the West simply can't afford to lose. In that case, you had better grit your teeth and pay up — and start thinking how to explain the deal to the Appropriations Committees. When to be hard, and to whom, is always a delicate question; but it is these little nuances which will make your job so interesting.

Hopefully yours,

Calculating Assistance by the Haves

U.S. CENSUS

What does a comparison of economic assistance to industrialized states during the Marshall Plan years and economic assistance to "underdeveloped" states since those years reveal? How extensive was the economic assistance program from 1948 to 1974?

Comparison of Average Annual Foreign Economic Assistance To "Developed" and "Underdeveloped" Countries With Select Domestic Governmental Expenditures.

(In billions of dollars except dollars per $1,000.00 of GNP. Excludes military aid.)

	Marshall Plan 1948–1952	Mutual Security Act 1953–1961	Agency For International Development 1962–1974
Average Annual Aid to Developed Countries	2.5	0.3	0.06
Average Annual Aid to Underdeveloped Countries	0.36	1.4	2.1
Average Annual Gross National Product	295.6	437.6	898.8

(Compiled from statistics cited in tables on gross national product, foreign economic assistance, and governmental expenditure by function as published in U.S. Bureau of the Census, *Statistical Abstract of the United States* (Washington: Government Printing Office, 1950–1976.)

	Marshall Plan 1948–1952	Mutual Se- curity Act 1953–1961	Agency For International Development 1962–1974
Average Annual Economic Assistance given per $1,000 of Gross National Product	$ 9.81	$ 4.29	$ 2.40
Average Annual Economic Assistance given to Under- developed Countries per $1,000 GNP	$ 1.22	$ 3.20	$ 2.34
Average Annual Public Welfare Expenditures per $1,000 of GNP.	$10.14 *	$ 8.46	$15.82
Average Annual Public Highway Expenditures per $1,000 of GNP	$13.19 *	$17.82	$16.82
Average Annual Police Expenditures per $1,000 of GNP	$ 3.04 *	$ 3.88	$ 4.98
Average Annual Public Higher Education Expendi- tures per $1,000 of GNP	$ 4.05 *	$ 5.02	$11.99

* Based on 1950 figures only.

Using the Have-Nots

SARGENT SHRIVER

What are the noneconomic consequences of the Peace Corps? What is meant by social progress? Is the Peace Corps more valuable for bringing economic progress to the Third World or an increased social awareness to the United States?

From U.S., Congress, Senate, *Congressional Record,* 88th Cong., 1st sess., June 25, 1963, vol. 109, pt. 9, pp. 11628–11629. From a speech by Peace Corps Director R. Sargent Shriver.

... [T]here has been a change in the nature of comment and criticism about the Peace Corps. In the beginning, the doubters worried about the callowness of youth and the ability of mortals to make any good idea work. The more recent criticism is more sophisticated and more substantive. Eric Sevareid recently observed: "While the Corps has something to do with spot benefits in a few isolated places, whether in sanitizing drinking water or building culverts, its work has, and can have, very little to do with the fundamental investments, reorganizations and reforms upon which the true and long-term economic development of backward countries depends." Mr. Sevareid acknowledges that "giving frustrated American youth a sense of mission and adding to our supply of comprehension of other societies fatten the credit side of the ledger." He adds: "If fringe benefits were all the Corps' originators had in mind, then this should be made clear to the country." I do not agree with him that the second and third purposes of the Peace Corps Act — representing America abroad in the best sense and giving Americans an opportunity to learn about other societies — are fringe benefits.

Fulton Freeman, the U.S. Ambassador in Colombia, believes the whole Peace Corps program could be justified by its creation of a new American resource in the volunteers who are acquiring language skills and intensive understanding of a foreign society. Former volunteers will be entering Government service (150 have already applied to join USIA), United Nations agencies, academic life, international business concerns and a host of other institutions which carry on the business of the United States throughout the world. Others will return to their homes, capable of exerting an enlightened influence in the communities where they settle. Many trite euphemisms of the ignorant and ready panaceas of the uninformed will clash immediately with the harsh facts that volunteers have learned to live with abroad.

Is the second purpose of the Peace Corps Act — to be a good representative of our society — a fringe benefit? Peace Corps volunteers are reaching the people of foreign countries on an individual basis at a different level from the influence of most Americans abroad. The Peace Corps volunteer lives under local laws, buys his supplies at local stores and makes his friends among local people. He leaves to the diplomat and the technicians the complex tools which are peculiarly their own while he sets out to work in the local environment as he finds it.

I am not suggesting that life for the volunteer is always hard. A visiting Ghanaian said: "The Peace Corps teachers in my country don't live so badly. After all, they live as well as we do." I agree that this is not so bad; nor is our objective discomfort for discomfort's sake, but rather a willingness to share the life of another people, to accept sacrifice when sacrifice is necessary and to show that material privilege has not become the central and indispensable ingredient in an American's life. It is interesting to note that the happiest volunteers are usually those with the most difficult living conditions.

Although I disagree with Mr. Sevareid's emphasis in dismissing two of the three purposes of the Peace Corps Act as fringe benefits, he does get to the heart of an important question when he compares the direct economic impact of the Peace Corps to fundamental investments, reorganizations and economic development. The Peace Corps' contribution has been less in direct economic development than in social development — health, education, construction and community organization. We are convinced that economic development directly depends on social development. In his valedictory report this past April as head of the Economic Commission for Latin America, Raul Prebisch observed that there are not "grounds for expecting that economic development will take place first and be followed in the natural course of events by social development. Both social and economic development must be achieved in measures that require the exercise of rational and deliberate action. There can be no speed-up in economic development without a change in the social structure." While they have their differences, Theodore W. Schultz and J. Kenneth Galbraith have no disagreement on the essential role of social development in economic progress. In contrast, some who argue from the European-North American experience overlook the vital need for social development which had already been substantially achieved in the countries of the Atlantic community. This is the basic difference between the problem of the Marshall plan, which was concerned with economic reconstruction in societies with abundant social resources, and the problem of forced-draft economic development in much of Asia, Africa, and Latin America.

Notwithstanding the Peace Corps' primary emphasis on social development, volunteers are making a direct economic contribution in a variety of situations. They are helping to organize farmers' cooperatives in Chile, Ecuador, and Pakistan; credit unions and savings and loan associations in Latin America; demonstration farms in the Near East. A group of volunteers in the Punjab sparked the creation of a poultry industry of some economic significance (using ground termite mounds for protein feed). These are grass roots projects. More of them will someday cause us to look back and wonder why it took so long to discover that people — human hands and enthusiasms — are an essential part of the relationship of mutual assistance which we must establish with our neighbors abroad.

A Jamaican radio commentator recently asserted that "a great distance between people is the best creator of good will. Jumble people up together on a sort of temporary basis of gratitude on one side and condescension on the other, and you'll have everyone at each other's throat in no time." If I believed this were inevitable, regardless of the attitude, preparation and mode of life of volunteers, I would advocate disbanding the Peace Corps — as well as most other programs oversea. But I have greater faith in the universality of men's aspirations and of men's ability to respect each other when they know each other. It is the American who lives abroad in isolation and the thoughtless tourist who create distrust and dislike.

I believe the Peace Corps is also having more impact than we may realize on our own society and among our own people. . . .

[Volunteers] will be coming home more mature, with a new outlook toward life and work. Like many other Americans, I have wondered whether our contemporary society, with its emphasis on the organizational man and the easy life, can continue to produce the self-reliance, initiative and independence that we consider to be part of our heritage. We have been in danger of losing ourselves among the motorized toothbrushes, tranquilizers, and television commercials. Will Durant once observed that nations are born stoic and die epicurean; we have been in danger of this happening to us.

The Peace Corps is truly a new frontier in the sense that it provides the challenge to self-reliance and independent action which the vanished frontier once provided on our own continent. Sharing in the progress of other countries helps us to rediscover ourselves at home.

The influence of the Peace Corps idea might be described as a series of widening circles, like the expanding rings from a stone thrown into a pond. The inner, most sharply defined circle represents the immediate effect of the program — accomplishments abroad in social and economic developments, skills, knowledge, understanding, institution-building, a framework for cooperative effort with private organizations, research and experiment in oversea Americanship, language training, and improvements in health.

The second ring moving outward on the water might be the Peace Corps' influence on our society, on institutions, and people on the creation of a new sense of participation in world events, an influence on the national sense of purpose, self-reliance and an expanded concept of volunteer service in time of peace.

There is still a wider circle and, being farthest from the splash, the hardest to make out clearly. Perhaps, I can explain it by describing the relationships I see between the Peace Corps and our American Revolution. The Revolution placed on our citizens the responsibility for reordering their own social structure. It was a triumph over the idea that man is incompetent or incapable of shaping his destiny. It was our declaration of the irresistible strength of a universal idea connected with human dignity, hope, compassion, and freedom. The idea was not simply American, of course, but arose from a confluence of history, geography, and the genius of a resolute few at Philadelphia.

We still have our vision, but our society has been drifting away from the world's majority: the young and raw, the colored, the hungry, and the oppressed. The Peace Corps is helping to put us again where we belong. It is our newest hope for rejoining the majority of the world without at the same time betraying our cultural, historic, political, and spiritual ancestors and allies. As Pablo Casals, the renowned cellist and democrat, said of the Peace Corps last year: "This is new, and it is also very old. We have come from the tyranny of the enormous, awesome, discordant machine, back to a realization that the beginning and the end are man — that it is man who is important, not the machine; and that it is man who accounts for growth, not just dollars and factories. Above all, that it is man who is the object of all our efforts."

Buying the Have-Nots

JOHN McDERMOTT

When the United States pumps economic aid into a country to foster its development, does it do more harm than good? Must massive economic aid result in the United States controlling the lives of the people it seeks to help?

In the late summer of 1954 a major American effort began in Vietnam, one calculated, it was hoped, to save the country from the until then victorious Communists of Ho Chi Minh. France appeared ready to abandon all political claims in the area and to U.S. policy makers this was perhaps the most hopeful sign of all, for the continued presence of the French had been undermining the efforts of anti-Communist Vietnamese nationalists to build a counterforce to the Communist-led Vietminh. The Vietnamese chief of state, former Emperor Bao Dai, was widely acknowledged to be a French puppet. He "ruled" through the French administration, and the French army protected him from the legions of Ho Chi Minh. Similarly, the Cao Dai and Hao Hoa religious sects and the squabbling politicians of Hanoi, Hué and Saigon were, according to the Americans, creatures of the French and tainted by collaboration with them: on the latter's departure they too would disappear from the scene and open the way for a genuine anti-colonialist and anti-Communist nationalism to assert itself. . . .

By the terms of the Geneva Agreements the Vietminh had withdrawn its main forces and cadres north of the 17th Parallel in late 1954, and it was into the chaos south of that demarcation line that the new U.S. presence and the new U.S. policy had already begun to take effect. Two leading ideas characterized this policy. First, in place of France's discredited colonial solution to Vietnam's problems the United States would try a nationalist solution. Allying itself with the forces of anti-Communist nationalism, the U.S. would work to preserve the southern zone from the Vietminh. Second, since it was the poverty, misery and gullibility of the peasantry which seem to have enabled it to be duped by the utopian and millennial appeals of the Communists, it was decided that a strong American commitment to economic development would help lead the country to prosperity, that the peasantry could thereby be won away from the Vietminh. Accordingly, even before the fall of Dienbienphu in May, the United States had thrown its support to one of the numerous anti-French Vietnamese nationalists, Ngo Dinh Diem. Under American pressure, Diem was finally appointed Prime Minister in late June and, together with him, U.S. officials worked to remove the French from the scene. This was sub-

From John McDermott, "Welfare Imperialism in Vietnam," *The Nation,* July 4, 1966, pp. 79–86. Reprinted with permission.

stantially achieved by early 1955. The first step in the American solution was complete; France was gone, South Vietnam was independent. There now remained the much more difficult task of counseling the new regime in the ways of building a firm political base and in bringing about the necessary economic development which promised the best long-run solution to South Vietnam's ills — internal and external. To this task fell not a narrow and limited segment of the American polity but the full force of the United States Government. . . .

U.S. influence was exerted at a remarkable diversity of points; no domestic competitor could match it. The Americans had influenced the choice of Diem in the first place. They gave technical and dollar support to a revamping of the entire Vietnamese educational system from elementary schools through the university and technical institute level. This included both teacher training and the rewriting of textbooks. They gave technical assistance in revising the banking and currency system and in framing general economic and monetary policy. The United States Operations Mission (USOM — the AID Mission) undertook planning and dollar support for the reconstruction and development of the entire Vietnamese transportation and communications network — railroads, canals, highways, civil aviation, coastal transport, radio and television, and the telephone system. They assisted in planning and executing the various agricultural programs, including crop diversification, land reclamation, land reform, agricultural extension and mass peasant regroupment (the Refugee Resettlement, Land Development, Agroville and later Strategic Hamlet Programs). Finally, they exerted extremely strong influence over the nation's two largest economic activities (exclusive of farming) — military operations and the import business. . . .

The American lobby was overwhelming. Possessing great prestige, spread throughout the Vietnamese government but clustered at the strategic points, well coordinated, with a near monopoly of technical information and armed with a significant stock of favors for its friends and threats for its foes, the U.S. interest in Vietnam was in a position to achieve almost any policy it desired. Provided it was determined enough, not even the dictator himself could withstand the U.S. choice.

Thus, it is understandable why and in what way the U.S. interest was more important for Vietnamese life than the French interest in the earlier period. The French controlled everyday affairs but directed that control to a relatively narrow range of Vietnamese events. Outside that range French influence was inadvertent and, therefore, blind. However disruptive their influence was on Vietnam's future the colonial French hardly controlled that future. The U.S. presence was far more important. The U.S. didn't care about everyday affairs. The U.S. was concerned about economic development, i.e., about the future of what are among the most decisive aspects of a culture: how a people work, what they work at, what they produce, the institutions which govern the distribution of that product, the principles which those institutions embody. In these areas the U.S. influence was focused and, I think it may fairly be said, the government of South Vietnam could not act independently. The policies it followed tended to be, in the final analysis, the policies of the U.S. government.

From the beginning American officials foresaw conflict between U.S. policy and the likely direction in which the peasantry — constituting the major part of the population — would assert its interests. The peasantry was understood to be politically unsophisticated and, as a result, infected by Communist sympathies. Superstitious and credulous, rural Vietnam seemed an easy mark for the semi-religious appeals of the Communists who seemed to promise a paradise in a future period called roughly "after the national revolution." The Americans saw the Communists not as the champion of the peasantry, but rather as infiltrators into its ranks — manipulators of its discontent, ruthless exploiters of its misery and ignorance. There were Communists and there were peasants: there could be no Communist peasants. Nevertheless, implicit in the situation was peasant opposition to U.S. policies. The likelihood of this opposition was reinforced in American eyes by the belief that the peasantry, beneath its Communist appearance, was fundamentally traditionalist and thus opposed to change even if that change meant emancipation from the miseries of its great poverty.

Viewing the matter in this way it was natural that the Americans should assign to the interests of the peasantry a low priority in the economic development process they were committed to bring about. They were committed to modernization and this implied that urban interests had to take precedence. . . .

. . . For Americans, economic development entailed a planned program to bring about a society of a definite kind — one that would set primary value on increasing productivity by means of the maximal exploitation of a given level of technical knowledge. The role of Americans and the influence of American attitudes were paramount here. The very meaning of economic development — with its emphasis on the production of consumer goods and a consumer class — reflects a desire on the part of most Americans to help developing nations follow the same course as American economic history.

But while most Americans think of economic development as something "scientific," out of the realm of politics, U.S. officials in Vietnam recognized that it was indeed a political matter. They understood that "modernization" required changes in Vietnam's institutions, and thus they were prepared to help design and execute the Agroville Program. They understood that it required profound social changes, for as the society and the economy changed and some classes and their functions became obsolete, new classes with new social roles had to arise. They recognized that outlooks and values would change inevitably under the impact of economic development, and so they concerned themselves with guiding those outlooks and values. They took a profound interest in the totality of the Vietnamese educational system, even to rewriting the textbooks; they undertook to establish and staff Vietnam's communications network in the early years and to advise it thereafter.

The conflict in Vietnam was and is in the very broadest sense a cultural one. The United States succeeded in imposing a development pattern which was but a thinly disguised version of modernization, American style. It succeeded in imposing this pattern but at the expense of allowing various elements in Vietnamese society to work out an alternative modernization pattern, one which would reflect the national past of Vietnam and not of the United States, one which would reflect the interests of the Vietnamese people not merely the desires of American technicians. The United States succeeded by damming up those social groups, particularly the peasant majority, which a normal pattern would have encompassed as its dynamic force. The pattern we brought about was imported — what was needed was a native one; it was bureaucratic — what was needed was a political one.

The French had proposed that their culture was relevant to Vietnam as something which, while remaining French, had universal aspects which could be shared in the form of a common heritage. By dominating the developmental process and imposing on it an imported pattern, American cultural influence attempted to determine the course of Vietnamese national life for the next epoch. Is it any wonder that good Vietnamese reject our pretty uniforms and strive desperately to throw us into the sea?

United States developmental policy in Vietnam is, to a large degree, the same policy that our government presses in the rest of the underdeveloped world. As in Vietnam, we attempt elsewhere to influence in a decisive way the process of economic development, the process which will choose the institutions, the social classes, and the values which will constitute the new nation that is coming to be.

To the other countries where we have development programs, we make the same forceful offer of our own economic experience; we expect it to be universally relevant, able to guide nations which differ in a thousand important ways from one another and ourselves. This requires the same dismissal of native interests and impulses. And as in Vietnam, the United States has the same overwhelming means to lobby its interest into effect.

America is building a curious empire, a kind which has never before been seen. It is committed not to the exploitation of the native peoples but to their welfare. One must not overlook this fact and think of our imperialism as a variant of the colonial imperialism of a past era. They are not analogous. Certainly venality, brutality, the urge to acquire illicit power are present in our executive bureaucracy no less than the bureaucracies of the French or Portuguese. Certainly we too have our share of seekers after martial glory — the Green Berets come to mind — and overseas profits. But most Americans, military and civilian, in government and in business, believe that to the best of our ability we are working to help the poorer nations — not merely to increase our own power.

We have been so blinded, however, by our commitment to the ideology of modernization that we fail to see the political imbalance we thereby create. There has been no effective democratic counterpoise to our welfare empire overseas. Not only has this counterpoise been missing but the central thrust of our development policy has been to prevent its inception — neutralize it, filter it out — until the developing nation has achieved "stability." Whether the politics of such imbalanced development will ever permit stable societies to come about is doubtful. But the question is now academic. For the present we may expect to see the bureaucratic power of the U.S. Government more and more opposed by armed resistance as native peoples seek to control their own future.

America's welfare imperialism promises to disrupt the life of other nations far more than did the older colonial imperialism of the British, French, Dutch and Portuguese. Each of these empires was exploitative in the sense of seeking monetary profit, prestige and military or naval standing. But the United States seeks more from the underdeveloped world; it is vitally concerned with the central processes of social and economic development. Colonial imperialism dealt mainly with questions of boundaries, ports and commodities. But U.S. imperialism extends into the lives of ordinary people and tries to control them, now and for the future.

Binding the Haves and Have-Nots

BARBARA WARD

Barbara Ward writes of fear, profit, and good will as motives for helping the Third World. On the basis of your study of American history, which motive do you think will be most influential in prompting Americans to act? Is Ward's call for a sense of community among all peoples realistic, or is nationalism too strong a force to be broken down?

As each Atlantic society began its process of development and drew the mass of the people into the new technological system based upon high savings, mechanized production, and a mass labour force, there came a time when the new possibilities and aspirations created by the system stood out in increasingly bitter contrast to its flagrant imbalance, unequal rewards, and urban misery. As the nineteenth century drew to a close, aggressive trade unionism, great strikes, violence in the streets scared cautious citizens in the United States into believing that the whole social order was being torn down around them. Anarchism grew as a force in Europe and advertized its cult of violence by carefully planned and highly visible assassinations. Russia boiled up, by way of peasant revolt, into the revolution of 1905. Even in Britain, where social peace had accompanied the great economic boom of the fifties and sixties, the mood grew more uncertain as the century waned. There were trade union riots in London in 1885 during the so-called Great Depression. Then, in the early 1900s, unrest increased again and one observer, speaking in 1909, made this analysis of the scene:

> If we [carry] on in the old happy-go-lucky way, the richer classes ever growing in wealth and in number, the very poor remaining plunged or plunging ever deeper into helplessness, hopeless misery, then I think there is nothing before us but savage strife between class and class and its increasing disorganization with the increasing waste of human strength and human virtue.

The speaker was Winston Churchill, and if his forecast proved wrong, it was in part because he himself at that time was deeply engaged in a most strenuous effort to introduce social insurance, end sweated labour, extend labour exchanges, impose minimum wage standards, and achieve a system of pensions for the aged. Where no such efforts were made — in Czarist Russia, for instance, or later in the miserable inter-war wreckage of China's 1911 Republic — the prediction proved correct. Once the mass of the people reach a certain level of awareness — of opportunity, of frustration — there are only two ways forward for society: to reform or blow up. There is every reason to suppose that in a planetary society in many ways more open, accessible, and aware of itself than was Russia or the United States in the 1880s, the choices are the same.

To those who believe that such a society can survive, to borrow the phrase of Mr. George Woods, former President of the World Bank, "half sated and half starved," that it can be held down by force or persuaded to forget the vast and growing disproportions between rich and poor, that the old "happy-go-lucky way" of keeping 80 per cent of the resources for 20 per cent of the people will peacefully endure, one can only say that every evidence of history refutes their optimism. Two thirds of humanity are on the verge of realizing what is the true context of wealth and poverty, affluence and misery, opportunity and frustration in this narrow world. Without reforms, without new ventures of generosity and justice, without sustained efforts of social innovation, then Winston Churchill's verdict, reversed at home precisely by such policies, could still be tragically vindicated in the world at large.

This is not an exercise designed to try, like Charles Dickens's Fat Boy, "to make yer flesh creep." It is a sober analysis of the only historical analogies we possess to guide us in policy-making today. And the chief reason why its relevance may seem dubious brings us back, once again, to the problem of context. We simply do not think about our planet as a community. We do not accept the comparison between what Professor Toynbee has called the "internal proletariat" and the "external proletariat," between the poor at home and the poor abroad. The nationalist framework of all our training keeps the poverty of the world at large outside our vision, beyond the reach of our imagination, and far away from any commitment of justice and good will. We live in the strangest dispensation in which lines on a map hem in the flow of wealth, pile it up higher and higher in one corner of the globe, and allow little of the spill-over that ended the exclusiveness of the feudal or Victorian elite and created the modern mass economy. Yet over, above, through, and round those same lines, the world surges on — in flight, in vision, in electronics, in trade, in wealth and ruin. Everything is unified, except our instruments of policy and our will to act. This is the basic reason for the paradoxes of our time. Our needs, our web of work and wealth, our institutions based upon gain — or upon fear — are worldwide in their impact. But the means of expressing our moral and humane obligations, our sense of justice and solidarity, our concern and our neighbourly love — these means are so weak that they can barely lift themselves over the lines on the map.

This is not an economic issue. It is political and moral. Societies growing in wealth by some $60,000 million a year are not confronted by any severe physical limitations on their ability to extend aid or share their increasing wealth more widely. No one doubts, for instance, that should the United States decide to spend anything from $5 billion to $50 billion on a new anti-missile system, the resources will be forthcoming. Particular difficulties such as the alleged strain of foreign aid on the balance of payments can be eased by "tying" aid — in other words, by seeing to it that all dollars are spent in America, all sterling in Britain. In any case, if the whole ring of wealthy states were all equally determined to aid development, they would make mutual arrangements to see that extra aid did *not* increase the strain — for instance, by agreeing not to convert into gold the proportion of currency represented by further capital assistance.

Similarly, if political leaders plead the impossibility of increasing internal budgetary commitments to economic assistance, they simply mean a *political* impossibility. Voters want the next annual round of growth in the economy — not less than $40,000 million in the case of the United States — to be spent on something else. Economically, $4,000 million more for aid would hardly be noticed. But political priorities are something else again and the next 3 or 4 per cent increase in national resources will follow them — for more defence, rebuilding the cities, coloured television, mink ear muffs, or whatever else the community believes to be of higher priority than pulling the rest of the human race across the threshold of the abundant life.

But in confronting what are basically political and moral decisions, we have the formidable hurdle of national exclusiveness to cross. The task is not, in the first place, to convince the citizens in wealthy countries that poverty should be attacked, opportunities increased, and a larger measure of justice extended to all the people. On balance, this battle, whose outcome seemed grim and uncertain only fifty years ago, has been largely won in Europe; and in the United States, it is hard to believe that the chief exception — urban poverty in the ghettoes — will be left to fester. The battle today is to convince the citizens who accept responsibility at home to accept it equally across the frontiers, across the lines on the map. And this is much more formidable.

We are all born tribalists. We all still live in the pretechnological structure of limited, separate, territorially circumscribed communities. We still derive our emotions from the millennia during which resources were scarce and the tribe or the empire or the nation were devices to safeguard a static share, if necessary by raiding and seizing other peoples' wealth. Even though wealth these days depends less and less on particular countries and more and more on the shared universe of men's minds, ideas, and research, we are hard put to it to overcome the emotional and territorial instincts bred of thousands of years of aggressive-protective conflict. Beneath our well washed skins and sophisticated hairdos still lurks the savage face of fearful, hungry, marauding tribal man. And the fact that nationalism was the first forcing house of the new technological society only increases our sense of its necessity. Like day-old chicks, we still find the world strange outside the incubator.

But to say that the task of persuasion and conversion is difficult does not mean that it should not be attempted or cannot be done. In the 1850s, Disraeli wrote of Britain as "two nations — the nation of the rich and the nation of the poor." The gulf between them was so great that he could describe it only in terms of the vast barriers which nationhood sets up between peoples of different culture and background. He did not, at that time, believe that the gulf could easily be bridged. His fear, indeed, was that it could not. But in the event, he underestimated the amount of reason, enlightened self-interest, informed apprehension and moral compassion the reformers could call on. Possibly we make the same underestimate today.

If we begin with the crudest motive — fear of violence and revolt — it is true that the sense of the Cold War has abated. The split between Russia and China has made obsolete all manner of dire foreboding about the "Sino-Soviet bloc" and its uncompromising hostility. Mechanized hordes of Communist divisions no longer threaten to sweep through Europe or Asia. However wasteful and terrifying, the nuclear deterrent at the level of the super-powers seems to work. On the other hand, the war in Vietnam has shown with what savage effectiveness guerrilla armies can take on forces that are vastly superior to them in equipment and firepower. If the big wars are contained, the small wars may not be, and the ordinary methods and weapons of modern war do not seem too effective in containing them. Possibly, then, they could be fought more effectively with less lethal instruments — with land reform, with cooperatives, with fertilizer and market roads, with urban housing, with the hope of schools and jobs. Land settlement has turned the dark lands of the Mau Mau into a lively, growing Kikuyu farming area. Rural works and cooperatives have brought some stability to some of the world's most overcrowded farm lands in East Pakistan. Earlier land reforms seem to lessen the appeal of guerrillas to the Bolivian peasant just as, first in the 1870s and then again under General MacArthur, they have stabilized and enriched the Japanese countryside.

Some people, of course, argue that neither armies nor aid need be considered. Let the poor go their own way while the Atlantic states, in isolated affluence, leave them to it. But it is difficult to envisage an American totally indifferent to a score of Cubas in Latin America. It is difficult to conceive of Europe steering completely clear of a long, desperate race war in Southern Africa. In the Middle East, the stakes are high enough to recreate the "Balkan" spiral, outside nations being drawn in to war by the struggles of local client states. In all these situations, sustained aid is not certain to contain or prevent conflict. But at least it has a chance of lessening the pressures that lead up to conflict. Of few other policies can so much be said.

Enlightened self interest points in the same direction. It is true that the developing world accounts for only about 20 per cent of the world's wealth and trade. Its trade with the wealthy nations is lower still — it provides only 14 per cent of their imports. Given their built-in capacities to raise output and increase productivity, they can in theory get on comfortably without the rest of the world. Yet they are intensely competitive. Their industrial goods jostle each other in the same markets. The response of many industries in the United States to livelier competition through falling tariffs is to demand the protection of a quota system. American food farmers resent Europe's protective agricultural levies. And the Atlantic stomach cannot push consumption beyond a certain point. All this suggests that, for Atlantic traders, a penumbra of over 2 billion people increasing their demands and their consumption and production enough to pay for the goods they want would be an admirable reassurance against the tougher forms of inter-Atlantic competition. Investment in development does raise skills and enlarge markets. As such, it is a useful if not an absolutely indispensable program against the day when "normal commerce" will have put colour TV in every room from Vladivostok to New York, and industry asks: Where next?

Even if we are not moved by either fear or profit, there are other motives — of reason, of good will, of conscience — and these played as large a part in domestic reform as any fear of the mob or hope of business interest. One needs no more than a reasonable acquaintance with history to realize that civil order is best maintained in societies with functioning institutions of law and police to see that peace is kept, and functioning policies of justice and welfare to see that it is worth keeping. This recognition of *fact* lies behind mankind's first experiments, in this century, with international peacekeeping through the United Nations and with international welfare and development through the World Bank, the U.N. Development Program, and all the other functional international agencies. If the world were not seen to be so small, vulnerable, and interdependent, these experiments would not have been undertaken. If the world were less "tribal," less divided and hostile, they would have been pursued more vigorously. But there at least they stand, a tribute to man's groping attempts to oppose reason to the drives of his millennial instincts. For it really does not stretch rationality very far to believe that nations cannot take themselves out of a world society which the astronaut strides round in 90 minutes — and science can blow up in 90 seconds. And if the nations are "in" without escape hatches, then clearly it is better to build and support the worldwide institutions — of peacekeeping, of development, of welfare — which in any society maintain the peace and in a nuclear society can prevent annihilation.

The trouble, it must be repeated, is that most traditional and customary feelings tend to point the other way: to withdrawal, to isolation, to obsessive concern with local interests, to indifference to the larger world. So reason, today, requires reinforcement from deeper commitments, from emotions which have some of the rootedness of tribal or nationalist devotion but not its large irrelevance to present reality. At this point, we return to where we started — to the vision society carries of its meaning and purpose, to the force of the images with which it tries to "invent" its future, to the picture not of where it is but of where it would like to be. And this, for the modern world, is still bound up with the vision of the unity of man.

We cannot escape it. The sense of a common, shared humanity — which is what we mean by the equality and unity of the human experiment — explodes in every revolution of the modern world. From the vision of the American Revolution, in which equal men came together for the political task of government, flows the Wilsonian concept of an orderly international system in which nations, equal in self-determination, come together to build a peaceful world. It is, in a sense, a highly respectable, gentlemanly version of humanity's travail. Yet it accepts the revolutionary need to pass beyond the nation in order to organize the world. From France and Marx and Russia, we inherit the turbulent, passionate version of the same faith. Now it is a question not of political forms and constitutional guarantees but of economic and social substance. Mankind will find out its unity when the barriers of exploitation and inequality have been thrown down; and the human family, in a world from which all states have withered away, will live in the perfect fraternity of shared and equal wealth.

Each version leaves out what the other brings in. The Americans have not shown much sense of the tragic incidence of inequality, exploitation, violence, and misery in the world on top of which an orderly international system is to be built up. The Russians have shown a remarkable lack of understanding of the political instruments, rule of law, and tough sacrifices of sovereignty demanded by a system in which Communist states, far from withering away, grow stronger and engage in all the traditional brouhaha of high diplomacy — frontier disputes, troop movements, spies, removals of envoys and long-range shouting matches. But the point here is not the deficiencies and imbalances of the two versions but rather the degree to which they are both committed, in their view of the world, to the single, inescapable community of man.

And this is not, after all, surprising, since both have their roots in the vision of humanity first formulated in the great ethical revolution of the world religions and transmitted to Western society through the mediation of Judeo-Christian culture. No doubt Chinese Communists will accept only with enormous reserve the idea of Western influences on Mao's thoughts. Russian Marxists tend to look no further than Lenin and Marx for their inheritance. But the situation in the Western world is odder still. Again and again, we hear its claim to be a "Christian civilization." But if it is, what do Christians suppose the words really mean? *Can* they mean that at a time when wealth beyond human imagining has been unlocked among the Atlantic nations by science and technology, their "Christian" response is to roll up the national income at a rate of $60,000 million a year and let the rest of the world fester in its miseries? This is a curious outcome for a faith in which Dives and Lazarus have become the symbols of selfish wealth heading for disaster and of helpless poverty waiting to be raised up.

Christians, of course, will disclaim selfishness, and indeed one can argue that it is not *intended* selfishness. The trouble, as we have seen, is that their indifference is rooted in something supposedly much more respectable — the total claims of national sovereignty and the explicit lack of obligations that go beyond national frontiers. We need no further explanation to tell us why national societies which will spend what is needed to build up a backward, poverty-stricken *Mezzogiorno* in Southern Italy or restore pockets of poverty like Appalachia have no sustained or unquestioned commitment to counter the infinitely deeper poverty of Andean villagers or the street-sleepers of Bombay. National governments have obligations only to national citizens. In return, citizens take these limits for granted, and so, at the frontiers, the flow of wealth, the sense of duty, the sustained and creative effort threatens to come to a full stop.

But can Christians accept such limits? Are they no more than nationalists or tribalists? Is their faith based on the formula "I will love my neighbour as myself — provided he is a fellow-American, Briton, Frenchman, German"? Must we rewrite every parable in the Bible to point out that the man in the ditch was really a Samaritan too, that Christ explicitly established that all the lepers were Jews before He cleansed them, that His condition for a cure was that the dumb man would only speak Hebrew, that the Centurion himself and his servant, far from being praised as Gentiles, had to accept citizenship in Israel before the healing words could be spoken?

If Christians allow their conscience to become thus determined by nation and race and culture, they can make no response to the profound and mysterious image of the Son of Man. They will not recognise "the least of these little ones" if the face is brown or black or yellow. They will staunch the flowing charity of God Himself and dam it up behind the arbitrary frontiers imposed by men across the wide bounty of the universe. And if this is their response to the deepest mystery of their faith — God's fatherhood of all mankind, God's providence which falls on just and unjust alike, God's love which embraces the whole family of man — then they will no doubt call down on the civilization they miscall Christian the anathema of destruction which Christ Himself defined for those who do not seek and find Him in every child of man. This is the full meaning and measure of the crisis which the Christian world confronts, a crisis forged in its complacency, confirmed in its indifference, and sealed by the judgment of a God who is not mocked.

◆ MODERN ESSAY ◆

Doomsday for Haves and Have-Nots?

ROBERT HEILBRONER

Can technology solve all of our problems? Can the industrial world produce enough goods to sustain our own high standard of living and lift the world's poor out of poverty? Robert Heilbroner doubts it. He sees limitations on the amount of wealth which can be produced, including environmental limitations. If there is not enough wealth to go around, will we hold on to most of it or will we share it? Faced with the question of human survival, how will the United States utilize its past experience? Must we reject our achievement ethic? Increase government control of our lives? Diminish liberty in the name of security? Given the basic split between rich and poor, what is the human prospect?

What is needed now is a summing up of the human prospect, some last reflections on its implications for the present and future alike.

The external challenges can be succinctly reviewed. We are entering a period in which rapid population growth, the presence of obliterative weapons, and dwindling resources will bring international tensions to dangerous levels for an extended period. Indeed, there seems no reason for these levels of danger to subside unless population equilibrium is achieved and some rough measure of equity reached in the distribution of wealth among nations, either by great increases in the output of the underdeveloped world or by a massive distribution of wealth from the richer to the poorer lands.

Whether such an equitable arrangement can be reached — at least within the next several generations — is open to serious doubt. Transfers of adequate magnitude imply a willingness to redistribute income internationally on a more generous scale than the advanced nations have evidenced within their own domains. The required increases in output in the backward regions would necessitate gargantuan application of energy merely to extract the needed resources. It is uncertain whether the requisite energy-producing technology exists, and, more serious, possible that its application would bring us to the threshold of an irreversible change in climate, as a consequence of the enormous addition of man-made heat to the atmosphere.

It is this last problem that poses the most demanding and difficult of the

---

challenges. The existing pace of industrial growth, with no allowance for increased industrialization to repair global poverty, holds out the risk of entering the danger zone of climatic change in as little as three or four generations. If that trajectory is in fact pursued, industrial growth will then have to come to an immediate halt, for another generation or two along that path would literally consume human, perhaps all, life. That terrifying outcome can be postponed only to the extent that the wastage of heat can be reduced, or that technologies that do not add to the atmospheric heat burden — for example, solar energy transformers — can be put to use. The outlook can also be mitigated by redirecting output away from heat-creating material outputs into the production of "services" that add only trivially to heat.

All these considerations make the designation of a timetable for industrial deceleration difficult to construct. Yet, under any and all assumptions, one irrefutable conclusion remains. The industrial growth process, so central to the economic and social life of capitalism and Western socialism alike, will be forced to slow down, in all likelihood within a generation or two, and will probably have to give way to decline thereafter. To repeat the words of the text, "whether we are unable to sustain growth or unable to tolerate it," the long era of industrial expansion is now entering its final stages, and we must anticipate the commencement of a new era of stationary total output and (if population growth continues or an equitable sharing among nations has not yet been attained) declining material output per head in the advanced nations.

These challenges also point to a certain time frame within which different aspects of the human prospect will assume different levels of importance. In the short run, by which we may speak of the decade or two immediately ahead, no doubt the most pressing questions will be those of the use and abuse of national power, the vicissitudes of political history, perhaps the short-run vagaries of the economic process, about which we have virtually no predictive capability whatsoever. From our vantage point today, a worsening of the situation in the Middle East, further Vietnams or Czechoslovakias, inflation, severe economic malfunction — or their avoidance — are sure to exercise the primary influences over the quality of existence, or even over the possibilities for existence.

In a somewhat longer time frame — extending perhaps for a period of a half century — the main shaping force of the future takes on a different aspect. Assuming that the day-to-day, year-to-year crises are surmounted in relative safety, the issues of the relative resilience and adaptability of the two great socio-economic systems come to the fore as the decisive questions. Here the properties of industrial socialism and capitalism as ideal types seem likely to provide the parameters within which and by which the prospect for man will be formed. We have already indicated what general tendencies seem characteristic of each of these systems, and the advantages that may accrue to socialist — that is, planning and probably authoritarian social orders — during this era of adjustment.

In the long run, stretching a century or more ahead, still a different facet of the human prospect appears critical. This is the transformational problem, centered in the reconstruction of the material basis of civilization itself. In this period, as indefinite in its boundaries but as unmistakable in its mighty dimensions as a vast storm visible on the horizon, the challenge devolves upon those deep-lying capabilities for political change whose roots in "human nature" we have just examined.

It is the challenges of the middle and the long run that command our attention when we speculate about the human prospect, if only because those of the short run defy our prognostic grasp entirely. It seems unnecessary to add more than a few words to underline the magnitude of these still distant problems. No developing country has fully confronted the implications of becoming a "modern" nation-state whose industrial development must be severely limited, or considered the strategy for such a state in a world in which the Western nations, capitalist and socialist both, will continue for a long period to enjoy the material advantages of their early start. Within the advanced nations, in turn, the difficulties of adjustment are no less severe. No capitalist nation has as yet imagined the extent of the alterations it must undergo to attain a viable stationary socio-economic structure, and no socialist state has displayed the needed willingness to subordinate its national interests to supranational ones.

To these obstacles we must add certain elements of the political propensities in "human nature" that stand in the way of a rational, orderly adaptation of the industrial mode in the directions that will become increasingly urgent as the distant future comes closer. There seems no hope for a rapid modification of the human character to bring about a peaceful, organized reorientation of life styles. Men and women, much as they are today, will set the pace and determine the necessary means for the social changes that will eventually have to be made. The drift toward the strong exercise of political power — a movement given its initial momentum by the need to exercise a much wider and deeper administration of both production and consumption — is likely to attain added support from the psychological insecurity that will be sharpened in a period of unrest and uncertainty. The bonds of national identity are certain to exert their powerful force, mobilizing men for the collective efforts needed, but inhibiting the international sharing of burdens and wealth. The myopia that confines the present vision of men to the short-term future is not likely to disappear overnight, rendering still more difficult a planned and orderly retrenchment and redivision of output.

Therefore the outlook is for convulsive change — change forced upon us by external events rather than by conscious choice, by catastrophe rather than by calculation. As with Malthus's much derided but all too prescient forecasts, nature will provide the checks, if foresight and "morality" do not. One such check could be the outbreak of wars arising from the explosive tensions of the coming period, which might reduce the growth rates of the surviving nation-states and thereby defer the danger of industrial asphyxiation for a period. Alternatively, nature may rescue us from ourselves by what John Platt has called a "storm of crisis problems." As we breach now this, now that edge of environmental tolerance, local disasters — large-scale fatal urban temperature inversions, massive crop failures, resource limitations such as the current oil shortage — may also slow down economic growth and give a necessary impetus to the piecemeal construction of an ecologically and socially viable social system.

Such negative feedbacks are likely to exercise an all-important cushioning effect on a crisis that would otherwise in all probability overwhelm the slender human capabilities for planned adjustment to the future. However brutal these feedbacks, they are apt to prove effective in changing our attitudes as well as our actions, unlike appeals to our collective foresight, such as the exhortations of the Club of Rome's *Limits to Growth,* or the manifesto of a group of British scientists calling for an immediate halt to growth. The problem is that the challenge to survival still lies sufficiently far in the future, and the inertial momentum of the present industrial order is still so great, that no substantial voluntary diminution of growth, much less a planned reorganization of society, is today even remotely imaginable. What leader of an underdeveloped nation, particularly one caught up in the exhilaration of a revolutionary restructuring of society, would call a halt to industrial activity in his impoverished land? What capitalist or socialist nation would put a ceiling on material output, limiting its citizens to the well-being obtainable from its present volume of production?

Thus, however admirable in intent, impassioned polemics against growth itself are exercises in futility today. Worse, they may even point in the wrong direction. Paradoxically, perhaps, the agenda for the moment lies in the temporary encouragement of the very process of industrial advance that is ultimately the mortal enemy. In the backward areas, the acute misery that is the potential source of so much international disruption can be remedied only to the extent that rapid improvements are introduced, including that minimal infrastructure needed to support a modern system of health services, education, transportation, fertilizer production, and the like. In the developed nations, what is required at the moment is the encouragement of technical advances that will permit the extraction of new resources to replace depleted reserves of scarce minerals, new sources of energy to stave off the collapse that would occur if present energy reservoirs were exhausted before substitutes were discovered, and above all, new techniques for the generation of energy that will minimize the associated generation of heat.

Thus there is a short period left during which we can probably continue on the present trajectory. It is possible that during this period a new direction will be struck that will greatly ease the otherwise inescapable adjustments. The underdeveloped nations, making a virtue of necessity, may redefine "development" in ways that limit technology and minimize the need for the accumulation of capital, stressing instead the education and vitality of their citizens. The possibilities of such a historic step would be much enhanced were the advanced nations to lead the way by a major effort to curtail the enormous wastefulness of industrial production as it is used today. If these changes took place, we might even look forward to a still more desirable redirection of history in a diminution of scale, a reduction in the size of the human community from the dangerous level of immense nation-states toward the "polis" that defined the appropriate reach of political power for the ancient Greeks.

All these are possibilities, but certainly not probabilities. The revitalization of the polis is hardly likely to take place during a period in which an orderly response to social and physical challenges will require an increase of centralized power and the encouragement of national rather than communal attitudes. The voluntary abandonment of the industrial mode of production would require a degree of self-abnegation on the part of its beneficiaries — managers and consumers alike — that would be without parallel in history. The redefinition of development on the part of the poorer nations would require a prodigious effort of will in the face of the envy and fear that Western industrial power and "affluence" arouse.

Thus in all likelihood we must brace ourselves for the consequences of which we have spoken — the risk of "wars of redistribution" or of "preemptive seizure," the rise of social tensions in the industrialized nations over the division of an ever more slow-growing or even diminishing product, and the prospect of a far more coercive exercise of national power as the means by which we will attempt to bring these disruptive processes under control.

From that period of harsh adjustment, I can see no realistic escape. Rationalize as we will, stretch the figures as favorably as honesty will permit, we cannot reconcile the requirements for a lengthy continuation of the present rate of industrialization of the globe with the capacity of existing resources of the fragile biosphere to permit or to tolerate the effects of that industrialization. Nor is it easy to foresee a willing acquiescence of humankind, individually or through its existing social organizations, in alterations of life in ways that foresight would dictate. If then, by the question: "Is there hope for man?" we ask whether it is possible to meet the challenges of the future without the payment of a fearful price, the answer must be: There is no such hope.

At this final stage of our inquiry, with the full spectacle of the human prospect before us, the spirit quails and the will falters. We find ourselves pressed to the very limit of our personal capacities, not only in summoning up the courage to look squarely at the dimensions of the impending predicament, but in finding words that can offer some plausible relief in a situation so bleak.

At this late juncture I have no intention of sounding a call for moral awakening or for social action on some unrealistic scale. Yet I do not intend to condone, much less to urge, an attitude of passive resignation, or a relegation of the human prospect to the realm of things we choose not to think about. Avoidable evil remains, as it always will, an enemy that can be defeated; and the fact that the collective destiny of man portends unavoidable travail is no reason, and cannot be tolerated as an excuse, for doing nothing.

This general admonition applies in particular to the intellectual elements of Western nations whose privileged role as sentries for society takes on a special importance in the face of things as we now see them. It is their task not only to prepare their fellow citizens for the sacrifices that will be required of them, but to take the lead in seeking to redefine the legitimate boundaries of power and the permissible sanctuaries of freedom for a future in which the exercise of power must inevitably increase and many present areas of freedom, especially in economic life, be curtailed.

Let me therefore put these last words somewhat more "positively," offsetting to some degree the bleakness of our prospect, without violating the facts or spirit of our inquiry. Here I must begin by stressing for one last time an essential fact. The human prospect is not an irrevocable death sentence. It is not apocalypse or Doomsday toward which we are headed, although the risk of enormous catastrophes exists. The prospect is better viewed as a formidable array of challenges that must be overcome before human survival is assured and *that can be overcome* by the saving intervention of nature, if not by the wisdom and foresight of man. The death sentence is therefore better viewed as a contingent life sentence — one that will permit the continuance of human society, but only on a basis very different from that of the present, and probably only after much suffering during the period of transition.

What sort of society might eventually emerge? As I have said more than once, I believe the long-term solution requires nothing less than the gradual abandonment of the lethal techniques, the uncongenial ways of life, and the dangerous mentality of industrial civilization itself. The dimensions of such a transformation into a "post-industrial" society have already been touched upon, and cannot be greatly elaborated here: in all probability the extent and ramifications of change are apt to be as unforeseeable from our contemporary vantage point as present-day society would have been unimaginable to a speculative observer a thousand years ago.

Yet I think a few elements of the society of the post-industrial era can be discerned. Although we cannot know on what technical foundation it will rest, we can be certain that many of the accompaniments of an industrial order must be absent. To repeat once again what we have already said, the societal view of production and consumption must stress parsimonious, not prodigal, attitudes. Resource-consuming and heat-generating processes must be regarded as necessary evils, not as social triumphs, to be relegated to as small a portion of economic life as possible. This implies a sweeping reorganization of the mode of production in ways that cannot be foretold, but that would seem to imply the end of the giant factory, the huge office, perhaps of the urban complex.

What values and ways of thought would be congenial with such a radical reordering of things we also cannot know, but it is likely that the ethos of "science," so intimately linked with industrial application, would play a much reduced role. In the same way, it seems probable that a true "post-industrial" society would witness the waning of much of the work ethic that is also intimately entwined with our industrial society. As one critic has pointed out, even Marx, despite his bitter denunciation of the alienating effects of labor in a capitalist milieu, placed his faith in the presumed "liberating" effects of labor in a socialist society, and did not consider a "terrible secret" — namely, that even the most creative work may be only "a neurotic activity that diverts the mind from the diminution of time and the approach of death."

It is therefore possible that a post-industrial society would also turn in the direction of many pre-industrial societies — toward the exploration of inner states of experience rather than the outer world of fact and material accomplishment. Tradition and ritual, the pillars of life in virtually all societies other than those of an industrial character, would probably once again assert their ancient claims as the guide to and solace for life. The struggle for individual achievement, especially for material ends, is likely to give way to the acceptance of communally organized and ordained roles.

This is by no means an effort to portray a future utopia. On the contrary, many of these possible attributes of a post-industrial society are deeply repugnant to my twentieth-century temper, as well as incompatible with my most treasured privileges. The search for scientific knowledge, the delight in intellectual heresy, the freedom to order one's life as one pleases are not likely to be easily contained within the tradition-oriented, static society I have depicted. To a very great degree, the public must take precedence over the private — an aim to which it is easy to give lip service in the abstract, but difficult for someone used to the pleasures of political, social, and intellectual freedom to accept in fact.

These are all necessarily prophetic speculations, offered more in the spirit of providing some vision of the future, however misty, than as a set of predictions to be "rigorously" examined. In these half-blind gropings there is, however, one element in which we can place credence, although it offers uncertainty as well as hope. This is our knowledge that some human societies have existed for millennia, and that others can probably exist for future millennia, in a continuous rhythm of birth and coming of age and death, without pressing toward those dangerous ecological limits, or engendering those dangerous social tensions, that threaten present day "advanced" societies. In our discovery of "primitive" cultures, living out their timeless histories, we may have found the single most important object lesson for future man.

What we do not know, but can only hope, is that future man can rediscover the self-renewing vitality of primitive culture without reverting to its levels of ignorance and cruel anxiety. It may be the sad lesson of the future that no civilization is without its pervasive "malaise," each expressing in its own way the ineradicable fears of the only animal that contemplates its own death, but at least the human activities expressing that malaise need not, as is the case in our time, threaten the continuance of life itself.

All this goes, perhaps, beyond speculation to fantasy. But something more substantial than speculation or fantasy is needed to sustain men through the long trials ahead. For the driving energy of modern man has come from his Promethean spirit, his nervous will, his intellectual daring. It is this spirit that has enabled him to work miracles, above all to subjugate nature to his will, and to create societies designed to free man from his animal bondage.

Some of that Promethean spirit may still serve us in good stead in the years of transition. But it is not a spirit that conforms easily with the shape of future society as we have imagined it; worse, within that impatient spirit lurks one final danger for the years during which we must watch the approach of an unwanted future. This is the danger that can be glimpsed in our deep consciousness, when we take stock of things as they now are: the wish that the drama run its full tragic course, bringing man, like a Greek hero, to the fearful end that he has, however unwittingly, arranged for himself. For it is not only with dismay that Promethean man regards the future. It is also with a kind of anger. If after so much effort so little has been accomplished; if before such vast challenges so little is apt to be done — then let the drama proceed to its finale, let mankind suffer the end it deserves.

Such a view is by no means the expression of only a few perverse minds. On the contrary, it is the application to the future of the prevailing attitudes with which our age regards the present. When men can generally acquiesce in, even relish, the destruction of their living contemporaries, when they can regard with indifference or irritation the fate of those who live in slums, rot in prisons, or starve in lands that have meaning only in so far as they are vacation resorts, why should they be expected to take the painful actions needed to prevent the destruction of future generations whose faces they will never live to see? Worse yet, will they not curse those future generations whose claim to life can be honored only by sacrificing present enjoyments; and will they not, if it comes to a choice, condemn them to nonexistence by choosing the present over the future?

The question, then, is how we are to summon up the will to survive — not perhaps in the distant future, where survival will call on those deep sources of imagined human unity, but in the present and near-term future, while we still enjoy and struggle with the heritage of our personal liberties, our atomistic existences.

At this last moment of reflection another figure from Greek mythology comes to mind. It is that of Atlas, bearing with endless perseverance the weight of the heavens in his hands. If man is to rescue life, he must first rescue the future from the angry condemnation of the present. Here the spirit of conquest and aspiration will not serve. It is Atlas, resolutely bearing his burden, that gives us the example we seek. If within us the spirit of Atlas falters there perishes the determination to preserve humanity at all cost and any cost, forever.

But Atlas is, of course, no other than ourselves. Myths have their magic power because they cast on the screen of our imaginations, like the figures of the heavenly constellations, immense projections of our own hopes and capabilities. We do not know with certainty that humanity will survive, but it is a comfort to know that there exist within us the elements of fortitude and will from which the image of Atlas springs.

1 2 3 4 5 6 7 8 9 0